토플 단어 만점 받자 !

TOEFL 滿
Vocabulary

1

TOEFL 滿
Vocabulary I

펴낸날 | 2008년 7월 3일

펴낸이 | 강 남 현

펴낸곳 | 월드컴출판사

등록 | 2000년 1월 17일

주소 | 서울시 구로구 구로동 222-8 코오롱디지탈타워 빌란트 II 1005호(우편번호 152-848)

전화 | 02)3273-4300(대표)

팩스 | 02)3273-4303

홈페이지 | www.wcbooks.co.kr

이메일 | wc4300@yahoo.co.kr

Preface

토플 영어단어 공부할 때 반드시 챙겨야 할 **TWO** 가지!!

Quantity

토 플 초보든, 토플 고수든, 그 누구를 막론하고 토플공부는 영어단어 학습으로 시작해서 영어단어 학습으로 끝이 난다고 해도 과언이 아니다. 아무리 독해력과 청취력이 뛰어난 사람이라고 해도 단어를 모르면 아무 소용없는 법. 세계가 급변하는 만큼 새로이 생겨나는 영어단어들도 그만큼 많아지고 있고, 반대로 쓰이지 않는 단어는 조용히 사라지기도 하는 것이 사실이다. 토플을 포함해 영어 공부할 때 단어는 당신의 재산이다. 영어 빈곤에 허덕이는 일이 없도록 영어의 곳간을 그득 채워 두자.

Quality

한 국어와 영어는 근본적으로 매우 다른 체계의 언어로, 영어단어의 뜻을 그대로 한국어로 옮기는 것은 불가능하다. 특히, 토플에 나오는 유의어 문제를 풀기 위해서는, 영어단어를 좀 더 깊이 있게 공부할 필요가 있다. 가령, 대부분 "greedy"를 "탐욕스러운"이라는 부정적인 뜻으로만 알고 있다. 하지만 영영사전을 찾아보면 "greedy"는 "필요한 것 보다 더 많은 것을 가지고 싶어 한다"는 뜻으로 긍정·부정 모두에 사용 가능하다. 즉, greedy for money는 "돈에 대한 탐욕", greedy for praise는 "칭찬을 많이 받고 싶은 열망"으로 해석이 가능한 것이다. 전자 greedy를 대체할 수 있는 난어는 avaricious, 빈면 후자는 eager로 대체할 수 있을 것이다. 이처럼 영한과 영영을 동시에 이용하는 질 높은 단어학습법은 단순히 단어를 아는데 그치는 것이 아니라, 실제로 그 단어를 석설하게 문장에 사용힐 수 있는 실용적 영어공부를 가능하게 한다.

이 책의 구성

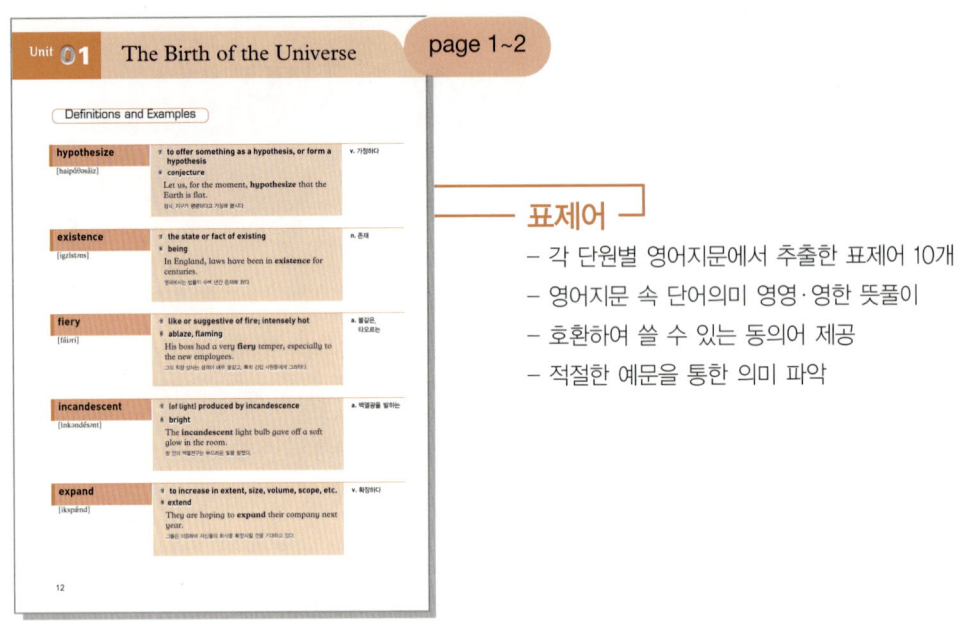

표제어

- 각 단원별 영어지문에서 추출한 표제어 10개
- 영어지문 속 단어의미 영영·영한 뜻풀이
- 호환하여 쓸 수 있는 동의어 제공
- 적절한 예문을 통한 의미 파악

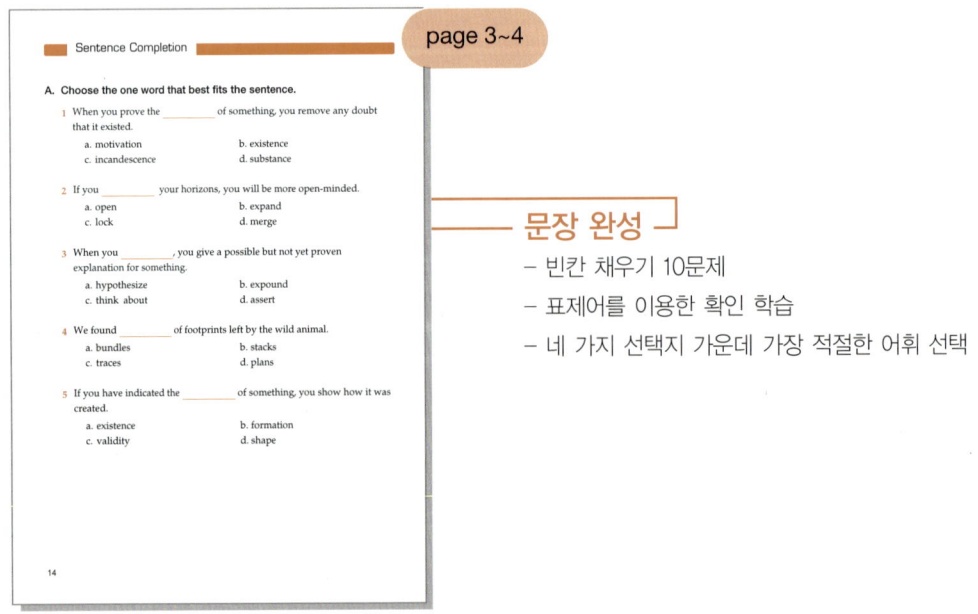

문장 완성

- 빈칸 채우기 10문제
- 표제어를 이용한 확인 학습
- 네 가지 선택지 가운데 가장 적절한 어휘 선택

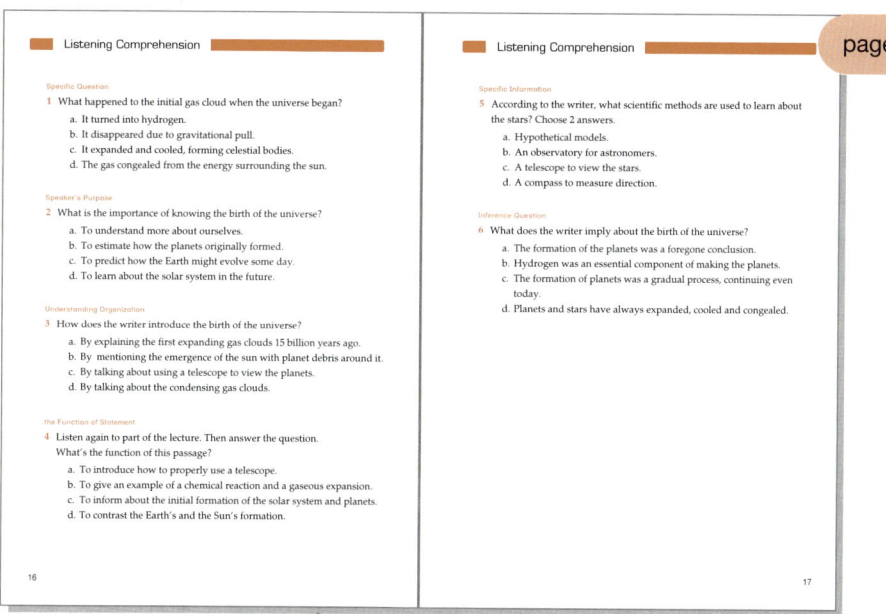

Listening Comprehension

Specific Question

1. What happened to the initial gas cloud when the universe began?
   a. It turned into hydrogen.
   b. It disappeared due to gravitational pull.
   c. It expanded and cooled, forming celestial bodies.
   d. The gas congealed from the energy surrounding the sun.

Speaker's Purpose

2. What is the importance of knowing the birth of the universe?
   a. To understand more about ourselves.
   b. To estimate how the planets originally formed.
   c. To predict how the Earth might evolve some day.
   d. To learn about the solar system in the future.

Understanding Organization

3. How does the writer introduce the birth of the universe?
   a. By explaining the first expanding gas clouds 15 billion years ago.
   b. By mentioning the emergence of the sun with planet debris around it.
   c. By talking about using a telescope to view the planets.
   d. By talking about the condensing gas clouds.

The Function of Statement

4. Listen again to part of the lecture. Then answer the question.
   What's the function of this passage?
   a. To introduce how to properly use a telescope.
   b. To give an example of a chemical reaction and a gaseous expansion.
   c. To inform about the initial formation of the solar system and planets.
   d. To contrast the Earth's and the Sun's formation.

16

Listening Comprehension

Specific Information

5. According to the writer, what scientific methods are used to learn about the stars? Choose 2 answers.
   a. Hypothetical models.
   b. An observatory for astronomers.
   c. A telescope to view the stars.
   d. A compass to measure direction.

Inference Question

6. What does the writer imply about the birth of the universe?
   a. The formation of the planets was a foregone conclusion.
   b. Hydrogen was an essential component of making the planets.
   c. The formation of planets was a gradual process, continuing even today.
   d. Planets and stars have always expanded, cooled and congealed.

17

토플 L/C 섹션

토플 유형별 문제 : 상세 질문, 화자의 의도, 구조 이해, 문장의 기능, 상세 정보, 추론

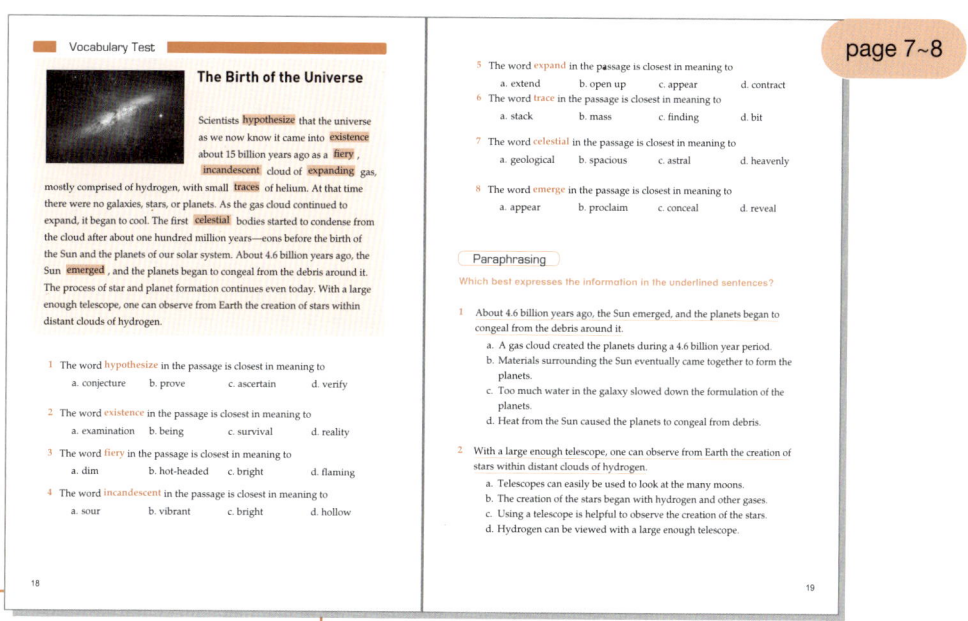

Vocabulary Test

The Birth of the Universe

Scientists hypothesize that the universe as we now know it came into existence about 15 billion years ago as a fiery , incandescent cloud of expanding gas, mostly comprised of hydrogen, with small traces of helium. At that time there were no galaxies, stars, or planets. As the gas cloud continued to expand, it began to cool. The first celestial bodies started to condense from the cloud after about one hundred million years—eons before the birth of the Sun and the planets of our solar system. About 4.6 billion years ago, the Sun emerged , and the planets began to congeal from the debris around it. The process of star and planet formation continues even today. With a large enough telescope, one can observe from Earth the creation of stars within distant clouds of hydrogen.

1. The word hypothesize in the passage is closest in meaning to
   a. conjecture   b. prove   c. ascertain   d. verify

2. The word existence in the passage is closest in meaning to
   a. examination   b. being   c. survival   d. reality

3. The word fiery in the passage is closest in meaning to
   a. dim   b. hot-headed   c. bright   d. flaming

4. The word incandescent in the passage is closest in meaning to
   a. sour   b. vibrant   c. bright   d. hollow

18

5. The word expand in the passage is closest in meaning to
   a. extend   b. open up   c. appear   d. contract

6. The word trace in the passage is closest in meaning to
   a. stack   b. mass   c. finding   d. bit

7. The word celestial in the passage is closest in meaning to
   a. geological   b. spacious   c. astral   d. heavenly

8. The word emerge in the passage is closest in meaning to
   a. appear   b. proclaim   c. conceal   d. reveal

Paraphrasing

Which best expresses the information in the underlined sentences?

1. About 4.6 billion years ago, the Sun emerged, and the planets began to congeal from the debris around it.
   a. A gas cloud created the planets during a 4.6 billion year period.
   b. Materials surrounding the Sun eventually came together to form the planets.
   c. Too much water in the galaxy slowed down the formulation of the planets.
   d. Heat from the Sun caused the planets to congeal from debris.

2. With a large enough telescope, one can observe from Earth the creation of stars within distant clouds of hydrogen.
   a. Telescopes can easily be used to look at the many moons.
   b. The creation of the stars began with hydrogen and other gases.
   c. Using a telescope is helpful to observe the creation of the stars.
   d. Hydrogen can be viewed with a large enough telescope.

19

실선 어휘문제

영어지문 읽고 동의어 찾기 & 적절한 paraphrasing 문장 고르기

TOEFL 滿 200% 활용하기

Ready!

■ 각 Unit별 표제어 10개를 먼저 습득한다.

> **▶ 滿 영단어 학습법**
> – 먼저 영영 뜻풀이를 읽어보고, 그 의미를 이미지로 파악해 본다.
> – 그런 다음, 생각한 이미지를 영한 뜻을 보며 눈으로 확인한다.
> – 예문 속에서 그 단어의 의미를 다시 한번 머리 속에 각인시킨다.
> – 마지막으로, 동의어를 익혀 단어를 확장시킨다.

Set!!

■ 빈칸 채우기 어휘문제 10개를 풀면서, 단어실력을 체크해본다.
■ 아울러, 실전에 들어가기에 앞서 mp3에 녹음된 지문을 대본 없이 소리로만 듣고, 관련한 L/C문제도 함께 풀어본다. 이때는 반드시 note-taking을 하면서 듣는다.

Go!!!

■ 본격적으로 iBT 토플 시험과 같은 유형의 어휘문제(8개)를 풀어 보면서, 실전감각을 익혀본다.
■ 어휘문제와 더불어, 독해력 향상을 위해 paraphrasing 문제도 함께 풀어본다.

Finish

■ 단어, 예문 및 LC문제와 영어지문이 녹음된 mp3 파일을 다운받아, 길에서든 지하철에서든 항상 들으면서 어휘력과 청취력의 동반 상승을 꾀하도록 한다.

iBT TOEFL 가이드

영 역	문 항	점수(비중)	시간	구 성
Listening	34~51	30(25%)	60~90분	– 대화형 2~3개, 강의형 4~6개의 지문으로 구성 – 대화당 5문제, 강의지문당 6문제 – 지문이 CBT보다 2~3개 길어짐 – CBT의 단문듣기 없어짐
Reading	36~70	30(25%)	60~100분	– 지문이 약 2배 길어짐 – 3~5개 지문, 각 지문당 12~14 문제 – 앞 지문으로 돌아갈 수 없음
Speaking	6	30(25%)	20분	– type 1 : 　한 가지 주제를 가지고 말하는 독립형 문제 　총 2문제. 15초 답변 생각 / 45초 말하기 – type 2 : 　읽기 / 듣기 / 말하기로 이어지는 통합형 문제 　총 2문제. 30초 답변 생각 / 60초 말하기 – type 3 : 　듣기 / 말하기가 연결된 통합형 문제 　총 2문제. 30초 답변 생각 / 60초 말하기
Writing	2	30(25%)	50분	– type 1 : 　읽기 / 듣기 / 쓰기의 영역이 통합된 문제 – type 2 : 　한 가지 주제를 가지고 견해를 밝히는 독립형 문제

iBT의 특징

1. Speaking영역이 추가되고, Structure영역이 사라진다.

2. 기존 CBT에서는 Listening Section과 Structure Section에서 응시자가 난이도와 배점이 다르게 설정된 문제를 풀지만, iBT 에서는 시험 영역 및 유형의 근본적인 변화로 인해 이 CAT(Computer Adaptive Test)이 방식이 폐지된다.

3. Listening, Speaking, Reading, Writing의 각 영역별 문제 외에도, Listening-Speaking, Reading-Listening-Speaking, Reading- Listening-Writing 과 같은 통합형 문제도 출제된다.

4. iBT의 총점은 120점, 시험시간은 약 4시간, 시험은 읽기, 듣기, 말하기, 쓰기의 순이다. 시험은 1년에 30~40회 정도 실시되고, 전용 컴퓨터 단말기가 마련된 ETS의 Test center에서 치러진다.

5. iBT는 인터넷을 이용해 시험 접수를 할 수 있을 뿐만 아니라, 시험 후 15일이면 시험 성적도 확인할 수 있고, 우편불로 수취노 가능하다. 또한, 성적은 총점과 함께 영역별 점수까지도 평가된다.

6. 네 개 시험 영역 모두 noto-taking이 허용되며, 문제를 풀 때 이 내용을 참고할 수 있다 note-taking 용지는 시험이 끝나면 모 두 수거된다.

TOEFL 滿 Vocabulary I
C o n t e n t s

TOEFL 滿 Vocabulary II

C o n t e n t s

The Birth of the Universe

Definitions and Examples

hypothesize

[haipáθəsàiz]

(영) to offer something as a hypothesis, or form a hypothesis

(동) conjecture

Let us, for the moment, **hypothesize** that the Earth is flat.

잠시, 지구가 평평하다고 가정해 봅시다.

v. 가정하다

---

existence

[igzístəns]

(영) the state or fact of existing

(동) being

In England, laws have been in **existence** for centuries.

영국에서는 법률이 수백 년간 존재해 왔다.

n. 존재

---

fiery

[fáiəri]

(영) like or suggestive of fire; intensely hot

(동) ablaze, flaming

His boss had a very **fiery** temper, especially to the new employees.

그의 직장 상사는 성격이 매우 불같고, 특히 신입 사원들에게 그러하다.

a. 불같은, 타오르는

---

incandescent

[ìnkəndésənt]

(영) (of light) produced by incandescence

(동) bright

The **incandescent** light bulb gave off a soft glow in the room.

방 안의 백열전구는 부드러운 빛을 발했다.

a. 백열광을 발하는

---

expand

[ikspǽnd]

(영) to increase in extent, size, volume, scope, etc.

(동) extend

They are hoping to **expand** their company next year.

그들은 이듬해에 자신들의 회사를 확장시킬 것을 기대하고 있다.

v. 확장하다

trace	영 a surviving mark, sign, or evidence of the former existence	n. 기미, 흔적
[treis]	동 bit	
	The C.S.I. investigator found **traces** of blood on the knife.	
	과학 수사대 수사관은 칼에서 피 묻은 흔적을 발견했다.	

celestial	영 pertaining to the sky or visible heaven	a. 천체의
[siléstʃəl]	동 astral	
	She stared at the **celestial** bodies through her telescope.	
	그녀는 자신의 망원경으로 천체를 바라보았다.	

emerge	영 to come forth into view or notice, as from concealment	v. 나타나다
[imə́:rdʒ]	동 appear	
	The burglar **emerged** from the shadows behind the store.	
	그 강도는 가게 뒤의 어두운 곳에서 나타났다.	

formation	영 the act or process of forming or the state of being formed	n. 형성
[fɔːrméiʃən]	동 creation	
	The **formation** of Hawaii was a result of volcanic activity.	
	하와이는 화산활동의 결과로 형성되었다.	

creation	영 the act of producing or causing to exist; the act of creating	n. 창조(물)
[kriːéiʃən]	동 conception	
	Designer Andre Kim's **creations** were applauded by the fashion industry.	
	디자이너 앙드레 김의 창조물은 패션업계의 찬사를 받았다.	

A. Choose the one word that best fits the sentence.

1 When you prove the _____ of something, you remove any doubt that it existed.

    a. motivation   b. existence

    c. incandescence   d. substance

2 If you _____ your horizons, you will be more open-minded.

    a. open   b. expand

    c. lock   d. merge

3 When you _____, you give a possible but not yet proven explanation for something.

    a. hypothesize   b. expound

    c. think about   d. assert

4 We found _____ of footprints left by the wild animal.

    a. bundles   b. stacks

    c. traces   d. plans

5 If you have indicated the _____ of something, you show how it was created.

    a. existence   b. formation

    c. validity   d. shape

B. Choose the one word that best fits the sentence.

1 The _____ temper of the supervisor eventually resulted in his dismissal.

    a. sizzling   b. great

    c. sweet   d. fiery

2 When you observe the _____ bodies, you will discover the wonders of astronomy.

    a. geological   b. celestial

    c. biographic   d. oceanic

3 Some talented musicians are willing to put their _____ online to download for free.

    a. creations   b. craftsmanship

    c. emergence   d. sculptures

4 When China _____ as a new superpower, it will influence the region for centuries.

    a. evolves   b. falls

    c. falters   d. emerges

5 The _____ light was bright enough for studying in the dark room.

    a. shallow   b. dull

    c. incandescent   d. reminiscent

Listening Comprehension

1 What happened to the initial gas cloud when the universe began?

    a. It turned into hydrogen.

    b. It disappeared due to gravitational pull.

    c. It expanded and cooled, forming celestial bodies.

    d. The gas congealed from the energy surrounding the sun.

Speaker's Purpose

2 What is the importance of knowing the birth of the universe?

    a. To understand more about ourselves.

    b. To estimate how the planets originally formed.

    c. To predict how the Earth might evolve some day.

    d. To learn about the solar system in the future.

Understanding Organization

3 How does the writer introduce the birth of the universe?

    a. By explaining the first expanding gas clouds 15 billion years ago.

    b. By mentioning the emergence of the sun with planet debris around it.

    c. By talking about using a telescope to view the planets.

    d. By talking about the condensing gas clouds.

the Function of Statement

4 Listen again to part of the lecture. Then answer the question.

What's the function of this passage?

    a. To introduce how to properly use a telescope.

    b. To give an example of a chemical reaction and a gaseous expansion.

    c. To inform about the initial formation of the solar system and planets.

    d. To contrast the Earth's and the Sun's formation.

Specific Information

5 According to the writer, what scientific methods are used to learn about the stars? Choose 2 answers.

    a. Hypothetical models.

    b. An observatory for astronomers.

    c. A telescope to view the stars.

    d. A compass to measure direction.

Inference Question

6 What does the writer imply about the birth of the universe?

    a. The formation of the planets was a foregone conclusion.

    b. Hydrogen was an essential component of making the planets.

    c. The formation of planets was a gradual process, continuing even today.

    d. Planets and stars have always expanded, cooled and congealed.

The Birth of the Universe

Scientists hypothesize that the universe as we now know it came into existence about 15 billion years ago as a fiery, incandescent cloud of expanding gas, mostly comprised of hydrogen, with small traces of helium. At that time there were no galaxies, stars, or planets. As the gas cloud continued to expand, it began to cool. The first celestial bodies started to condense from the cloud after about one hundred million years—eons before the birth of the Sun and the planets of our solar system. About 4.6 billion years ago, the Sun emerged, and the planets began to congeal from the debris around it. The process of star and planet formation continues even today. With a large enough telescope, one can observe from Earth the creation of stars within distant clouds of hydrogen.

1 The word **hypothesize** in the passage is closest in meaning to

    a. conjecture   b. prove   c. ascertain   d. verify

2 The word **existence** in the passage is closest in meaning to

    a. examination   b. being   c. survival   d. reality

3 The word **fiery** in the passage is closest in meaning to

    a. dim   b. hot-headed   c. bright   d. flaming

4 The word **incandescent** in the passage is closest in meaning to

    a. sour   b. vibrant   c. bright   d. hollow

5 The word **expand** in the passage is closest in meaning to

    a. extend   b. open up   c. appear   d. contract

6 The word **trace** in the passage is closest in meaning to

    a. stack   b. mass   c. finding   d. bit

7 The word **celestial** in the passage is closest in meaning to

    a. geological   b. spacious   c. astral   d. heavenly

8 The word **emerge** in the passage is closest in meaning to

    a. appear   b. proclaim   c. conceal   d. reveal

Paraphrasing

Which best expresses the information in the underlined sentences?

1   About 4.6 billion years ago, the Sun emerged, and the planets began to congeal from the debris around it.

    a. A gas cloud created the planets during a 4.6 billion year period.
    b. Materials surrounding the Sun eventually came together to form the planets.
    c. Too much water in the galaxy slowed down the formulation of the planets.
    d. Heat from the Sun caused the planets to congeal from debris.

2   With a large enough telescope, one can observe from Earth the creation of stars within distant clouds of hydrogen.

    a. Telescopes can easily be used to look at the many moons.
    b. The creation of the stars began with hydrogen and other gases.
    c. Using a telescope is helpful to observe the creation of the stars.
    d. Hydrogen can be viewed with a large enough telescope.

The Big Bang

Definitions and Examples

attempt
[ətémpt]

- 영 to try to perform, make, or achieve
- 동 aim

Her **attempted** jokes were terrible — no one laughed.

그녀가 한 농담은 끔찍하게도 재미가 없었기 때문에 아무도 웃지 않았다.

v. 시도하다

---

phenomenon (pl. -na)
[finámənàn]

- 영 a fact, occurrence, or circumstance observed
- 동 anomaly

The scientists set out to study the **phenomena** of nature.

과학자들은 자연 현상 연구에 착수했다.

n. 현상

---

unanswered
[ʌnǽnsərd]

- 영 not responded to in kind
- 동 incomplete, unknown

There are still a lot of **unanswered** questions about the event.

그 사건에 대해 답변을 받지 못한 질문이 아직 많이 있다.

a. 대답이 없는

---

observation
[àbzərvéiʃən]

- 영 the act of noting and recording something with instruments
- 동 inspection

The **observations** of planet Saturn indicated three new moons.

토성을 관측한 결과, 세 개의 새로운 위성이 발견되었다.

a. 관측

---

calculate
[kǽlkjəlèit]

- 영 to determine by reasoning, mathematical methods, or practical experience
- 동 account, estimate

The experts **calculated** the odds of winning the presidential election.

전문가들은 대통령 선거에서 당선될 확률을 추정했다.

v. 추정하다

explode
[iksplóud]

ⓥ to burst forth violently or emotionally, usually from chemical reaction

ⓢ blow up

High above the desert, the bombs were **exploding** around the city.

사막 위로 높이, 폭탄이 도시 주위에서 폭발하고 있었다.

v. 폭발하다

occur
[əkə́:r]

ⓥ take place; come to pass

ⓢ happen

It suddenly **occurred** to him that he had slept in that morning.

별안간, 그는 그날 아침 늦잠잤던 일이 떠올랐다.

v. 발생하다
(머리에)떠오르다

infinitely
[ínfənətli]

ⓥ without bounds

ⓢ greatly, considerably

Every moment is **infinitely** precious to me.

매 순간이 나에게는 매우 중요하다.

ad. 무한하게

shrink
[ʃriŋk]

ⓥ to draw back, as in retreat or avoidance

ⓢ contract

The clothes **shrink** in the dryer.

그 옷들은 건조기에 넣으면 줄어든다.

v. 수축하다

contraction
[kəntrǽkʃən]

ⓥ an act or instance of contracting

ⓢ reduction

The expectant mother was having **contractions** every five minutes.

그 임산부는 5분마다 진통(자궁 수축)을 겪고 있었다.

n. 수축

A. Choose the one word that best fits the sentence.

1   If your phone calls go _____ , then maybe the other person doesn't want to talk to you.

   a. unanswered   b. unseen

   c. unintelligent   d. unrealized

2   Sometimes when you _____ your finances properly, you will be able to make a good budget.

   a. sift   b. expound

   c. calculate   d. destroy

3   When you study _____ , you are studying something unusual.

   a. occurrences   b. events

   c. phenomena   d. occasions

4   If you _____ something, you try until you either succeed or fail.

   a. give up   b. attempt

   c. tempt   d. make

5   His theory was downplayed, because it was not based on thorough _____ .

   a. looks   b. observations

   c. appearances   d. stereotypes

B. Choose the one word that best fits the sentence.

1 If you don't exercise regularly, your muscles will _____.

   a. fall   b. shrink

   c. kick off   d. dissuade

2 The _____ dynamite destroyed the entire building.

   a. discharging   b. electrifying

   c. tracing   d. exploding

3 When you start to feel the _____, then it's time to go to the hospital to have the baby.

   a. sorrows   b. muscles

   c. contractions   d. pounding

4 It _____ to him that he had better study harder in order to learn about the Big Bang theory.

   a. occurred   b. criticized

   c. thought   d. dawned

5 We were talking about what our lives would be like if we were _____ wealthy.

   a. repeatedly   b. infinitely

   c. nervously   d. dully

Listening Comprehension

Specific Question

1 What's the Big Bang theory?

    a. A law that regulates the movement of the planets and stars.

    b. A theory that the universe is expanding from a central point.

    c. A prediction that God created the universe.

    d. A contraction in the universe that occurred 15 billion years ago.

Speaker's Purpose

2 Why does the writer explain the Big Bang theory?

    a. To better understand how and why the planets move about in space.

    b. To estimate the speed of the planets.

    c. To predict how many asteroids there are.

    d. To observe phenomena everywhere.

Understanding Organization

3 How does the writer introduce the Big Bang theory?

    a. Through vetting theories about the universe used by scientists.

    b. Through estimating the origin of space explosions.

    c. Through observing phenomena from stars and nebulas.

    d. Through detecting patterns at incredible speeds.

the Function of Statement

4 Listen again to part of the lecture. Then answer the question.
What's the function of this passage?

    a. To introduce a new cosmological theory.

    b. To give an example of how scientists can observe space.

    c. To describe the demolition of the universe.

    d. To apply a theory to explain known information about the universe's origins.

Specific Information

5 According to the writer, what main factor contributed to Edward Hubble's theory? Choose 2 answers.

    a. He observed stars and nebulas.

    b. He calculated that objects in the universe were moving away from each other.

    c. He predicted that the universe was contracting from two points.

    d. The universe was expanding from a central point.

Inference Question

6 What does the writer imply about the Big Bang theory?

    a. Contractions are very interesting and need further study.

    b. There is much information to be learned.

    c. It offers the best theory about the universe based on careful observations.

    d. We can learn more about Mars and Saturn.

The Big Bang

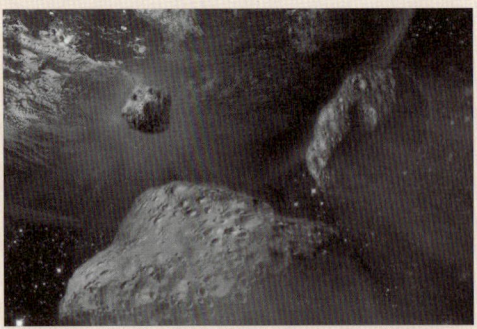

The Big Bang is a cosmological theory that attempts to explain the origin of the universe. It accounts for some phenomena, but it still leaves many questions unanswered. In 1929 an American astronomer, Edwin Hubble, made careful observations of the light from stars and nebulas. Using these observations, he calculated that all objects in the universe are moving away from each other at incredible speeds. He concluded that the universe is expanding as if it were exploding from one central point. That explosion — the Big Bang — is supposed to have occurred about 15 billion years ago, when all matter was contained in an infinitely small point. What caused that point to explode? Will the universe continue to expand, or will it, at some future time, begin to shrink, repeating a cycle of expansions and contractions ad infinitum? Science as yet has no answers to these questions.

1 The word **attempt** in the passage is closest in meaning to

    a. persevere   b. prove   c. aim   d. continue

2 The word **phenomena** in the passage is closest in meaning to

    a. anomaly   b. things   c. occurrences   d. festivals

3 The word **unanswered** in the passage is closest in meaning to

    a. ushered   b. unappealing   c. mysterious   d. unknown

4 The word **observation** in the passage is closest in meaning to

    a. response   b. inspection   c. result   d. discovery

5 The word **calculate** in the passage is closest in meaning to

    a. add   b. make sure   c. account   d. dismiss

6 The word **explode** in the passage is closest in meaning to

    a. blow up   b. expand   c. implode   d. die

7 The word **occur** in the passage is closest in meaning to

    a. observe   b. happen   c. come to   d. pass

8 The word **infinitely** in the passage is closest in meaning to

    a. only   b. minutely   c. considerably   d. definitely

Paraphrasing

Which best expresses the information in the underlined sentences?

1 That explosion — the Big Bang — is supposed to have occurred about 15 billion years ago, when all matter was contained in an infinitely small point.

    a. Big Bang is a phrase summarizing the start of the universe following an explosion.
    b. The universe exploded inward from a central point.
    c. The beginning of the solar system occurred billions of years ago.
    d. The planets and galaxies formed from an infinitely small amount of matter.

2 Will the universe continue to expand, or will it, at some future time, begin to shrink, repeating a cycle of expansions and contractions in an infinitum?

    a. Scientists are examining the expansion and contraction of the universe.
    b. When the universe shrinks, it will go back to its original state before the Big Bang.
    c. It is unknown whether the universe goes through a continuous cyclical period.
    d. The universe is constantly changing.

The Origin of the Earth

Definitions and Examples

excess [iksés]	영 the amount or degree by which one thing exceeds another 동 extra, surplus The **excess** amount of food gives us more calories than our requirement. 과다한 양의 음식을 섭취하면 필요 이상의 칼로리가 우리 몸에 축적된다.	a. 과다한
region [rí:dʒən]	영 an extensive, continuous part of a surface 동 area Russia's land mass covers the **regions** of Europe and Asia. 러시아의 땅덩어리는 유럽과 아시아 지역에 이른다.	n. 지역
solid [sálid]	영 firm or compact in substance 동 hard Under extremely high temperatures, one can melt **solid** materials like steel and iron. 극도의 고온에서는 강철이나 무쇠와 같은 고체를 녹일 수 있다.	a. 고체의 딱딱한
relatively [rélətivli]	영 in a relative manner 동 comparatively Mexican food is **relatively** spicy compared to Western cuisine. 멕시코 음식은 서구 요리에 비해 비교적 맵다.	ad. 비교적
chunk [tʃʌ́ŋk]	영 a thick mass or lump of anything 동 mass The rats were eating the **chunk** of cheese on the floor. 그 쥐들은 바닥에 놓인 치즈 덩어리를 먹고 있었다.	n. 덩어리

radioactive

[rèidiouǽktiv]

⑱ exhibiting, or caused by radioactivity

The nuclear power plant is highly **radioactive**.

그 원자력 발전소에서는 방사능이 강하게 유출된다.

a. 방사능(성)의

---

decay

[dikéi]

⑱ to break down into component parts

⑧ rot

Over the years, the cables on the bridge **decayed** until they broke.

여러 해가 지나면서, 다리 위의 케이블이 부식되어 끊어졌다.

v. 부식하다
(방사능 물질이)
자연붕괴하다

---

melt

[melt]

⑱ to become liquefied by warmth or heat, as ice, snow, butter, or metal

⑧ liquefy

The plane's fuselage **melted** after it crashed and burned on the runway.

그 비행기의 동체는 활주로에 추락한 뒤 불타 녹아버렸다.

v. 녹다

---

belch

[beltʃ]

⑱ to eject gas spasmodically or violently; give forth

⑧ erupt

The chimney **belched** dark puffs of smoke.

그 굴뚝은 검은 연기를 내뿜었다.

v. (기체를) 내뿜다

---

combination

[kàmbənéiʃən]

⑱ the act of combining or the state of being combined

⑧ mixture

A **combination** of Coca-Cola and chips will give you a high calorie diet.

코카콜라와 감자 칩의 조합은 칼로리가 높다.

n. 조합

Sentence Completion

A. Choose the one word that best fits the sentence.

1 Some matter is made from liquids, gases and others from _____ components.

    a. solid   b. expansive

    c. nutritious   d. mellow

2 When taking a _____ out of your hair, then you cut a large part of your hair.

    a. specimen   b. heat

    c. chunk   d. fraction

3 When traveling through a large area, you are going through a(an)

_____.

    a. bounty   b. acre

    c. neighborhood   d. region

4 When you do _____ work, you are doing more than what is required.

    a. overindulgent   b. excess

    c. recessive   d. minimal

5 If you are _____ faster at running than someone, it means you are faster compared to them.

    a. hastily   b. relatively

    c. slowly   d. quickly

B. Choose the one word that best fits the sentence.

1 The car _____ exhaust fumes into the air.

    a. pointed   b. swerved

    c. belched   d. convulsed

2 How many times did I tell you that the nuclear power plant is _____?

    a. radioactive   b. rusted

    c. inert   d. expensive

3 Spaghetti is made from a(an) _____ of noodles and tomato sauce.

    a. amalgamation   b. combination

    c. grouping   d. solution

4 Radioactive material _____ in space, contributing to the formation of the planets.

    a. clouded   b. decayed

    c. ripened   d. juiced

5 The students learned that billions of years ago, much of the iron in the Earth's surface _____.

    a. combined   b. softened

    c. merged   d. melted

Specific Question

1 How did the Earth originate?

    a. Iron melted below the surface.

    b. An expansion of gas swirled around the sun.

    c. Excess gas cooled, forming a chunk of iron and other materials.

    d. Solid bodies were formed from gas.

Speaker's Purpose

2 Why does the writer explain the origin of the Earth?

    a. To make a connection between iron and gases.

    b. To estimate how material in space came together and formed our planet.

    c. To predict more about geology.

    d. To detect patterns in the solar system.

Understanding Organization

3 How does the writer introduce the Earth's origins?

    a. Laws of physics were involved.

    b. Releasing energy helped form the Earth.

    c. Excess gas from stars can sometimes create planets like Earth.

    d. Radioactive material is essential to creating planets.

the Function of Statement

4 Listen again to part of the lecture. Then answer the question.
   What's the function of this passage?

    a. To introduce the origin of the Earth from a religious perspective.

    b. To give an example of the formation of the sun and other stars.

    c. To describe volcanic activity.

    d. To tell how gas combines with other material like iron and forms planetary matter.

Specific Information

5 According to the writer, what factors contributed to creating the planet
   Earth? Choose 2 answers.

   a. Decaying radioactive material.

   b. The melting of the inner mantle in the Earth.

   c. Cooling gas.

   d. Cooling gas and igneous rocks.

Inference Question

6 What does the writer imply about the Earth's origins?

   a. Understanding chemistry is important.

   b. The Earth was one big primordial mass due to inert gases.

   c. Changes in gases and metals produced energy to create the planet.

   d. Understanding biology is important.

The Origin of the Earth

Stars like the Sun are formed from clouds of gas. In the wake of this process, excess gas remains in the region around the star. The leftover gas cools and forms solid bodies, planets like the Earth. When the Earth took shape some four billion years ago, it was a relatively cool, solid chunk of iron and some other materials. There were also small amounts of radioactive elements in the Earth's primordial mass. The radioactive material decayed over millions of years, releasing a great deal of energy. That energy melted the iron, which sunk to the center of the Earth, nearly four thousand miles below the surface. At the same time, the surface was rent by violent Earthquakes. Volcanoes belched gas clouds containing hydrogen and oxygen, the combination of which formed water. And that water accumulated to form the first large oceans.

1 The word **excess** in the passage is closest in meaning to

    a. extra   b. extracted   c. unnecessary   d. fewer

2 The word **region** in the passage is closest in meaning to

    a. land   b. area   c. acre   d. sphere

3 The word **solid** in the passage is closest in meaning to

    a. hard   b. durable   c. improvable   d. gaseous

4 The word **relatively** in the passage is closest in meaning to

    a. just   b. similarly   c. demonstrably   d. comparatively

5 The word **chunk** in the passage is closest in meaning to

   a. particle   b. solid   c. mass   d. thing

6 The word **decay** in the passage is closest in meaning to

   a. thrive   b. fall apart c. rot   d. lose

7 The word **melt** in the passage is closest in meaning to

   a. congeal   b. liquefy   c. water   d. harden

8 The word **belch** in the passage is closest in meaning to

   a. erupt   b. throw   c. absorb   d. reflect

Paraphrasing

Which best expresses the information in the underlined sentences?

1 That energy melted the iron, which sunk to the center of the Earth, nearly four thousand miles below the surface.

   a. The energy sunk into the middle of the Earth.
   b. Most of the iron was melted by sheer energy below the Earth's surface.
   c. Some of the center of the Earth (4,000 miles below the surface) is very hot.
   d. Too much of the Earth is unsuitable for metals to exist.

2 Volcanoes belched gas clouds containing hydrogen and oxygen, the combination of which formed water.

   a. Many of the gases in clouds come from condensation and volcano water.
   b. The air does not contain much hydrogen or oxygen, thus forming volcanoes.
   c. Too much water results in the belching of gas clouds.
   d. Volcanoes threw up various kinds of gases to create water.

The Conquistadors

Definitions and Examples

soldier of fortune [sóuldʒər ʌv fɔ́ːrtʃən]	영 one who will serve in any army or undertake risky tasks for personal gain 동 military adventurer In Iraq, a **soldier of fortune** can earn up to $700 a day. 이라크에서 용병은 하루에 최대 700달러까지도 벌 수 있다.	n. 용병
brave [bréiv]	영 possessing or exhibiting courage or courageous endurance 동 fearless The **brave** human rights activist in Myanmar challenged the police. 미얀마의 용감한 그 인권운동가는 경찰에 저항했다.	a. 용감한
ruthless [rúːθlis]	영 without pity or compassion 동 cruel The **ruthless** Russian mobster lit up a cigarette in his face. 그 무자비한 러시아 조직원은 그의 면전에서 담배에 불을 붙였다.	a. 무자비한
greedy [gríːdi]	영 excessively or inordinately desirous of wealth, profit, etc. 동 rapacious Many businessmen become **greedy** after years in the business. 수많은 사업가들이 여러 해 동안 사업에 손을 댄 뒤 탐욕스러워진다.	a. 탐욕스러운
convert [kənvə́ːrt]	영 to change (something) into a different form or properties 동 alter She asked her fiancé to **convert** to Judaism before getting married. 그녀는 결혼 전 자신의 약혼자에게 유대교로 개종할 것을 부탁했다.	v. 개종하다

lower
[lóuər]

- 영 bottom half, southern portion; situated, placed, or occurring not far above the ground, floor
- 동 under

The **lower** part of Manhattan is filled with all sorts of cafes and shops.

맨해튼 남부 지역에는 다양한 종류의 카페와 상점이 가득하다.

a. 남부의, 밑의

man-made
[mǽn-méid]

- 영 produced artificially
- 동 artificial

The new airports in Hong Kong and Osaka were built on **man-made** islands.

홍콩과 오사카에 새롭게 생긴 공항은 인공 섬 위에 지어졌다.

a. 인공의

encounter
[enkáuntər]

- 영 to come upon or meet with, esp. unexpectedly
- 동 happen upon

She feared to **encounter** her ex-boyfriend as they worked in the same building.

그녀는 옛 남자친구와 같은 건물에서 일하기 때문에 마주칠 일이 걱정이었다.

v. (우연히) 만나다

majesty
[mǽdʒisti]

- 영 wonder, amazement; regal, lofty, or stately dignity
- 동 excellence

The **majesty** of the Taj Mahal was simply beyond breathtaking.

타지마할의 웅장함은 놀라움, 그 이상이었다.

n. 웅장함

rich
[ritʃ]

- 영 abounding in natural resources
- 동 bountiful

The **richer** the planet, the more resources there are.

행성은 풍요로울수록 더욱 많은 자원을 보유하고 있다.

a. 풍요로운

A. Choose the one word that best fits the sentence.

1 If you are _____ , then you will be feared by many and admired by some.

    a. sympathetic   b. warm-blooded

    c. sickly   d. ruthless

2 When someone decides to _____ their religion, they choose to change to a new one.

    a. translate   b. renovate

    c. convert   d. redirect

3 When someone is _____ , they are not afraid of tremendous difficulties and pain.

    a. lucky   b. brave

    c. timid   d. arrogant

4 If you fight like a _____ , then you probably are very skilled with weapons.

    a. supervisor   b. technician

    c. soldier of fortune   d. goalie

5 If you are _____ , then you like money and can be financially selfish.

    a. satiable   b. greedy

    c. ravenous   d. queer

Sentence Completion

B. Choose the one word that best fits the sentence.

1 His _____, the King of Portugal, is ready to receive you now in the palace.

    a. multitude   b. majesty

    c. celebrity   d. indecency

2 He has strong arms but a weak _____ body.

    a. lesser   b. lower

    c. subordinate   d. reduced

3 Luckily, the European explorers found _____ lands in the New World.

    a. battered   b. poorer

    c. richer   d. middle-class

4 He _____ an Alaskan grizzly bear in the middle of the trail and quickly ran away.

    a. encountered   b. encouraged

    c. diverged   d. shoved into

5 One of the most marvelous _____ structures is the Great Wall of China.

    a. accumulated   b. synthesized

    c. manufactured   d. man-made

1 Who did the conquistadors bring with them?

    a. Christian missionaries and natives.

    b. Some explorers to help navigate the New World.

    c. Christian missionaries and Catholics.

    d. Conquerors and their families.

2 Why does the writer explain conquistadors?

    a. Because native Indian populations initially welcomed the Europeans.

    b. Because they were brave, courageous men who swept through the New World.

    c. Because significant trade occurred between the Christians and Coloradans.

    d. Because religion was wiped out in California, Colorado, and Kansas.

3 How does the writer introduce conquistadors?

    a. Through explaining how the European soldiers of fortune came over by ship.

    b. By estimating the farm yields in Kansas and the mid-west.

    c. By predicting how much European soldiers of fortune found in gold and treasure.

    d. By recounting stories about Christian priests.

the Function of Statement

4   Listen again to part of the lecture. Then answer the question.
    What's the function of this passage?

>   a. To introduce the effect that Europeans had on the New World.

>   b. To give an example of man-made and natural wonders.

>   c. To describe the Aztec natural wonders found by the Indians.

>   d. To contrast Christian priests and Buddhist monks.

Specific Information

5   According to the writer, what two things did the conquistadors discover
    on their journeys? Choose 2 answers.

>   a. Aztec civilizations.

>   b. A land with few natural resources.

>   c. Grand Canyon natural wonders.

>   d. Bountiful corn crops.

Inference Question

6   What does the writer imply about conquistadors?

>   a. The conquistadors were lucky to discover new land.

>   b. The explorers relied on outdated technology to defeat the Indians.

>   c. Christianity was an evil religion and harmed the pagan Indians.

>   d. They were domineering and aggressive invaders who ventured forth
>   in North America.

The Conquistadors

In the 16th century, European soldiers of fortune in search of treasure and adventure made the dangerous journey across the Atlantic Ocean to the New World. The conquistadors — the Spanish word meaning conquerors — were brave, ruthless, greedy men. They were accompanied by groups of Christian priests, who wanted to convert the native Indian populations to Christianity. Their expeditions ranged from what is now Mexico to places as distant as lower California, Colorado, and Kansas. Few of the stories about the New World circulating in Europe at the time prepared them for the man-made and natural wonders they actually encountered. From the fabulous cities of the Aztecs to the stunning majesty of the Grand Canyon, the conquistadors discovered a land far richer than any they had ever dreamed of.

1 The word **soldier of fortune** in the passage is closest in meaning to
   a. slave   b. merchant
   c. worker   d. military adventurer

2 The word **brave** in the passage is closest in meaning to
   a. champion   b. timid   c. fearless   d. weak-kneed

3 The word **ruthless** in the passage is closest in meaning to
   a. cruel   b. cunning   c. merciful   d. special

4 The word **greedy** in the passage is closest in meaning to
   a. aspiring   b. trying   c. lustful   d. rapacious

5 The word **convert** in the passage is closest in meaning to

    a. rework   b. amend   c. alter   d. fixate

6 The word **lower** in the passage is closest in meaning to

    a. under   b. over   c. increased   d. quarter

7 The word **man-made** in the passage is closest in meaning to

    a. cloned   b. reproduced   c. artificial   d. chemical

8 The word **encounter** in the passage is closest in meaning to

    a. stumble   b. happen upon   c. kick   d. bounce

Paraphrasing

Which best expresses the information in the underlined sentences?

1 Their expeditions ranged from what is now Mexico to places as distant as lower California, Colorado, and Kansas.

    a. The expeditions in Mexico were wonderful adventures to behold.
    b. The explorers traveled from the Spanish territories to southern California and beyond.
    c. Too much water in southern California was polluted in the 16th century.
    d. Mexicans should have fought harder to preserve their land.

2 From the fabulous cities of the Aztecs to the stunning majesty of the Grand Canyon, the conquistadors discovered a land far richer than any they had ever dreamed of.

    a. Aztec life was preserved thanks to the scientific work of the conquistadors.
    b. Discovery of new lands is a foregone conclusion, even back then.
    c. The New World was wealthier in resources and beauty than anyone had imagined.
    d. Dreams are good because sometimes they come to fruition.

Definitions and Examples

throughout
[θrúːáut]

- 영 in or to every part of, everywhere in
- 동 across

The children ran **throughout** the house, screaming and laughing.

아이들은 웃고 소리치며 집안 곳곳을 뛰어다녔다.

prep. 도처에

---

anthropologist
[æ̀nθrəpάlədʒist]

- 영 a person who specializes in anthropology
- 동 ethnologist

Some **anthropologist**s have discovered oldest human-like fossils.

일부 인류학자들이 가장 오래되고 인간과 흡사한 화석을 발견했다.

n. 인류학자

---

argue
[άːrgjuː]

- 영 to put forth reasons for or against
- 동 debate

The couple **argued** almost every week and their shouting upset the baby.

그 부부는 거의 매주 말싸움을 했으며 이들의 고함 소리 때문에 아기는 불안해했다.

v. 논쟁하다

---

population
[pàpjəléiʃən]

- 영 the total number of persons inhabiting a country, city, or any district or area
- 동 inhabitant

The **population** of Mexico City was much larger than that of Shanghai.

멕시코 시티의 인구는 상해보다 훨씬 많다.

n. 인구

---

estimate
[éstəmèit]

- 영 an approximate calculation of a quantity or value
- 동 appraisal

His **estimate** is that the project should be finished in three weeks.

그의 추정치에 따르면 그 프로젝트는 분명히 삼 주 안에 끝난다.

n. 추정치

Humanities I

dwelling

[dwéliŋ]

(영) **a place to live in**

(동) **house**

Many of the **dwellings** were a little bit bland regarding their design.

디자인 상으로 볼 때 이 주거지의 상당수는 다소 개성이 없었다.

n. 주거지

---

elaborate

[ilǽbərèit]

(영) **worked out with great care and nicety of detail; executed with great minuteness**

(동) **intricate**

This art gallery has a much more **elaborate** exhibit than the others.

이 미술관은 다른 곳보다 훨씬 더 정교한 전시물을 보유하고 있다.

a. 정교한

---

cluster

[klʌ́stər]

(영) **to gather or grow into bunches**

(동) **huddle, gather**

They **clustered** in groups of three and four.

이들은 세 명씩 또는 네 명씩 무리지어 있었다.

v. 밀집하다
무리지어 있다

---

constitute

[kánstətjùːt]

(영) **to be the elements or parts of**

(동) **compose, make up**

These children **constitute** a very diverse group in terms of their national origins.

이 아이들은 출신국가로 볼 때 상당히 다양한 구성을 이루고 있다.

v. 이루다
구성하다

---

transportation

[trænspərtéiʃən]

(영) **a means of conveyance**

(동) **transport**

Lack of **transportation** is making life difficult for many students in the area.

운송수단이 부족하기 때문에 이 지역에 사는 많은 학생들이 생활에 어려움을 느끼고 있다.

n. 운송 (수단)

A. Choose the one word that best fits the sentence.

1 If you _____ , then you are likely to raise your voice and get very emotional.

    a. soothe   b. argue

    c. disagree   d. joust

2 When you are given _____ , it means that is the best information available at the time.

    a. guesstimates   b. estimates

    c. hearsay   d. esteem

3 If you are a(an) _____ , you are interested in the scientific study of people, society and culture.

    a. biologist   b. psychologist

    c. anthropologist   d. geologist

4 Clues that this house was haunted were found _____ the house.

    a. right into   b. throughout

    c. aside from   d. sometimes

5 When the _____ gets bigger in a city, the amount of people increases.

    a. resident   b. habitation

    c. population   d. demographics

B. Choose the one word that best fits the sentence.

1 Three major branches _____ the American government.

    a. compart   b. constitute

    c. subdivide   d. consist

2 When their _____ were torn down by the government, the family had nowhere to go.

    a. structures   b. shafts

    c. dwellings   d. sheds

3 The subway is a popular form of _____ in Seoul.

    a. transmission   b. freight

    c. correspondence   d. transportation

4 There isn't a more _____ hotel than the Burj Al Arab Hotel in Dubai.

    a. convoluted   b. elaborate

    c. entangled   d. dexterous

5 People _____ around the entertainer to get his autograph.

    a. scattered   b. dispersed

    c. uncovered   d. clustered

Listening Comprehension

Specific Question

1 What did anthropologists argue about?

    a. Whether the European should have battled the Indians for food.

    b. An estimate of dwellings that suited the environment.

    c. The variety and size of Indian dwellings.

    d. Patterns in the river populations.

Speaker's Purpose

2 Why does the writer explain North American natives?

    a. To show how Indians lived in a variety of dwellings suited to the environment.

    b. To estimate means of transportation in the community.

    c. To predict how one civilization can conquer another.

    d. To indicate that the interior areas were much better than the coastal areas.

Understanding Organization

3 How does the writer introduce North American native life?

    a. By showing who was living there at the time of Columbus.

    b. By analyzing their hunting strategies near the Great Lakes.

    c. Through illustrating that Columbus came from Spain.

    d. Through discussing elaborate wooden structures.

the Function of Statement

4 Listen again to part of the lecture. Then answer the question.
What's the function of this passage?

    a. To introduce the term Inuit to supplant the word Eskimo.

    b. To give an example of homes clustered near rivers.

    c. To describe the living conditions of the native tribes.

    d. To contrast varieties in dwellings.

Specific Information

5 According to the writer, what two types of structures did native Indians live in? Choose 2 answers.

      a. Large mud and clay huts.

      b. Canvas tents.

      c. Elaborate wooden homes.

      d. Ice boxes.

Inference Question

6 What does the writer imply about North American natives?

      a. Anthropologists have long argued over the size of dwellings.

      b. Native Indians were well organized with a good food supply chain.

      c. Anthropologists predict the population was not that large.

      d. Eskimos had a far healthier diet than the inland Indians.

North America (1)

At the time Columbus discovered America, Indians could be found living throughout the North American continent. Although anthropologists have long argued over the size of the Indian population at that time, many now believe that it may have been as high as 10 to 20 million, figures much higher than early estimates. The Indians lived in a variety of dwellings suited to the environment, from simple tents to elaborate wooden structures to the grass and snow igloos of Eskimos in the north. The Indians tended to be concentrated around the Great Lakes and in the southwest of what would later become the United States. Tribes that lived in the interior areas of the continent clustered near rivers, which constituted a supply of food and an important means of transportation.

1 The word **throughout** in the passage is closest in meaning to

    a. across   b. inside   c. during   d. outside

2 The word **anthropologist** in the passage is closest in meaning to

    a. assistant   b. ethnologist   c. researcher   d. philologist

3 The word **argue** in the passage is closest in meaning to

    a. debate   b. fuss   c. compromise   d. cluster

4 The word **population** in the passage is closest in meaning to

    a. conjecture   b. rodents   c. inhabitants   d. numbers

5 The word **estimate** in the passage is closest in meaning to

    a. assertion   b. appraisal   c. hunch   d. fact

6 The word **dwelling** in the passage is closest in meaning to

    a. agony   b. apartment   c. interior   d. house

7 The word **elaborate** in the passage is closest in meaning to

    a. intricate   b. decrepit   c. fashionable   d. structured

8 The word **cluster** in the passage is closest in meaning to

    a. crawl   b. prove   c. gather   d. scatter

Paraphrasing

Which best expresses the information in the underlined sentences?

1 Although anthropologists have long argued over the size of the Indian population at that time, many now believe that it may have been as high as 10 to 20 million, figures much higher than early estimates.

    a. After much discussion, academic research points to new evidence.

    b. Anthropologists have long debated the accuracy of the Indian population.

    c. Too little is known about eating habits of the Cree Indians.

    d. Substantial amounts of food were available, given the large population densities.

2 Tribes that lived in the interior areas of the continent clustered near rivers, which constituted a supply of food and an important means of transportation.

    a. Interior inhabitants often located near bountiful rivers.

    b. Tribes that lived in the interior often fought with those near rivers.

    c. They clustered near rivers because they were short on food.

    d. Salmon constituted most of their diet near transportation hubs.

Definitions and Examples

purchase
[pə́:rtʃəs]

- 영 acquisition by the payment of money
- 동 buying

The Louisiana **Purchase** was the smartest real estate deal ever completed by the U.S. government.

루이지애나 매입은 미국 정부가 이룬, 가장 영리한 부동산 거래였다.

n. 매입

acquisition
[æ̀kwəzíʃən]

- 영 the act of acquiring or gaining possession
- 동 gain

The **acquisition** of the semiconductor company was almost final.

그 반도체 회사 인수는 거의 마지막 단계에 이르렀다.

n. 획득, 인수

range
[réindʒ]

- 영 to vary within certain limits
- 동 vary, extend

The hockey player had a slap shot **ranging** in speed from 80-100 m.p.h.

그 하키 선수는 시속 80~100마일에 이르는 슬랩 샷을 날렸다.

v. 이르다

double
[dʌ́bəl]

- 영 to become double
- 동 make twofold

Sales at Hewlett Packard more than **doubled** in the first quarter.

휴렛 팩커드 사의 매출액은 1/4분기에 두 배 이상 늘어났다.

v. 두 배로 늘어나다

seek
[síːk]

- 영 to go in search or quest of
- 동 look for

She **sought** out a new boyfriend by using online dating sites.

그녀는 온라인 데이트 사이트를 이용해 새 남자친구를 찾았다.

v. 찾다

wilderness

[wíldərnis]

영 a wild and uninhabited area left in its natural condition

동 wilds

Much of the Canadian **wilderness** is vast, cold and forbidding.

캐나다 황야 중 대부분은 면적이 광대하고 날씨가 추우며 접근하기도 어렵다.

n. 황야

expedition

[èkspədíʃən]

영 an organized group of people undertaking a journey for a particular purpose

동 explorers

An **expedition** was sent to examine and survey the river.

그 강을 조사할 목적으로 탐험대가 파견되었다.

n. 탐험대

veteran

[vétərən]

영 a person who has served in a military force, especially one who has fought in a war

동 ex-serviceman

The Vietnam **veteran** suffered from post-traumatic stress disorder.

그 베트남전 참전 군인은 외상후 스트레스 장애를 겪었다.

n. 퇴역 군인

outline

[áutlàin]

영 to draw the outline of

동 plan

She **outlined** the new advertising campaign for the summer.

그녀는 여름을 겨냥한 새 광고 캠페인의 윤곽을 그렸다.

v. 윤곽을 그리다

route

[rú:t]

영 a course, way, or road for passage or travel

동 path

When you drive through the mountainous **route**, make sure to use snow tires.

산악 길(도로)을 운전해 지나갈 경우 반드시 스노타이어를 사용해라.

v. 길(도로)

A. Choose the one word that best fits the sentence.

1 If a firm makes a(an) _____ , then it buys another company.

    a. possessive   b. acquisition

    c. sellout   d. merger

2 If you _____ the value of your house, then it increased in value by a factor of two.

    a. gave up   b. doubled

    c. raised   d. tripled

3 Going from the battlefield to the business world is something most _____ have to do at some point.

    a. technicians   b. retailers

    c. veterans   d. conscientious objectors

4 Most of these wearers made _____ of two or four boxes at a time.

    a. assets   b. contacts

    c. returns   d. purchases

5 When prices for apples are _____ from $1 to $15 at the market, that is a large range.

    a. ranging   b. stunning

    c. dominating   d. expanding

B. Choose the one word that best fits the sentence.

1 When the team leader _____ plans for a fresh advertising campaign, the staff was enthused.

    a. forced   b. outlined

    c. misused   d. solved

2 They had _____ out a small cottage in the countryside near a bubbling brook.

    a. hunted for   b. fanned

    c. sought   d. dished

3 Decades ago, one could drive for days from Illinois to California along _____ 66.

    a. route   b. trail

    c. pathway   d. bikeway

4 Lewis and Clark made their way through treacherous _____, hostile Indians and the Rockies.

    a. trees   b. backyards

    c. sludge   d. wilderness

5 A large _____ of pilgrims made their trip on the Mayflower.

    a. journey   b. handful

    c. expedition   d. exhibit

1 What relationship was Lewis to President Jefferson?

    a. He was the nephew to Clark.

    b. He was captain to Jefferson's secretary.

    c. He acted as a lieutenant in the White House.

    d. He was Jefferson's personal secretary.

Speaker's Purpose

2 Why does the writer explain the American West?

    a. To show how to organize an expedition.

    b. To show how it was a vast untamed wilderness, full of potential.

    c. To advocate the expansion of British territories.

    d. To indicate that anyone can forge a new society.

Understanding Organization

3 How does the writer introduce the opening of the American West?

    a. Through complimenting the French on their generosity.

    b. Through advocating giving back the western states to Mexico.

    c. By describing Jefferson's relationship with the French ambassador.

    d. By explaining the Louisiana Purchase and its tremendous effect.

the Function of Statement

4 Listen again to part of the lecture. Then answer the question.
What's the function of this passage?

    a. To introduce how President Thomas Jefferson gave away 2.6 million kilometers of land.

    b. To give an example of Clark's journey to reach the source of the Columbia River.

    c. To describe how nations can have cordial relations.

    d. To show the fascinating exploratory history of the early American West.

Specific Information

5 According to the writer, what two areas did Lewis and Clark explore? Choose 2 answers.

   a. Columbia River.

   b. Montana-Canadian border.

   c. Northern Idaho.

   d. Missouri River.

Inference Question

6 What does the writer imply about Lewis and Clark?

   a. The veterans of the early Indian wars were able explorers.

   b. The Southern Rockies was probably a better route to travel through.

   c. They were pioneers who helped open up early America.

   d. They were British turncoats who betrayed their country.

North America (2)

The opening of the American West began in 1803, following the purchase of more than 2.6 million square kilometers of land from France by President Thomas Jefferson. With this acquisition, called the Louisiana Purchase, the United States gained an area ranging from New Orleans to the Northern Rockies, and the size of the country more than doubled. Jefferson sought a useful route across this wilderness and organized an expedition to be led by his personal secretary, Captain Meriwether Lewis, and Lieutenant William Clark, both of whom were veterans of the early Indian wars. Jefferson outlined the route they were to follow: first they were to travel up to the source of the Missouri River, then spend a day carrying their boats over the western mountains to reach the source of the Columbia River, and finally float down the Columbia to the Pacific Ocean.

1 The word **purchase** in the passage is closest in meaning to

    a. auction   b. buying   c. rummage   d. fire sale

2 The word **acquisition** in the passage is closest in meaning to

    a. liability   b. gain   c. enticement   d. merger

3 The word **range** in the passage is closest in meaning to

    a. extend   b. mainstream   c. zigzag   d. shrink

4 The word **double** in the passage is closest in meaning to

    a. bend   b. be twosome

    c. join up   d. be made twofold

5 The word **seek** in the passage is closest in meaning to

    a. visualize   b. look for   c. remember   d. observe

6 The word **wilderness** in the passage is closest in meaning to

    a. wetland   b. jungle   c. toy store   d. wilds

7 The word **expedition** in the passage is closest in meaning to

    a. missionaries   b. task forces

    c. helpers   d. a party of explorers

8 The word **veteran** in the passage is closest in meaning to

    a. sniper   b. expert   c. sergeant   d. ex-serviceman

Paraphrasing

Which best expresses the information in the underlined sentences?

1 With this acquisition, called the Louisiana Purchase, the United States gained an area ranging from New Orleans to the Northern Rockies, and the size of the country more than doubled.

    a. The idea of such a large transfer of land is inconceivable today.

    b. Mexico was nice to grant the U.S. such a large piece of land.

    c. The United States must be very grateful for this large acquisition.

    d. Such a large acquisition doubled the size of the United States.

2 First they were to travel up to the source of the Missouri River, then spend a day carrying their boats over the western mountains to reach the source of the Columbia River.

    a. Lewis and Clark carried a lot of supplies on their backs with no help.

    b. Their plans were to go over the western mountains to the Columbia.

    c. Such a trip is very arduous, particularly for the older Clark.

    d. Their plans went astray after the canoes broke down.

Animal Behavior (1)

Definitions and Examples

---

infancy
[ínfənsi]

- 영 the state or period of being an infant
- 동 incipient stage

The new start-up company was still in its **infancy**.

그 신생 회사는 아직 초기 단계에 있었다.

n. 유아기(초기)

---

thought
[θɔ́:t]

- 영 the product of mental activity
- 동 notion

His **thought** about asking her out on a date was nothing but a dream.

그녀에게 데이트 신청을 하려는 그의 생각은 단지 허황된 꿈에 불과했다.

n. 생각

---

scholar
[skálər]

- 영 a learned or erudite person
- 동 academic

The eminent **scholar** made a presentation at the seminar.

그 저명한 학자는 세미나에서 발표를 하였다.

n. 학자

---

instinctive
[instíŋktiv]

- 영 arising from instinct or from a natural ability
- 동 intuitive

The mother bear had an **instinctive** feeling about her cubs.

그 어미 곰은 자신의 새끼들에게 본능적인 감정(모성애)을 지녔다.

a. 본능(직관)적인

---

laboratory
[lǽbərətɔ̀:ri]

- 영 any place equipped to conduct scientific experiments, tests, investigations, etc.
- 동 testing room

The C.S.I. **laboratory** was equipped with the latest in technology.

과학수사대 실험실에는 최신 기술 장비가 갖춰져 있었다.

n. 실험실

Life Science I

determine [ditə́:rmin]	영 to decide (a dispute, question) by an authoritative or conclusive decision 동 decide The principal will **determine** the appropriate punishment. 교장선생님이 적절한 처벌을 결정할 것이다.	v. 결정하다
adaptive [ədǽptiv]	영 serving or able to adapt 동 flexible Many animals are quite **adaptive** to their surroundings in Nature. 많은 동물들은 주변의 자연환경에 잘 적응할 수 있다.	a. 적응력이 있는
technique [tekní:k]	영 a practical method or art applied to some particular task 동 method, skill, ability The sushi chef had an amazing **technique**, especially with his knife. 그 초밥 요리사는 놀라운 솜씨를 가지고 있었으며, 특히 칼 솜씨가 대단했다.	n. 테크닉(솜씨) 기법
gosling [gázliŋ]	영 a young goose The baby **gosling** followed its mother through the pond. 그 거위 새끼는 어미를 따라 연못을 지나갔다.	n. 새끼 거위
substitute [sʌ́bstitjù:t]	영 a person or thing acting or serving in place of another 동 replacement The **substitute** worked for three weeks in the class. 대체 교사가 3주 동안 그 반을 맡았다.	n. 대역, 대체(물)

A. Choose the one word that best fits the sentence.

1 When a person is a _____ , then he is knowledgeable and an expert in their field.

    a. chemist   b. scholar

    c. youngster   d. taxi driver

2 When someone works in a(an) _____ , he examines and analyzes things there.

    a. laboratory   b. office

    c. race track   d. station

3 When you are in your _____ , you are very very young.

    a. infancy   b. retirement home

    c. middle age   d. grave

4 If you had a _____ about something, then you considered it.

    a. craving   b. runway

    c. thought   d. disillusion

5 If you are _____ , you have a natural intuition and feeling about something.

    a. funny   b. humorous

    c. instinctive   d. creative

B. Choose the one word that best fits the sentence.

1 The young _____ was looking for her mother by the bird feed stand.

    a. piglet   b. gosling

    c. foal   d. cub

2 He couldn't _____ whether to buy tickets for the Chinese opera or Russian symphony.

    a. establish   b. determine

    c. find out   d. hypothesize

3 This _____ is not as good as the original one.

    a. substitute   b. liability

    c. separation   d. necessity

4 Some insects are highly _____ in order to survive in the wild.

    a. adaptive   b. luxurious

    c. rigid   d. borderline

5 The best _____ for listening is concentrating fully on the other person.

    a. meditation   b. expertise

    c. technique   d. knowledge

1 Why do scientists study animal behavior?

    a. To dismiss European academic techniques.

    b. To learn how animals and birds behave in their natural surroundings.

    c. To predict how young goslings find a new parent.

    d. To study animal "language" in minute detail.

2 Why does the writer explain animal behavior techniques?

    a. To gain the respect of all scientific groups.

    b. To show that new scientific approaches are always possible.

    c. To predict how other scientists will react to published articles on the subject.

    d. To show patterns in young goslings and Lorenz.

3 How does the writer introduce animal behavior?

    a. By outlining the two commonly heard attitudes toward animal behavior.

    b. By estimating how many goslings each mother gives birth to.

    c. By predicting how to observe animal life, particularly birds.

    d. By talking about adaptive animal "language."

the Function of Statement

4 Listen again to part of the lecture. Then answer the question.
What's the function of this passage?

    a. To indicate that animal behavior is highly developed and difficult to analyze.

    b. To show that many scientists disagree over how to study bird life.

    c. To indicate that there are three schools of thought for studying animal life.

    d. To show that Lorenz was innovative in studying mating habits.

Specific Information

5 According to the writer, what two factors were commonly used to study animal behavior? Choose 2 answers.

    a. Studying animals in controlled laboratory conditions.

    b. Looking at physical features of baby birds.

    c. Studying animals in their natural surroundings.

    d. Having a group discussion about animals in a seminar session.

Inference Question

6 What does the writer imply about animal behavior?

    a. An entirely new set of discoveries can be made if one uses new techniques.

    b. Natural surroundings are the best place for studying birds.

    c. Nothing much can be learned from new behavior methods.

    d. Controlled laboratory conditions are the only proven method for studying birds.

Animal Behavior (1)

When the science of animal behavior was still in its infancy, researchers split into two schools of thought. European scholars stressed instinctive behavior, preferring to observe and test animals in their natural surroundings. American scientists, on the other hand, studied animals under controlled laboratory conditions. One man, however, had the respect of both groups: Konrad Z. Lorenz of Austria. He developed a new approach based on the idea that an animal's behavior is determined by its struggle for survival and is therefore the product of adaptive evolution, just as an animal's physical features are. He studied a wide variety of creatures: frogs, dogs, ducks, and monkeys, among others. One of his techniques was to learn the "language" of animals so that he could approach them better. Among his discoveries was that if goslings lose their mother, they will accept a substitute. In fact, a group of such goslings adopted Lorenz as their mother, happily following him around.

1   The word **infancy** in the passage is closest in meaning to
    a. discovery   b. youngster   c. maturity   d. incipient stage

2   The word **thought** in the passage is closest in meaning to
    a. measurement b. proof   c. notion   d. information

3   The word **scholar** in the passage is closest in meaning to
    a. university   b. academic   c. assistant   d. pupil

4   The word **instinctive** in the passage is closest in meaning to
    a. behavioral   b. required   c. intuitive   d. common

5 The word **laboratory** in the passage is closest in meaning to

    a. washroom   b. office space   c. conditioner   d. testing room

6 The word **determine** in the passage is closest in meaning to

    a. decide   b. despise   c. implore   d. renounce

7 The word **adaptive** in the passage is closest in meaning to

    a. rigorous   b. flexible   c. theoretical   d. informal

8 The word **technique** in the passage is closest in meaning to

    a. judgment   b. fluency   c. method   d. system

Paraphrasing

Which best expresses the information in the underlined sentences?

1 He studied a wide variety of creatures: frogs, dogs, ducks, and monkeys, among others.

    a. Most interesting are the mating habits of the green frog.

    b. He studied many species of reptiles, animals and birds, including mammals.

    c. Too many species of animal life were available to study.

    d. He studied many species of whales, bees and birds, including mammals.

2 Among his discoveries was that if goslings lose their mother, they will accept a substitute.

    a. Most discoveries were not that interesting and didn't need further study.

    b. Many goslings, but not all, can find a new mother.

    c. There is too much difficulty for baby goslings to find a new father.

    d. It is common for lost goslings to adopt a new mother.

Animal Behavior (2)

Definitions and Examples

extent

[ikstént]

- 영 the space or degree to which a thing extends
- 동 range

The **extent** of his cruelty was absolutely amazing.

그가 가진 잔인함의 정도는 너무 놀라웠다.

n. 정도

---

hydrophone

[háidrəfòun]

- 영 a device for locating sources of sound under water, as for detecting submarines by the noise of their engines

A **hydrophone** was used to detect the enemy submarine.

적 잠수함을 감지하는 데 수중 청음기가 사용되었다.

n. 수중 청음기

---

submarine

[sʌ́bmərìːn]

- 영 a vessel that can be submerged under water, usually built for warfare
- 동 submersible

The **submarine** USS Ohio was an essential component of the U.S. Navy.

USS 오하이오호 잠수함은 미 해군의 핵심 구성 요소였다.

n. 잠수함

---

vast

[væst]

- 영 of very great area or extent
- 동 wide

The **vast** tundra in the Canadian north extended for hundreds of miles.

캐나다 북쪽의 방대한 툰드라 지역은 그 크기가 수백 마일에 이르렀다.

a. 방대한

---

sonar

[sóunɑːr]

- 영 a method or device for detecting and locating objects submerged in water by echolocation
- 동 asdic

Sonar can often be used to detect sounds of whales, dolphins and ships.

수중 음파 탐지기는 고래, 돌고래, 함선의 음파를 탐지하는 데 종종 사용될 수 있다.

n. 수중 음파 탐지기 또는 그 방식

emit
[imít]

- 영 to send forth (liquid, light, heat, sound, particles, etc.)
- 동 give off

The radio waves from Russia began to **emit** signals into the Far East.

러시아에서 발생한 라디오 전파가 극동 지역으로 신호를 보내기 시작했다.

v. (신호·소리를) 보내다

obstacle
[ábstəkəl]

- 영 something that obstructs or hinders progress
- 동 impediment

The university entrance exam was an **obstacle** to getting into UCLA.

대입고사가 캘리포니아 주립대학 입학에 장애물이 되었다.

n. 장애물

utilize
[jú:təlàiz]

- 영 to make use of something in a practical way
- 동 use, employ

The company was **utilizing** its advertising budget to the fullest.

그 회사는 자사의 광고 예산을 최대로 사용하고 있었다.

v. 사용하다

suffocation
[sʌ̀fəkéiʃən]

- 영 the condition of being deprived of oxygen
- 동 choking, asphyxia

He died of **suffocation** after his wife shoved a pillow on his face.

아내가 베개로 그의 얼굴을 누른 후 그는 질식사했다.

n. 질식

stranding
[strǽndiŋ]

- 영 the condition of driving or running ashore
- 동 beaching

There have been too many recent **strandings** on beaches by whales.

최근 들어 해변에는 고래들의 스트랜딩이 너무 많이 발생하고 있다.

n. 스트랜딩(고래가 해안으로 밀려온 뒤 돌아가지 못하고 죽는 현상)

A. Choose the one word that best fits the sentence.

1 To go in a _____ is to go underwater, submerged in the ocean.

    a. toy boat   b. skiff

    c. schooner   d. submarine

2 You use _____ to detect underwater sound waves.

    a. guideline   b. sonar

    c. pianos   d. power plants

3 The _____ to which you try hard is the degree to which you apply yourself.

    a. extent   b. position

    c. possibility   d. association

4 A _____ is a measuring device for recording underwater sounds.

    a. hydroplane   b. hydrophone

    c. clarinet   d. microphone

5 If you have a _____ fortune, then you have a lot of money and investments.

    a. vast   b. moderate

    c. minute   d. small

Sentence Completion

B. Choose the one word that best fits the sentence.

1 The _____ of the young child was such a tragedy; the whole family was shocked.

    a. humor   b. suffocation

    c. development   d. credit

2 That whale might _____ sounds if we listen carefully.

    a. radiate   b. emit

    c. pass on   d. beam

3 There are too many whale _____ happening on the California coastline each summer.

    a. beaches   b. intestines

    c. successes   d. strandings

4 There's no _____ that is too difficult for me to surmount.

    a. fountain   b. summons

    c. obstacle   d. windfall

5 When you _____ all your skills at work, you will likely get a promotion.

    a. manufacture   b. abuse

    c. hurdle   d. utilize

Listening Comprehension

1 Why were hydrophones developed?

    a. To help submarines avoid whales and dolphins.

    b. To help biologists study marine and bird life.

    c. To predict how submarines could communicate.

    d. To detect submarines during World War II.

Speaker's Purpose

2 What do whales and dolphins use sound for?

    a. To locate other obstacles in the ocean using echoes.

    b. To develop a highly sophisticated method of social communication.

    c. To predict how to find other marine life.

    d. To detect hydrophones in the ocean.

Understanding Organization

3 How does the writer introduce marine life sounds?

    a. By talking about sonar language.

    b. By talking about social communication in dolphins.

    c. By explaining about communication gear during World War II.

    d. By analyzing patterns in whale "language" via sonar.

the Function of Statement

4 Listen again to part of the lecture. Then answer the question.
What's the function of this passage?

    a. To show that scientific equipment can sometimes help understand marine life.

    b. To give an example of sonar language.

    c. To describe the limitations of social communication.

    d. To contrast whale and dolphin lives.

Specific Information

5 According to the writer, what two factors contributed to whale strandings? Choose 2 answers.

    a. Places where whales cannot get sharp echoes from the ocean floor.

    b. Submarines that send conflicting signals.

    c. Gently sloping sandy or muddy bottoms.

    d. Other large whales.

Inference Question

6 What does the writer imply about communication?

    a. A vast array of information about sonar language is needed.

    b. Social communication is highly overrated.

    c. If we understand more about whale and dolphin communication, we could save them.

    d. Strandings by whales are not that common.

Animal Behavior (2)

It is common knowledge that whales and dolphins can hear and make sounds, but the extent to which sea animals use sound to communicate and navigate was not known until World War II. During the war, hydrophones were developed to detect submarines, but they also picked up a vast array of sounds produced by sea mammals. As well as using sonar language for social communication, whales were found to emit sounds to help them detect obstacles by bouncing sounds off of them — in other words, by utilizing echoes. This phenomenon may help to explain why whales sometimes appear to commit "suicide" by heading into shallow waters where they get stuck and die of suffocation, when no longer supported by the sea, the weight of their bodies makes it impossible for them to breathe. It has been found that such strandings almost always occur on gently sloping sandy or muddy bottoms, where whales cannot get the same sharp echoes they can get from steep rocky coasts.

1 The word **extent** in the passage is closest in meaning to

    a. range   b. security   c. method   d. sum

2 The word **submarine** in the passage is closest in meaning to

    a. boat   b. submersible   c. mate   d. ship

3 The word **vast** in the passage is closest in meaning to

    a. narrow   b. short   c. thin   d. wide

4 The word **sonar** in the passage is closest in meaning to

    a. echo   b. asdic   c. emitter   d. transmitter

5 The word **emit** in the passage is closest in meaning to

    a. give off   b. receive   c. improvise   d. send in

6 The word **obstacle** in the passage is closest in meaning to

    a. catalyst   b. gate   c. aid   d. impediment

7 The word **utilize** in the passage is closest in meaning to

    a. hinder   b. use   c. facilitate   d. better

8 The word **suffocation** in the passage is closest in meaning to

    a. manslaughter   b. pressing   c. choking   d. heading

Paraphrasing

Which best expresses the information in the underlined sentences?

1 This phenomenon may help to explain why whales sometimes appear to commit "suicide" by heading into shallow waters where they get stuck and die of suffocation.

    a. This theory helps explain the strandings that occur so often amongst whales.

    b. Getting stuck on shallow shores is easily rectified.

    c. Committing "suicide" is not that common in marine mammals.

    d. Committing "suicide" is an unfortunate side effect of being a whale.

2 It has been found that such strandings almost always occur on gently sloping sandy or muddy bottoms, where whales cannot get the same sharp echoes they can get from steep rocky coasts.

    a. The saturation of a whale's skin does not suffice on rocky coasts.

    b. Gentle slopes are not adequate for sonar echo waves to bounce back from.

    c. Too much shallow water is not healthy for whales.

    d. Whales easily receive sonar signals in all types of water.

Animal Behavior (3)

Definitions and Examples

intelligent

[intélədʒənt]

영 having good understanding or a high mental capacity; quick to comprehend

동 brilliant

What is the most **intelligent** animal on this planet?

지구상에서 가장 지적인 동물은 무엇인가?

a. 지적인

---

note

[nóut]

영 to observe carefully

동 notice

I **noted** that he had dark circles under his eyes.

나는 그의 눈 밑에 다크서클이 생긴 것에 주목했다.

v. 주목하다

---

hatch

[hǽtʃ]

영 to bring forth (young) from the egg

동 bear

It was the first time to **hatch** an egg for the young mother hen.

어린 어미 암탉이 처음으로 알을 부화했다.

v. 부화하다

---

infant

[ínfənt]

영 a child during the earliest period of its life

동 baby

The **infant** slept peacefully most nights to the amazement of the mother.

그 유아는 거의 매일 밤 조용히 잠들어서 엄마를 놀라게 했다.

n. 유아, 갓난아기

---

efficient

[ifíʃənt]

영 doing well and thoroughly with no waste of time, money or energy

동 effective

He considers the **efficient** use of energy a very important issue.

그는 효과적인 에너지 사용이 매우 중요한 문제라고 생각한다.

a. 효과적인

Life Science I

exhibit [igzíbit]	영 to show outwardly 통 display, present Recently, the company has **exhibited** the latest models of cell phones. 근래에 그 회사는 최신 휴대 전화 모델을 선보였다.	v. 보여주다
competent [kámpətənt]	영 having suitable or sufficient skill, knowledge, experience, etc., for some purpose 통 capable She was the most **competent** professor on campus. 그 여자는 캠퍼스에서 가장 능력 있는 교수였다.	a. 능력 있는
wriggle [rígəl]	영 to twist to and fro; writhe 통 squirm The worm was **wriggling** in her hand. 벌레가 그녀의 손에서 꿈틀거리고 있었다.	v. 꿈틀거리다
motion [móuʃən]	영 the action or process of moving or of changing place or position; movement 통 action The **motion** of the piston in the Formula One racecar was very fast. 포뮬러 원 경주용 자동차의 피스톤 움직임은 매우 빨랐다.	n. 움직임
wavy [wéivi]	영 moving in a wavelike form 통 sinuous Our teacher showed us some **wavy** letters from the unique language. 우리 선생님은 독특한 언어에서 물결 모양의 문자를 몇 개 보여주셨다.	a. 물결 모양의

A. Choose the one word that best fits the sentence.

1 When a bird tries to _____ an egg, it is giving birth to an infant bird.

    a. send out   b. experience

    c. nurture   d. hatch

2 A(An) _____ is a newborn life form, typically human, not animal.

    a. toddler   b. teenager

    c. infant   d. twin

3 I _____ that your hair was wet this morning.

    a. noted   b. downplayed

    c. denoted   d. deserved

4 If you think in a(an) _____ way, then you are quite knowledgeable and smart.

    a. energetical   b. intelligent

    c. functional   d. furtive

5 The museum _____ all recent archaeological findings.

    a. divulges   b. exhibits

    c. propitiates   d. outrages

B. Choose the one word that best fits the sentence.

1 There's no point trying to avoid the _____ snake; just let it go
   away on its own.

    a. soft   b. squeamish

    c. wriggling   d. delicious

2 Many people doubt how _____ this strategy is.

    a. efficient   b. expansive

    c. adept   d. heated

3 The vehicle is now in _____ .

    a. motion   b. laser

    c. disruption   d. event

4 The young woman executive had to be very _____ to pass the
   management test.

    a. slow   b. competent

    c. incoherent   d. well-groomed

5 The child was born with _____ hair.

    a. curvacious   b. wavy

    c. shaky   d. daring

1 How long does it take an infant human to walk?

    a. Until they learn more about adaptive behavior skills.

    b. Much less than most ducklings.

    c. About a year to go from crawling to walking.

    d. A similar length of time as the butterfly.

Speaker's Purpose

2 Why does the writer explain intelligence in animals?

    a. We can all learn better ways to learn how to walk as youngsters.

    b. He is certain that intelligence is better than instinct.

    c. Instinct sometimes offers animals an advantage over humans, in the case of flying and swimming.

    d. Much remains to be known about both animal and human behavior.

Understanding Organization

3 How does the writer introduce animal and human actions?

    a. By outlining examples of intelligence and instinctual behavior.

    b. By estimating the longevity of butterflies.

    c. Through discussing the evolution of the tadpole.

    d. Through a pattern of comparison.

the Function of Statement

4 Listen again to part of the lecture. Then answer the question.
What's the function of this passage?

    a. That adaptive behavior is a learning process in humans, but not for all animals.

    b. That frogs exhibit extremely competent behavior.

    c. A description of the comparative limitations of "language" theory.

    d. A contrast in the jumping motion of the frog.

5 According to the writer, what two animals can do things that humans cannot? Choose 2 answers.

   a. Green frogs.

   b. Ducklings.

   c. Most tadpoles.

   d. Butterflies.

6 What does the writer imply about intelligence in animals?

   a. Butterflies are more amazing than most human beings.

   b. Intelligence is more efficient than instinctive methods.

   c. It is presumptive to think that only humans are intelligent.

   d. Even tadpoles are as slow to learn as humans.

Animal Behavior (3)

It has been said that animals act instinctively but human beings act intelligently. While this is not completely true — as some animals do show intelligent behavior — it should also be noted that instinct does offer animals certain advantages. A newly hatched butterfly, for example, can fly immediately, and a duckling can make a perfect dive into the water only two hours after being born. On the other hand, it takes a human infant well over a year to learn how to walk. Human beings must learn most of their adaptive behavior, and this is in many cases not as efficient as instinct. There are many animals, however, like human beings, that do not exhibit highly competent behavior from birth, and many of their behavior patterns change throughout their lives. Take, for example, the frog. As an egg, the frog displays wriggling motions; after it hatches into a tadpole, wavy swimming motions; and when it is full grown, the jumping motions of an adult frog.

1 The word **intelligent** in the passage is closest in meaning to
   a. brilliant   b. probable   c. likely   d. retarded

2 The word **note** in the passage is closest in meaning to
   a. ignore   b. notice   c. disregard   d. overlook

3 The word **hatch** in the passage is closest in meaning to
   a. open   b. contrive   c. bear   d. propel

4 The word **infant** in the passage is closest in meaning to
   a. baby   b. miniscule   c. minor   d. cousin

5 The word **efficient** in the passage is closest in meaning to

    a. eminent   b. effective   c. ineffectual   d. reproductive

6 The word **exhibit** in the passage is closest in meaning to

    a. conceal   b. conspire   c. present   d. evaluate

7 The word **competent** in the passage is closest in meaning to

    a. capable   b. informal   c. emotional   d. strange

8 The word **wriggling** in the passage is closest in meaning to

    a. stiff   b. flexible   c. dodging   d. squirming

Paraphrasing

Which best expresses the information in the underlined sentences?

1 On the other hand, it takes a human infant well over a year to learn how to walk.

    a. In contrast, it takes a baby at least a year to walk.

    b. Many tadpoles do not walk until much later in life.

    c. Too much time is spent on learning how to walk.

    d. In contrast, it takes a human at most a year to walk.

2 As an egg, the frog displays wriggling motions; after it hatches into a tadpole, wavy swimming motions; and when it is full grown, the jumping motions of an adult frog.

    a. The main point is to continually practice wriggling motions.

    b. A tadpole quickly learns to wriggle, swim and later jump.

    c. Wavy swimming motions are best for young tadpoles.

    d. Much of the time spent during a tadpole's youth is spent jumping.

Victorian Architecture

Definitions and Examples

full swing [fúl swíŋ]	영 **greatest activity** 동 **full operation** By the time he arrived, the party was in **full swing**. 그가 도착할 즈음에는 파티가 한창이었다.	**n.** 한창, 최고조
fabulously [fǽbjələsli]	영 **almost impossible to believe** 동 **wonderfully** They were **fabulously** wealthy but extremely arrogant. 그들은 굉장히 부자면서 매우 거만한 사람들이었다.	**ad.** 굉장히
lack [lǽk]	영 **to be without or deficient in** 동 **not have, want** She **lacked** any formal education but her husband loved her deeply. 그 여자는 정규 교육이 부족했지만 남편은 그녀를 깊이 사랑했다.	**v.** 부족하다
sophistication [səfístəkéiʃən]	영 **sophisticated character, ideas, tastes, as the result of education, worldly experience** 동 **elegance, refinement** He had gained a worldly **sophistication** due to his extensive travels. 여러 곳을 여행한 덕분에 그는 폭넓은 지적 교양을 쌓았다.	**n.** 지적 교양(세련)
taste [téist]	영 **the sense of what is fitting, harmonious, or beautiful** 동 **style** Your **taste** in clothes is absolutely atrocious. 너의 패션 감각은 정말 형편없다.	**n.** 미적 관념, 감각

brand
[brǽnd]

영 kind, grade, or make, as indicated by a stamp, trademark, or the like

동 type

Some younger kids really like wearing **brand** name clothes.

일부 아이들은 유명 상표의 옷을 입고 싶어한다.

n. (특별한)종류, 상표

---

architecture
[ɑ́ːrkətèktʃər]

영 the art of planning, designing, and constructing buildings

동 building design

Most apartment buildings in large Asian cities lack unique **architecture** styles.

아시아의 대도시에는 독특한 건축 양식이 부족한 아파트가 대부분이다.

n. 건축

Renaissance
[rènəsɑ́ːns]

영 a revival of intellectual or artistic achievement and vigor

동 rebirth, restoration

The **Renaissance** was a time of true innovation and cultural rebirth.

르네상스 시대는 진정한 변혁기이자 문예 부흥기였다.

n. 르네상스
문예 부흥

---

chalet
[ʃæléi]

영 a kind of farmhouse, low and with wide eaves, common in Alpine regions

동 cottage, cabin

Staying at winter **chalets** can be a great way to experience skiing.

샬레에서 겨울을 보낸다면, 스키 체험에 아주 좋은 방법이 될 수 있다.

n. 샬레
(스위스풍 별장)

---

clutter
[klʌ́tər]

영 to fill or litter with things in a disorderly manner

동 litter

The roads were **cluttered** with debris from the night's storm.

밤 사이에 몰아친 폭풍 때문에 도로가 잔해로 어지러워졌다.

v. 어지르다

A. Choose the one word that best fits the sentence.

1 When you are said to _____ cultural knowledge, then you have little information about it.

    a. love   b. lack

    c. dispose   d. offer

2 I don't like his _____ in music.

    a. stench   b. ordeal

    c. taste   d. nirvana

3 If your party is in _____, then it is full of people who are having a good time.

    a. trouble   b. full swing

    c. the can   d. strain

4 If you are _____ wealthy, then you have a lot of money and are affluent.

    a. freshly   b. meagerly

    c. fabulously   d. seldom

5 If your friends think of you as someone with _____, then you are stylish and cultured.

    a. sophistication   b. erudition

    c. cleverness   d. foxiness

B. Choose the one word that best fits the sentence.

1 Staying at _____ in the Swiss or Italian Alps could be a wonderful experience.

    a. ponds   b. gates

    c. chalets   d. schools

2 A famous and renowned running shoe _____ must surely be Nike.

    a. sorting   b. oddity

    c. advertiser   d. brand

3 The room was _____ with toys.

    a. equipped   b. paneled

    c. padded   d. cluttered

4 The _____ of the late 19th century was a weird mixture of styles.

    a. designer   b. sect

    c. architecture   d. mannerism

5 During the _____, many famous painters came into their own like Monet and Manet.

    a. eclipse   b. Renaissance

    c. Neolithic Age   d. civil war

1 What were ancient Egyptian forms decorated with?

    a. Jewelry from Swiss chalets.

    b. Artwork from Swiss castles.

    c. Ornaments from Swiss chalets.

    d. Sculpture from Swiss shanties.

2 Why does the writer explain Victorian architecture?

    a. To show that it was artistically ugly.

    b. To explain that it was a wild mixture of European classical and contemporary styles.

    c. To explain about the cluttered collections.

    d. To show patterns in crass opulence.

3 How does the writer introduce Victorian architecture?

    a. By explaining at the turn of the 18th century, many people were prosperous.

    b. By showing that at the turn of the 19th century, American businessmen became fabulously poor.

    c. By predicting that classical and contemporary architecture would come into vogue.

    d. By describing how the Industrial Revolution made many people millionaires.

the Function of Statement

4 Listen again to part of the lecture. Then answer the question.
What's the function of this passage?

    a. To introduce how to blend Italian and Greek styles.

    b. To give an example of mixtures of ancient, modern, foreign, and domestic architecture.

    c. To describe the limitations of contemporary Greek styles.

    d. To contrast Swiss and Chinese ancient screens.

Specific Information

5 According to the professor, what two factors did wealthy Americans lack?
Choose 2 answers.

    a. Taste and sophistication.

    b. Their own architectural style.

    c. Sophistication and values.

    d. Building extremely small homes.

Inference Question

6 What does the writer imply about Victorian architecture?

    a. Japanese paper umbrellas clashed with Victorian style.

    b. American architecture borrowed heavily from others.

    c. Rich people should have more sophistication.

    d. Italian Renaissance domes were tacky.

Victorian Architecture

In the late 19th century, the Industrial Revolution was in full swing, and many American businessmen became fabulously wealthy. By 1889, there were more than 100 millionaires in the United States, and all their income was tax free. Many of the rich lacked sophistication and taste, and this could clearly be seen in the odd houses they had built for themselves. America had an unusual brand of Victorian architecture that was a wild mixture of European classical and contemporary styles. Greek columns supported Italian Renaissance domes. Ancient Egyptian forms were decorated with details from Swiss chalets. The only rule seemed to have been: more is better. The interiors were studies in crass opulence, cluttered with collections of Roman statues, Japanese paper umbrellas, French cabinets, Chinese screens, and American pianos — a strange mixture of ancient, modern, foreign, and domestic objects.

1 The word **full swing** in the passage is closest in meaning to

    a. improvement   b. full operation   c. slowing   d. motion

2 The word **fabulously** in the passage is closest in meaning to

    a. squalidly   b. wonderfully   c. randomly   d. sometimes

3 The word **lack** in the passage is closest in meaning to

    a. conceive   b. prove   c. improve   d. do not have

4 The word **sophistication** in the passage is closest in meaning to

    a. supremacy   b. elegance   c. difficulty   d. arrogance

5 The word **taste** in the passage is closest in meaning to

    a. savor   b. style   c. fragrance   d. flavor

6 The word **brand** in the passage is closest in meaning to

    a. advertisement   b. verification   c. stigma   d. type

7 The word **architecture** in the passage is closest in meaning to

    a. planning   b. building design   c. home   d. mansion

8 The word **clutter** in the passage is closest in meaning to

    a. arrange   b. litter   c. constitute   d. build

Paraphrasing

Which best expresses the information in the underlined sentences?

1   Ancient Egyptian forms were decorated with details from Swiss chalets.

    a. The ancient Egyptians were very skilled at decorating Switzerland.

    b. Swiss chalets are similar in design to pensions.

    c. Too much variation in interior design produces dreadful results.

    d. Egyptian style was used in conjunction with Swiss design.

2   The only rule seemed to have been: more is better.

    a. The bigger the better and particularly the less expensive too.

    b. Many wealthy people preferred very large vacation homes.

    c. There didn't seem to be a definition of too much.

    d. Too many ostentatious homes denigrate the city.

Jazz Age Chronicler

Definitions and Examples

credit
[krédit]

영 commendation or honor given for some action, quality, etc.

동 recognition

She was given due **credit** for working hard on the marketing project.

그녀는 마케팅 기획에서 열심히 일한 것에 대해 응당 공로를 인정받았다.

n. 공로(인정)

blame
[bléim]

영 an act of attributing fault

동 condemnation

She is always trying to put the **blame** on others.

그녀는 늘 다른 사람을 비난하려고 한다.

n. 비난

overnight
[óuvərnàit]

영 for or during the night

동 almost instantly

FedEx tries to send most of its packages and parcels **overnight**.

페덱스 사는 대부분의 소포를 하룻밤 사이에 운송하도록 노력한다.

ad. 하룻밤 사이에

witty
[wíti]

영 possessing wit in speech or writing

동 clever

He was charming and **witty** and all the women laughed at his jokes.

그는 매력적이고 재치가 넘쳐서 모든 여자들이 그의 농담에 웃음을 터뜨렸다.

a. 재치 있는

unstable
[ʌnstéibəl]

영 not stable

동 unbalanced, unsettled

The emotionally **unstable** worker was asked to leave after two years.

정서가 불안정한 그 근로자는 2년 후 퇴직을 권고 받았다.

a. 불안정한

behavior

[bihéivjər]

- 영 manner of behaving or acting.
- 동 manner, action

Your **behavior** has much improved these last few months.

너의 행동은 지난 몇 달 사이 많이 좋아졌다.

n. 행동

---

disrupt

[disrʌ́pt]

- 영 to cause disorder or turmoil in
- 동 disturb

Persons who **disrupt** the meeting by not adhering to the rules may be asked to leave.

규칙을 지키지 않아서 회의를 혼란에 빠뜨린 사람들은 퇴장을 요구 받을 수 있다.

v. 혼란에 빠뜨리다

---

lavishly

[lǽviʃli]

- 영 in a wasteful manner; very generously
- 동 extravagantly

It would be wonderful if we could afford a **lavishly** designed wedding dress.

돈을 많이 들여 디자인한 웨딩 드레스를 살 수 있다면 정말 기분이 좋을 텐데.

ad. 사치스럽게

---

drunken

[drʌ́ŋkən]

- 영 given to drunkenness
- 동 intoxicated

The **drunken** businessman stumbled home and fell on his face on the bed.

술에 취한 사업가가 비틀거리며 집까지 걸어가서 침대에 코를 박고 쓰러졌다.

a. 술에 취한

---

serve

[sə:rv]

- 영 to contribute to; to be useful or of service to
- 동 help

The news **served** to raise awareness of the consequences of fatigue behind the wheel.

이 뉴스가 운전 중 피로로 인해 야기되는 결과에 대한 사람들의 인식을 높이는 데 공헌했다.

v. 공헌하다

A. Choose the one word that best fits the sentence.

1 If you send a parcel _____ by courier, then it takes 24 hours to arrive.

    a. fortnight   b. overnight

    c. next week   d. 48 hours

2 If a psychiatrist diagnoses you as _____, then you have emotional problems.

    a. arrogant   b. robust

    c. unstable   d. lethargic

3 When you incur _____ for something, you are criticized for it.

    a. sabotage   b. acclamation

    c. blame   d. indignation

4 If you are given _____ for doing something at work, then you are acknowledged.

    a. culpability   b. censure

    c. food   d. credit

5 When a person is very _____, he is humorous and usually charming to talk to.

    a. crazy   b. witty

    c. mental   d. psychotic

B. Choose the one word that best fits the sentence.

1 When _____ soccer players get together, there can be really rowdy parties afterwards.

    a. happy   b. drunken

    c. beaming   d. decent

2 When his _____ gets better, we can let him out of his room and have dinner.

    a. mannerism   b. style

    c. behavior   d. geniality

3 F. Scott Fitzgerald often held _____ decorated parties well into the night.

    a. harshly   b. weakly

    c. sensitively   d. lavishly

4 She _____ the development of the design industry.

    a. handed out   b. gave

    c. served   d. ate

5 The partygoers from the nightclub next door _____ the neighborhood.

    a. tranquilized   b. organized

    c. disrupted   d. suppressed

Listening Comprehension

Specific Question

1 How did Fitzgerald pay for his lifestyle?

    a. Through promoting his unstable wife's career.

    b. Through renting out his lavish New York home.

    c. By hosting drunken parties and selling tickets.

    d. By writing novels and essays.

Speaker's Purpose

2 Why does the writer explain the Jazz Age?

    a. To explain that the royal couples receive better treatment.

    b. To show that if you were witty and famous, the 1920s was a great time.

    c. To explain that wealth created many weird characters.

    d. To illustrate how successful novelists were arrogant.

Understanding Organization

3 How does the writer introduce the Jazz Age?

    a. By describing New York City's Fifth Avenue.

    b. Through introducing Fitzgerald's first novel "The Sun Also Rises."

    c. By illustrating Fitzgerald's influence on youth culture.

    d. Through introducing Fitzgerald's first novel "This Side of Paradise."

the Function of Statement

4 Listen again to part of the lecture. Then answer the question.
   What's the function of this passage?

    a. To introduce a dashing young couple in the 1920s.

    b. To give an example of the Gilded Age of the 1920s.

    c. To describe the limitations of excessive wealth.

    d. To contrast F. Scott and his wife Zelda.

Specific Information

5 According to the professor, what two factors made the Fitzgerald couple seem wild? Choose 2 answers.

    a. Laughing during inopportune moments.

    b. Writing awful movie reviews on Fifth Avenue.

    c. Riding on the hoods of taxis.

    d. Being quite calm at movies.

Inference Question

6 What does the writer imply about the Jazz Age?

    a. Entertaining lavishly is something everyone should aspire to.

    b. Success can lead to extravagant lifestyles.

    c. They lived the good life and were an example for all.

    d. Crying noisily over jokes is healthy behavior.

Jazz Age Chronicler

F. Scott Fitzgerald deserves much of the credit — and the blame — for the youth culture of the 1920's. In 1920, at the age of 24, Fitzgerald became famous overnight with the publication of his first novel, *This Side of Paradise*. The book was a huge success, and, in the words of a fellow writer, Fitzgerald became "a kind of king of our American youth." If he was king, the queen was his beautiful, witty, and unstable wife, Zelda. The royal couple became almost as well known for their wild behavior as for his writing. They rode on the hoods of taxis down New York City's Fifth Avenue, disrupted plays by laughing during the sad parts and crying noisily over the jokes, and entertained lavishly at drunken parties. To pay for their extravagant life style, Fitzgerald wrote the stories and novels that record — and partly served to create — the period.

1 The word **credit** in the passage is closest in meaning to

  a. recognition   b. accusation   c. censure   d. exoneration

2 The word **blame** in the passage is closest in meaning to

  a. prospect   b. congeniality   c. dissension   d. condemnation

3 The word **overnight** in the passage is closest in meaning to

  a. gradually   b. unhurriedly   c. hesitantly   d. almost instantly

4 The word **witty** in the passage is closest in meaning to

  a. slow   b. clever   c. retarded   d. dull

5 The word **unstable** in the passage is closest in meaning to

    a. steady   b. dizzy   c. unsettled   d. intelligent

6 The word **behavior** in the passage is closest in meaning to

    a. inertia   b. thought   c. action   d. assertion

7 The word **disrupt** in the passage is closest in meaning to

    a. separate   b. dismantle   c. disturb   d. arrange

8 The word **lavishly** in the passage is closest in meaning to

    a. extravagantly   b. thriftily   c. passively   d. compliantly

Paraphrasing

Which best expresses the information in the underlined sentences?

1 The royal couple became almost as well known for their wild behavior as for his writing.

    a. The royal couple were well known for their hospitality.
    b. Being royal is especially difficult, even in England.
    c. Many of Fitzgerald's parties were wild and flamboyant.
    d. The Fitzgerald couple was renowned for their behavior.

2 They rode on the hoods of taxis down New York City's Fifth Avenue, disrupted plays by laughing during the sad parts, and entertained lavishly at drunken parties.

    a. Behaving extravagantly and boorishly was how they acted.
    b. Riding on taxis is a good strategy, especially when they are full.
    c. It is hard to get a taxi on New York City's Fifth Avenue.
    d. Entertaining lavishly at drunken parties was quite common.

Real Jazzmen

Definitions and Examples

symphonic
[simfánik]

- 영 of or pertaining to symphony or harmony of sounds.
- 동 **harmonious**

The **symphonic** music soothed her wounded soul.

조화로운 음악이 그녀의 상처 받은 영혼을 위로했다.

a. 교향악의
조화로운

---

pass (for)
[pǽs]

- 영 to be accepted as or be considered
- 동 **be regarded (as)**

If he was a bit taller and wore a gray suit, he could **pass for** a professor at our school.

키가 조금 더 크고 회색 양복을 입었다면, 그는 우리 학교에서 교수로 통할 수 있었을 것이다.

v. 통하다

---

obscurity
[əbskjúərəti]

- 영 the condition of being unknown
- 동 **anonymity**

He traveled in relative **obscurity** throughout Afghanistan and Iran.

익명으로 아프가니스탄과 이란의 곳곳을 여행했다.

n. 익명, 무명

---

frankly
[frǽŋkli]

- 영 in a frank manner
- 동 **honestly**

Frankly speaking, it is time you tried harder to get married.

솔직하게 말해서, 결혼하려면 더 열심히 노력해야 할 때다.

ad. 솔직하게

---

label
[léibəl]

- 영 to designate or describe by or on a label
- 동 **brand, tag**

The new hip hop album by 50 Cent was **labeled** offensive.

50 Cent의 새 힙합 앨범은 무례한 음악으로 분류되었다.

v. (라벨로) 분류하다

inferior [infíəriər]	영 lower in station, rank, degree, or grade 동 lesser Japanese and Korean cars are considered **inferior** to many German cars. 일본과 한국산 자동차는 독일산 자동차에 비해 하급으로 취급된다.	a. 하급의
glorious [glɔ́:riəs]	영 brilliantly beautiful or magnificient; splendid 동 dazzling, superb The **glorious** days of the Montreal Canadians hockey team are over. 몬트리올 캐나디언스 하키 팀의 영광의 날이 끝이 났다.	a. 영광스러운 멋진
toot [tu:t]	영 to make a sound resembling that of a horn, whistle, or the like 동 honk The children were **tooting** their horns at the birthday party celebration. 아이들은 생일 축하 파티에서 호른을 불고 있었다.	v. 불다
rattletrap [rǽtltræp]	영 worn-out, rickety or rattling 동 dilapidated The **rattletrap** train car was so old that it almost fell apart. 낡아빠진 기차의 차량은 너무 오래되어서 거의 다 부서졌다.	a. 낡아빠진
triumphant [traiʌ́mfənt]	영 having achieved victory or success 동 successful The **triumphant** Korean soccer team returned from the 2002 World Cup. 2002년 월드컵에서 좋은 성과를 거둔 한국 축구팀이 돌아왔다.	a. 승리를 얻은

A. Choose the one word that best fits the sentence.

1 If you live in _____ , then you live a relatively quiet and secret
  lifestyle.

  a. obscurity   b. gloomy times

  c. spotlight   d. basements

2 When something is _____ , it is categorized and given an
  explanation.

  a. hidden   b. labeled

  c. stuck   d. written

3 If you can compose _____ music, then you are a highly talented
  composer.

  a. chemical   b. cute

  c. unharmonious   d. symphonic

4 His sophisticated manners allow him to _____ for a gentleman.

  a. hop   b. pass
  c. hunker   d. root

5 If you speak _____ to your co-worker, then you are being honest
  and forthright.

  a. often   b. naively
  c. frankly   d. deceptively

Sentence Completion

B. Choose the one word that best fits the sentence.

1 If you ride in a _____ vehicle, don't be surprised if it falls apart on your mid-trip.

    a. metal   b. luxurious

    c. rattletrap   d. BMW

2 Japanese cars used to be _____ but now Lexus, Infinity and Acura are fine luxury cars.

    a. superior   b. inferior

    c. luxurious   d. fashionable

3 Some historians lament that the _____ days of the United States are beginning to end.

    a. depressing   b. jiffy

    c. glorious   d. poverty-stricken

4 Louis Armstrong eventually made a _____ career out of jazz and is world renowned.

    a. trifling   b. triumphant

    c. boring   d. comeback

5 There's no point _____ your horn.

    a. tooting   b. pulling

    c. exhaling   d. telling

1 What advantages did the concert organizers like Whiteman have over real jazzmen?

    a. They promoted New Orleans jazz.

    b. They encouraged Louis Armstrong to sell records.

    c. They produced jazz concerts for record sums.

    d. They owned rattletrap luxury cars.

Speaker's Purpose

2 Why does the writer explain jazz artists?

    a. To illustrate the U.S. contribution to music.

    b. In order to show the birth of a new musical era.

    c. To show how bad the third-rate dance bands were.

    d. To promote the great Louis Armstrong.

Understanding Organization

3 How does the writer introduce jazz artists?

    a. Through analyzing Armstrong's illustrious career.

    b. By discussing Black neighborhoods.

    c. By describing symphonic jazz, the roots of jazz.

    d. Through illustrating neglected music.

the Function of Statement

4 Listen again to part of the lecture. Then answer the question.

  What's the function of this passage?

    a. To introduce the disparities between races regarding music.

    b. To give an example of how jazzmen traveled in rattletrap cars.

    c. To describe the limitations of becoming a promoter.

    d. To contrast various musical genres.

5 According to the professor, what two places was the first jazz music played in? Choose 2 answers.

    a. Black dance halls in Cincinnati.

    b. Obscure and remote venues.

    c. Old Chicago minstrel shows.

    d. Black dance halls in Harlem.

6 What does the writer imply about jazz artists?

    a. It is hard for true musicians to earn a living.

    b. The beginning of early jazz was a difficult time for musicians.

    c. There is success in being a concert promoter.

    d. Real music was being produced in Chicago.

Real Jazzmen

"Symphonic jazz" and most of the other music that passed for jazz in the 1920's were not real jazz at all. The real music was being produced in relative obscurity. It had moved up river from New Orleans, its birthplace, but it was still heard mainly in black dance halls in Harlem and Chicago, and on records that were frankly labeled "race records" and sold only in black neighborhoods. And while concert organizers like Paul Whiteman were making a quarter of a million dollars a year producing jazz concerts of an inferior quality, the real jazzmen were often broke. The great Louis Armstrong had to play in dubious show bands, while Bix Beiderbecke wasted his glorious cornet tone tooting for third-rate dance bands. The real jazzmen traveled from date to date in rattletrap cars with the luggage tied to the roof. But the musicians were tough and so was the music, and it survived the neglect of the age to become America's one triumphant contribution to the world's music.

1 The word **symphonic** in the passage is closest in meaning to
   a. messy   b. harmonious   c. cacophonous   d. wondrous

2 The word **pass for** in the passage is closest in meaning to
   a. be provided for   b. be furnished with
   c. be replaced by   d. be regarded as

3 The word **obscurity** in the passage is closest in meaning to
   a. gloom   b. limbo   c. glare   d. anonymity

4 The word **frankly** in the passage is closest in meaning to
   a. freely   b. credulously   c. honestly   d. properly

5 The word **label** in the passage is closest in meaning to

    a. manipulate   b. tag   c. print   d. level

6 The word **inferior** in the passage is closest in meaning to

    a. interior   b. lesser   c. well-known   d. infamous

7 The word **glorious** in the passage is closest in meaning to

    a. notorious   b. bright   c. superb   d. divine

8 The word **toot** in the passage is closest in meaning to

    a. implode   b. sound   c. honk   d. blip

Paraphrasing

Which best expresses the information in the underlined sentences?

1 The great Louis Armstrong had to play in dubious show bands, while Bix Beiderbecke wasted his glorious cornet tone tooting for third-rate dance bands.

    a. The dubious show bands were in fact, highly underrated.
    b. Armstrong started in lowly show bands, despite his immense talent.
    c. Bix Beiderbecke was an established clarinet player.
    d. Cornet tone singing is revered today.

2 The real jazzmen traveled from date to date in rattletrap cars with the luggage tied to the roof.

    a. Real jazzmen traveled in old beat-up cars to venues.
    b. Rattletrap cars were especially designed for holding instruments.
    c. Real jazzmen traveled together and stayed in motels.
    d. The breaking point for many musicians was the arduous road trip.

Definitions and Examples

topsoil	영 **the fertile, upper part of the soil**	n. 표토
[tápsɔ̀il]	동 **surface soil**	
	Much of the **topsoil** in the Sahara is highly eroded.	
	사하라 사막의 표토 중 대부분은 침식 정도가 심각하다.	

deteriorate	영 **to make or become worse or inferior in character, quality, value, etc.**	v. 나빠지다 악화되다
[ditíəriərèit]	동 **degenerate, worsen**	
	The company decided to let their older products **deteriorate**.	
	그 회사는 예전 상품을 개선하지 않고 그냥 두기로 했다.	

drought	영 **a period of dry weather, esp. a long one that is injurious to crops**	n. 가뭄
[dràut]	동 **dryness, dry spell**	
	Much of the arid plains in Bangladesh routinely suffer from **drought**.	
	방글라데시의 메마른 평원 중 상당 부분이 일상적으로 가뭄을 겪는다.	

severe	영 **unnecessarily extreme**	a. 맹렬한, 심각한
[sivíər]	동 **awful, serious**	
	Her injuries were so **severe** that she couldn't complete her training.	
	그녀의 상처는 너무 심각해서 훈련을 끝마칠 수가 없었다.	

considerable	영 **rather large or great in size, distance, extent, etc.**	a. 상당한
[kənsídərəbəl]	동 **substantial, sizable**	
	They had **considerable** financial resources but squandered it all.	
	그들은 상당한 자금을 보유하고 있었지만 전부 탕진해 버렸다.	

Earth Science I

erosion [iróuʒən]	⑱ condition in which the earth's surface is worn away by the action of water and wind ⑧ destruction, washing away The **erosion** of the hillside was threatening the school below. 산허리가 침식되면서 산허리 아래에 있는 학교에서 불안해하고 있었다.	**n.** 침식
plant [plǽnt]	⑱ to put or set in the ground for growth, as seeds, young tress, etc. ⑧ grow Which indian taught the pilgrims to **plant** corn? 어떤 인디언이 청교도 이주자들에게 옥수수를 심으라고 가르쳤을까?	**v.** 심다
paucity [pɔ́:səti]	⑱ smallness of quantity; scarcity; scantiness ⑧ lack The **paucity** of her generosity was noted by all her co-workers. 그녀가 너그러움이 부족하다는 것은 주위 동료들도 모두 아는 사실이었다.	**n.** 부족
residue [rézidjù:]	⑱ something that remains after a part is removed, disposed of, or used; ⑧ leftover Police officer Murphy was pleased to discover chemical **residue** on the victim's shoes. 머피 경찰관은 희생자의 신발에 묻은 화학 물질 찌꺼기를 발견하고 기뻐했다.	**v.** 찌꺼기
apprehension [æ̀prihénʃən]	⑱ anticipation of adversity or misfortune; suspicion or fear of future trouble or evil. ⑧ fear In **apprehension** of losing jobs, the workers themselves hid signs of their infection. 해고에 대한 우려때문에 직원들은 자신의 감염 사실을 숨겼다.	**n.** 우려

A. Choose the one word that best fits the sentence.

1 If a farmer has a _____ on his farm, then there is no water for a long time.

    a. bug   b. drought

    c. flood   d. scab

2 When you have a _____ amount of money, then you have lots of money and are wealthy.

    a. bare   b. mere

    c. considerable   d. destitute

3 When something starts to _____, then it is breaking down.

    a. put together   b. resolve

    c. deteriorate   d. cry out

4 If you dig up _____, then you are digging up the upper part of the soil.

    a. seedlings   b. topsoil

    c. flowers   d. creosote

5 If you have a _____ headache, then it is very bad and painful.

    a. severe   b. mild

    c. mediated   d. painless

Sentence Completion

B. Choose the one word that best fits the sentence.

1 The thief left _____ from his gun at the scene of the crime, a vital clue for police.

    a. material   b. residue

    c. tissue   d. hair dregs

2 One of the primary causes of _____ is massive rainstorms, wind and mud slides.

    a. cavity   b. rust

    c. erosion   d. weather

3 There's no point trying to _____ that seedling; the soil is too dry.

    a. lodge   b. sew

    c. dig   d. plant

4 She generally seemed to avoid moments of _____ during her life.

    a. meditation   b. apprehension

    c. relaxation   d. calm

5 There is a(an) _____ of rain in the hot dry plains of the Indian Punjab province.

    a. abundance   b. deluge

    c. paucity   d. expansiveness

1 What can make soil erosion worse?

    a. Farmers who plant many crops.

    b. Weak crop roots in good quality topsoil.

    c. Topsoil that is laced with chemicals.

    d. High winds, coupled with weak soil conditions.

Speaker's Purpose

2 Why does the writer explain soil erosion?

    a. To demonstrate the difficulties farmers have in producing crops.

    b. To estimate erosion in winter months.

    c. To analyze the yields of specific corn crops.

    d. To show how the rains cause further damage to wetlands.

Understanding Organization

3 How does the writer introduce soil erosion?

    a. By describing dangerous residues in agricultural chemicals.

    b. Through talking about storms in Texas and Arkansas.

    c. By reviewing farming patterns on the Great Plains.

    d. By recounting the Dust Bowl days of the 1930's.

the Function of Statement

4 Listen again to part of the lecture. Then answer the question.
What's the function of this passage?

    a. To introduce an alternative to fixing susceptibility to wind erosion.

    b. To give examples of erosion by wind, winter and spring rains.

    c. To describe agricultural chemicals in everyday life.

    d. To contrast industrial and farming techniques in the mid-west.

Specific Information

5 According to the writer, what two factors contributed to wind erosion? Choose 2 answers.

    a. Farmland that is susceptible to drought.

    b. Severe storms over farmland.

    c. Topsoil in the Dust Bowl region.

    d. Weak crop roots in poor quality topsoil.

Inference Question

6 What does the writer imply about soil erosion?

    a. Fighting erosion is a severe problem because we all rely on food.

    b. Dangerous residues of chemicals abound everywhere.

    c. Less and less rainfall is due over the coming decades.

    d. We haven't lost this much topsoil since the Dust Bowl.

Soil

The condition of the topsoil on the ranches and farms of the Great Plains of the United States has continued to deteriorate. In recent years drought and severe storms with high winds have caused considerable erosion of the soil. During periods of drought, farmers tend to plant fewer crops, and the resultant paucity of crop roots that hold the soil in place increases susceptibility to wind erosion. Water erosion by winter and spring rains causes further damage. And when there is no rain, dangerous residues of agricultural chemicals remain in the soil. Farms and ranches in the Great Plains region haven't lost this much topsoil since the Dust Bowl days of the 1930's, and there is considerable cause for apprehension.

1 The word **topsoil** in the passage is closest in meaning to

    a. dry land   b. compost   c. surface soil   d. gravel

2 The word **deteriorate** in the passage is closest in meaning to

    a. worsen   b. cause   c. rot   d. improve

3 The word **drought** in the passage is closest in meaning to

    a. desiccate   b. dryness   c. dampness   d. drizzle

4 The word **severe** in the passage is closest in meaning to

    a. stubborn   b. awful   c. impressive   d. bearable

5 The word **considerable** in the passage is closest in meaning to

    a. sizable   b. essential   c. main   d. wretched

6 The word **erosion** in the passage is closest in meaning to

    a. running amok   b. washing away

    c. casting out   d. building up

7 The word **plant** in the passage is closest in meaning to

    a. pluck   b. brush   c. delve   d. grow

8 The word **paucity** in the passage is closest in meaning to

    a. fertility   b. lack   c. abundance   d. density

Paraphrasing

Which best expresses the information in the underlined sentences?

1 During periods of drought, farmers tend to plant fewer crops, and the resultant paucity of crop roots that hold the soil in place increases susceptibility to wind erosion.

    a. The lack of plant roots leads to high erosion from winds.

    b. Periods of drought are often followed by substantial rains.

    c. Too much rain leads to competition among plants.

    d. Too many plant roots uses up water resources.

2 Farms and ranches in the Great Plains region haven't lost this much topsoil since the Dust Bowl days of the 1930's, and there is considerable cause for apprehension.

    a. Topsoil resources are diminishing, even more than in the 1930's.

    b. Apprehension exists in Great Plains farmers' minds.

    c. Farms and ranches are using too much water.

    d. Topsoil resources are on the decline, even in the Great Plains.

Unit 14 Groundwater

Definitions and Examples

groundwater
[gráundwɔ̀:tər]

영 **water beneath the surface, most of which has seeded down from above**

The Near the nuclear power plant they discovered contaminated **groundwater**.

원자력 발전소 근처에서 사람들은 오염된 지하수를 발견했다.

n. 지하수

peak
[píːk]

영 **the pointed top of a mountain or ridge**

동 **top**

The **peaks** in the Karakoram Mountains in Pakistan are some of the most spectacular on Earth.

파키스탄에 있는 카라코람 산맥의 여러 봉우리는 지구에서 볼 수 있는 장관에 속한다.

n. 봉우리

surge
[sə́ːrdʒ]

영 **to wise and move, as in waves or billows**

동 **rush**

Large waves **surged** across the beach and spilled over the highway.

거대한 파도가 해안으로 밀어닥쳐와 고속도로를 덮쳤다.

v. 밀어닥치다
넘치다

support
[səpɔ́ːrt]

영 **to provide everything necessary so that someone or something can live or exist**

동 **sustain, maintain**

The men were almost dead with fatigue, but hope **supported** them.

그 사람들은 피로로 인해 거의 죽음에 이르렀으나 희망이 그들을 지탱해 주었다.

v. 지탱하다

scarce
[skέərs]

영 **insufficient to satisfy the need or demand; not abundant**

동 **insufficient**

Water is the last thing a nation like Canada will be **scarce** of.

캐나다 같은 나라는 절대 물 부족을 겪을 리 없다.

a. 부족한

Earth Science I

irrigation [ìrəgéiʃən]	영 the artificial application of water to land to assist in the production of crops. The **irrigation** ditch had not been full of water for three years. 관개 수로는 지난 3년 동안 물이 가득 찬 적이 없었다.	n. 관개
seep [síːp]	영 to flow slowly and in small quantities through or into something 동 leak, permeate Water **seeped** through the walls during the hurricanes. 허리케인이 발생한 동안 물이 벽에 스며들었다.	v. 스며들다
pump [pʌmp]	영 to force a liquid to flow in that direction using a pump 동 pull out of The villagers tried to prevent the well from being **pumped** dry. 지나친 펌프질로 인한 우물 고갈을 막기 위해 마을 주민들은 노력했다.	v. 펌프로 퍼 올리다
map [mæp]	영 to make a map of 동 chart **Mapping** the Earth is now done by geosynchronous orbiting satellites. 지구의 지도를 만드는 일을 오늘날에는 정지 궤도 위성이 일임한다.	v. 지도를 만들다
conservation [kànsəːrvéiʃən]	영 the act of conserving; prevention of injury, decay, waste, or loss 동 preservation Much more **conservation** needs to be done in sub-Saharan Africa. 사하라 사막 이남의 아프리카 지역은 지금보다 훨씬 많은 관리를 받아야 한다.	n. (자연) 보호, 관리

Sentence Completion

A. Choose the one word that best fits the sentence.

1 When your tap water in the bathroom _____, then it comes out very fast.

    a. wanders   b. surges

    c. heaves   d. pitches

2 If the planet's oil resources become _____, then all the drilling has used them up.

    a. scarce   b. improving

    c. abundant   d. half full

3 If you climb to the _____, then you have finally reached the top of it.

    a. bottom   b. peak

    c. edge   d. side

4 If you don't have anyone _____ you, then no one will be there to help you.

    a. carrying   b. impeding

    c. giving   d. supporting

5 When you dig into ground and hit _____, then you have struck a water source.

    a. dirt   b. drip

    c. groundwater   d. hose

B. Choose the one word that best fits the sentence.

1 Many cartographers travel around the Earth _____ out new geographic areas.

    a. mapping   b. dimming

    c. eclipsing   d. repressing

2 Many farmers routinely pipe in water to fill their _____ ditches.

    a. refuse   b. chemical

    c. irrigation   d. sewage

3 In order to prevent _____ through cracks, it is necessary to seal the concrete of the wall.

    a. insulting   b. viewing

    c. appropriating   d. seeping

4 In Africa, there have been recent _____ efforts to protect elephants and cheetahs.

    a. greed   b. saturation

    c. savagery   d. conservation

5 When you are _____ up your mountain bike tire, the air will inflate the inner tube.

    a. hitting   b. slugging

    c. spiking   d. pumping

1 Why do some people fight over the rights to groundwater?

    a. Because they have excessive amounts of crops to water.

    b. Because water is so expensive in some communities.

    c. Water is crucial to supporting farm life in deserts.

    d. In some communities with little water, groundwater is essential for helping crops grow.

2 Why does the writer explain groundwater use?

    a. Because most of mankind's usable water comes from below the surface.

    b. To suggest that people start to conserve their tap water.

    c. To show that water is available everywhere under the Earth's surface, from beneath the deserts to coastlines.

    d. To discourage better management and conservation.

3 How does the writer introduce groundwater use?

    a. By showing how people in the Himalayas use their water.

    b. By talking about advances in irrigation technology.

    c. By predicting future droughts given the scarcity of water.

    d. Through describing all the places one can find groundwater, from mountains to deserts.

4 Listen again to part of the lecture. Then answer the question.
   What's the function of this passage?

   a. To explain that hundreds of scientists spend their time mapping locations.
   b. To show the necessity for conserving groundwater given how vital it is to society and our sources of food.
   c. To describe the limitations of conservation programs.
   d. To contrast desert and mountain water usage.

5 According to the writer, what two aspects do scientists measure about groundwater wells? Choose 2 answers.

   a. The original location of groundwater.
   b. Prior areas where groundwater has been conserved.
   c. How fast groundwater flows.
   d. Small Death Valley communities.

6 What does the writer imply about groundwater use?

   a. Management and conservation issues need to be better funded by the government.
   b. We need to predict how fast wells will dry up.
   c. Hundreds of scientists spend their time mapping well locations.
   d. The proper use of groundwater, from wells or springs is essential for mankind.

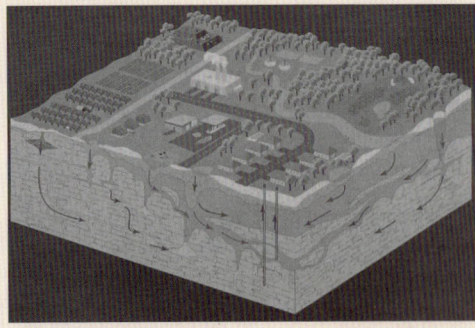

Groundwater

Groundwater is a major source of mankind' usable water. It is found everywhere under the earth's surface, from beneath the deserts of Death Valley to the highest peaks of the Himalayas. It surges up through wells and springs, supporting life on farms and in towns as well as supplying large cities. When surface water is scarce, groundwater serves as a vital supply for irrigation, and people have even fought over the rights to it. Groundwater can rarely be seen except when it seeps up into a well or flows from a spring, but scientists can estimate how much is stored at a given location, how fast it is moving, how soon pumping a well will affect other wells, where the water comes from, and where it will be found years in the future. So important is groundwater that hundreds of scientists spend their time mapping its location for the purpose of management and conservation.

1 The word **peak** in the passage is closest in meaning to

    a. curve   b. side   c. top   d. nadir

2 The word **surge** in the passage is closest in meaning to

    a. tackle   b. rush   c. confront   d. underline

3 The word **support** in the passage is closest in meaning to

    a. satisfy   b. deteriorate   c. improve   d. sustain

4 The word **scarce** in the passage is closest in meaning to

    a. insufficient   b. stupendous   c. sufficient   d. harmless

5 The word **seep** in the passage is closest in meaning to

  a. foam   b. permeate   c. ripple   d. weep

6 The word **pump** in the passage is closest in meaning to

  a. push in   b. pull out of   c. shove   d. inoculate

7 The word **map** in the passage is closest in meaning to

  a. chart   b. mop   c. illuminate   d. process

8 The word **conservation** in the passage is closest in meaning to

  a. squandering   b. observation   c. storage   d. preservation

Paraphrasing

Which best expresses the information in the underlined sentences?

1 Groundwater can rarely be seen except when it seeps up into a well or flows from a spring, but scientists can estimate how much is stored at a given location, and how fast it is moving.

  a. Scientists can estimate the flow of water, but they don't know where it is going.

  b. Calculating the amount and source of groundwater is vital.

  c. Too few spring wells in deserts do not provide sufficient water for farmers.

  d. Any given location has plentiful well, but extracting it is another matter.

2 So important is groundwater that hundreds of scientists spend their time mapping its location for the purpose of management and conservation.

  a. More funding needs to be funneled into mapping projects.

  b. Mapping out groundwater locations is central to managing water resources.

  c. The location of groundwater wells needs to be put in a central database.

  d. Too much overlapping maps have been drawn up by scientists.

Definitions and Examples

---

adequate

[ǽdikwit]

ⓔ as much or as good as necessary for some requirement or purpose

ⓢ **sufficient**

They do not have enough money to acquire **adequate** food for a healthy life.

건강한 삶을 위해 충분한 음식을 얻기에는 그들이 가진 돈이 부족하다.

a. 충분한

---

vital

[váitl]

ⓔ **necessary to continued existence or effectiveness**

ⓢ **essential, indispensable**

It is **vital** that the United States keeps a military presence in the Middle East.

미국 군대의 지속적인 중동 주둔은 매우 중요하다.

a. 매우 중요한

---

organism

[ɔ́:rɡənìzəm]

ⓔ **a form of life composed of mutually interdependent parts that maintain various vital processes**

ⓢ **living thing, creature**

Almost all life forms start as an **organism**, and then develop after that.

거의 모든 생물은 유기체로 시작한 후 진화한다.

n. 유기체

---

dissolve

[dizálv]

ⓔ **to make a solution of, as by mixing with a liquid**

ⓢ **melt**

If you put icing sugar into a glass of Pepsi, it quickly **dissolves**.

콜라가 든 잔에 가루 설탕을 넣으면 금방 녹는다.

v. 녹다

---

distribute

[distríbjuːt]

ⓔ **to divide and give out in shares**

ⓢ **deliver**

The paperboy **distributes** the newspaper every morning.

신문 배달 소년은 매일 아침 신문을 배달한다.

v. 배달하다

Earth Science I

circulation [sə̀:rkjəléiʃən]	영 movement in a circle or circuit, especially the movement of blood through bodily vessels as a result of the heart's pumping action 동 flow Blood **circulation** plays an important part in our being. 혈액 순환은 우리의 생존에 중요한 역할을 한다.	**n.** 순환
thirst [θə́:rst]	영 a sensation of dryness in the mouth and throat caused by need of liquid; strong or eager desire 동 dryness I quenched my **thirst** with water from the well. 나는 우물물을 마시고 갈증을 해소했다.	**n.** 갈증
biochemist [bàioukémist]	영 someone with special training in biochemistry The **biochemists** at the university were conducting amazing research. 그 대학교의 생화학자들은 놀라운 실험을 진행 중이었다.	**n.** 생화학자
venture [véntʃər]	영 to make or embark on a venture; dare to go 동 chance The young Asian girl had never **ventured** beyond her home country. 나이 어린 그 아시아계 소녀는 고국을 떠나 본 적이 없었다.	**v.** 모험을 감행하다 과감히 하다
ancestor [ǽnsestər]	영 a person from whom one is descended 동 antecedent Anthropologists have determined that most of our **ancestors** date back to what is now Kenya. 인류학자들은 우리 조상 중 대다수가 현재의 케냐 지역에서 살았다는 결론을 내렸다.	**n.** 조상

Sentence Completion

A. Choose the one word that best fits the sentence.

1 If you are working on a(an) _____ in science class, then you are playing with a basic life form.

    a. toy   b. organism

    c. individual   d. projectile

2 When a delivery person _____ a product, they are sending it to its destination.

    a. shares   b. buys

    c. distributes   d. scatters

3 Your height is _____ for a professional basketball player.

    a. erudite   b. polished

    c. adequate   d. cellular

4 If you hurt your _____ organs, then you damage important internal organs.

    a. vital   b. external

    c. insignificant   d. subordinate

5 When something _____ in a liquid, then it is being mixed up in the liquid.

    a. congeals   b. dissolves

    c. breaks up   d. creates

B. Choose the one word that best fits the sentence.

1 If you have _____ forth into the world of travel, then you have discovered many amazing cultures.

    a. foregone   b. retreated

    c. ventured   d. hesitated

2 If you cut off the _____ in your hand, then no more blood will flow to it.

    a. sweat glands   b. nerve

    c. routes   d. circulation

3 After running exhausted for 16 kilometers, her _____ for water increased markedly.

    a. thirst   b. perspiration

    c. pain   d. disgust

4 Some of our most ancient _____ were highly capable of finding groundwater.

    a. associates   b. acquaintances

    c. ancestors   d. friends

5 There's one _____ who is conducting amazing chemical research work on zebras.

    a. accounting supervisor   b. biochemist

    c. choreographer   d. journalist

Specific Question

1 What vital elements does the body distribute?

    a. Nitrogen, oxygen and plasma.

    b. Carbon dioxide, oxygen, and salt.

    c. Carbon monoxide, oxygen, and salt.

    d. Carbon dioxide, sulfur, and salt.

Speaker's Purpose

2 Why does the writer explain the function of water?

    a. To explain that an adequate supply of water is vital for all forms of animal and plant life.

    b. To estimate that an organism loses 50% of its water through excretion.

    c. To explain that water is absolutely necessary, as the body distributes vital elements, circulates blood and removes waste.

    d. To explain that salt levels are central to blood circulation.

Understanding Organization

3 How does the writer introduce the function of water?

    a. Water is vital for all organisms, from the smallest ameba to the tallest tree.

    b. Water makes up about 60 percent of every living organism.

    c. Water is vital for all organisms except large mammals and fauna.

    d. Humans still carry water within their bodies from their ancestors.

the Function of Statement

4   Listen again to part of the lecture. Then answer the question.
    What's the function of this passage?

      a. To introduce how the human body replaces vital nutrients.

      b. To examine the concentration of salt in human beings.

      c. To state that water is vital for all living things.

      d. To contrast how evaporation must constantly be replaced in the body.

Specific Information

5   According to the writer, what two elements does the body lose? Choose 2
    answers.

      a. Muscle tissue.

      b. Excretion.

      c. Nitrogen.

      d. Evaporation.

Inference Question

6   What does the writer imply about the function of water?

      a. Next to blood cells, water is invaluable.

      b. Without water, a human being could not even open his eyes.

      c. All life functions in essence, on water and the nutrients contained
        within.

      d. The water from human ancestors helps us survive.

Bodywater

An **adequate** supply of water is **vital** for all forms of animal and plant life, from the smallest ameba to the tallest tree. Water makes up about 50 percent of every living **organism**. A person would die if he lost more than 15 percent of his body's water. In the body, water **dissolves** and **distributes** vital elements such as carbon dioxide, oxygen, and salt. It is essential for blood **circulation**, the removal of wastes, and the movement of muscles. Without water, a human being could not even open his eyes. The water that an organism loses through excretion and evaporation must constantly be replaced. This never-ending **thirst** is believed to be a legacy of the ocean origins of life. The concentration of salt in human beings is about 0.9 percent, a level that biochemists believe is the same as that of the sea 400 million years ago — when the first organisms ventured from the oceans to the land. So, in one sense, human beings still carry within their bodies the water from which their **ancestors** evolved long ago.

1   The word **adequate** in the passage is closest in meaning to

    a. available   b. deficient   c. subpar   d. sufficient

2   The word **vital** in the passage is closest in meaning to

    a. unavailable   b. typical   c. essential   d. unnecessary

3   The word **organism** in the passage is closest in meaning to

    a. termination   b. scamp   c. mammal   d. creature

4 The word **dissolve** in the passage is closest in meaning to

    a. melt   b. disprove   c. merge   d. disappear

5 The word **distribute** in the passage is closest in meaning to

    a. accompany   b. deliver   c. take   d. retrieve

6 The word **circulation** in the passage is closest in meaning to

    a. flow   b. route   c. division   d. allotment

7 The word **thirst** in the passage is closest in meaning to

    a. contentment   b. dryness   c. apathy   d. satisfaction

8 The word **ancestor** in the passage is closest in meaning to

    a. descendant   b. successor   c. antecedent   d. offspring

Paraphrasing

Which best expresses the information in the underlined sentences?

1   The water that an organism loses through excretion and evaporation must constantly be replaced.

    a. Water must be replaced once a organism duplicates itself.
    b. Water loss is common in most organisms.
    c. Too much water replacement is bad for organism development.
    d. The water lost through excretion must be replaced.

2   So, in one sense, human beings still carry within their bodies the water from which their ancestors evolved long ago.

    a. When ancestors do evolve, they are not likely to change that much.
    b. In essence, humans have water that dates back to their ancestors.
    c. Too much water in our ancestors needed to be expelled.
    d. Ancestors evolved so long ago that nothing remains from them.

Machine (1)

Definitions and Examples

commonly

[kámənli]

- 영 usually; ordinarily
- 동 generally

The agency controls the prescription of **commonly** abused drugs.

그 기관은 일반적으로 남용되는 약물에 대해 규제한다.

ad. 일반적으로
흔히

---

device

[diváis]

- 영 a thing made for a particular purpose
- 동 instrument

The **devices** used in computer servers are made to high tolerances.

컴퓨터 서버에 사용되는 장치는 내구력이 높다.

n. 장치

---

contraption

[kəntrǽpʃən]

- 영 a mechanical contrivance
- 동 apparatus, gadget

It turned out that this **contraption** never worked.

알고보니 이 새 고안물은 절대 작동되지 않는 것이었다.

n. 새 고안물
도구, 기계

---

finding

[fáindiŋ]

- 영 something that has been found
- 동 discovery

The scientific **findings** were very shocking and revealing about humanity.

그 과학적인 발견은 매우 충격적이었으며, 우리가 알지못한 인류에 대한 새로운 것을 보여주었다.

n. 발견(물)
연구결과

---

convert

[kənvə́:rt]

- 영 to change into a different form or properties
- 동 alter, transform

The gas **converted** to tiny droplets of sulfuric acid.

그 기체는 작은 황산 방울로 변했다.

v. 변환하다

Social Science II

capable [kéipəbəl]	⑱ having the ability or capacity for ⑧ able The country has missiles **capable** of hitting the United States. 그 나라는 미국을 공격할 수 있는 미사일을 보유하고 있다.	**a.** 능력 있는 할 수 있는
awesome [ɔ́:səm]	⑱ showing or characterized by awe ⑧ amazing The fireworks were **awesome** and full of sparkles and explosions. 불꽃과 폭음 소리가 가득한, 굉장히 멋진 불꽃놀이였다.	**a.** 굉장히 멋진
blow (up) [blóu]	⑱ to cause to explode ⑧ explode, blast Several rebels **blew up** the houses, so they had nowhere to go. 몇몇 폭도들이 주택을 폭파하여 그들은 갈 곳이 없었다.	**v.** 폭파하다
trap [trǽp]	⑱ to prevent from escaping or getting free ⑧ hold The atmospheres of some planets are able to **trap** energy just like a greenhouse. 몇몇 행성의 대기권은 온실처럼 에너지를 가둬둘 수 있다.	**v.** 가두다 잡아두다
revert [rivə́:rt]	⑱ to return to a former condition, practice, subject, or belief ⑧ return, go back Considering a few faults in the new system, they decided to **revert** to their old system. 새 시스템의 결점을 고려한 후, 그들은 이전 시스템으로 되돌아가기로 결정했다.	**v.** 되돌아가다

Sentence Completion

A. Choose the one word that best fits the sentence.

1 When you own a _____ , it is a mechanism or machine.

    a. convention   b. concept

    c. contraption   d. confirmation

2 If you read some scientific _____ , then you have read the conclusions.

    a. matters   b. introductions

    c. findings   d. bodies

3 If you own many electronic _____ , then you are likely an early adopter.

    a. desktops   b. classics

    c. refrigerators   d. devices

4 The pencil is a _____ used writing utensil.

    a. splendidly   b. hopefully

    c. hasslingly   d. commonly

5 Ice _____ to water when melted.

    a. converts   b. innovates

    c. relocates   d. transfers

Sentence Completion

B. Choose the one word that best fits the sentence.

1 The animals were _____ inside a cage.
   - a. regenerated
   - b. impeded
   - c. trapped
   - d. invigorated

2 Women are just as _____ as men at doing 99 percent of all available jobs.
   - a. nurturing
   - b. inexperienced
   - c. helpless
   - d. capable

3 That was the most _____ depiction of mid 17th century life in Europe I have every read.
   - a. awesome
   - b. delicious
   - c. lucrative
   - d. expensive

4 If our society ever _____ to using non-digital telephones and analog TVs, it will be terrible.
   - a. jumps forward
   - b. advances
   - c. releases
   - d. reverts

5 The bomb _____ up after 30 seconds.
   - a. screwed
   - b. blew
   - c. tussled
   - d. grasped

1 What invention was devised in Greece?

    a. An expansion device.

    b. A device that opened doors.

    c. A parallel apparatus that forced doors.

    d. A steam-assisted door closure.

2 Why does the writer explain steam machines?

    a. To show how Torricelli made the Italians proud.

    b. To estimate present-day uses of steam power.

    c. To show the basics of steam power and history.

    d. To illustrate patterns in Hero and Watt's accounts.

3 How does the writer introduce steam machines?

    a. By talking about the conception of Hero as inventor.

    b. Through discussing the conception of Watt as inventor.

    c. By suggesting that water and ions revert back to their natural state.

    d. By showing the principles of steam and hybrid batteries.

the Function of Statement

4 Listen again to part of the lecture. Then answer the question.
What's the function of this passage?

    a. To introduce how steam was made more efficient more than 300 years ago.
    b. To give an example of James Watt's failures.
    c. To introduce how steam has been with mankind for longer than 300 years.
    d. To contrast the dangers of boilers and electric toasters.

Specific Information

5 According to the professor, what two factors contribute to an exploding boiler? Choose 2 answers.

    a. Expanding steam with no escape outlet.
    b. Trapped steam over prolonged periods.
    c. Faulty boiler lids.
    d. Trapped steam over short periods.

Inference Question

6 What does the writer imply about steam machines?

    a. Pure water is needed to produce 1,600 liters of steam.
    b. They were a simple, yet ingenious idea centuries ago.
    c. Galileo and Torricelli did not try hard enough to perfect their design.
    d. At a rate of 1/1,600 liters, steam is very energy efficient.

Machine (1)

The age of steam power is commonly thought to have started with James Watt, but the history of steam technology in fact goes back much further. In ancient Greece, Hero of Alexandria wrote about devices, such as an automatic door-opening contraption, which were powered by steam. Many centuries later, Galileo, Torricelli, and De Caus determined the basic principles of steam technology. Among their 17th century findings were that water converts to steam when boiled and that steam expands during this process, with a liter of water capable of producing about 1,600 liters of steam. These scientists also discovered the awesome power produced by this conversion — not only can the steam produced raise the lid off a pot but it can also blow up a boiler in which it is trapped. They also found that when steam cools, it reverts back to water and that if this process occurs in a closed container, it creates a vacuum.

1 The word **commonly** in the passage is closest in meaning to

    a. comprehendingly   b. quizzically

    c. generally   d. rarely

2 The word **device** in the passage is closest in meaning to

    a. instrument   b. PDA   c. stationery   d. hallmark

3 The word **contraption** in the passage is closest in meaning to

    a. intervention   b. apparatus   c. trapping   d. scion

4 The word **finding** in the passage is closest in meaning to

    a. discovery   b. ruling   c. seeking   d. verdict

5 The word **convert** in the passage is closest in meaning to

    a. invert   b. transform   c. combine   d. fixate

6 The word **capable** in the passage is closest in meaning to

    a. incompetent   b. inert   c. gifted   d. able

7 The word **awesome** in the passage is closest in meaning to

    a. essential   b. amazing   c. ubiquitous   d. appalling

8 The word **blow up** in the passage is closest in meaning to

    a. hassle   b. honk   c. explode   d. expand

Paraphrasing

Which best expresses the information in the underlined sentences?

1   Many centuries later, Galileo, Torricelli, and De Cause determined the basic principles of steam technology.

    a. Galileo and Torricelli improved the basic concept of steam fusion.
    b. Air can not be condensed within a steam pipe.
    c. The three men figured out the basic concepts of steam.
    d. Galileo and De Caus improved the principles of steam.

2   Among their 17th century findings were that water converts to steam when boiled and that steam expands during this process.

    a. The saturation point of steam comes after boiling for 37 minutes.
    b. In the 17 century, water was more manageable for steaming.
    c. Too much water in a boiler cannot be turned into steam.
    d. Converting water to steam was a discovery from the 17th century.

Machine (2)

Definitions and Examples

assembly line
[əsémbli làin]

- ⑧ an arrangement of workers and machines in which each worker handles only one part of a product
- ⑧ production line

  Henry Ford invented the modern **assembly line** to make Ford motorcars.

  헨리 포드는 포드 자동차를 생산할 현대적인 조립 라인을 고안했다.

n. 조립 라인

specialist
[spéʃəlist]

- ⑧ one who is devoted to a particular occupation or branch of study or research
- ⑧ expert

  There were many **specialists** working on the secret Project X program.

  비밀 프로젝트 X 프로그램에 참여하고 있는 전문가들이 많았다.

n. 전문가

historic
[histɔ́(:)rik]

- ⑧ well-known or important in history
- ⑧ notable, significant

  The **historic** fortress in Suwon, just outside of Seoul is simply amazing.

  서울외곽인 수원에 위치한, 역사적으로 유명한 그 요새는 정말 굉장하다.

a. 역사상 유명한

standardize
[sténdərdàiz]

- ⑧ to cause to conform to a standard
- ⑧ homogenize

  The cell phone company needed to **standardize** their products with those in other countries.

  그 휴대 전화 회사는 자사의 제품을 다른 국가의 제품과 규격을 통일해야 했다.

v. 규격을 통일하다

interchangeable
[ìntərtʃéindʒəbəl]

- ⑧ capable of being put or used in the place of each other
- ⑧ exchangeable

  You will need several **interchangeable** parts to fix your laptop.

  노트북 컴퓨터를 수리하려면 호환할 수 있는 부품이 몇 개 필요할 것이다.

a. 호환할 수 있는

task
[tǽsk]

- (영) a piece of work assigned or done as part of one's duties
- (동) job, duty

He has a mountainous **task** ahead of him.

그는 할 일이 산더미처럼 있다.

n. 일

rule
[rú:l]

- (영) a principle or regulation governing conduct, action, procedure, arrangement, etc.
- (동) principle

If you play by the **rules**, then you are likely to succeed in life.

규칙에 따라 행동하면, 성공인생을 누릴 공산이 크다.

n. 규칙

possibly
[pásəbli]

- (영) in a possible manner
- (동) apparently

Sammy has all the money she can **possibly** use.

새미에게는 어떻게든 자신이 사용할 수 있는 돈이 충분히 있다.

ad. 어쩌면
어떻게든

avoid
[əvɔ́id]

- (영) to keep away from or keep out of the way of someone or something
- (동) evade, shun

Many of the workers want to **avoid** overwork.

대다수 노동자들은 초과 근무를 피하고 싶어한다.

v. 피하다

stoop
[stú:p]

- (영) to bend the head and shoulders, or the body forward and downward
- (동) bend over, crouch

Try and **stoop** over so you can reach past your knees to your toes.

무릎을 지나서 발까지 닿을 수 있도록 한번 허리를 구부려 보세요.

v. 허리를 구부리다

A. Choose the one word that best fits the sentence.

1 If there is a(an) _____ palace, then it means it is very old or
  historically important.

    a. ground-breaking   b. remarkable

    c. historic   d. academic

2 If you make a device with _____ parts, they will work in different
  models or brands.

    a. potable   b. incompatible

    c. interchangeable   d. transportable

3 If you hire _____, then you are employing trained people who can
  do a particular task.

    a. amateurs   b. novices

    c. left wingers   d. specialists

4 When you work along a(an) _____, you stand in a line and put
  together things.

    a. assembly line   b. procession line

    c. main line   d. power line

5 When there are _____ practices, they are copied in many different
  regions.

    a. varying   b. standardized

    c. haphazard   d. ineffectual

B. Choose the one word that best fits the sentence.

1 Make sure your children _____ dark alleys or other "dangerous" places where strangers might be hiding or lurking.

    a. avoid   b. frequent

    c. snatch   d. stride

2 Recently taking on a(an) _____ that required more than his ability, he has difficulty sleeping at night with all the worries about the work.

    a. chance   b. task

    c. turn   d. initiative

3 There's no point disobeying the _____ because your supervisor will likely yell at you.

    a. rule   b. constitution

    c. ridicule   d. explanation

4 If you _____ down too much, you might end up hurting your back.

    a. erect   b. stoop

    c. drop   d. alternate

5 I'm not saying "don't bathe," but "don't scrub" if you can _____ avoid it.

    a. ludicrously   b. excessively

    c. infinitely   d. possibly

1 What was Sorensen nicknamed after?

    a. A iron worker's machine.

    b. Some cast iron aluminum.

    c. Some molten hot iron.

    d. Several cast members from a play.

2 Why does the writer explain assembly lines?

    a. To illustrate how the Model F was built.

    b. To show how industry modernized.

    c. To help the Japanese modernize their auto industry.

    d. To indicate patterns in industry efficiency.

3 How does the writer introduce assembly lines?

    a. By telling how Ford and Sorensen made the assembly line.

    b. By estimating assembly lines in Michigan.

    c. Through predicting worker break times.

    d. By talking about 5,000 unique parts.

4 Listen again to part of the lecture. Then answer the question. What's the function of this passage?

    a. To introduce an alternative method to making cars.

    b. To illustrate how Ford took the task to the worker.

    c. To describe the limitations of assembly lines.

    d. To contrast production specialist's methods.

Specific Information

5 According to the professor, what two rules did Henry Ford implement along the assembly line? Choose 2 answers.

    a. Don't walk more than one step.

    b. Try not to take too many bathroom breaks.

    c. Do not stoop over to pick something up.

    d. Make every other car black.

Inference Question

6 What does the writer imply about assembly lines?

    a. Huge advances were made helping workers' back problems.

    b. Workers deserve more movement on the factory floor.

    c. Assembly lines are outdated now that robots are used.

    d. Huge advances were made streamlining auto plants.

Machine (2)

The assembly line was born in 1913 in the automobile factory of Henry Ford. With the help of Charles E. ("Cast-Iron Charlie") Sorensen and other production specialists, Ford developed the assembly line into the form it takes even today. The car produced on that first assembly line was the historic Model T. Made up of about 5,000 standardized and interchangeable parts, the car was available in any color of the rainbow, Ford said, "so long as it is black." Principle No. 1 of Ford's line was to take the task to the worker, instead of the worker to the task. Other basic rules were that no worker should ever have to take more than a single step if possible (if it could possibly be avoided), nor did workers ever have to stoop.

1 The word **assembly line** in the passage is closest in meaning to

    a. invention line   b. gathering line

    c. production line   d. grid line

2 The word **specialist** in the passage is closest in meaning to

    a. expert   b. gold digger

    c. lawyer   d. consultant

3 The word **historic** in the passage is closest in meaning to

    a. notable   b. stupendous

    c. pathetic   d. fatal

4 The word **interchangeable** in the passage is closest in meaning to

    a. awkward   b. incompatible

    c. congealable   d. exchangeable

5 The word **task** in the passage is closest in meaning to

    a. device   b. gadget   c. job   d. dough

6 The word **rule** in the passage is closest in meaning to

    a. responsibility   b. punishment   c. belief   d. principle

7 The word **possibly** in the passage is closest in meaning to

    a. apparently   b. improbably   c. formerly   d. sometimes

8 The word **avoid** in the passage is closest in meaning to

    a. distinguish   b. confront   c. evade   d. refute

Paraphrasing

Which best expresses the information in the underlined sentences?

1 Made up of about 5,000 standardized and interchangeable parts, the car was available in any color of the rainbow, Ford said, "so long as it is black."

    a. Cars are made of many different interchangeable designs.

    b. Ford decided to make the interchangeable parts rainbow colored.

    c. The Ford could only be ordered in black and had many parts.

    d. The rainbow was the basis for the Ford paint scheme.

2 Principle No. 1 of Ford's line was to take the task to the worker, instead of the worker to the task.

    a. The Ford lineup is not tough enough to beat the Chrysler one.

    b. Bringing the job to the worker was the most efficient strategy.

    c. Too much efficiency makes the worker lazy and inept.

    d. The prime responsibility was to bring various tasks to supervisors.

Flying Machine

Definitions and Examples

touch [tʌtʃ]	영 **a slight added action or effort in doing or completing any piece of work** 동 **stroke** The sculptor needs to add some final **touches** before it's ready for delivery. 조각가는 배달하기 전에 마지막으로 작품을 조금 만져서 다듬어야 했다.	**n.** 손질
telegram [téləgræm]	영 **a message or communication sent by telegraph** 동 **telegraph** A hundred years ago, it was common to send a **telegraph** across town. 백 년 전에는 도시에서 전보를 치는 일이 흔했다.	**n.** 전보
urge [ə́:rdʒ]	영 **to try to persuade or request earnestly** 동 **encourage, exhort** She was **urging** her husband to work harder and be more assertive. 그녀는 남편이 더 열심히 일하고 보다 자기 주장을 분명히 하도록 격려하였다.	**v.** 격려하다, 권하다
secrecy [sí:krəsi]	영 **the state or condition of being secret, hidden, or concealed** 동 **confidentiality** They often whispered in **secrecy** to each other in the hallways. 그들은 종종 복도에서 비밀스럽게 속삭였다.	**n.** 비밀
flimsy [flímzi]	영 **without material strength or solidity** 동 **weak, fragile** Don't rent a **flimsy** chair that feels like it's going to break when you sit in it. 앉았을 때 부서질 것 같은 약한 의자는 빌리지 마라.	**a.** 약한

Social Science II

jerry-built [dʒéri bílt]	⑲ built very quickly and cheaply, without much care for safety or quality ⑧ unsubstantial, shoddy They lived in a little **jerry-built** house in the suburbs. 그들은 교외에 다소 날림으로 지은 집에서 살았다.	a. 날림으로 지은
wobbly [wábəli]	⑲ inclined to shake as from weakness or defect ⑧ shaky, unsteady One leg of the metal table was **wobbly**, irritating the student. 금속 탁자의 다리 하나가 흔들거려서 그 학생은 짜증이 났다.	a. 불안정한 흔들거리는
last [lǽst]	⑲ to go on or continue in time ⑧ continue There was little hope for a **lasting** peace in the Middle East. 중동 지역에 평화가 계속된다는 희망은 거의 없었다.	v. 계속되다
demonstrate [démənstrèit]	⑲ to exhibit the operation or use of (a device, process, product, or the like) ⑧ show, manifest She **demonstrated** how efficient the system was by increasing sales. 그녀는 판매 증가로 그 시스템이 얼마나 효율적인지 보여주었다.	v. 보여주다
awaken [əwéikən]	⑲ to make aware ⑧ awake, waken The international community has belatedly begun to **awaken** to the danger of climate change. 국제 사회는 기후 변화의 위험성에 대해 뒤늦게 자각하기 시작했다.	v. 자각하다

A. Choose the one word that best fits the sentence.

1 When someone is _____ you to do something, they are requesting
   you to do it.

   a. urging   b. patronizing

   c. discouraging   d. mitigating

2 It's easy to discern a _____ building from a solid one — hollow
   doors, shaky floors, and crooked walls give it away.

   a. durable   b. staunch

   c. flimsy   d. sound

3 When you put the final _____ on a project, you are finishing it.

   a. square one   b. touches

   c. moments   d. brew

4 If your grandparents ever sent a(an) _____, then they lived prior to
   World War II.

   a. telepathy   b. cable car

   c. telegram   d. email message

5 If you can maintain _____ between friends, then the relationship
   will be healthy.

   a. strain   b. enmity

   c. secrecy   d. silence

Sentence Completion

B. Choose the one word that best fits the sentence.

1   The Wright brothers tried to _____ for all of mankind that flight was indeed possible.

　　a. demonstrate　　　　　　　　b. exhume
　　c. develop　　　　　　　　　　d. withhold

2   The building is so _____ that nobody would ever have dared stay in it.

　　a. substantial　　　　　　　　b. practical
　　c. handy　　　　　　　　　　　d. jerry-built

3   When something becomes _____, it is not even or level with the ground.

　　a. steadfast　　　　　　　　　b. wobbly
　　c. welcoming　　　　　　　　　d. struggling

4   If we _____ to the fact that our environment is being destroyed, we may save it.

　　a. falter　　　　　　　　　　　b. awaken
　　c. rejoice　　　　　　　　　　　d. deny

5   There's no _____ peace in many African nations due to tribal conflict and civil war.

　　a. volatile　　　　　　　　　　b. lasting
　　c. stop-gap　　　　　　　　　　d. possessive

Listening Comprehension

1 What did Orville send to his father?

    a. A telegraphic code.

    b. A telegram explaining a secret.

    c. A letter to government officials.

    d. A telegram telling of the flimsy glider.

2 Why does the writer explain the Wright brothers?

    a. To demonstrate that manned flight is hard, but not impossible.

    b. To show that North Carolina is ripe for testing planes.

    c. To explain that Orville was overconfident of succeeding.

    d. To show that no engineering feat is impossible.

3 How does the writer introduce the Wright brothers?

    a. Through explaining the doubts of Orville's mom.

    b. By showing that the "flying machine" failed.

    c. Through illustrating the doubts of others.

    d. By explaining about the poorly built plane.

4 Listen again to part of the lecture. Then answer the question. What's the function of this passage?

    a. To introduce an alternative to official aeronautics policy.

    b. To give an example of wobbly aircraft in Ohio.

    c. To describe how two men conquered the doubts of others.

    d. To contrast Ohio and North Carolina as flight centers.

Listening Comprehension

5 According to the professor, what two factors broke the limited news about the Kitty Hawk flight? Choose 2 answers.

    a. Government orders for planes.

    b. A demonstration for the US government.

    c. The Wright brothers' sales pitch.

    d. Increased news after 1908.

6 What does the writer imply about the Wright brothers?

    a. The law of gravitation works against pilots.

    b. That it was foolish to doubt man's ability to fly.

    c. Improved versions of balsa wood planes are now popular.

    d. That it was dangerous to even try to fly.

Flying Machine

In the year 1903 almost nobody believed that men would ever fly. At least two men knew better. In December 1903, on a stretch of sand at Kitty Hawk, North Carolina, Orville and Wilbur Wright were putting the last touches on a "flying machine" they had built at their bicycle shop in Dayton, Ohio, and shipped to Kitty Hawk for tests. Confident of success, Orville sent a telegram to his father in Dayton urging secrecy. Then quite suddenly, on December 17, it happened. The two brothers piloted their flimsy, jerry-built machine on a series of wobbly flights, the longest one lasting 59 seconds and covering 852 feet. The next day, only two newspapers across the entire United States carried the story. Not until 1908, after Wilbur and Orville demonstrated an improved version of their airplane to United States government officials, did the public awaken to the fact that men were truly flying.

1 The word **touch** in the passage is closest in meaning to
   a. plan   b. stroke   c. sense   d. flight

2 The word **telegram** in the passage is closest in meaning to
   a. telegraph   b. email   c. messenger   d. typography

3 The word **urge** in the passage is closest in meaning to
   a. dishearten   b. intimidate   c. scorn   d. exhort

4 The word **secrecy** in the passage is closest in meaning to
   a. confidentiality b. contemplation c. breaking news d. solemnity

5 The word **flimsy** in the passage is closest in meaning to

    a. feasible   b. flamboyant   c. fragile   d. formidable

6 The word **jerry-built** in the passage is closest in meaning to

    a. sturdy   b. false   c. unsubstantial   d. oppressive

7 The word **wobbly** in the passage is closest in meaning to

    a. solid   b. shaky   c. touchy   d. steady

8 The word **last** in the passage is closest in meaning to

    a. shorten   b. lack   c. appraise   d. continue

Paraphrasing

Which best expresses the information in the underlined sentences?

1   The two brothers piloted their flimsy, jerry-built machine on a series of wobbly flights, the longest one lasting 59 seconds and covering 852 feet.

    a. The two brothers managed to fly their home-made contraption for 852 feet.

    b. Warm air helps lift planes for longer flights.

    c. Too much oversteering is often caused by newly built planes.

    d. The brothers often took out their planes for a wobbly flight.

2   The next day, only two newspapers across the entire United States carried the story.

    a. Too much TV coverage followed the short flight.

    b. The U.S. media was so excited about flying machines.

    c. Too little news coverage followed the amazing flight.

    d. The flight was on a holiday, so only two papers carried the story.

Definitions and Examples

caldron [kɔ́:ldrən]	영 a large vessel, such as a kettle or vat, used for boiling 동 vessel The witch was stirring her secret stew in the large **caldron**. 그 마녀는 커다란 솥에 담긴 신비한 스튜를 휘젓고 있었다.	n. 솥
proximity [prɑksíməti]	영 nearness in place, time, order, occurrence, or relation 동 nearness The **proximity** of the meteor to the planet was too close, said NASA. 미 항공 우주국은 유성이 지구에 너무 근접해 있다고 발표했다.	n. 근접
crystal [krístl]	영 a solid formed by a three-dimensional pattern of atoms, ions, or molecules Snow **crystals** are very beautiful during the winter. 눈 결정은 겨울 동안 매우 아름답다.	n. 결정(체)
prerequisite [pri:rékwəzit]	영 something that is required in advance 동 requirement It was a **prerequisite** for the businessman to have management experience. 경영을 해 본 경험이 있는지가 사업가의 필수조건이었다.	n. 필수 조건
theory [θíəri]	영 a proposed explanation whose status is still not proven 동 belief The Big Bang **theory** is criticized by many evangelical Christians. 빅뱅 학설은 많은 복음주의 기독교인들에게서 비판을 받는다.	n. 학설, 이론

unnumbered

[ʌ̀nnʌ́mbərd]

- 영 countless; innumerable
- 동 incalculable

When I first saw the room, its walls were blackened with the smoke of **unnumbered** years.

내가 그 방을 처음 보았을 때, 방안의 벽은 수많은 해 동안 연기에 그을려 검게 변해있었다.

a. 수많은

civilization

[sìvəlizéiʃən]

- 영 a human society with its own social organization and culture
- 동 culture, society

The Hindu, Roman and Chinese **civilizations** rank amongst the greatest.

힌두, 로마, 중국 문명은 가장 위대한 문명에 속한다.

n. 문명

speculate

[spékjəlèit]

- 영 to believe especially on uncertain or tentative grounds
- 동 guess, surmise

Experts **speculated** that oil prices would persist in the short run.

전문가들은 짧은 기간 동안 석유 가격이 현상을 유지할 것이라고 추측했다.

v. 추측하다

cataclysm

[kǽtəklìzəm]

- 영 any violent upheaval, esp. one of a social or political nature
- 동 disaster, upheaval

The **cataclysm** of the Russian Revolution was a terrible event in the early 20th century.

러시아 혁명이라는 격변은 20세기 초에 일어난 끔찍한 사건이었다.

n. 격변

schedule

[skédʒu(:)l]

- 영 to plan for a certain date
- 동 plan, slate

The meeting is **scheduled** for Wednesday.

그 모임은 수요일로 예정되어있다

v. 예정하다

A. Choose the one word that best fits the sentence.

1 If you are going to make salt _____ , you need to heat the water to around 140 degrees.

    a. cornflakes   b. ions

    c. crystals   d. proteins

2 Having a _____ is much different than having proof for that specific belief.

    a. theory   b. declaration

    c. ratification   d. cuisine

3 If the _____ of your car is too close to another one, there might be an accident.

    a. volume   b. proximity

    c. majority   d. smell

4 When you cook something in a _____ , you are using a kind of large pot.

    a. caldron   b. mug

    c. scoop   d. lid

5 English is generally a _____ for university degrees in this country.

    a. cosmetics   b. prerequisite

    c. custom   d. pretense

B. Choose the one word that best fits the sentence.

1 If there is a(an) _____ , then the future of our country might be in jeopardy.

    a. tranquility   b. cataclysm

    c. trace   d. affluence

2 He confessed his inability to solve the _____ problems.

    a. fractured   b. unnumbered

    c. easygoing   d. unbending

3 One of the most amazing _____ would surely be the Persian Empire.

    a. religions   b. counties

    c. civilizations   d. philosophies

4 Our previously _____ show was cancelled for the actor's personal reasons.

    a. estimated   b. deregulated

    c. marred   d. scheduled

5 He _____ that there is life on the planet Mars.

    a. speculated   b. ploted

    c. disrupted   d. schemed

1 Can Mars be capable of supporting life?

    a. Pictures from the Viking spacecraft are inconclusive.

    b. Mars could have life due to its proximity to Earth.

    c. Presently, there is evidence of complex life forms on Mars.

    d. Some primitive forms of life may have existed, but not now.

2 Why does the writer think Mars may have had life?

    a. Sending more spacecraft like the Viking missions is a good idea.

    b. Water on Mars (leading to life) is just a theory.

    c. Mars atmosphere, full of ice crystals, could lead to water and basic life.

    d. Scientists should return to Mars in the future.

3 How does the writer introduce life on Mars?

    a. Through explaining the laws of gravity.

    b. Mars' similarity to Earth may give it a similar atmosphere that supports life.

    c. By predicting how much it would cost to send a spacecraft there.

    d. Through talking about complex life forms on Mars.

4 Listen again to part of the lecture. Then answer the question.
What's the function of this passage?

    a. To introduce an explanation of life on Mars.

    b. To learn which planets are most like our Earth.

    c. To describe NASA's exploration program.

    d. To analyze ice crystals in space.

Specific Information

5 According to the writer, what two factors were discovered by the spacecraft? Choose 2 answers.

    a. Venus is similar in shape to Earth.

    b. There likely once was water on Mars.

    c. There was a cold atmosphere and ice crystals.

    d. Cataclysms were found by the manned missions.

Inference Question

6 What does the writer imply about the planet Mars?

    a. Life is only possible on Earth and Venus.

    b. An estimate of the distance between Mars and Venus.

    c. There may have been life on Mars, given its environment.

    d. A pattern of river formations on Mars.

Mars

While a caldron-like Venus is the planet in closest proximity to the Earth, Mars is the most Earthlike. It has a thin, cold atmosphere containing ice crystals, frozen water that is the necessary prerequisite for life. Eerie pictures from NASA's spacecraft, Viking 1 and Viking 2, lend evidence to the theory that there may have been water on Mars at one time. Some go so far as to suggest that unnumbered millennia ago, Mars was a warm, wet world with rivers, oceans, and maybe even an advanced civilization. But there is no evidence of complex life forms on Mars now. What happened to Mars, and did Martians, in fact, ever exist? Scientists have speculated that the planet may have fallen victim to some natural cataclysm. Or did the Martians destroy each other in a fratricidal war? The answers to these questions must await human exploration of the planet in manned missions scheduled for the first decades of the next century.

1 The word **caldron** in the passage is closest in meaning to

    a. vessel   b. planet   c. hamper   d. pottage

2 The word **proximity** in the passage is closest in meaning to

    a. immediacy   b. junction   c. nearness   d. gap

3 The word **prerequisite** in the passage is closest in meaning to

    a. direction   b. requirement   c. option   d. auxiliary

4 The word **theory** in the passage is closest in meaning to

    a. academic   b. proof   c. belief   d. assertion

5 The word **unnumbered** in the passage is closest in meaning to

    a. identified   b. finite   c. disproved   d. incalculable

6 The word **civilization** in the passage is closest in meaning to

    a. regression   b. elitism   c. culture   d. savagery

7 The word **speculate** in the passage is closest in meaning to

    a. donate   b. guess   c. concentrate   d. assert

8 The word **cataclysm** in the passage is closest in meaning to

    a. catalyst   b. disaster   c. selection   d. satellite

Paraphrasing

Which best expresses the information in the underlined sentences?

1 Scientists have speculated that the planet may have fallen victim to some natural cataclysm.

    a. The planet Earth has fallen victim to too many cataclysms.

    b. A few scientists believe that a natural disaster helped the planet come into being.

    c. Much of the molten lava at the center of the Earth was created by a natural cataclysm.

    d. The main theory held by the scientific community is that a cataclysmic event occurred.

2 The answers to these questions must await human exploration of the planet in manned missions scheduled for the first decades of the next century.

    a. The answers to most questions about mankind's origins must come from further deep space research.

    b. Scientist hope to explore space in the next 50 years.

    c. To find out more proof, we must explore further into the deepest reaches of space.

    d. Manned missions are very effective for exploring the Earth.

Stars

Definitions and Examples

atom
[ǽtəm]

영 the smallest component of an element
동 particle

Atoms comprise the smallest elements in nature.
원자는 자연에서 가장 작은 요소를 구성한다.

n. 원자

dense
[déns]

영 having the component parts closely compacted together
동 thick

The **dense** fog drifted through the skyscrapers in Shanghai.
짙은 안개가 상하이 시의 고층 건물 사이에 떠 있었다.

a. 짙은, 자욱한

swirl
[swə́:rl]

영 to move with a twisting or whirling motion; eddy
동 whirl, spin

The **swirling** tornado lifted up the pickup and tossed it across the field.
소용돌이치는 토네이도는 픽업 트럭을 들어 올려 평야 저편으로 내동댕이쳤다.

v. 소용돌이치다

central
[séntrəl]

영 of or forming the center
동 middle, main

Central to the idea of feminism is the concept of equality amongst all.
페미니즘 사상의 중심에는 모든 사람이 평등하다는 개념이 자리잡고 있다.

a. 중심의

searing
[síəriŋ]

영 intense or burning
동 blazing

The **searing** heat along the Vietnamese coastline caused many sunburns.
베트남 해안의 몹시 뜨거운 열기 때문에 많은 사람들이 화상을 입었다.

a. 몹시 뜨거운

Astronomy & Physics II

equivalent [ikwívələnt]	영 equal in value, measure, force, effect, significance 동 same, parallel The Hiroshima bomb was **equivalent** to 15,000 tons of TNT explosives. 히로시마에 투하된 폭탄의 위력은 15,000톤의 TNT 폭약의 위력에 상당했다.	a. 상당하는, 같은
countless [káuntlis]	영 too numerous to count 동 innumerable The player had to repeat the same action **countless** times. 그 선수는 같은 동작을 수없이 많이 반복해야만 했다.	a. 수없이 많은
collapse [kəlǽps]	영 to fall or cave in; crumble suddenly 동 fall down, founder The **collapsing** of the World Trade Center towers shocked a nation. 세계무역센터 건물 붕괴는 미국에 충격을 안겨 주었다.	v. 붕괴되다
peacefully [píːsfəli]	영 in a peaceful manner 동 quietly The plane disappeared **peacefully** into the darkness. 그 비행기는 어둠 속으로 조용히 사라졌다.	ad. 조용히
spew [spjuː]	영 to discharge the contents of the stomach through the mouth; vomit 동 eject, spit out The volcano was **spewing** molten lava and ash across the county. 그 화산은 그 지역 전체에 뜨거운 용암과 화산재를 내뿜고 있었다.	v. 내뿜다

Sentence Completion

A. Choose the one word that best fits the sentence.

1 If something is _____ , it is going around and around in circles.

   a. triangulating   b. motioning

   c. swirling   d. wondering

2 If the temperature outside is _____ , then it is very very hot.

   a. damp   b. gusty

   c. frigid   d. searing

3 If a material is the opposite of thin and light, it is probably _____ .

   a. dense   b. soft

   c. penetrable   d. experienced

4 Part of the building blocks of matter include basic elements like

_____ .

   a. evidence   b. atoms

   c. electricities   d. jammers

5 If you have a _____ office, then it is probably your headquarters.

   a. branch   b. central

   c. lethal   d. secondary

B. Choose the one word that best fits the sentence.

1 There's no point hoping to solve the problems in the Middle East
_____.

    a. peacefully   b. belligerently

    c. outstandingly   d. hostilely

2 A mile is _____ to about 1.6 kilometers.

    a. equivalent   b. diverse

    c. likely   d. incompatible

3 _____ failings in the system resulted in a massive recall.

    a. Limited   b. Countable

    c. Countless   d. Considerate

4 When the volcano is _____ lava, you had better run away fast if
you want to live.

    a. swallowing   b. expanding

    c. sidestepping   d. spewing

5 If a star is found to be _____, then a black hole will be formed.

    a. rising   b. collapsing

    c. glittering   d. veering

Specific Question

1 How are stars formed?

    a. The collapse of hydrogen atoms brings about concentrated mass.

    b. Nuclear reactions, equivalent to H-bombs, create high temperatures.

    c. Hydrogen atoms in dense clouds come together, creating chain reactions.

    d. Gravity pulls in stars, combining them together.

Speaker's Purpose

2 Why does the writer explain the creation of stars?

    a. To learn about the smallest of planets.

    b. To explain how helium converges and forms dense matter.

    c. To describe the birth and death.

    d. To analyze patterns in the orbits of planets.

Understanding Organization

3 How does the writer introduce the formation of stars?

    a. By explaining swirling gas clouds of helium.

    b. Through searing heat and the theory of atomic fission.

    c. By talking about the makeup of the sun.

    d. By talking about hydrogen atoms colliding and increasing mass.

the Function of Statement

4 Listen again to part of the lecture. Then answer the question.
What's the function of this passage?

    a. To describe how new stars pull in mass, creating tremendous amounts of energy.

    b. To explain how when mass increases, energy is created.

    c. To analyze the limitations of gravitational theory.

    d. To talk about how high pressure causes fusion reactions.

5 According to the writer, what two factors signal the collapse of stars?
   Choose 2 answers.

   a. The gravitation pull of stars gets stronger.
   b. All hydrogen gets used up in the star.
   c. Some explode in colors of yellow.
   d. Old stars become larger and turn red.

6 What does the writer imply about stars?

   a. One must study gravitational center forces.
   b. Stars undergo constant change, from birth to death.
   c. Hydrogen is the key to the creation of stars.
   d. A pattern exists between energy and hydrogen atoms.

Stars

Stars are formed when hydrogen atoms in dense, swirling gas clouds are pulled toward the center of the cloud by gravity. As the central mass increases, more atoms are pulled in, and as they fall to the center, they pick up speed, emitting a great deal of energy. This energy heats the gas to increasingly higher temperatures, and after several million years, the temperature reaches about 10 million degrees Celsius. The searing heat and titanic pressure cause fusion reactions equivalent to the power of countless H-bombs. As the reactions progress, hydrogen and helium begin to build heavier atoms through nuclear reactions. At this point, a true star is said to exist. But the process of hydrogen atoms collapsing toward the gravitational center continues until all of the hydrogen is used up. Aging stars swell and turn red. Small, old stars collapse peacefully. Larger ones explode violently, spewing their contents into space.

1 The word **atom** in the passage is closest in meaning to

    a. mass   b. particle   c. depiction   d. chunk

2 The word **dense** in the passage is closest in meaning to

    a. weighty   b. thick   c. wispy   d. impervious

3 The word **swirling** in the passage is closest in meaning to

    a. triangular   b. confusing   c. whirling   d. subsiding

4 The word **central** in the passage is closest in meaning to

    a. outer   b. middle   c. minor   d. secondary

5 The word **searing** in the passage is closest in meaning to

    a. biting   b. blazing   c. freezing   d. caustic

6 The word **equivalent** in the passage is closest in meaning to

    a. same   b. dissimilar   c. slight   d. dejected

7 The word **countless** in the passage is closest in meaning to

    a. finite   b. limited   c. innumerable   d. few

8 The word **collapse** in the passage is closest in meaning to

    a. founder   b. obey   c. ravage   d. surge

Paraphrasing

Which best expresses the information in the underlined sentences?

1 The searing heat and titanic pressure cause fusion reactions equivalent to the power of countless H-bombs.

    a. The saturation point of H-bombs is similar to a fusion reaction.

    b. The pressure in a fusion reaction is equivalent to many H-bombs.

    c. H-bombs are the main cause of searing heat and friction.

    d. Much more research needs to be done to connect fusion and pressure.

2 But the process of hydrogen atoms collapsing toward the gravitational center continues until all of the hydrogen is used up.

    a. The gravitational center of stars involves the dissolution of hydrogen atoms.

    b. Hydrogen atoms use an unlimited amount of ions.

    c. All the hydrogen atoms get used up after a star collapses toward the gravitational center.

    d. Collapsing typically involves hydrogen atoms and a distant star.

Definitions and Examples

exhaust

[igzɔ́ːst]

ⓔ **to wear out or use up completely**
ⓢ **use up, consume**

The fuel supply in the car was **exhausted** after the long trip.

긴 여행 후 차의 연료가 고갈되었다.

v. 고갈하다

---

vast

[vǽst]

ⓔ **of very great area or extent; immense**
ⓢ **large**

The **vast** farms of Montana go on and on for hundreds of miles.

몬태나 주에 있는 방대한 규모의 농장은 수백 마일에 걸쳐져 있다.

a. 방대한

---

produce

[prədʒúːs]

ⓔ **to bring forth or yield**
ⓢ **generate, create**

High winds **produced** a dramatic dust storm in the region.

강한 바람이 불어 그 지역에 엄청난 모래폭풍이 형성되었다.

v. 만들어내다

---

tide

[tàid]

ⓔ **the periodic rise and fall of the sea level under the gravitational pull of the moon**
ⓢ **current**

Tides go in and out every day, influenced by the pull of the moon.

달의 인력 때문에 조수는 매일 밀물과 썰물을 반복한다.

n. 조수

---

harness

[háːrnis]

ⓔ **to bring something under your control and use it**
ⓢ **utilize, control**

The country looks to **harness** wind power in the face of skyrocketing oil prices.

고공 행진하는 유가 상승에 맞서 국가에서는 풍력 이용에 관심을 갖는다.

v. 이용하다

Astronomy & Physics II

meet [míːt]	영 to comply with; fulfill 통 satisfy He is struggling to **meet** the expectations of his parents. 그는 부모님의 기대를 충족시키기 위해 피나는 노력을 하고 있다.	v. (기대, 요건 등을) 충족시키다
concentrate [kánsəntrèit]	영 to put or bring into a single place, group, etc. 통 focus The nation's wealth is **concentrated** in a few people. 그 나라의 부는 소수 사람들에게 집중되어 있다.	v. 집중하다
match [mǽtʃ]	영 to equal; be equal to 통 equal, fit The blood did not **match** the sample in the police department. 그 혈액은 경찰서에 보관된 샘플과 일치하지 않았다.	v. 필적하다 일치하다
nonrenewable [nɑn rinʃúːwəbəl]	영 that cannot be renewed, usually a natural resource 통 non-recyclable Oil is a **nonrenewable** resource that is dwindling in supply. 공급이 점점 줄고있는 석유는 재생 불가능한 자원이다.	a. 재생 불가능한
limitless [límitlis]	영 without limit; boundless 통 infinite The boundaries of space are **limitless**, going on forever. 우주의 경계는 무한하여 끝없이 이어진다.	a. 무한한

A. Choose the one word that best fits the sentence.

1   I live in an area that receives little wind so my wind generators have never
    _____ a lot of energy.

    a. consumed   b. conceived

    c. put aside   d. produced

2   When the _____ come in, the sea rises up and down.

    a. tides   b. marshes

    c. aridity   d. seaweeds

3   If the land is _____ , it is very expansive in range and far-reaching.

    a. vast   b. congested

    c. peaceful   d. narrow

4   When you _____ something, you used it up.

    a. created   b. exhausted

    c. saved   d. augmented

5   Most states desirably _____ power of renewable energy.

    a. abuse   b. harness

    c. spoil   d. pollute

B. Choose the one word that best fits the sentence.

1 Much of the world's natural oil resources is _____.

    a. potable   b. nonrenewable

    c. fractured   d. tantamount

2 She did not _____ the expectations of fans in the movie.

    a. involve   b. meet

    c. upset   d. deceive

3 His scientific interests were rightly _____ on the problem considering its importance.

    a. digressed   b. dispersed

    c. concentrated   d. spread

4 There is a _____ supply of wind-powered energy.

    a. mysterious   b. weathered

    c. tedious   d. limitless

5 The space shuttle cannot _____ the speed of light.

    a. match   b. result in

    c. offset   d. evaluate

1 Why is there concern about the world's energy supplies?

    a. Because little money can be made from natural energy sources.

    b. Because the petroleum companies want to increase profits.

    c. Because most nonrenewable energy will eventually be gone, given recent fears.

    d. Because many new businesses want to develop water and wind resources.

2 Why does the writer emphasize using natural resources?

    a. Because stocks in wind power companies could be very profitable.

    b. Because hydroelectric power can produce up to 80% of our energy needs.

    c. Because solar energy is equally as powerful.

    d. Because humans are currently using over 17% of hydroelectric power.

3 How does the writer introduce energy power?

    a. By suggesting we are going to run out of nonrenewable energy very soon.

    b. By estimating how much fuel can be burned in one day.

    c. By predicting how much fuel supply is left in the Middle East.

    d. By contrasting the power of the sun with wind power.

the Function of Statement

4 Listen again to part of the lecture. Then answer the question.
   What's the function of this passage?

     a. To introduce alternative ideas to energy sources.
     b. To stress hydroelectric power uses.
     c. To describe the limitations of petroleum technology.
     d. To contrast our past usage of wind power.

Specific Information

5 According to the writer, what two types of energy could help save the
   planet? Choose 2 answers.

     a. Tidal power.
     b. Windmill power.
     c. Hydroelectric power.
     d. Solar panels on motorcycles.

Inference Question

6 What does the writer imply about energy sources?

     a. Many obstacles stand in the way of making tidal power effective.
     b. Most energy problems are unfixable.
     c. There are solutions to our planet's energy problems if we are
        inventive enough.
     d. Most energy solutions are too expensive.

Energy (1)

Fears abound that the world's nonrenewable energy supplies will eventually be exhausted. However, human beings use but a fraction of the vast amount of energy produced by nature every day. Human beings use only one or two percent of the power produced by rivers, for example, but such hydroelectric power could meet 80 percent of our needs. Wind power could produce twice as much electricity as water does now. If the power of the tides could be harnessed, it could meet half of the world's energy needs. The greatest producer of energy is the sun. If the total supply of all the world's fuel was concentrated in one place and burned at a rate to match the sun's energy, it would be consumed within three days. So, even as the world's nonrenewable energy supplies decrease, limitless energy possibilities remain to be tapped.

1 The word **exhaust** in the passage is closest in meaning to

    a. use up   b. accumulate   c. tire   d. stock up

2 The word **vast** in the passage is closest in meaning to

    a. weighty   b. large   c. meager   d. bound

3 The word **produce** in the passage is closest in meaning to

    a. generate   b. unite   c. measure   d. splurge

4 The word **tide** in the passage is closest in meaning to

    a. current   b. ocean   c. water   d. seaweed

5 The word **harness** in the passage is closest in meaning to

  a. water   b. misuse   c. utilize   d. harass

6 The word **meet** in the passage is closest in meaning to

  a. overfulfill   b. inundate   c. satisfy   d. demand

7 The word **concentrate** in the passage is closest in meaning to

  a. mingle   b. focus   c. disperse   d. tap

8 The word **match** in the passage is closest in meaning to

  a. counter   b. prove   c. improve   d. equal

Paraphrasing

Which best expresses the information in the underlined sentences?

1 If the total supply of all the world's fuel was concentrated in one place and burned at a rate to match the sun's energy, it would be consumed within three days.

  a. The world's fuel supply could be used up in several days.
  b. The sun has immense energy reserves.
  c. All of the world's fuel, burning at the rate of the sun, would be quickly used up.
  d. The Earth needs to consume more energy to match that of the sun.

2 So, even as the world's nonrenewable energy supplies decrease, limitless energy possibilities remain to be tapped.

  a. Energy hopes for Earth lie in developing new energy possibilities.
  b. Much of the Earth's energy remains to be tapped.
  c. Too much alternative energy sources will help decrease supply.
  d. The world's energy supplies are dwindling fast.

Definitions and Examples

unsettled

[Ʌnsétld]

영 not populated or settled, as a region

동 uninhabited

In early days much of the land was **unsettled** and taxes were comparatively small.

그 땅의 여러 지역이, 초창기에는 정착 주민이 적었고 세금도 비교적 적었다.

a. 사람이 살지 않는

generation

[dʒénəréiʃən]

영 all of the offspring that are at the stage of descent from a common ancestor

동 age group, contemporary

For **generations**, the family had lived in the large Tudor home.

수 세대에 걸쳐 그 가족은 튜더 왕가의 넓은 집에서 거주했다.

n. 세대

remarkable

[rimá:rkəbəl]

영 notably or conspicuously unusual

동 extraordinary, notable

It was **remarkable** how gifted and articulate he was.

그는 놀라울 정도로 타고난 재능의 소유자이자 생각이 명확한 사람이었다.

a. 놀랄만한

carve

[ká:rv]

영 to cut (a solid material) so as to form something

동 cut

The wind-**carved** rocks, called ventifacts, created a landscape found nowhere else on Earth.

자갈, 즉 바람에 깎여 만들어진 돌더미가 지구상 어디에서도 발견할 수 없는 풍경을 만들어 냈다.

v. 깎아내다

preserve

[prizə́:rv]

영 to keep in perfect or unaltered condition

동 conserve, keep

We should **preserve** wilderness areas for their own sake and for the benefit of future generations. 야생지역을 보호해야 하는 이유는 그 지역 자체를 위해서, 그리고 미래 세대들을 위해서이다.

v. 보호하다

geyser	⑧ a hot spring that intermittently sends up fountain like jets of water and steam into the air	n. 간헐천
[gáizər]	⑤ hot spring	
	If you go to Wyoming, you will surely see some **geysers**.	
	와이오밍 주에 가면 분명히 간헐천을 보게 될 거다.	

advance	⑧ a forward movement; progress in space	n. 진군, 전진
[ədvǽns]	⑤ forward movement, procession	
	They were making maximum effort to stop the **advance** of the troops toward their area bases.	
	그들은 자신들의 기지로 진군해 오는 병력을 저지하기 위해 온 힘을 쏟았다.	

rarity	⑧ something rare, unusual, or uncommon	n. 희귀(한 것)
[rɛ́ərəti]	⑤ scarcity	
	Sadly, it seems that a man with a conscience is a **rarity** these days.	
	안타깝게도 요즘에는 양심적인 사람들이 희귀한 것 같다.	

state	⑧ to declare definitely or specifically	v. (분명히) 말하다
[stéit]	⑤ declare, say	
	He **stated** his goal was to protect and enhance the quality of life.	
	자신의 목표는 삶의 질 보호 및 강화임을 분명히 말했다.	

contradiction	⑧ direct opposition between things compared	n. 모순
[kàntrədíkʃən]	⑤ inconsistency	
	It was a **contradiction** to see the billionaire drive a simple Honda sedan.	
	수수한 혼다 세단을 몰고 다니는 억만장자를 본 일은 모순이었다.	

A. Choose the one word that best fits the sentence.

1 When something is _____ , it is truly quite extraordinary.

    a. sophomoric   b. sullen

    c. worn   d. remarkable

2 Some opponents of homosexual marriage believe that the whole society should _____ the traditional definition of marriage.

    a. spoil   b. redefine

    c. preserve   d. disrupt

3 The state was only created in 1981, having evolved from an unknown and almost entirely _____ zone over the previous thirty years.

    a. renowned   b. unsettled

    c. populated   d. highlighted

4 It's our obligation to give the next _____ an opportunity to enjoy the beautiful and unique nature of the Earth.

    a. forefathers   b. resources

    c. generations   d. timeframes

5 The flow of water _____ both land and ice into graceful curves.

    a. stamped   b. envisioned

    c. carved   d. cherished

B. Choose the one word that best fits the sentence.

1　I found major differences in his campaign position on illegal immigration, compared to his _____ position on the same topic in his book.

    a. freaked   b. radiating

    c. stated   d. itchy

2　You can find a beautiful spouting _____ in Yellowstone National Park in Wyoming.

    a. iceberg   b. incineration

    c. geyser   d. wheat field

3　Critics argued that there was a little bit of a _____ in the president's new health care policies compared to his old one.

    a. vestige   b. sadness

    c. development   d. contradiction

4　The family desperately want to move to any place where violent crime is a _____ .

    a. spur   b. fad

    c. rarity   d. pester

5　This wall was surrounded by a water-filled ditch, a defensive barrier to prevent the _____ of soldiers, horses and war machines.

    a. shield   b. advance

    c. procedure   d. discord

1 Why did the sequoia, bison, and elk survive?

    a. Because Theodore Roosevelt established a special park for them.

    b. Because hunting and logging were not permitted in their habitat.

    c. Because elk meat tasted too bitter for humans to eat.

    d. Because scientists accurately predicted elk mating habits.

2 Why does the writer explain the park system?

    a. To promote glacier-carved granite cliffs.

    b. That it is very difficult to protect nature from humanity.

    c. To indicate how all of humanity can benefit from parks.

    d. To discourage others to save the area's natural wonders.

3 How does the writer introduce the park system?

    a. By talking about the Alberta-Montana park system.

    b. By talking about individuals who were motivated to save wilderness areas.

    c. By predicting how to preserve the Yellowstone River.

    d. Through criticizing the National Park Service.

4 Listen again to part of the lecture. Then answer the question.
What's the function of this passage?

    a. To introduce a system that showcases American natural wonders.

    b. To display America's natural wonders to foreigners.

    c. To describe the limitations of the mining industry in parks.

    d. To contrast how some countries do not protect nature from humanity.

Specific Information

5 According to the writer, what two factors make Yosemite Valley a success today? Choose 2 answers.

    a. Its natural history museum.

    b. Its glacier-carved granite cliffs.

    c. Its traditional hot dog and hamburger stands.

    d. Its recreation areas for the public.

Inference Question

6 What does the writer imply about the park system?

    a. To show that unsettled lands need to be preserved.

    b. To warn of chemical fluctuations in the geysers.

    c. To indicate a model for other European countries to copy.

    d. To show that nature and man can live side by side.

North America (3)

Although the West was still relatively unsettled in the mid-1800's, a few individuals were motivated to save the area's natural wonders for future generations. In 1864 Congress established the Yosemite Valley, remarkable for its glacier-carved granite cliffs, as a park for "public use, resort and recreation." More than 809,000 hectares were set aside eight years later to preserve the Yellowstone River's source, known for its geysers and hot springs. With the advance of settlers across the North American continent, wilderness became a rarity, and sequoia, bison, and elk survived only where axes and guns were not permitted. Thus, the United States park system was established, serving two main functions: to display America's natural wonders and to protect nature from humanity. Still today, the stated purpose of the parks is to serve as places to be used by the public. Resolving this contradiction will always be a compromise, which the National Park Service can only achieve with the help of the public.

1 The word **unsettled** in the passage is closest in meaning to

    a. unknown   b. unproven   c. uninhabited   d. non-functioning

2 The word **generation** in the passage is closest in meaning to

    a. contemporary   b. production   c. hustler   d. ancestor

3 The word **remarkable** in the passage is closest in meaning to

    a. suspicious   b. extraordinary   c. disillusioned   d. adorable

4 The word **carve** in the passage is closest in meaning to

    a. cut   b. mince   c. crack   d. highlight

5 The word **preserve** in the passage is closest in meaning to

    a. abandon   b. exhaust   c. procure   d. conserve

6 The word **advance** in the passage is closest in meaning to

    a. aggression   b. backward movement

    c. forward movement   d. stalemate

7 The word hot **rarity** in the passage is closest in meaning to

    a. affluence   b. scarcity   c. affliction   d. excess

8 The word **state** in the passage is closest in meaning to

    a. repeal   b. denounce   c. declare   d. resent

Paraphrasing

Which best expresses the information in the underlined sentences?

1 With the advance of settlers across the North American continent, wilderness became a rarity, and sequoia, bison, and elk survived only where axes and guns were not permitted.

    a. Many loggers decimated the trees and the abundant forests.

    b. Sequoia, bison, and elk survived only in Canadian provincial parks.

    c. Trappers killed off many of the elk, bison and sequoia trees.

    d. The settlers, advancing across the continent, hunted much of the wildlife.

2 Resolving this contradiction will always be a compromise, which the National Park Service can only achieve with the help of the public.

    a. The National Park Service is not known for its ability to compromise.

    b. Establishing national parks is always a tradeoff between nature and modernization.

    c. Too much park service initiatives will lead to an increase in wildlife.

    d. More mining is needed in some of the larger national parks.

The Puritans (1)

Definitions and Examples

purify
[pjúərəfài]

- 영 to make pure; free from anything that debases, pollutes, adulterates, or contaminates
- 동 cleanse

Those judges have interfered to '**purify**' the political system.

그 판사들은 정치 제도를 깨끗이 하는 데 방해물 역할을 해왔다.

v. 깨끗이 하다

---

withdrew
[wiðdrú:]

- 영 to draw back, away, or aside
- 동 retire, retreat

The soldiers were forced to **withdraw** to outlying areas.

병사들은 변방으로 물러날 수 밖에 없었다.

v. 물러나다
후퇴하다

---

persecution
[pə:rsikjú:ʃən]

- 영 the act of persecuting
- 동 ill-treatment, oppression

Much **persecution** of gay and Black people in the U.S. is motivated by prejudice.

미국에서, 동성애자와 흑인에 대한 수많은 박해는 편견에서부터 시작되었다.

n. 박해

---

homeland
[hóumlænd]

- 영 one's native land
- 동 birthplace, motherland

She longed to return to her **homeland** after an absence of 12 years.

그녀는 12년 동안 이국에서 생활한 후 자신의 조국으로 돌아갈 날을 애타게 기다렸다.

n. 조국

Puritan
[pjúərətən]

- 영 a group of Protestants in the 16th century within the Church of England, demanding greater strictness in religious discipline

The **Puritans** first settled along the New England coast four centuries ago.

청교도들은 4세기 전 뉴 잉글랜드 지역의 해안가를 따라서 정착 생활을 시작했다.

n. 청교도

Humanities II

corruption [kərʌ́pʃən]	영 **the act of corrupting or state of being corrupt; lack of integrity or honesty** 통 **dishonesty** There is too much **corruption** in many Asian countries, but that is changing. 많은 아시아 국가에서 부패가 만연해 있지만 변화가 일어나고 있는 중이다.	n. 부패
community [kəmjúːnəti]	영 **a group of people living in the same locality and under the same government** 통 **neighborhood, society** **Communities** form the backbone of neighborhood values. 공동체는 이웃의 가치를 형성하는 데 중추적인 역할을 한다.	n. 공동체, 지역사회
obedience [oubíːdiəns]	영 **the state or quality of being obedient** 통 **compliance, submission** The **obedience** of the high school students was superb. 그 고등학교 학생들은 대단히 순종적이었다.	n. 복종, 순종
legacy [légəsi]	영 **anything handed down from the past, as from an ancestor or predecessor** 통 **heritage** His **legacy** was donating money to build public libraries. 그는 유산으로 공공 도서관 설립에 필요한 돈을 기부했다.	n. 유산
self-government [sélf-gʌ́vərnmənt]	영 **control of the government of a state, community, or other body by its own members** 통 **autonomy, self-rule** There was a time when Quebec wanted its own **self-government**. 퀘벡 주에서 자치를 원했던 시기가 있었다.	n. 자치

A. Choose the one word that best fits the sentence.

1 If you are under _____ , then you are being tormented or harassed.

    a. operation   b. spotlight

    c. persecution   d. justice

2 If your family was part of the _____ group, then you have historic American family roots.

    a. Kenyan   b. Puritan

    c. Lutheran   d. Aborigine

3 If you _____ something, then you make it extremely clean.

    a. soil   b. soften

    c. purify   d. stultify

4 If the chess master decides to _____ from the competition, he will quit the match.

    a. ratchet up   b. oversee

    c. emerge   d. withdraw

5 When you return to your _____ , you are going back to where you were born or raised.

    a. hideout   b. homeland

    c. IRS   d. office cubicle

B. Choose the one word that best fits the sentence.

1 Many hockey players have great careers, but the _____ of Wayne Gretzky was unparalleled.

    a. hopelessness   b. principle

    c. legacy   d. birthright

2 A lot of _____ comes about because people do not respect existing social institutions.

    a. credit   b. integrity

    c. corruption   d. friskiness

3 Eritrea, once part of Ethiopia, now is ruled by _____.

    a. conquistadors   b. self-government

    c. righteousness   d. conglomerates

4 The _____ of her new German Shepherd dog was exemplary.

    a. agreement   b. obedience

    c. permission   d. inferiority

5 Many Puritan _____ were known for their low crime rates and good school attendance.

    a. shanties   b. slums

    c. bumpers   d. communities

1 When did the Puritans think they could return to England?

    a. When the King of England granted them a pardon.

    b. When there was no more religious corruption.

    c. When the Anglican Church collapsed.

    d. When England had more natural wonders like New England.

Speaker's Purpose

2 Why does the writer explain the Puritans?

    a. To give a better sense of how they fled corruption and persecution.

    b. To show the roots of American individualism.

    c. To learn more about the Mayflower ship.

    d. To predict ways to found new colonies.

Understanding Organization

3 How does the writer introduce the Puritans?

    a. Through examining the Mayflower route to the New World.

    b. By estimating the distance between England and Plymouth Rock.

    c. By explaining how the Puritans withdrew into their own communities.

    d. Through analyzing the founding of a new nation in the wilderness.

the Function of Statement

4 Listen again to part of the lecture. Then answer the question.
What's the function of this passage?

    a. To introduce how early English settlers made their own decisions, collectively.

    b. To give an example of Plymouth Rock as the foundation of the U.S.

    c. To describe the limitations of founding new religions.

    d. To contrast British and New England religions.

5 According to the writer, what two aspects symbolized the Mayflower Compact? Choose 2 answers.

    a. Illiberal democracy.

    b. That obedience was paramount.

    c. Self-government as an eventual goal.

    d. That community decisions trumped those of the individual.

6 What does the writer imply about the Puritans?

    a. The Church of England was a resilient institution.

    b. New communities can lay new foundations to escape their tormentors.

    c. They were the founders of modern Protestant churches.

    d. Self-government is essential for any autocratic thinking society.

The Puritans (1)

Having failed to " purify " the Church of England, the Puritans withdrew into their own religious communities. Then, in order to escape persecution in their homeland , they set sail for North America. Many Puritans believed that one day England would change, free itself of the religious corruption they opposed, and welcome them back. None of them believed they were helping to found a new nation in the wilderness of North America. Before they landed at Plymouth Rock, Massachusetts, on December 21, 1620, they had already laid the foundations for a tradition that would influence future communities . While still on board their ship, the Mayflower, they signed the Mayflower Compact, in which they pledged obedience to all decisions made by the community for the common good. That document helped establish the legacy of democratic self-government for those who would come after them.

1 The word **purify** in the passage is closest in meaning to
  a. make hygienic
  b. cleanse
  c. unseal
  d. expel

2 The word **withdraw** in the passage is closest in meaning to
  a. eradicate
  b. advance
  c. retire
  d. confiscate

3 The word **persecution** in the passage is closest in meaning to
  a. oppression
  b. abdication
  c. reward
  d. guilt

4 The word **homeland** in the passage is closest in meaning to
  a. neighborhood
  b. guild
  c. province
  d. birthplace

5 The word **corruption** in the passage is closest in meaning to

    a. candor   b. dishonesty   c. kickback   d. acquaintance

6 The word **community** in the passage is closest in meaning to

    a. locksmith   b. ground   c. communism   d. society

7 The word **obedience** in the passage is closest in meaning to

    a. agreement   b. duty   c. compliance   d. irregularity

8 The word **legacy** in the passage is closest in meaning to

    a. heritage   b. legitimacy   c. endowment   d. legality

Paraphrasing

Which best expresses the information in the underlined sentences?

1 Before they landed at Plymouth Rock, Massachusetts, on December 21, 1620, they had already laid the foundations for a tradition that would influence future communities.

    a. The Puritans started a tradition that would go on for decades.
    b. Plymouth Rock was an important Connecticut shipping port.
    c. Too much freedom would undo the Puritan foundation.
    d. The Mayflower Compact helped establish the U.S. constitution.

2 That document helped establish the legacy of democratic self-government for those who would come after them.

    a. The Mayflower Compact established a national banking system.
    b. Establishing a legacy was not the intentions of the settlers.
    c. This document set the foundation for self-government from England.
    d. The legacy of the Puritans will forever be enshrined in U.S. history.

The Puritans (2)

Definitions and Examples

force	㉦ power to influence, affect, or control another person or thing	n. 영향력
[fɔ́ːrs]	㉤ influence, power	
	The last meeting showed that the conservative party was no longer a political **force**.	
	지난 번 회동으로 보수당에게는 더 이상 정치적으로 영향력이 없는 것이 드러났다.	

influential	㉦ having or exerting influence, esp. great influence	a. 영향력이 있는
[ìnfluénʃəl]	㉤ powerful	
	Bill Gates is a very **influential** business leader and power broker.	
	빌 게이츠는 정계 및 재계에 막강한 영향력을 미치는 인물이다.	

sincerity	㉦ the quality of being open and truthful	n. 성실(진심), 정직
[sinsérəti]	㉤ honesty, candor	
	With all **sincerity**, I give you my sincerest apologies.	
	진심으로 당신에게 심심한 사과의 말을 전합니다.	

intolerant	㉦ unwilling to tolerate differences in opinions, practices, or beliefs, especially religious beliefs	a. 편협한
[intálərənt]	㉤ narrow-minded	
	It's wrong to be **intolerant** towards other religions. 다른 종교에 대해서 편협한 태도를 취하는 것은 옳지 못하다.	

attitude	㉦ a way of thinking or acting etc.	n. 태도
[ǽtitʃùːd]	㉤ stance, position	
	Challenge the ideas, beliefs and **attitudes** you hold about your life.	
	인생에 대한 당신의 생각, 믿음, 태도에 비판적 시각을 가져보라.	

guarantee

[gæ̀rəntíː]

- 영 to secure, as by giving or taking security
- 동 promise, secure

The government focuses on building the legal institutions and structures that will **guarantee** human rights in the long term.

정부는 장기적으로 향후 인권을 보장할 법률 제도 및 기구 구성에 집중한다.

v. 보증(보장)하다

champion

[tʃǽmpiən]

- 영 to act as champion of
- 동 defend, support

She had always **championed** her children when they played sports.

그녀는 아이들이 운동 경기를 할 경우 늘 아이들의 힘을 북돋았다.

v. 옹호하다
힘을 북돋우다

initiative

[iníʃiətiv]

- 영 readiness and ability in initiating action
- 동 lead

If you don't take the **initiative**, then time will pass you by.

솔선수범하지 않으면 시간만 낭비하게 될 것이다.

n. 솔선(수범)

morality

[mɔ(ː)rǽləti]

- 영 conformity to the rules of right conduct
- 동 ethics

The **morality** of the Catholic Church has recently been called into question.

가톨릭 교회의 도덕성은 최근 의심을 받고 있다.

n. 도덕(성)

hardheadedness

[hɑːrd hedid nis]

- 영 the quality of not being easily moved or deceived
- 동 stubbornness, willfulness

His **hardheadedness** often gets in the way of negotiations.

그의 완고함이 종종 협상에 방해가 된다.

n. 완고함, 고집

A. Choose the one word that best fits the sentence.

1 If you give someone your _____, then you are very thankful to them.

    a. contempt   b. zeal

    c. sorrow   d. sincerity

2 If you have strong _____, then you are likely someone who is opinionated.

    a. horizons   b. attitudes

    c. affections   d. pertinency

3 Brought to India in the 8th century by traders, Islam became a dominant religious _____ in the country during the Moghul Empire.

    a. assent   b. fury

    c. force   d. efficacy

4 When someone is _____, they hold a lot of power and are highly respected.

    a. unknown   b. influential

    c. sarcastic   d. impotent

5 When someone is _____, then they are narrow-minded.

    a. unusual   b. adverse

    c. intolerant   d. forbearing

B. Choose the one word that best fits the sentence.

1 _____ is something that the Puritans believed was very important.

    a. Binge drinking   b. Corruption

    c. Self-indulgence   d. Morality

2 She _____ that the quarterly report would be finished, but now it's delayed a month.

    a. doubted   b. escalated

    c. guaranteed   d. mesmerized

3 The religious democratic activists _____ freedom of the people, meaning that the wishes of a majority of the people had to be respected.

    a. outlined   b. opposed

    c. traced   d. championed

4 Your _____ is not going to get you guys anywhere; it's only going to deteriorate the relationship.

    a. thoughtfulness   b. hardheadedness

    c. consideration   d. remission

5 The people who become successful in life are usually those who take the

_____ .

    a. passing   b. disadvantage

    c. initiative   d. backseat

Listening Comprehension

Specific Question

1 Why were church and state separated in the constitution?

    a. To prevent intolerant religions from controlling the government.

    b. To prevent intolerance amongst Protestant branches.

    c. To prevent a love of learning in New England.

    d. To prevent the English from taking over the colonies.

Speaker's Purpose

2 Why does the writer explain the way Puritans were treated?

    a. To teach a lesson in religious tolerance.

    b. To learn more about where American values came from.

    c. To predict that Americans will become less religiously tolerant.

    d. To show how Puritans challenged traditional authority.

Understanding Organization

3 How does the writer introduce the Puritanism ethic?

    a. By talking about the decline in the power of Puritanism.

    b. By estimating the future of higher education institutions like Harvard.

    c. Through advocating a strong sense of morality.

    d. By outlining how the church is no longer an important political force.

the Function of Statement

4 Listen again to part of the lecture. Then answer the question.
What's the function of this passage?

    a. To introduce Puritan tolerance of other religious groups.

    b. To give an example of how churches can set up universities.

    c. To describe the beginnings of separation of church and state.

    d. To contrast an influential part of American life.

Specific Information

5 According to the writer, what two factors contributed to the decline of
   Puritan power? Choose 2 answers.

     a. An independent judiciary.

     b. Their intolerance of other religious groups.

     c. The rise of Protestantism.

     d. That the U.S. Constitution limited their influence.

Inference Question

6 What does the writer imply about Puritanism?

     a. A love of learning should be sought by all.

     b. The American strong sense of morality had its roots in Puritanism.

     c. Some of the traits of modern Americans would scare older Puritans.

     d. It is ironic that the Puritan movement created intolerance.

The Puritans (2)

Even after Puritanism was no longer an important political force in the United States, its culture remained an influential part of American life. In a negative sense, for all its dedication and sincerity, Puritanism unfortunately encouraged many of the intolerant attitudes its believers had left England to escape. But reaction to Puritan intolerance of other religious groups helped produce the separation of church and state that is guaranteed in the Constitution of the United States. In a more positive vein, Puritans challenged traditional authority and championed the virtues of personal initiative. Their love of learning led to the enactment of laws for compulsory public education and the founding of Harvard and other colleges. The Puritan character can still be seen in some of the traits of modern Americans — their strong sense of morality (and their hardheadedness), practicality, and militant enthusiasm for humanitarian causes.

1 The word **force** in the passage is closest in meaning to

  a. influence   b. suggestion   c. personality   d. status

2 The word **influential** in the passage is closest in meaning to

  a. susceptible   b. powerful   c. coercive   d. suspicious

3 The word **sincerity** in the passage is closest in meaning to

  a. iniquity   b. challenge   c. sin   d. honesty

4 The word **intolerant** in the passage is closest in meaning to

  a. annoying   b. open-minded   c. bearable   d. narrow-minded

5 The word **attitude** in the passage is closest in meaning to

  a. movement   b. sensitivity

  c. stance   d. stumbling block

6 The word **guarantee** in the passage is closest in meaning to

  a. correct   b. promise   c. tone down   d. honor

7 The word **champion** in the passage is closest in meaning to

  a. improve   b. preside   c. perish   d. support

8 The word **initiative** in the passage is closest in meaning to

  a. lead   b. affair   c. impatience   d. scheme

Paraphrasing

Which best expresses the information in the underlined sentences?

1   In a more positive vein, Puritans challenged traditional authority and championed the virtues of personal initiative.

  a. The positive point of authority is that religion cannot dominate.
  b. Personal initiative was a key facet of being Puritan.
  c. Puritans challenged authority but couldn't beat the government.
  d. The Puritans dominated authority far too often.

2   The Puritan character can still be seen in some of the traits of modern Americans — their strong sense of morality (and their hardheadedness), practicality, and militant enthusiasm for humanitarian causes.

  a. The character of Puritans is embodied in much of American culture.
  b. Character is highly overrated by most people.
  c. Too many Puritan characteristics are still evident today.
  d. Militant enthusiasm is not practical for many Americans.

Mammals

Definitions and Examples

perish [périʃ]	⑨ to die or be destroyed through violence, privation, etc. ⑧ die, pass away Sadly, his parents **perished** in the horrible earthquake. 불행히도 그의 부모는 끔찍한 지진 사고로 죽었다.	**v.** 죽다
trait [tréit]	⑨ a distinguishing characteristic or quality, esp. of one personal nature: bad traits of character ⑧ characteristic, feature An interesting **trait** of Americans is that they are very independent. 미국인들이 갖고 있는 흥미로운 특징은 매우 독립심이 강하다는 점이다.	**n.** 특징, 형질
suited [súːtid]	⑨ fitted, or appropriate (to or for) ⑧ proper, suitable The hockey player was well **suited** to playing defense. 그 하키 선수는 수비 포지션에 아주 적합했다.	**a.** 적합한
offspring [ɔ́(ː)fspriŋ]	⑨ a child or animal in relation to its parent or parents ⑧ children, descendant After three children, she didn't want to have any more **offspring**. 3명의 아이를 낳은 후 그녀는 더 이상 자식을 원하지 않았다.	**n.** 자식
favorable [féivərəbəl]	⑨ affording advantage, opportunity, or convenience ⑧ advantageous, helpful My company occupied a **favorable** position in the negotiations. 우리 회사는 그 협상에서 유리한 위치를 점했다.	**a.** 유리한

Life Science Ⅱ

variation

[vὲəriéiʃən]

- 영 the act, process, or accident of varying in condition, character, or degree
- 통 aberration

There was too much **variation** in the accounting books to satisfy the taxman. 회계 장부에 변동 사항이 너무 많아서 그 세금 징수원은 그 장부에 확신이 서지 않았다.

n. 변화, 다양

---

injurious

[indʒúəriəs]

- 영 harmful, hurtful, or detrimental
- 통 hurtful

Going to work when you are really sick can be **injurious** to others.

몸이 많이 아플 때 직장에 출근하면 다른 사람들에게 해로울 수 있다.

a. 해로운

---

fit

[fit]

- 영 successfully adapted to survive and produce viable offspring in a particular environment
- 통 appropriate

To Darwin, the **fittest** animal is the one that can survive the longest.

다윈의 말을 빌리자면, 가장 적응력 있는 동물이 가장 오래 생존할 수 있는 동물이다.

a. 적응성 있는

---

species

[spí:ʃi(:)z]

- 영 a group whose members are so similar or closely related as to be able to breed together
- 통 breed

Many **species** have died out over the years due to disease and hunting.

많은 종이 질병과 사냥 때문에 오랜 시간에 걸쳐 차차 소멸되었다.

n. 종

---

disappear

[dìsəpíər]

- 영 to cease to exist
- 통 vanish, die out

Will the rare Siberian tiger **disappear** over the next few decades?

희귀 송인 시베리아 호랑이가 향후 몇 십 년 안에 멸종할까?

v. 소멸되다 사라지다

Sentence Completion

A. Choose the one word that best fits the sentence.

1 If you are well-_____ for your partner, then you have good chemistry in your relationship.

    a. canvassed   b. suited

    c. finessed   d. financed

2 You should take advantage of _____ situations and avoid ones that could get too tricky.

    a. favorable   b. ominous

    c. parochial   d. ludicrous

3 If you _____ , you will no longer exist.

    a. perish   b. are reborn

    c. live   d. rehabilitate

4 When a species exhibits a particular _____ , it has a certain characteristic.

    a. calculation   b. dimension

    c. trait   d. disqualification

5 If you have many _____ , then you have many children.

    a. relatives   b. forebears

    c. offspring   d. co-workers

B. Choose the one word that best fits the sentence.

1 Which of the animal _____ in the Galapagos Islands did Darwin study the most?

    a. precursors   b. subordinates

    c. tributaries   d. species

2 All stones have shade _____.

    a. amenities   b. variations

    c. amounts   d. indolence

3 Try not to be too _____ to the other football team when you hit them on the field.

    a. empty   b. influential

    c. injurious   d. picky

4 He said he would _____ for a while, but I didn't know it would vanish for that long.

    a. disappear   b. sprout

    c. flourish   d. dwindle

5 We are still living in the jungle of modern society where the strongest and the _____ will survive.

    a. most vulnerable   b. fittest

    c. corniest   d. supplest

Specific Question

1 What's the meaning of survival of the fittest?

    a. Weaker animals sometimes conquer the strong.

    b. Some have more luck in the animal kingdom than others.

    c. Darwin was not quite sure of his theory.

    d. Stronger animals successfully adapt to their surroundings and weaker ones don't.

Speaker's Purpose

2 Why does the writer explain the evolution theory?

    a. Science is on a constant quest to quantify, ascertain and observe Nature.

    b. Understanding the theory of natural selection is key to understanding Nature.

    c. Darwin was trying to get his theory published in scientific journals.

    d. There were many competing theories about how animals evolve and survive.

Understanding Organization

3 How does the writer introduce the evolution theory?

    a. Adapting is only necessary for larger animals in the tropics.

    b. By discussing the importance of offspring.

    c. Animals either adapt or die off if they cannot become suited to their environment.

    d. By concluding that offspring are not that important.

the Function of Statement

4 Listen again to part of the lecture. Then answer the question.
What's the function of this passage?

   a. That Darwin's theory explains that large amounts of offspring have a greater chance to succeed and adapt.
   b. That Darwin's theory of evolution is largely dependent on offspring.
   c. To describe the limitations of Darwin's theory.
   d. To contrast how Darwin and Newton viewed scientific evidence.

Specific Information

5 According to the writer, what two factors typify the evolution theory?
Choose 2 answers.

   a. Natural selection (destruction of the weak).
   b. Differentiation in the plant kingdom.
   c. Favorable individual differences.
   d. A pattern in the spacing of the planets.

Inference Question

6 What does the writer imply about evolution?

   a. Evolution is an unestablished theory that conflicts with the Bible.
   b. Central to understanding Nature is the theory of evolution and perishing.
   c. Evolution is largely unproven in religious circles.
   d. Adapting to life is the essence of survival in the animal and plant world.

Mammals

Mammals, like all other creatures, must either adapt to their environment or perish. Adaptation occurs when an animal with traits suited to survival produces offspring. Conversely, an organism with disadvantageous or harmful traits will, as a rule, have fewer or no offspring. This is the basis of Darwin's theory of evolution. In his book On the Origin of Species, which outlines this theory, Darwin wrote: "The preservation of favorable individual differences and variations and the destruction of those which are injurious, I have called natural selection, or the survival of the fittest." By "fittest," Darwin did not mean the largest, smartest, or strongest members of a group. Instead, he used the term to refer to those members of a species that produce the largest number of surviving offspring. If a species cannot leave offspring that can adapt to an environment, that species will sooner or later disappear.

1 The word **perish** in the passage is closest in meaning to

    a. die   b. languish   c. replenish   d. regenerate

2 The word **trait** in the passage is closest in meaning to

    a. profile   b. personae   c. characteristic   d. function

3 The word **suited** in the passage is closest in meaning to

    a. tantamount   b. proper   c. similar   d. opposite

4 The word **offspring** in the passage is closest in meaning to

    a. species   b. relatives   c. groups   d. children

5 The word **favorable** in the passage is closest in meaning to

    a. advantageous   b. willing   c. sullen   d. adverse

6 The word **variation** in the passage is closest in meaning to

    a. aberration   b. strangeness   c. deficiency   d. rejection

7 The word **injurious** in the passage is closest in meaning to

    a. hurtful   b. improper   c. unexpected   d. abusive

8 The word **fit** in the passage is closest in meaning to

    a. strict   b. appropriate

    c. tight   d. inflexible

Paraphrasing

Which best expresses the information in the underlined sentences?

1 By "fittest," Darwin did not mean the largest, smartest, or strongest members of a group.

    a. He meant that large families were counterproductive.

    b. He has much work to do on his theory.

    c. He referred to species that had a larger offspring than others.

    d. The smartest are not always those that last the longest.

2 If a species cannot leave offspring that can adapt to an environment that species will sooner or later disappear.

    a. The natural selection theory advocates that animals need a balance in life.

    b. Most ecological habitats are not suited to natural selection.

    c. Central to the natural selection theory is that some species will die if they don't adapt.

    d. The tipping point in Nature is when the strong eat their young.

Unit 26   The Grizzly Bear

Definitions and Examples

state

[stéit]

영 the condition of a person or thing, as with respect to circumstances or attributes

동 condition

The **state** of affairs for the government were recently not that good.

최근 정부의 상황이 그다지 좋지 않았다.

n. 상태, 상황

---

hibernation

[háibə́:rnéiʃən]

영 the torpid or resting state in which some animals pass the winter

동 resting period, winter sleep

The grizzly bear was in **hibernation** for the winter months.

그 회색곰은 겨울 동안 동면에 들어갔다.

n. 동면

---

bodily

[bádəli]

영 of or pertaining to the body

동 physical

The doctor said to be careful of contacting infected **bodily** fluids.

의사는 감염된 체액과 접촉하지 않도록 당부했다.

a. 신체상의

---

litter

[lítər]

영 a number of young brought forth by a multiparous animal at one birth

동 babies, brood

The mother cat had a **litter** of six kittens.

그 어미 고양이는 여섯 마리의 새끼를 낳았다.

n. (한 배에서 태어난) 새끼

---

gestation

[dʒestéiʃən]

영 the period of development in the uterus from conception until birth

동 pregnancy

The **gestation** period for many insects is just a few weeks.

많은 곤충들의 경우 임태기간이 단지 몇 주에 불과하다.

n. 임태

average
[ǽvəridʒ]

- 영 usual or ordinary in kind or character
- 동 common

The **average** French person smokes a lot of cigarettes.

보통의 프랑스인은 담배를 많이 피운다.

a. 보통의

agile
[ǽdʒəl]

- 영 quick and well-coordinated in movement
- 동 quick, nimble

She was very **agile**, especially when playing badminton.

그녀는 매우 민첩했으며, 배드민턴을 칠 때 특히 그러했다.

a. 민첩한

rough
[rʌf]

- 영 having a coarse or uneven surface, as from projections, irregularities, or breaks; not smooth
- 동 irregular, rugged

The surface of the highway was very **rough**.

그 고속도로의 노면은 매우 험했다.

a. 험한

terrain
[təréin]

- 영 the surface features of an area of land
- 동 area, ground

Much of the **terrain** was too difficult for the tanks and armored vehicles to cross.

탱크와 장갑차가 건너가기에는, 그 지형의 대부분이 너무 험했다.

n. 지형

savage
[sǽvidʒ]

- 영 fierce, ferocious, or cruel
- 동 wild, brutal

His methods were **savage** and vicious, but very effective on the K-1 tour.

그의 방식은 사납고 잔인하였지만 K-1 원정 경기에서는 매우 효과적이었다.

a. 사나운, 포악한

A. Choose the one word that best fits the sentence.

1 If you have no _____ fluids, then you are probably dead.

   a. monetary   b. cellular
   c. material   d. bodily

2 It begins with conception, goes through _____, results in a birth, and continues on to nurture and development.

   a. gestation   b. progress
   c. evolution   d. construction

3 The _____ of economy is in fine shape and the manufacturing sector is doing well.

   a. state   b. denial
   c. downside   d. recession

4 When an animal is in _____, then it is sleeping for a long time.

   a. overcrowding   b. hibernation
   c. pain   d. farmland

5 If an animal gives birth to a _____, then it has several babies.

   a. puddle   b. litter
   c. plague   d. mob

Sentence Completion

B. Choose the one word that best fits the sentence.

1 There's no point trying to climb the _____ in the Karakoram Mountains; it's too steep.

    a. wake   b. brook

    c. landscape   d. terrain

2 The _____ height of Korean teenagers rose several centimeters over the past decade.

    a. massive   b. abnormal

    c. exacting   d. average

3 The best gymnasts were very quick and _____ on the gymnastics floor.

    a. wasteful   b. slovenly

    c. agile   d. ponderous

4 The _____ grizzly bear routinely killed many moose on the Canadian plains.

    a. savage   b. industrious

    c. meek   d. credible

5 The _____ surface made it difficult for forensic investigators to gather evidence.

    a. smooth   b. rough

    c. well-paved   d. hygienic

Specific Question

1 What's hibernation?

    a. It's a habit adopted by some animals to look for food.

    b. It refers to the distance between an animal's home and hunting area.

    c. It's a prolonged state of resting for some mammals.

    d. It's a pattern of migration to other regions.

Speaker's Purpose

2 Why does the writer explain grizzly bears?

    a. To talk about their unique way of resting and why they are effective killers.

    b. To learn more about the bear's competitors.

    c. Because their gestation period is quite common.

    d. Because to detect these patterns in bears, scientists must study them for years.

Understanding Organization

3 How does the writer introduce grizzly bears?

    a. Much of the public despises bears, especially large ones.

    b. By explaining about female grizzlies.

    c. They are found in three regions throughout the world.

    d. A pattern is emerging that grizzly litters are getting smaller.

the Function of Statement

4 Listen again to part of the lecture. Then answer the question.
What's the function of this passage?

    a. To introduce the basics of grizzly bear life.

    b. To give an example of how we can save grizzlies.

    c. To describe the limitations of hibernation in cold winters.

    d. To contrast black and grizzly bears.

Specific Information

5 According to the writer, what two methods do grizzly bears use when
fighting? Choose 2 answers.

    a. Using its teeth.

    b. Using its babies as a buffer zone.

    c. Using its claws.

    d. Being agile and moving through the forest.

Inference Question

6 What does the writer imply about grizzly bears?

    a. They are highly dangerous and territorial.

    b. More grizzlies are moving to regions in Asia.

    c. Many bears make good house pets.

    d. Some grizzlies have a lot of fur.

The Grizzly Bear

Grizzly bears are found in the western part of North America and in parts of Europe and Asia. During the winter, they remain in a state similar to hibernation, except for the fact that their bodily functions continue, and body temperature remains normal. Each year the female grizzly has a litter of one to four young after a gestation period of six to nine months. The grizzly bear has a huge, muscular body covered with fur. An average adult grizzly is about 2.5 meters long and weighs 360 kilograms, yet the animal is very agile and can move quickly through forests and over rough mountainous terrain. If cornered, the grizzly is among the most dangerous of animals. It will defend itself by striking with its claws and tearing with its teeth. But in spite of being capable of such savage behavior, grizzly bears can be tamed and will remain docile.

1 The word **state** in the passage is closest in meaning to

    a. place   b. condition   c. region   d. position

2 The word **hibernation** in the passage is closest in meaning to

    a. winter sleep   b. warming   c. spite   d. siesta

3 The word **bodily** in the passage is closest in meaning to

    a. anatomical   b. watery   c. physical   d. abstract

4 The word **litter** in the passage is closest in meaning to

    a. garbage   b. selection   c. babies   d. supplies

5 The word **gestation** in the passage is closest in meaning to

    a. evolution   b. advancement   c. behavior   d. pregnancy

6 The word **average** in the passage is closest in meaning to

    a. rare   b. common   c. peculiar   d. divisive

7 The word **agile** in the passage is closest in meaning to

    a. intelligent   b. creeping   c. quick   d. smooth

8 The word **rough** in the passage is closest in meaning to

    a. irregular   b. even   c. refined   d. rejectable

Paraphrasing

Which best expresses the information in the underlined sentences?

1 During the winter, they remain in a state similar to hibernation, except for the fact that their bodily functions continue, and body temperature remains normal.

    a. When a bear hibernates, it goes completely into shut down mode.
    b. Air currents can often awake a bear from hibernation.
    c. Hibernation is not a state of complete sleep; many bodily functions still work.
    d. The body temperature often rises several degrees in the winter.

2 But in spite of being capable of such savage behavior, grizzly bears can be tamed and will remain docile.

    a. The savage behavior of grizzlies can be tamed by professionals.
    b. Much of the anger in bears can be treated with scientific methods.
    c. Too much open territory is bad for male grizzlies.
    d. Despite their erratic behavior, bears make cuddly friends.

Life in the Sea

Definitions and Examples

endless

[éndlis]

영 having or seeming to have no end, limit, or conclusion

동 boundless, infinite

The chemistry test seemed **endless**, with countless pages of difficult questions.

어려운 문제들로 가득 찬 수많은 페이지의 화학 시험은 끝이 없는 듯 보였다.

a. 끝없는

---

wonder

[wʌ́ndər]

영 the feeling aroused by something strange and surprising

동 admiration, astonishment

I've read the book a couple of times and still felt **wonder** at the creativity of the story.

그 책을 두어 번 읽었지만 창의적인 이야기 때문에 지금까지도 신비로움을 느낀다.

n. 신비로움, 경이

---

teeming

[tíːmiŋ]

영 abounding or swarming with something, as with people

동 swarming, filled

The ants nest was **teeming** with activity as hundreds of ants swarmed about.

그 개미집은 떼지어 이리저리 돌아다니는 개미 수백 마리로 들끓었다.

a. 들끓는

---

trillion

[tríljən]

영 a million million

The Iraq War might easily cost a **trillion** dollars or more.

이라크 전쟁 비용은 족히 1조 이상에 이를 수도 있다.

n. 무수, 1조

---

aid

[éid]

영 help or support

동 help, assistance

The poor in Africa need the **aid** of many other countries.

아프리카의 빈민들은 다른 여러 나라들의 도움을 필요로 한다.

n. 도움

Life Science Ⅱ

dweller

[dwélər]

영 a person or an animal that inhabits a particular place

동 inhabitant

He was a **dweller** of old buildings that were ready to be demolished.

그는 철거를 앞둔 낡은 건물에 사는 거주자였다.

n. 거주자

---

roam

[róum]

영 to walk, go, or travel without a fixed purpose or direction

동 wander

Mammoths once **roamed** the plains of Central Asia millions of years ago.

수백 만년 전 매머드는 중앙 아시아의 평원을 돌아다녔었다.

v. 돌아다니다

---

conceivable

[kənsí:vəbəl]

영 capable of being conceived

동 imaginable

It is **conceivable** that U.F.O.s do exist in outer space.

미확인 비행물체 UFO가 우주공간에 존재한다는 생각은 충분히 가능한 일이다.

a. 생각할 수 있는 상상할 수 있는

---

cling

[klíŋ]

영 to come or be in close contact with

동 attach, stick

The red dress **clings** to the body and falls smoothly.

그 붉은 드레스는 몸에 딱 달라붙으며, 선이 부드럽다.

v. 달라붙다

---

flatten

[flǽtn]

영 to make flat or flatter

동 level

Their job was to **flatten** the surrounding buildings and clean up the debris.

그들의 일은 주변의 건물을 무너뜨리고 잔해를 깨끗하게 청소하는 것이었다.

v. 평평하게 만들다 (무너뜨리다)

Sentence Completion

A. Choose the one word that best fits the sentence.

1 When the pool is _____ with exotic fish, then it is full of exotic fish.

    a. storming   b. emptying

    c. sparse   d. teeming

2 When you get rid of a _____ on your property, then you send the person away.

    a. surface   b. misfortune

    c. dweller   d. contract

3 If you drive for _____ hours, then you are driving for a very long time.

    a. endless   b. counting

    c. inclusive   d. purposeful

4 They gazed with _____ at the rich palaces and mighty churches.

    a. hazard   b. wonder

    c. phenomenon   d. creativity

5 If your company has sales of a(an) _____ dollars, then it is a large successful company.

    a. mediocre   b. trillion

    c. inadequate   d. meager

B. Choose the one word that best fits the sentence.

1 A piece of toilet paper _____ to her high heel shoe.

    a. hugged   b. grabbed

    c. loosed   d. clung

2 The organization has increased humanitarian _____ to the country by more than half.

    a. aid   b. sanction

    c. threat   d. blockade

3 Did you know that rhinoceroses used to _____ in ancient China?

    a. lurch   b. thrash

    c. blunder   d. roam

4 The baker _____ the cake out and put it in the oven.

    a. flattened   b. strode

    c. hazed   d. splattered

5 It is not _____ to count all the marine life in all the oceans.

    a. reckless   b. conceivable

    c. incredible   d. devious

Specific Question

1 What's the most amazing mammal in the oceans?

    a. The Antarctic blue whale, which reaches up to 30 meters in length.

    b. The coral reefs along the Australian coastline.

    c. The common orange starfish.

    d. The strange goosefish with its flattened head

Speaker's Purpose

2 Why does the writer explain life in the sea?

    a. To focus on the amazing variety of life forms.

    b. To talk about the hideous-looking goosefish.

    c. To predict the relationship of the blue whale to other organisms.

    d. To talk about patterns on new life forms on the seabed.

Understanding Organization

3 How does the writer introduce life in the sea?

    a. By mentioning the trillions of organisms on the planet.

    b. Through counting the number of living organisms in the oceans.

    c. By predicting the future health of the oceans.

    d. By comparing the dinosaur and blue whale.

the Function of Statement

4 Listen again to part of the lecture. Then answer the question.

What's the function of this passage?

    a. That much of marine life has already been catalogued by scientists.

    b. To make us more curious about the wonder of the oceans.

    c. That there is a vast array of interesting marine life in our oceans.

    d. That dinosaurs are much more interesting than blue whales.

Specific Information

5 According to the writer, what two forms of marine life are quite
   interesting? Choose 2 answers.

   a. Antarctic blue whales.
   b. Blue dolphins.
   c. Starfish on coral branches.
   d. Sea horses.

Inference Question

6 What does the writer imply about the oceans?

   a. Much of marine life is as interesting, if not more so than life on land.
   b. Coral branches are in danger due to pollution from mankind.
   c. He predicts that the blue whale will become extinct.
   d. He detects patterns in the life cycle of starfish.

Life in the Sea

The variety and beauty of life beneath the surface of the sea is an endless source of wonder. The number of living organisms in the sea is greater than the number of stars in the sky. The waters are teeming with trillions upon trillions of creatures that can only be seen with the aid of a microscope, not to mention a wide variety of larger animals. The largest sea dweller, the Antarctic blue whale, averages 30 meters in length and weighs 135 metric tons, well over three times the weight of the largest dinosaur that ever roamed the face of the Earth. Life in the sea comes in every conceivable size, shape, and form. Starfish cling to the pink coral branches of living stone forests, while hideous-looking goosefish, with large flattened heads and enormous mouths, filled with sharp, pointed teeth, prowl the ocean depths in search of prey.

1 The word **endless** in the passage is closest in meaning to

    a. intermittent   b. temporary   c. infinite   d. ongoing

2 The word **wonder** in the passage is closest in meaning to

    a. admiration   b. approval   c. success   d. struggle

3 The word **teeming** in the passage is closest in meaning to

    a. educating   b. swarming   c. attending   d. strolling

4 The word **aid** in the passage is closest in meaning to

    a. starvation   b. hindrance   c. assistant   d. help

5 The word **dweller** in the passage is closest in meaning to

    a. ulcer   b. inhabitant   c. homeowner   d. translator

6 The word **roam** in the passage is closest in meaning to

    a. look for   b. spread   c. wander   d. subject

7 The word **conceivable** in the passage is closest in meaning to

    a. impossible   b. incredible   c. enough   d. imaginable

8 The word **cling** in the passage is closest in meaning to

    a. separate   b. pound   c. stick   d. pass

Paraphrasing

Which best expresses the information in the underlined sentences?

1 The largest sea dweller, the Antarctic blue whale, averages 30 meters in length and weighs 135 metric tons, well over three times the weight of the largest dinosaur that ever roamed the face of the Earth.

    a. Many whales are large, but none as big as the blue whale.
    b. The largest marine mammal is one that is three times the weight of the largest dinosaur.
    c. The largest marine mammal is one that is three times the length of the largest dinosaur.
    d. The Antarctic blue whale has the largest appetite of all mammals.

2 Starfish cling to the pink coral branches of living stone forests, while hideous-looking goosefish, with large flattened heads and enormous mouths, filled with sharp, pointed teeth, prowl the ocean depths in search of prey.

    a. The ocean floor is saturated with a wide variety of marine life.
    b. Goosefish can easily eat coral with their large teeth.
    c. Too much variety of ocean life is harmful to the marine biological balance.
    d. Much of pink coral attracts plankton for the blue whale.

Unit 28 Engineer (1)

Definitions and Examples

prototype
[próutoʊtàip]

영 the original or model on which something is based or formed

동 example, original

Some clever engineers are making an electric car **prototype**.

일부 영리한 공학자들은 전기 자동차 견본을 개발하고 있다.

n. 원형, 견본

---

assemble
[əsémbəl]

영 to bring together or gather into one place, company, body, or whole

동 gather, bring together

The Secretary-General then addressed the **assembled** troops.

그런 다음 사무 총장은 집합한 병사들에게 연설했다.

v. 모으다

---

mechanic
[məkǽnik]

영 a type of worker that fixes, repairs or works on mechanical mechanisms

동 engineer

The **mechanics** worked all night designing the complex iPod that involved lots of circuitry.

기계공들은 밤새 수많은 회로가 탑재된 복잡한 아이팟의 설계 작업을 했다.

n. 기계공

---

objective
[əbdʒéktiv]

영 something that one's efforts or actions are intended to attain or accomplish

동 purpose, goal

His **objective** was to eventually get a university job in three years.

3년 안에 대학과 관련된 직업을 구하는 것이 그의 목표였다.

n. 목표

---

patent
[pǽtənt]

영 special permission granting an investor sole rights to an invention

동 copyright

A **patent** is applied for to protect the idea of a new innovative product.

특허는 혁신적인 새 상품의 아이디어를 보호하기 위해 신청하는 것이다.

n. 특허

organized
[ɔ́ːrgənàizd]

영 having a formal organization or structure
동 arranged, methodical

Being **organized** was a central part to his life, both at work and home.

직장과 가정에서, 조직적인 생활이란 그의 삶에서 중심적인 역할을 한다.

a. 조직적인
짜임새있는

strive
[stràiv]

영 to exert much effort or energy
동 try, endeavor

With my goals and destination clearly set, I **strived** to achieve them.

목표와 목적지를 분명히 정해두고, 나는 그것을 성취하기 위해 노력했다.

v. 노력하다

generator
[dʒénərèitər]

영 a machine which produces electricity
동 dynamo, power producer

In Iraq, it is necessary to have **generators** in case the power goes out.

이라크에서는 전력 공급이 끊길 경우를 대비해 발전기를 비치해야 한다.

n. 발전기

conduit
[kándʒuit]

영 a pipe, tube, or the like, for conveying water or other fluid
동 main, duct

There are many **conduits** in a large building for air conditioning.

큰 빌딩에는 냉방을 목적으로 사용하는 도관이 많이 있다.

n. (수도·전기)도관

novelty
[návəlti]

영 something new and strange
동 curiosity, oddity

We are way past the point where teaching the Internet is a **novelty**.

인터넷 교육이 신기한 일로 여겨졌던 시대는 훨씬 지났다.

n. 신기한 것

A. Choose the one word that best fits the sentence.

1 The _____ take apart the BMW and retool the engine overnight.

    a. practitioners   b. solicitors

    c. servicemen on active duty   d. mechanics

2 If you are the first one with _____ on a product, then you have exclusive rights.

    a. civil rights   b. patents

    c. legislations   d. bounties

3 If you make a(an) _____, you are designing the very first copy of something.

    a. benchmark   b. anomaly

    c. prototype   d. ballpark figure

4 He entered and the _____ members stood from the chairs.

    a. dispersed   b. assembled

    c. destroyed   d. accumulated

5 If you set out to achieve a(an) _____, then you are trying to do something.

    a. objective   b. accumulation

    c. summit   d. windfall

B. Choose the one word that best fits the sentence.

1 When you install _____ for air conditioning systems, make sure you have enough materials.

a. specimens
b. conduits
c. funnels
d. sewages

2 The Holocaust was a calculated, highly _____ plan to eliminate certain ethnic groups, primarily, the Jews.

a. oriented
b. organized
c. reveted
d. venerated

3 The power plant is a _____ on the prairie, the first in the country to burn animal litter.

a. uniformity
b. custom
c. novelty
d. route

4 When the _____ turn off, we will not have any power to run the hospital.

a. suppliers
b. shredders
c. generators
d. ditches

5 Millions of people are _____ to escape their shattered society, where most of the basics of normal life have collapsed.

a. striving
b. dismembering
c. loitering
d. fancying

Specific Question

1 What was Edison's most famous invention?

    a. An under-the floor-heating system.

    b. The telegraph pole.

    c. The incandescent bulb.

    d. The radar system for planes.

Speaker's Purpose

2 Why does the writer explain Edison?

    a. To show the impracticability of the incandescent lamp.

    b. To show the depth of Edison's engineering success.

    c. To indicate the frustration that he went through.

    d. To promote engineering labs in New Jersey.

Understanding Organization

3 How does the writer introduce Edison?

    a. By talking about his "invention factory".

    b. Through explaining his relationship with his assistants.

    c. By predicting his success regarding electricity.

    d. By praising his 400 patent applications.

the Function of Statement

4 Listen again to part of the lecture. Then answer the question.
What's the function of this passage?

    a. To introduce how to solve unique problems.

    b. To give an example of Edison's organized approach to problem solving.

    c. To describe the limitations of the incandescent bulb.

    d. To contrast Edison and Bell's techniques.

5 According to the professor, what two factors contributed to the discovery of light bulb? Choose 2 answers.

    a. Having a dedicated research staff.

    b. Using transferable technology from the phonograph.

    c. A thorough process for vetting inventions.

    d. Having major inventions goals scheduled at intervals.

6 What does the writer imply about Edison?

    a. That more ingenious inventors are needed nowadays.

    b. Perseverance eventually pays off with great inventions.

    c. Making minor inventions every 10 days is not sufficient.

    d. Developing generators, fuses, and conduits is an arduous process.

Engineer (1)

In 1876, Thomas Edison established an "invention factory," the prototype for today's engineering laboratories, in Menlo Park, New Jersey. There he assembled a handful of young assistants and a dozen mechanics to do nothing but work on inventions. Edison's goal was "a minor invention every 10 days and a big thing every six months or so," an objective that was readily achieved. By the time he left the laboratory in 1887, Edison had received almost 400 patents, including one for a practical incandescent lamp, one for an electric system, and one for the phonograph. Perhaps Edison's greatest invention, however, was his organized approach to problem solving. Edison explored every aspect of a problem and its possible solutions, striving to solve even those unique problems associated with his inventions. For example, by developing generators, fuses, and conduits, Edison made the electric light a practical reality rather than a mere novelty.

1 The word **prototype** in the passage is closest in meaning to
    a. skepticism   b. original   c. test type   d. illustration

2 The word **assemble** in the passage is closest in meaning to
    a. pull together   b. put apart   c. bring together   d. pull off

3 The word **mechanic** in the passage is closest in meaning to
    a. engineer   b. kerchief   c. technicality   d. pundit

4 The word **objective** in the passage is closest in meaning to
    a. rationale   b. principal   c. statement   d. purpose

5 The word **patent** in the passage is closest in meaning to

    a. copyright   b. law   c. niche   d. suggestion

6 The word **organized** in the passage is closest in meaning to

    a. given   b. dribbled   c. arranged   d. premeditated

7 The word **strive** in the passage is closest in meaning to

    a. ramble   b. solicit   c. endeavor   d. bolster

8 The word **generator** in the passage is closest in meaning to

    a. power producer   b. catalyst

    c. circuit   d. fuselage

Paraphrasing

Which best expresses the information in the underlined sentences?

1 Perhaps Edison's greatest invention, however, was his organized approach to problem solving.

    a. The greatest invention was yet to come for Edison.

    b. His organized approach was too methodical.

    c. Edison was a great inventor but a poor manager.

    d. Problem solving was something that Edison was very organized at.

2 Edison explored every aspect of a problem and its possible solutions, striving to solve even those unique problems associated with his inventions.

    a. The problems associated with Edison's inventions never went away.

    b. Striving to solve every permutation was what Edison tried to do.

    c. Too much exploration can lead to untried solutions.

    d. Some people associated inventions with Edison.

Engineer (2)

Definitions and Examples

skill [skíl]	영 the ability, coming from one's knowledge, practice, aptitude, etc., to do something 동 technique, art Her **skills** were paramount in the office where her supervisor relied upon her. 그녀의 기술은 사무실 내에서 최고이기 때문에 상사도 그녀를 신뢰했다.	n. 기술
apprentice [əpréntis]	영 a person who works for another in order to learn a trade 동 learner, trainee The **apprentice** was fired by Donald Trump after screwing up on the project. 도널드 트럼프는 견습생이 프로젝트를 망치자 그를 해고했다.	n. 도제, 견습생
intensive [inténsiv]	영 of, relating to, or characterized by intensity 동 concentrated, thorough The institution boasts that its **intensive** instruction helps students with reading problems. 그 기관은 집중교육이 독서에 어려움이 있는 학생들에게 도움이 된다고 호언장담한다.	a. 집중적인
concept [kánsept]	영 a general notion or idea 동 idea, theory Some **concepts** were extremely hard to grasp for the physicist student. 일부 개념은 그 물리학도가 파악하기에 너무 어려웠다.	n. 개념
broad [brɔ́:d]	영 of great extent; large 동 wide, extensive Across the **broad** avenue in Moscow was a procession of military tanks. 모스크바에 있는 넓은 광장을 전차들이 행진하며 지나갔다.	a. 넓은

exposure
[ikspóuʒər]

ⓔ the act of subjecting someone to an influencing experience

ⓢ experience

The **exposure** of traveling was great for her overall education of other cultures.

그녀가 다른 문화에 대해 포괄적으로 이해할 수 있었던 이유는 여행 경험 때문이었다.

n. 경험, 체험

aesthetic
[esθétik]

ⓔ pertaining to a sense of the beautiful or to the science of aesthetics

ⓢ artistic, refined

Much of Hong Kong is designed with a sense of **aesthetic** values.

홍콩 지역 대부분은 미적 감각으로 설계된다.

a. 미적인

prepared
[pripέərd]

ⓔ properly expectant, organized, or equipped

ⓢ ready, set

Are you **prepared** to take the TOEFL test this week?

이번 주 토플 시험칠 준비가 되었습니까?

a. 준비된

vast
[vǽst]

ⓔ of very great area or extent

ⓢ broad, massive

The **vast** tundra of the Canadian north goes on and on forever.

캐나다 북부에 있는 방대한 툰드라 지대는 끝없이 이어져 있다.

a. 방대한

array
[əréi]

ⓔ a large group, number, or quantity of people or things

ⓢ a lot, plenty

He had quite an **array** of books on politics and international relations.

그는 성지학과 국제 관계에 관한 다량의 책을 보유하고 있었다.

n. 다량

Sentence Completion

A. Choose the one word that best fits the sentence.

1 When someone deals with _____ , they are considering ideas, thoughts and beliefs.

    a. coherences   b. conscience

    c. concepts   d. conscription

2 If you have substantial job _____ , then you are highly trained in a specific task.

    a. pleas   b. clumsiness

    c. cubicles   d. skills

3 If you receive substantial _____ to travel, then you will learn new cultures.

    a. kinship   b. classics

    c. exposure   d. divulgence

4 If you are considered a(an) _____ at work, then you are new at the job like an intern.

    a. apprentice   b. software developer

    c. globalist   d. chief editor

5 If you have an open and _____ mind, then you will likely learn many things.

    a. narrow   b. broad

    c. stigmatic   d. separate

Sentence Completion

B. Choose the one word that best fits the sentence.

1 The _____ choices of courses at MIT resulted in higher admissions that year.

    a. spatial   b. vast

    c. shallow   d. mediocre

2 If you visit the museum in Madrid, the _____ beauty of Picasso's Guernica will astound you.

    a. sodden   b. overdelicate

    c. dilapidated   d. aesthetic

3 The 37 poor readers in the _____ reading program outpaced the 12 poor readers in the standard instruction groups.

    a. intensive   b. capacious

    c. haphazard   d. eventful

4 The _____ of radio telescope satellites stationed in Peru were aimed into deep space.

    a. lack   b. shortage

    c. regalia   d. array

5 If you are not _____ before climbing Mt. Everest, then disaster will likely happen.

    a. agitated   b. unwilling

    c. prepared   d. summoned

1 What is MIT trying to teach now?

    a. Humanities studies coupled with structural engineering.

    b. Training in specific scientific concepts.

    c. Practical concepts for learning old techniques.

    d. Humanities lessons coupled with civil engineering.

Speaker's Purpose

2 Why does the writer explain engineering?

    a. To encourage growth in more technical colleges.

    b. To give broad exposure to practical applications.

    c. To show the evolution of a technical field.

    d. To illustrate patterns in French and U.S. schools.

Understanding Organization

3 How does the writer introduce engineering?

    a. By encouraging students to move to France.

    b. By showing the evolution of trades to professions.

    c. By indicating how to enter the United States.

    d. By preparing students for the MIT test.

the Function of Statement

4 Listen again to part of the lecture. Then answer the question.
What's the function of this passage?

    a. To introduce a well-rounded approach to engineering school.

    b. To reopen the Rensselaer Polytechnic Institute.

    c. To describe the limitations of engineering schools.

    d. To contrast intensive scientific training studies.

5 According to the professor, what two forms of study do students receive? Choose 2 answers.

> a. Some concepts that are practical.
>
> b. A sense of beauty and design.
>
> c. A sense of fair play and fun.
>
> d. A vast array of social problems.

6 What does the writer imply about engineering?

> a. That the Ecole Polytechnique has an edge over MIT.
>
> b. That skills have declined since 1794.
>
> c. That aesthetic values can be of value for an engineer.
>
> d. That future engineers will be acquainted with the arts.

Engineer (2)

With skills being passed on from master to apprentice, engineering was regarded as a trade rather than a profession up until the late 18th century. Then, in 1794, the first school for engineers was established, the Ecole Polytechnique, in Paris. America's first engineering school, the Rensselaer Polytechnic Institute, was opened 30 years later. Today, over 280 schools grant 65,000 engineering degrees in the United States alone. Schools such as the Massachusetts Institute of Technology are working to create a new type of engineer. Students there receive intensive training in scientific concepts and practical applications; at the same time, they receive broad exposure to the humanities. By encouraging their students to develop aesthetic values and a sense of fun, teachers at MIT believe these future engineers will be better prepared to deal with the vast array of problems that society faces.

1   The word **skill** in the passage is closest in meaning to
   a. habit   b. awkwardness   c. art   d. sorrow

2   The word **apprentice** in the passage is closest in meaning to
   a. trainee   b. counselor   c. intermediate   d. expert

3   The word **intensive** in the passage is closest in meaning to
   a. shrewd   b. attentive   c. whimsical   d. concentrated

4   The word **concept** in the passage is closest in meaning to
   a. allusion   b. idea   c. impression   d. guess

5 The word **broad** in the passage is closest in meaning to

    a. underlying   b. narrow   c. confusing   d. extensive

6 The word **exposure** in the passage is closest in meaning to

    a. confession   b. rejection   c. experience   d. contrition

7 The word **aesthetic** in the passage is closest in meaning to

    a. artistic   b. candid   c. demonic   d. visual

8 The word **prepared** in the passage is closest in meaning to

    a. ripened   b. conceived   c. ready   d. reluctant

Paraphrasing

Which best expresses the information in the underlined sentences?

1 Schools such as the Massachusetts Institute of Technology are working to create a new type of engineer.

    a. The administrators at MIT are trying to churn out a new type of engineer.
    b. MIT administrators are revamping their school.
    c. MIT engineers are refashioning their curriculum.
    d. Schools like MIT are trying to churn out a new type of engineer.

2 Students there receive intensive training in scientific concepts and practical applications; at the same time, they receive broad exposure to the humanities.

    a. Scientific concepts alone are not enough.
    b. Intensive training is for fast-track international students.
    c. The humanities department is ideally suited for arts oriented students.
    d. Broader exposure is needed so students will comprehend concepts.

Unit 30 Roman Citizenship

Definitions and Examples

status
[stéitəs]

영 position relative to that of others
동 position, standing

Her **status** in the law firm rose after she drove her new BMW to work.

BMW 신차를 타고 출근한 뒤로 법률 회사에서 그녀의 위신이 높아졌다.

n. 지위, 위신

---

class
[klǽs]

영 one of a number of economic/social groups
동 group, rank, caste

In India, there are many social **classes** based upon education.

인도에서는 교육 수준에 따른 여러 사회 계층이 존재한다.

n. 계층

---

property
[prápərti]

영 something that a person owns
동 possession

I paid for the film posters and they are my **property**.

영화 포스터에 대한 돈을 지불했기 때문에 이제 그것은 내 소유다.

n. 재산, 소유(물)

---

second class
[sékənd klǽs]

영 less valuable and less important than other people
동 inferior, secondary

Too many airlines treat our children as **second-class** citizens.

너무나 많은 항공사가 우리의 아이들을 2등 시민으로 취급한다.

a. 2등의

---

privileged
[prívəlidʒd]

영 confined to an exclusive or chosen group of individuals
동 favored

Only the **privileged** class was permitted to fly on the new Airbus A380.

오직 특권층만이 새 항공기인 에어버스 A380 탑승이 허용되었다.

a. 특권이 있는

Social Science Ⅲ

citizenship
[sítəzənʃip]

영 the state of being vested with the rights, privileges, and duties of a citizen.

동 civil rights

It is very hard to get **citizenship** in Korea, but not so hard in Canada.

한국의 시민권을 획득하기란 정말 어렵지만 캐나다의 시민권은 그렇게 어렵지 않다.

n. 시민권
시민의 신분

automatically
[ɔ̀:təmǽtik]

영 in a reflex manner

동 mechanically, naturally

Every morning, he **automatically** orders a cafe mocha at Starbucks.

매일 아침 그는 스타벅스 커피점에서 기계적으로 카페 모카 커피를 주문한다.

ad. 자동으로
기계적으로

outstanding
[àutstǽndiŋ]

영 marked by superiority or distinction

동 excellent, superior

Her performance on the oral test was simply **outstanding**.

그녀는 구술 시험에서 아주 뛰어난 성적을 받았다.

a. 뛰어난

gradually
[grǽdʒuəli]

영 by small degrees or little by little

동 slowly, steadily

The effects of global warming are happening **gradually**.

지구 온난화의 영향이 점점 나타나고 있다.

ad. 점점

inhabitant
[inhǽbətənt]

영 a person who inhabits a particular place

동 resident, dweller

Many **inhabitants** of rural areas are moving to large urban cities in Asia.

아시아에서는 시골 지역 거주자들 가운데 상당수가 대도시로 몰려들고 있다.

n. 거주자

245

A. Choose the one word that best fits the sentence.

1 When I saw that he touched my _____ in an attempt to damage it, I became pretty upset.

    a. junk   b. property

    c. nerve   d. weakness

2 The racist politician was criticized for treating immigrants as _____ people.

    a. second class   b. exclusive

    c. entitled   d. primary

3 If you have high _____ in society, then you are regarded with respect.

    a. categories   b. status

    c. scores   d. ill fame

4 He and his wife make about $60,000 combined each year, placing them in the middle _____ .

    a. brigade   b. swarm

    c. class   d. battalion

5 When you come from a(an) _____ class in society, try not to become too arrogant.

    a. estranged   b. poor

    c. remedial   d. privileged

B. Choose the one word that best fits the sentence.

1 Climbing a mountain like K2 is something you must try and do
   _____ .

   a. dejectedly   b. half-heartedly
   c. gradually   d. hostilely

2 There's no point applying for _____ in Canada unless you plan on
   learning English.

   a. performance records   b. citizenship
   c. expulsion   d. ownership

3 The children of Roman citizens were _____ given citizenship if they
   were males.

   a. dishonorably   b. forcibly
   c. spiritlessly   d. automatically

4 There are very few _____ in Greenland because of the harsh weather
   conditions.

   a. inhabitants   b. homeowners
   c. loaner   d. creditors

5 His excessively _____ academic record was questioned by the
   admissions committee.

   a. vain   b. outstanding
   c. morose   d. copyrighted

Listening Comprehension

1 Who was divided into three classes?

    a. Emperors, slaves and concubines.

    b. Slaves, inhabitants and citizens.

    c. Women, children and foreign slaves.

    d. Slaves, inheritants and citizens.

2 Why does the writer explain Roman citizenship?

    a. To show that male inhabitants dominated the Empire.

    b. To criticize Roman emperors for their treatment of women.

    c. To demonstrate the importance of granting full citizenship.

    d. To tell how unprivileged many men were.

3 How does the writer introduce Roman citizenship?

    a. By talking about living in the territories.

    b. Through demonstrating how citizenship in Rome was privileged.

    c. By telling how to receive full Roman citizenship.

    d. Through showing the merits of owning slaves.

4 Listen again to part of the lecture. Then answer the question.
What's the function of this passage?

    a. To introduce Constitutio Antoniniana's new laws.

    b. To show the disparities between slave and citizen life.

    c. To describe the limitations of holding public office.

    d. To explain about citizens who were quickly given citizenship.

Specific Information

5   According to the writer, what two rights did woman not have in Rome?
Choose 2 answers.

   a. They couldn't vote.

   b. They couldn't bear children for senators.

   c. They couldn't be citizens.

   d. They couldn't plant vegetables.

Inference Question

6   What does the writer imply about Roman citizenship?

   a. That women should not have been a separate class from men.

   b. That citizenship largely determined a person's life.

   c. That Roman territories were for slaves.

   d. That holding public office was very serious.

Roman Citizenship

Citizenship in Ancient Roman was a privileged status enjoyed by only a few. People living within the Roman Empire could be divided into three classes: slave, inhabitants of the Empire, and citizens. Slaves were considered property and had only very limited rights. Surprisingly, a slave who was freed by his owner automatically received full Roman citizenship. People who lived within the Roman territories could be given a limited form of Roman citizenship, a sort of second class citizen. Full Roman citizens were the privileged class in the Empire. Women were a class apart from men. They could never be granted full citizenship and as such could not vote or hold public office. There were various ways of obtaining Roman citizenship. All male children of Roman citizens were automatically given citizenship, freed slaves and their male children were given full citizenship, and some individuals were granted full citizenship for outstanding service to the Empire. Rome gradually began granting citizenship to whole provinces; and in the 3rd century, Constitutio Antoniniana granted citizenship to all male inhabitants of the Empire.

1 The word **status** in the passage is closest in meaning to

    a. statue   b. holding   c. standing   d. status quo

2 The word **class** in the passage is closest in meaning to

    a. assembly   b. lecture   c. caste   d. rating

3 The word **property** in the passage is closest in meaning to

    a. attribute   b. feature   c. possession   d. deliberation

4 The word **second class** in the passage is closest in meaning to

    a. higher   b. inferior   c. standard   d. superior

5 The word **privileged** in the passage is closest in meaning to

    a. marginalized   b. working-poor c. favored   d. overestimated

6 The word **citizenship** in the passage is closest in meaning to

    a. custody   b. care provider c. detention   d. civil rights

7 The word **automatically** in the passage is closest in meaning to

    a. in a rut   b. mechanically c. habitually   d. nominally

8 The word **outstanding** in the passage is closest in meaning to

    a. squalid   b. superior   c. average   d. eclipsed

Paraphrasing

Which best expresses the information in the underlined sentences?

1   Women were a class apart from men.

    a. Women were granted more rights than most men.
    b. Women were above and beyond men in Rome.
    c. Women were treated as a separate class from men.
    d. Some women were seen as superior to men.

2   They could never be granted full citizenship and as such could not vote or hold public office.

    a. They couldn't vote because they were not legal nationals.
    b. They could not vote in municipal elections.
    c. Being granted full legal rights was forbidden.
    d. Being denied full citizenship adversely affected their voting rights.

Water (1)

Definitions and Examples

hydroelectric [hàidrouiléktrik]	영 generating electricity by conversion of the energy of running water 동 energy-producing Much of Canada's power comes from **hydroelectric** dams. 캐나다가 소비하는 전력 중 대부분은 수력 발전 댐에서 생산된다.	**a.** 수력 발전의
produce [prədjúːs]	영 to bring into existence; give rise to 동 cause, generate The report emphasizes the link between vehicle-**produced** air pollution and negative health effects. 그 보고서는 차량에서 야기된 대기 오염과 건강에 미치는 악영향 사이의 연관성을 강조한다.	**v.** 만들어내다 야기하다
light [làit]	영 to make (an area or object) bright with or as if with light 동 illuminate At night, he would use a flashlight to **light** up bricks on the Great Wall of China. 밤이 되면 그는 손전등을 이용해 만리장성의 벽을 밝게 비추곤 했다.	**v.** 밝게 비추다
run [rʌ́n]	영 to cause to function 동 operate The factory **ran** the machines 24 hours a day. 그 공장은 24시간 기계를 가동했다.	**v.** 가동하다
nuclear [njúːkliər]	영 using or derived from the energy of atomic nuclei 동 atomic **Nuclear** power has a much better reputation than it did in the 1970s. 원자력 발전에 대한 평판이 1970년대에 비해 좋아졌다.	**a.** 핵의

Earth Science Ⅱ

huge	영 of exceedingly great size, extent, or quantity	a. 거대한
[hjú:dʒ]	동 colossal, enormous	
	Once done with the churches, we went to see the **huge** windmill that is visible from the train.	
	우선 교회를 구경한 후, 우리는 기차에서도 보이는 거대한 풍차를 보러 갔다.	

marvel	영 something that causes wonder, admiration, or astonishment	n. 경이
[má:rvəl]	동 wonder	
	Dolly the sheep was hailed as a **marvel** of science but she also sparked off ethical rows.	
	복제양 돌리는 과학의 경이로 환영 받았지만 동시에 윤리적 논란을 불러일으켰다.	

impressive	영 making a great impression on a person's mind, feelings etc	a. 인상적인
[imprésiv]	동 striking, remarkable	
	Her husband showed her their **impressive** new home.	
	남편은 부인에게 인상적인 새 보금자리를 보여주었다.	

bed	영 the bottom of a lake, river, sea, or other body of water	n. 바닥
[bed]	동 bottom	
	No one ever saw an emerald, because the emeralds were hidden in the **bed** of the sea.	
	에메랄드는 바다 밑바닥에 숨겨져 있어서 이제껏 아무도 그것을 본 적이 없었다.	

attraction	영 a person, place, thing, or event that is intended to attract	n. (관광) 명소 인기거리
[ətrǽkʃən]	동 appeal, lure	
	The main **attraction** was a long torchlit carnival procession held at dusk on Wednesday.	
	최고의 인기는 수요일, 해가 질 무렵에 시작하는 횃불 카니발의 긴 행렬이었다.	

Sentence Completion

A. Choose the one word that best fits the sentence.

1 The fires that _____ the hall fill the air with a slight tinge of smoke that tickles my throat.

    a. fade   b. dust

    c. light   d. shadow

2 The company found it difficult to procure even the raw materials to _____ the plants due to paucity of funds.

    a. water   b. disrupt

    c. eradicate   d. run

3 If your home has _____ power, then it is powered by water-powered electricity.

    a. watery   b. hydroelectric

    c. ductile   d. battery

4 If you _____ energy, you generate it.

    a. produce   b. foil

    c. terminate   d. resurrect

5 When a(an) _____ reaction reaches a certain intensity, it can "run away" or "go critical", which could be deadly.

    a. nuclear   b. initial

    c. herbal   d. hydrogenous

B. Choose the one word that best fits the sentence.

1 Some believe that a small volcanic eruption may have occurred on the
_____ of the lake.

   a. bunk   b. coral

   c. moor   d. bed

2 The woman was happily wearing a _____ diamond ring on her left
ring finger.

   a. fusing   b. composed
   c. huge   d. flabby

3 The building is being touted as a _____ of modern architecture.

   a. sense   b. gravel
   c. marvel   d. degradation

4 Recently, there have been a lot of new tourist _____ near China's
hydroelectric dams.

   a. attractions   b. tricks
   c. temperaments   d. appellants

5 It was so _____ that her father ran the marathon in record time for
his age group.

   a. dreadful   b. impressive
   c. unremarkable   d. tantalizing

1 Why is the Hoover Dam impressive?

    a. It is taller than any other hydroelectric dam in the Western Hemisphere.

    b. It provides 11 billion kiloliters of water a day.

    c. Many tourists flock to see the dam's height.

    d. It provides lots of power for Colorado.

2 Why does the writer explain hydroelectric power plants?

    a. They are marvels of architectural engineering.

    b. A trillion kilowatt-hours of electricity is produced at Niagara Falls.

    c. They are an important power source for the U.S.

    d. They are amazing engineering feats, dating back to 1895.

3 How does the writer introduce hydroelectric power plants?

    a. By trying to draw thousands of visitors to Hoover Dam.

    b. By outlining the history of hydroelectric plants, starting with Niagara Falls.

    c. By contrasting American and Canadian hydroelectric systems.

    d. Through analyzing tourist patterns at Colorado dams.

the Function of Statement

4 Listen again to part of the lecture. Then answer the question.
   What's the function of this passage?

   a. To contrast Arizona and Nevada hydro projects.

   b. To give an example of one of the marvels of modern engineering.

   c. To describe the necessity and importance of hydroelectric dams.

   d. To introduce Herbert Hoover, an American president.

Specific Information

5 According to the writer, what two types of power plants contribute to U.S.
   electricity needs? Choose 2 answers.

   a. Windmill plants.

   b. Steam generator plants.

   c. Corn ethanol plants.

   d. Nuclear power plants.

Inference Question

6 What does the writer imply about hydroelectric power plants?

   a. Steam plants, although underused, are an important key to our
      future energy needs.

   b. The tallest hydroelectric dam is in the Western Hemisphere .

   c. Hydroelectric power plants can produce an immense amount of
      power.

   d. With the right engineering advances, the U.S. can boost its
      production to 21 billion kiloliters of water a day.

Water (1)

The first large hydroelectric power plant in the United States was built in 1895 at Niagara Falls. By 1968 there were more than 1,500 hydroelectric plants operating in the United States. More than one trillion kilowatt-hours of electricity was being produced to light homes and run factories by 1975. Of this power, steam plants, including nuclear power plants, provided 84.3 percent, and hydroelectric plants produced about 15 percent. Taken together, steam plants and hydroelectric plants used 11 billion kiloliters of water a day. Huge hydroelectric dams are one of the marvels of modern engineering. The Hoover Dam is an especially impressive example, standing 221 meters above the bed of the Colorado River between Nevada and Arizona. The Hoover Dam is the tallest hydroelectric dam in the Western Hemisphere and has become a major tourist attraction, drawing thousands of visitors annually.

1 The word **produce** in the passage is closest in meaning to

   a. consume   b. generate   c. plant   d. subdue

2 The word **light** in the passage is closest in meaning to

   a. stir up   b. illuminate   c. darken   d. clarify

3 The word **run** in the passage is closest in meaning to

   a. operate   b. discontinue   c. invigorate   d. force

4 The word **nuclear** in the passage is closest in meaning to

   a. biological   b. small   c. powerful   d. atomic

5 The word **huge** in the passage is closest in meaning to

    a. hectic   b. enormous   c. diminutive   d. annual

6 The word **marvel** in the passage is closest in meaning to

    a. wonder   b. point   c. scream   d. limitation

7 The word **impressive** in the passage is closest in meaning to

    a. dominant   b. insignificant   c. remarkable   d. trendy

8 The word **bed** in the passage is closest in meaning to

    a. shore   b. sideline   c. berth   d. bottom

Paraphrasing

Which best expresses the information in the underlined sentences?

1   Huge hydroelectric dams are one of the marvels of modern engineering.

    a. The point will come when we run out of potable water.
    b. Hydroelectric dams are amazing engineering feats.
    c. More energy alternatives needed to be explored and funded.
    d. Too many dams have ruined the ecological environments of rivers.

2   The Hoover Dam is the tallest hydroelectric dam in the Western Hemisphere and has become a major tourist attraction, drawing thousands of visitors annually.

    a. If there is not adequate control over the amount of tourists, then the dam will be overwhelmed.
    b. Cracks are appearing in the Hoover Dam on the western edge.
    c. The Hoover Dam was named after a failed Republican president.
    d. The tallest dam in the Western Hemisphere has an abundance of visitors.

Water (2)

Definitions and Examples

deviation
[dìːvíéiʃən]

영 the act of deviating or turning aside

동 departure, anomaly

The society feels tattoos are a **deviation** from the norm.

그 사회에서 문신은 평범함에서 벗어난, 이례적인 것으로 생각된다.

n. 이례, 이탈

---

pattern
[pǽtərn]

영 a natural or chance marking, arrangement, or design

동 form, mode

Many of the **patterns** in the rug seem similar to ancient Persian rugs.

그 융단의 수많은 패턴은 고대 페르시아 시대 융단과 흡사한 것 같다.

n. 양식, 패턴

---

portion
[pɔ́ːrʃən]

영 a part of any whole, either separated from or integrated with it

동 part, share

She told her boyfriend that his **portion** of pizza was too big.

남자친구의 피자 조각(부분)이 너무 크다고 그녀가 말했다.

n. 부분

---

climatologist
[klàimətálədʒist]

영 someone who is an expert in climatology(기후학)

동 meteorologist

Some **climatologists** predict that the Arctic icecap will melt by 2040.

일부 기후학자들은 2040년경 북극의 만년설이 녹아 사라질 것이라고 예측한다.

n. 기후학자

---

mild
[màild]

영 not cold, severe, or extreme, as air or weather

동 temperate, genial

The summer months in Vancouver are usually quite **mild**.

보통 밴쿠버의 여름은 보통 꽤 따뜻하다.

a. 따뜻한, 순한

Earth Science II

long-term [láŋgtə̀ːrm]	영 covering a relatively long period of time According to her horoscope, her **long-term** prospects looked promising. 별점대로 라면 그녀의 장기적인 전망은 좋았다.	a. 장기적인
trend [trénd]	영 the general course or prevailing tendency 동 tendency, drift It is a recent **trend** in many companies these days to increase the basic pay to some extent. 요즘 많은 기업에서 기본급을 일정 수준 인상하는 추세다.	n. 경향, 추세
fossil fuel [fásl fjúːəl]	영 any combustible organic material, as oil, coal, or natural gas, derived from the remains of former life Saudi Arabia is running out of **fossil fuels** 사우디 아라비아에서는 화석 연료가 부족하다.	n. 화석 연료
trap [trǽp]	영 to prevent from escaping or getting free 동 catch Greenhouse gases are **trapped** in a lower part of the atmosphere, where they can alter the Earth's climate. 온실가스가 대기권 하층부에 갇히고, 그 지점에서 온실가스로 인한 지구 기후 변화가 일어날 수 있다.	v. 잡아두다
upset [ʌpsét]	영 to disturb or derange completely; put out of order; throw into disorder 동 disturb Innovations should not **upset** the system and should lead to sustained changes. 기술 혁신으로 체계가 혼란해 져서는 안되고 지속적인 변화가 이루어져야 한다.	v. 혼란하게 하다

Sentence Completion

A. Choose the one word that best fits the sentence.

1 If you eat a large _____ of a pizza, then you take a significant part of the pizza.

    a. potion
               b. friction

    c. portion
               d. constriction

2 If you want a _____ hot sauce on your food, then you want a sauce that is not too hot.

    a. piercing
               b. spicy

    c. stupefying
            d. mild

3 If you make _____ from your path, then you depart from your original direction.

    a. deviations
           b. progressions

    c. differences
          d. declarations

4 There are common _____ of behavior exhibited by many species.

    a. guidebooks
          b. patterns

    c. cliches
            d. quartets

5 When _____ give a weather report, they are acting like a meteorologist.

    a. engineers
          b. clients

    c. climatologists
       d. sculptors

B. Choose the one word that best fits the sentence.

1 Two-piece long underwear called long johns has superior ability to
_____ heat and keep you warm.

   a. trap   b. collapse

   c. shut out   d. mangle

2 Many wise farmers often devise _____ goals to get through periods
of drought.

   a. inebriated   b. implausible

   c. long-term   d. rickety

3 One recent _____ in Korean society is for more women to openly
smoke cigarettes in public.

   a. editorial   b. affinity

   c. trend   d. habituation

4 Such a ridiculous rule should be eliminated because it threatens and
_____ the society's values and sense of order.

   a. upsets   b. fortifies

   c. cherishes   d. enhances

5 There's no point denying that one day, the world will run out of most of its
_____ resources.

   a. wind   b. regent

   c. stimulation   d. fossil fuel

1 Why did droughts occur in the U.S.?

    a. More than mild temperatures in north central states.

    b. A mixture of fossil fuel emissions from automobiles and humidity.

    c. More than mild temperatures in tropic regions.

    d. A possible rise in carbon dioxide concentrations.

2 Why does the writer explain climate change?

    a. To state that the world is getting warmer or cooler, depending on the region.

    b. To show how fossil fuel use by mankind is changing our climate.

    c. To mention fossil fuel concentrations in the atmosphere.

    d. To offer scientists a chance to research alternative wind power devices.

3 How does the writer introduce climate change?

    a. By explaining that droughts are not the norm in climate behavior.

    b. By estimating the effect of droughts on water supplies.

    c. By predicting the damage of droughts on the California water basin.

    d. By showing drought patterns in the North Central Africa region.

4 Listen again to part of the lecture. Then answer the question.
   What's the function of this passage?

   a. To explain that it is not possible to predict when or where droughts
      will occur.
   b. To give an example of the frequency of droughts.
   c. To describe the limitations of drought prevention technology.
   d. To show the power of small changes in our climate.

Specific Information

5 According to the writer, what two factors contributed to the phenomenon
   known as the "greenhouse effect?" Choose 2 answers.

   a. Concentrations in the atmosphere.
   b. Carbon dioxide trapping heat from the sun.
   c. Measuring concentrations in carbon dioxide.
   d. Burning fossil fuels.

Inference Question

6 What does the writer imply about climate change?

   a. Our world is getting warmer, not cooler, especially in the Sahel
      region.
   b. Water supplies are quickly diminishing.
   c. Scientists cannot predict when or where droughts will occur.
   d. Small changes by mankind in our climate can upset weather patterns.

Water (2)

Droughts have always been considered deviations from normal weather patterns, but, in fact, they occur somewhere in the world every year. In some places they come and go on an almost regular basis. For example, the Sahel region of North Central Africa suffered major droughts from 1910 to 1913 and then again from 1938 to 1942. In the United States, a severe drought struck the western portion of the country in the 1930's and then again in the 1950's. It is not possible to predict when or where droughts will occur. Many climatologists believe that the generally mild weather over much of the globe from 1890 to 1945 was a deviation from a long-term global cooling trend. The short break from this cooling trend may have been caused by a rise in carbon dioxide concentrations in the atmosphere due to the burning of fossil fuels. Carbon dioxide tends to trap heat from the sun, a phenomenon known as the "greenhouse effect." Regardless of whether the world is getting warmer or cooler, it is certain that even small changes in climate can upset weather patterns, which have a direct effect on water supplies and other aspects of the environment.

1   The word **deviation** in the passage is closest in meaning to

    a. derivation   b. device   c. departure   d. density

2   The word **pattern** in the passage is closest in meaning to

    a. collection   b. form   c. effect   d. understanding

3   The word **portion** in the passage is closest in meaning to

    a. half   b. potion   c. assignment   d. part

4 The word **climatologist** in the passage is closest in meaning to

    a. meteorologist   b. Doppler   c. dermatologist   d. ob-gyn

5 The word **mild** in the passage is closest in meaning to

    a. fussy   b. extreme   c. temperate   d. brittle

6 The word **trend** in the passage is closest in meaning to

    a. tantrum   b. tendency   c. tenancy   d. trauma

7 The word **trap** in the passage is closest in meaning to

    a. gasp   b. catch   c. repeal   d. escape

8 The word **upset** in the passage is closest in meaning to

    a. disturb   b. straighten   c. refute   d. infuriate

Paraphrasing

Which best expresses the information in the underlined sentences?

1   Many climatologists believe that the generally mild weather over much of the globe from 1890 to 1945 was a deviation from a long-term global cooling trend.

    a. The mild weather we are having is here to stay.
    b. Mild weather is a recent phenomenon that will go away.
    c. Too much mild weather will cause more droughts.
    d. Climatologists believe that mild weather is contrary to a cooling trend.

2   Carbon dioxide tends to trap heat from the sun, a phenomenon known as the "greenhouse effect."

    a. Carbon dioxide traps heat, causing a cooling effect.
    b. Clean air is key to driving back carbon dioxide emissions.
    c. Greenhouse gases are dangerous to small rodents who depend on cool air.
    d. Carbon dioxide traps heat, causing a warming effect.

Water (3)

Definitions and Examples

waste [wéist]	영 any materials unused and rejected as worthless or unwanted 동 refuse, trash Most families in modern countries throw out too much **waste**. 현대 국가에서 대부분의 가정은 너무 많은 쓰레기를 배출한다.	n. 쓰레기
pollutant [pəlúːtənt]	영 something that pollutes, especially a waste material that contaminates air, soil, or water 동 contaminant The **pollutant**s in Hong Kong's atmosphere are much worse than in Seoul. 대기권에 있는 오염 물질은 홍콩이 서울보다 훨씬 더 심각하다.	n. 오염 물질
waterway [wɔ́ːtərwèi]	영 a canal, river, or narrow channel of sea which ships or boats can sail along 동 watercourse **Waterways** in downtown Los Angeles often run dry. 로스앤젤레스 중심가에 있는 수로가 말라버렸다.	n. 수로
raw [rɔ́ː]	영 being in a natural condition; not processed or refined 동 unprocessed, crude **Raw** water should not be considered safe for drinking or washing without further treatment. 정화되지 않은 물은, 향후 처리 과정 없이 식수와 세탁용으로 안전하지 못하다.	a. 정화되지 않은 원료 그대로의
invisible [invízəbəl]	영 not visible 동 unseen, imperceptible Although the air appears to be clean, there are many **invisible** pollutants. 공기는 깨끗해 보이지만 그 안에는 보이지 않는 오염 물질이 많다.	a. 보이지 않는

Earth Science II

organic [ɔːrgǽnik]	영 **of, relating to, or derived from living organisms** Some household cleaning products contain **organic** solvents such as petroleum distillates. 일부 가정용 청소 용품에는 석유 증류액과 같은 유기체 용해 성분이 포함되어 있다.	a. 유기체의
harmless [háːrmlis]	영 **without the power or desire to do harm** 동 **innocuous, safe** Much of the food we eat is relatively **harmless**, but it's good to be careful. 우리가 먹는 음식 가운데 대부분은 비교적 무해하지만 조심해서 나쁠 것은 없다.	a. 무해한
fertilizers [fɚ́ːrtəlàizər]	영 **any substance used to fertilize the soil, especially a commercial or chemical manure** 동 **chemical, manure** **Fertilizers** are a key component to large agriculture businesses. 비료는 대규모 경작 사업에 중요한 요소다.	n. 비료
tend [tend]	영 **to have a tendency or disposition to do or be something** 동 **be inclined, be apt** Believe it or not, short-haired cats **tend** to shed more than longhaired cats. 믿거나 말거나, 털이 짧은 고양이는 털이 긴 고양이보다 털이 더 많이 빠지는 경향이 있다.	v. (~한) 경향이 있다.
nerve tissue [nɚ́ːrv tíʃuː]	영 **tissue composed of neurons** 동 **nervous tissue** Her **nerve tissue** was damaged after the motorcycle accident. 그녀는 오토바이 사고 이후 신경 조직에 손상을 입었다.	n. 신경 조직

A. Choose the one word that best fits the sentence.

1 If the boat travels on _____, then it is going along a river or stream.

    a. dugouts   b. watering spots

    c. waterways   d. freeways

2 If you can become _____, then no one will be able to see you.

    a. unclear   b. invisible

    c. detectable   d. traceable

3 If you recycle your _____, then you reuse it again and again.

    a. desecration   b. DVD

    c. obligation   d. waste

4 When there are _____ in your drinking water, then there is something potentially harmful.

    a. ferments   b. tonics

    c. pollutants   d. papayas

5 Recently, the prices of _____ materials in the international market soared up mainly due to expanding universal demand.

    a. ubiquitous   b. raw

    c. nocuous   d. overdone

B. Choose the one word that best fits the sentence.

1 It is a problem that frustration in society _____ to be vented on someone weak.

    a. fizzles   b. tends

    c. subsidies   d. aspires

2 The bacteria that is already present in water uses _____ matter to multiply and at the same time it removes oxygen from the water.

    a. organic   b. detrimental

    c. fluctuating   d. inanimate

3 The kitten is _____ and will not scratch you, so be gentle with it.

    a. unruly   b. harmless

    c. detrimental   d. articulate

4 If the doctor damages your _____ in your spine, then you could be paralyzed.

    a. textile   b. nerve tissue

    c. pores   d. bandana

5 The agribusiness uses a lot of _____ to spray its large farms and crops.

    a. implements   b. parasites

    c. fertilizers   d. slimes

1 What forms do pollutants come in?

    a. Pollutants can come from hybrid vehicles and diesel trucks.

    b. Pollutants can come from raw sewage and invisible toxic chemicals.

    c. Pollutants can come from outer space.

    d. Pollutants can come from toilets and laboratory clinics.

Speaker's Purpose

2 Why does the writer explain pollutants?

    a. To tell about pollutants that pass through the food chain to humans.

    b. To discuss punishment for industrial polluters.

    c. To predict how mankind can combat pollutants.

    d. To compare pollutants that break down with those that do not.

Understanding Organization

3 How does the writer introduce pollutants?

    a. By analyzing how some pollutants are inorganic and do not break down.

    b. By discussing how pollutants take a range of forms.

    c. By explaining how pollutants are harmless.

    d. By talking about liquid-waste pollutants in our water systems.

the Function of Statement

4 Listen again to part of the lecture. Then answer the question.
What's the function of this passage?

    a. To introduce nitrates, fluorides, and phosphates that are finding their way into water supplies.

    b. To give an example of pollutants that multiply in the water.

    c. To describe the limitations of killing fish.

    d. To contrast groundwater pollution and oceanic pollution.

Specific Information

5 According to the writer, what two pollutants are harmful? Choose 2 answers.

    a. Pollutants that consume oxygen and kill fish.

    b. Pollutants that are made of liquid enzymes.

    c. Pollutants that multiply rapidly.

    d. Pollutants that are resilient to chemicals.

Inference Question

6 What does the writer imply about pollutants?

    a. Pollutants multiply rapidly and consume all of the oxygen in the water.

    b. Public health is at risk from water-borne pollutants.

    c. It will take a miracle to clean up our waterways.

    d. A minor amount of pollutants passes through the food chain to humans.

Water (3)

Billions of liters of liquid-waste pollutants are dumped into the world's waterways every day. The pollutants take a range of forms, from raw sewage to invisible toxic chemicals. Many of them are organic, some break down into harmless elements, but others thrive so well that they multiply rapidly and consume all of the oxygen in the water, killing fish. Other pollutants are inorganic and do not break down. (The number of chemicals from new pesticides, fertilizers, and other new products found in water is increasing.) Nitrates, fluorides, and phosphates are also finding their way into water supplies from groundwater pollution. These pollutants pass through the food chain to humans, where they tend to build up in nerve tissue. The public health significance of these chemicals is not yet fully known.

1 The word **waste** in the passage is closest in meaning to

    a. produce   b. broth   c. refuse   d. extravagance

2 The word **pollutant** in the passage is closest in meaning to

    a. element   b. contaminant   c. purity   d. organ

3 The word **waterway** in the passage is closest in meaning to

    a. watercourse   b. chain   c. ditch   d. pathway

4 The word **raw** in the passage is closest in meaning to

    a. unscrupulous   b. unproven
    c. uncooked   d. unprocessed

5 The word **invisible** in the passage is closest in meaning to

    a. revealed   b. imperceptible c. secreted   d. opaque

6 The word **harmless** in the passage is closest in meaning to

    a. suspicious   b. rueful   c. innocuous   d. offensive

7 The word **fertilizer** in the passage is closest in meaning to

    a. manure   b. fertility   c. agent   d. heroin

8 The word **tend** in the passage is closest in meaning to

    a. be unlikely   b. attend   c. be inclined   d. tantalize

---

Paraphrasing

Which best expresses the information in the underlined sentences?

1 Many of them are organic, some breaking down into harmless elements, but others thriving so well that they multiply rapidly and consume all of the oxygen in the water, killing the fish.

    a. Some pollutants are organic, easily breaking down into harmless components.

    b. Pollutants can easily multiply into the millions.

    c. Some pollutants are inorganic, easily breaking down and killing the fish.

    d. Many pollutant molecules routinely take up all the oxygen in the water.

2 These pollutants pass through the food chain to humans, where they tend to build up in nerve tissue.

    a. The food chain is an essential component for survival.

    b. Passing pollutants from the water to humans is a natural process.

    c. Too many contaminants are unhealthy for nerve tissue.

    d. Humans need to be more careful about what they put in their diet.

Definitions and Examples

wide-ranging

[wáid rèindʒiŋ]

영 extending over a large area

동 broad, extensive

His personal library was **wide-ranging**, from biographies to sociology.

그의 개인 도서관에는 전기문에서부터 사회학에 이르기까지 광범위한 종류의 도서가 있었다.

a. 광범위한

---

statesman

[stéitsmən]

영 a person who is experienced in the art of government or versed in the administration of government affairs

동 politician

Winston Churchill was a great **statesman** during the 20th century. 윈스턴 처칠은 20세기 위대한 정치가였다.

n. 정치가

---

architect

[á:rkitèkt]

영 a person who engages in the profession of architecture

동 building designer

It would be my dream to live in a home designed by an **architect**.

건축가가 설계한 집에 사는 것이 내 꿈이었다.

n. 건축가

---

philosopher

[filásəfər]

영 a person who studies or writes about philosophy

동 thinker

Plato was one of the first profound Greeks and a great **philosopher**. 플라톤은 최초로 심오한 사상을 지닌 그리스인들 가운데 한 사람이자 위대한 철학자였다.

n. 철학자

---

jarring

[dʒá:riŋ]

영 startling or harsh

동 unpleasant, discordant

The driving instructor showed us a **jarring** picture of an accident that had occurred two years ago.

운전 강사는 2년 전에 일어난 사고를 담은, 매우 거슬리는 사진을 보여주었다.

a. 조화되지 않은 (귀에) 거슬리는

endow [indáu]	⑲ to furnish, as with some talent, faculty, or quality ⑧ bestow, furnish Nature has **endowed** the four-year-old boy with great ability. 조물주는 그 네 살짜리 소년에게 위대한 능력을 주었다.	**v.** 부여하다
skeptic [sképtik]	⑲ a person who has doubts about things that other people believe ⑧ unbeliever Many **skeptics** have predicted that the planet will run out of petroleum. 많은 회의론자들은 지구가 석유부족을 겪게 될 것이라고 예측했다.	**n.** 회의론자
frugality [fruːgǽləti]	⑲ prudence in avoiding waste ⑧ economy, prudence Some wealthy billionaires dispense with **frugality** and spend like the wind. 일부 억만장자들은 절약하지 않고 돈을 흥청망청 쓴다.	**n.** 절약
sum [sʌm]	⑲ an indefinite amount or quantity, especially of money ⑧ amount, quantity How can beginner businessmen start business by a small **sum** of money? 초보 사업자가 소량의 자본금으로 어떻게 사업을 시작할 수 있을까?	**n.** 총계, 금액
squander [skwándər]	⑲ to spend or use (money, time, etc.) extravagantly or wastefully ⑧ waste, lavish She inherited a fortune and was found **squandering** it in Las Vegas. 그녀는 많은 재산을 상속받았지만 라스베이거스에서 모두 탕진했다.	**v.** 탕진하다

A. Choose the one word that best fits the sentence.

1 When you want a(an) _____ to build your home, it means you want someone to design it.

    a. caterer   b. architect

    c. plumber   d. engineer

2 When something is _____, it is a really shocking and jolting experience.

    a. spanking   b. buzzing

    c. jarring   d. pushing

3 If you have a(an) _____ gun collection, then you have a large selection of weapons.

    a. common   b. wide-ranging

    c. unique   d. ancient

4 If you are called a(an) _____, then you are influential, diplomatic and powerful.

    a. arsonist   b. wanted man

    c. traitor   d. statesman

5 When someone is praised as a _____, they are commended for their profound thinking.

    a. subordinate   b. go-between

    c. philosopher   d. pupil

B. Choose the one word that best fits the sentence.

1   If you develop a habit of saving after spending, you will never be able to save a good _____ of money.

    a. sum   b. subtraction

    c. calculation   d. aid

2   Human beings are _____ with good natural resources like air, water land, biodiversity, forest, mountains and glaciers.

    a. deplored   b. endowed

    c. mastered   d. conquered

3   Thomas Jefferson didn't believe in God; he was a _____ regarding the existence of God.

    a. humorist   b. performer

    c. skeptic   d. priest

4   As man continues to _____ the Earth's resources, the climate could change in such a way that it is no longer benevolent to mankind.

    a. harbor   b. squander

    c. preserve   d. regenerate

5   His financial philosophy was based on _____, never spending more than $5 a day.

    a. annulment   b. conceit

    c. wealth   d. frugality

Specific Question

1 Why was the Louisiana Purchase considered a waste by some?

    a. The French wanted it back after selling it to the U.S.

    b. $15 million was a huge amount in the 1700's.

    c. Many thought that more land in the U.S. was not needed.

    d. Others did not want Jefferson to be successful.

Speaker's Purpose

2 Why does the writer explain Jefferson?

    a. To contrast Jefferson's poor money management.

    b. To show how Jefferson campaigned for basic human rights for Whites.

    c. To show the merits of the pursuit of happiness theory.

    d. To explain how Jefferson sought for better conditions for all.

Understanding Organization

3 How does the writer introduce Jefferson?

    a. As an enemy of God himself and a critic of organized religion.

    b. As a fabulous plantation and slave owner.

    c. Through describing how he squandered government resources.

    d. By outlining his role as Declaration of Independence author and president.

the Function of Statement

4 Listen again to part of the lecture. Then answer the question.
What's the function of this passage?

    a. To introduce the wise decisions that Jefferson made (in hindsight).

    b. To give an example that ordinary men can do great things.

    c. To describe the need for more land acquisitions.

    d. To contrast the hypocrisy in Jefferson's own marriage.

Specific Information

5   According to the writer, what two things did Jefferson achieve as president? Choose 2 answers.

   a. He freed the slaves with Lincoln.

   b. He campaigned for wise spending in government.

   c. He wrote the Declaration of Independence.

   d. He purchased Louisiana Territory.

Inference Question

6   What does the writer imply about Jefferson?

   a. All men are not created equal.

   b. He was a great man despite some contradictions.

   c. There could have been greater presidents.

   d. Jefferson's place in history is overrated.

Thomas Jefferson

Thomas Jefferson, the author of the Declaration of Independence and America's third President, was a man of wide-ranging interests and many talents. He was a statesman, a politician, an architect, a philosopher, and an inventor. But he also possessed some jarring contradictions. In the Declaration of Independence, for example, he wrote, "… all men are created equal," but he himself was a slave owner. He wrote that God had endowed men with the right to "life, liberty, and the pursuit of happiness," yet he was a skeptic, who questioned the existence of God. Jefferson campaigned for frugality in government but paid $15 million, a huge sum at the time, for the Louisiana Purchase. His critics accused him of squandering the money on a worthless expanse of wilderness. But it turned out to be a wise investment that more than doubled the area of the United States.

1 The word **wide-ranging** in the passage is closest in meaning to

    a. open   b. overseas   c. massive   d. extensive

2 The word **statesman** in the passage is closest in meaning to

    a. politician   b. heroine   c. geologist   d. renegade

3 The word **architect** in the passage is closest in meaning to

    a. draftsman   b. structural engineer
    c. building designer   d. electrician

4 The word **philosopher** in the passage is closest in meaning to

    a. panhandler   b. practitioner   c. tamer   d. thinker

5   The word **endow** in the passage is closest in meaning to

     a. bestow   b. demand   c. deprive   d. behold

6   The word **skeptic** in the passage is closest in meaning to

     a. optimist   b. unbeliever   c. sycophant   d. worshipper

7   The word **frugality** in the passage is closest in meaning to

     a. indulgence   b. pursuit   c. generosity   d. prudence

8   The word **squander** in the passage is closest in meaning to

     a. waste   b. summon   c. improve   d. resent

Paraphrasing

Which best expresses the information in the underlined sentences?

1   He wrote that God had endowed men with the right to "life, liberty, and the pursuit of happiness," yet he was a skeptic, who questioned the existence of God.

    a. Life, liberty and the pursuit of happiness is for the slaves.

    b. God gave people basic rights that couldn't be taken away.

    c. Too much freedom will lead to a revolt.

    d. It is normal to question the existence of God.

2   His critics accused him of squandering the money on a worthless expanse of wilderness.

    a. The critics were highly jealous people with a grudge to bear.

    b. Jefferson's critics couldn't see the wisdom of his decision.

    c. Too much money was being spent of trees and unknown forest land.

    d. The point of spending money is to use it all up.

Unit 35　The American Revolution (1)

Definitions and Examples

complexity

[kəmpléksəti]

- 영 the state or quality of being complex
- 동 intricacy, complication

  Much of the world is mired in **complexity**, far above our heads.

  이해할 수 없을 정도로 세상의 많은 부분이 복잡하게 뒤섞여 있다.

n. 복잡

---

tremendous

[triméndəs]

- 영 extraordinarily great in size, amount, or intensity
- 동 huge, enormous

  There are **tremendous** travel opportunities in Asia.

  아시아에는 여행할 곳이 어마어마하게 많다.

a. 어마어마한

---

impact

[ímpækt]

- 영 the effect or impression of one thing on another
- 동 influence, effect

  The **impact** of the financial crisis was felt throughout the economy.

  금융 위기로 인한 충격이 경제 전반에서 느껴졌다.

n. 충격, 영향

---

rebellion

[ribéljən]

- 영 open, armed, and organized resistance to a constituted government
- 동 revolt, uprising

  The likelihood of **rebellion** in the Middle East could become more common.

  중동에서 저항 운동이 일어날 가능성이 더욱 높아질 수도 있다.

n. 저항 운동

---

full-scale

[fúl-skéil]

- 영 using all possible means, facilities, etc.
- 동 all-out, complete

  Napoleon launched a **full-scale** naval assault on the British.

  나폴레옹은 영국에 대해 해상에서의 전면적인 군사공격을 개시했다.

a. 전면적인

distinguished

[distíŋgwiʃt]

- 영 made conspicuous by excellence
- 동 conspicuous, outstanding, marked

French food can be **distinguished** by its delicious sauces and lack of spices.

프랑스 음식은 맛 좋은 소스와 소량의 향신료로 그 맛이 두드러진다.

a. 두드러진
특징적인

nationalism

[nǽʃənəlìzəm]

- 영 an devotion and loyalty to one's own nation
- 동 patriotism

Nationalism is very prevalent in Korea and Japan, often leading to prejudice.

한국과 일본, 양국에서 민족주의가 만연하여, 종종 적대감을 불러일으킨다.

n. 애국심, 민족주의

prominent

[prámənənt]

- 영 leading, important, or well-known
- 동 important, eminent

There are several **prominent** politicians running this year for the presidency.

올해 대통령 선거에 출마한 중요 정치인들이 몇몇 있다.

a. 중요한, 유명한

colonist

[kálənist]

- 영 an inhabitant of a colony

Initially, it was a hard time for the **colonists** to survive.

초창기는 식민지 주민들이 생존하기 힘든 시기였다.

n. 식민지 주민

reject

[ridʒékt]

- 영 to refuse to have, take, recognize, etc.
- 동 rebuff, refuse

Due to their dress code, they were **rejected** from entering the hip hop nightclub.

복장 규정 때문에 힙합 나이트 클럽에서 그들의 입장을 거절했다.

v. 거절하다

285

A. Choose the one word that best fits the sentence.

1 When something has large _____, then it has great influence.

    a. pretense   b. vileness

    c. contact   d. impact

2 When the military launches a(an) _____ attack, they use all their forces to face the enemy.

    a. full-scale   b. partial

    c. parochial   d. incomplete

3 If a situation is full of _____, then it is very difficult to resolve.

    a. density   b. complexity

    c. commitment   d. tolerance

4 If you have _____ strength, then you would be very good at weight lifting.

    a. conditional   b. puny

    c. tremendous   d. tiny

5 If there is a(an) _____, there usually is much bloodshed and a change in government.

    a. lawfulness   b. rebellion

    c. anniversary   d. banquet

B. Choose the one word that best fits the sentence.

1 In colonial times, many of the first American _____ believed the British king was too arrogant.

    a. CEOs   b. traitors

    c. colonists   d. buffs

2 The renowned dean of the law school was _____ by a grand ceremony when he left.

    a. outshone   b. distinguished

    c. betrayed   d. repealed

3 One of the benefits of _____ is that the entire country feels united toward a cause.

    a. altruism   b. egoism

    c. nationalism   d. provincialism

4 Absurdly, the supervisor of the department wanted to _____ 98% of the job applications.

    a. estimate   b. amount to

    c. reject   d. mobilize

5 When the _____ judge handed down his ruling, the public obeyed it fully.

    a. disregarded   b. prominent

    c. ridiculous   d. incapable

1 What action did the colonists want the King to execute?

    a. To end the annexation of Upper Canada.

    b. To end military behavior against the colonies.

    c. To rule for another term.

    d. To stop invading European neighbors like France.

2 Why does the writer explain the American Revolution?

    a. To detail the growth of nationalism in the U.S.

    b. To estimate the admiration for the English.

    c. To illustrate how Americans fought for their legal rights.

    d. To show patterns in rebellions around the world.

3 How does the writer introduce the American Revolution?

    a. Through explaining the profound effect of the revolution.

    b. By showing the merits of political independence.

    c. By talking about the First Continental Congress.

    d. Through showing the suffering made by the King.

4 Listen again to part of the lecture. Then answer the question.
What's the function of this passage?

    a. To introduce how Englishmen admired King George.

    b. To give an example of defending colonists' rights.

    c. To describe the American Revolution and the lack of concern for the law.

    d. To illustrate how revolutions can overhaul an entire nation.

Specific Information

5 According to the writer, what two aspects did the colonists fight for?
   Choose 2 answers.

     a. Legal rights as Englishmen.
     b. Separate taxation for the colonies.
     c. Less nationalistic feelings.
     d. Gradual political independence.

Inference Question

6 What does the writer imply about the American Revolution?

     a. Complex changes came about after the revolution.
     b. A concerted effort for independence.
     c. A deep reverence for the law is needed.
     d. Rights should not be guaranteed for Englishmen.

The American Revolution (1)

The American Revolution was an event of enormous complexity and tremendous impact. It began as a series of rebellions in defense of the rights of the colonies and only gradually became a full-scale war for political independence. Unlike most revolutions that were to follow, the American Revolution was distinguished by a deep concern for the law. The colonists fought for the rights they believed were guaranteed them as Englishmen. Most colonists at the time considered King George III to be above criticism, and despite the growth of nationalism, very few prominent colonists blamed their sufferings on the King himself. Even after many bloody battles had been fought, the First Continental Congress rejected calls for independence from England and continued to ask the King to end military actions against the colonies until a compromise could be worked out.

1 The word **complexity** in the passage is closest in meaning to

    a. selflessness   b. intricacy   c. obscurity   d. action

2 The word **tremendous** in the passage is closest in meaning to

    a. huge   b. feeble   c. insignificant   d. detained

3 The word **impact** in the passage is closest in meaning to

    a. rear-ender   b. fender   c. smack   d. effect

4 The word **rebellion** in the passage is closest in meaning to

    a. naughtiness   b. revolt   c. obedience   d. menace

5 The word **full-scale** in the passage is closest in meaning to

    a. unfortunate   b. far-flung   c. all-out   d. sparse

6 The word **distinguished** in the passage is closest in meaning to

    a. surpassed   b. conspicuous   c. criticized   d. documented

7 The word **nationalism** in the passage is closest in meaning to

    a. patriotism   b. treachery   c. controlling freak   d. jingoism

8 The word **prominent** in the passage is closest in meaning to

    a. conventional   b. enterprising   c. important   d. peripheral

Paraphrasing

Which best expresses the information in the underlined sentences?

1 Unlike most revolutions that were to follow, the American Revolution was distinguished by a deep concern for the law.

    a. All too often, revolutions (France, Russia) lead to vast corruption.

    b. A democratic constitution is more important than specific laws.

    c. Too much concern for the law is never a bad thing.

    d. The American Revolution was known for its emphasis on the law.

2 Most colonists at the time considered King George III to be above criticism.

    a. King George III was not open-minded.

    b. Kings throughout Europe were arrogant and too powerful.

    c. King George III shouldn't be criticized.

    d. King George III listened to his subject some of the time.

The American Revolution (2)

Definitions and Examples

---

negotiate
[nigóuʃièit]

- 영 **to arrange or settle by discussion and mutual agreement**
- 동 **work out, arrange**

The company hired a capable lawyer to **negotiate** the settlement of the claim.

그 회사는 배상 청구 문제 협상에 나설 유능한 변호사를 고용했다.

v. 협상(교섭)하다

---

compromise
[kámprəmàiz]

- 영 **a settlement of differences in which each side makes concessions**
- 동 **agreement, concession**

The two sides have finally reached a **compromise** on major issues.

양측은 주요 사안에 대해 마침내 타협에 이르렀다.

n. 타협

---

eloquent
[éləkwənt]

- 영 **characterized by forceful and appropriate expression**
- 동 **expressive**

John F. Kennedy's speeches were often **eloquent** and moving.

케네디 대통령의 연설은 보통 표현력이 뛰어나고, 감동적이었다.

a. 감명적인
표현력이 뛰어난

---

persuasive
[pərswéisiv]

- 영 **able, fitted, or intended to persuade**
- 동 **convincing, effective**

Although the CEO was frequently **persuasive**, he was quite rude.

그 최고경영자는 설득력은 뛰어난 편이지만, 매우 무례한 사람이었다.

a. 설득력이 있는

---

propaganda
[prὰpəgǽndə]

- 영 **information, ideas, or rumors deliberately spread to help or harm a person, nation**
- 동 **information, publicity, hype**

During World War II, the Nazis disseminated **propaganda** via radio.

2차 세계 대전 중 나치는 라디오를 통해 선전 활동을 하였다.

n. 선전(물)

---

revolt

[rivóult]

영 to break away from or rise against constituted authority, as by open rebellion

동 rebel

The Buddhist monks in Burma are **revolting** against an oppressive and violent government.

버마의 불교 승려들은 강압적이고 난폭한 정부에 반대하는 혁명을 일으켰다.

v. 혁명을 일으키다

principle

[prínsəpl]

영 an accepted or professed rule of action or conduct

동 belief, rule

The **principle** of equality for women should be applied everywhere.

남녀 평등 원칙은 어느 곳이든 적용되어야 한다.

n. 원칙

consent

[kənsént]

영 agreement in sentiment, opinion, a course of action, etc.

동 permission, agreement

The mother did not give **consent** to her daughter to drive the car.

어머니는 딸의 자동차 운전을 허가하지 않았다.

n. 동의, 허가

govern

[gʌ́vərn]

영 to rule over by right of authority

동 rule, manage

Although we are **governed**, the power rests with us, the people.

우리는 통치를 받고 있지만 권력은 우리들, 즉 국민에게 있다.

v. 통치하다

treasure

[tréʒər]

영 to keep or regard as precious; value highly

동 value, cherish

People **treasure** the constitution more than anything else.

국민은 그 무엇보다도 헌법을 가장 귀중하게 여긴다.

v. 귀중하게 여기다

A. Choose the one word that best fits the sentence.

1 If you write a(an) _____ poem, then the words flow with precision and beauty.

    a. expansive   b. sarcastic

    c. eloquent   d. indecent

2 When someone hands out _____, it is likely to be inflammatory and provocative.

    a. facts and figures   b. truths

    c. propaganda   d. buzz words

3 This is not to say that _____ an agreement is the best course for every situation.

    a. negotiating   b. sabotaging

    c. mocking   d. averting

4 When someone makes a(an) _____ presentation, they are convincing to the audience.

    a. inquisitive   b. improbable

    c. misleading   d. persuasive

5 Many experts have painted the rosy picture that the two sides are likely to seek a _____ about the thorny issue.

    a. contention   b. compromise

    c. conflict   d. contempt

B. Choose the one word that best fits the sentence.

1 The government has responsibility to make sure that the _____ are not exposed to a health threat like mad cow disease.

   a. accused   b. governed
   c. administration   d. deceased

2 Whenever a government becomes oppressive, the people have a right to _____.

   a. obey   b. conform
   c. revolt   d. proliferate

3 One _____ in the U.S. constitution is that the people ultimately decide their own fate.

   a. principle   b. deceit
   c. release   d. fundamentalism

4 She _____ her 24 karat diamond necklace the most, compared to her other numerous possessions.

   a. supports   b. impeaches
   c. treasures   d. rages

5 The teenage daughters did not receive their mothers' _____ to go to the Beyonce concert.

   a. red light   b. consent
   c. dissent   d. agitation

1 What was the style of the Declaration of Independence?

    a. Awkward and wordy.

    b. Informative with some clever phrases.

    c. Eloquent and persuasive.

    d. Demeaning and offensive.

2 Why does the writer explain the Declaration of Independence?

    a. To show how the Founding Fathers came up with powerful political ideas.

    b. To illustrate the disenfranchisement of half a million people.

    c. To show how a new nation came up with an eloquent document.

    d. To show patterns in nicely written legislation.

3 How does the writer introduce the Declaration of Independence?

    a. Through advocating the abolition of slavery.

    b. By stating that Jefferson wanted to increase the number of slaves.

    c. By describing the negotiations with the colonists.

    d. By suggesting more amendments to it.

the Function of Statement

4 Listen again to part of the lecture. Then answer the question.
   What's the function of this passage?

   a. To suggest that slaves should be included in the writing of documents.

   b. To give an example of half a million people who were shut out of the system.

   c. To describe the limitations of writing constitutional documents.

   d. To inform about an influential document that guides American life.

Specific Information

5 According to the writer, what two ideas were contained within the Declaration of Independence? Choose 2 answers.

   a. Politicians must be eloquent.

   b. All men are created equal.

   c. People chose the government, not vice versa.

   d. Consent is needed for ratification of major documents.

Inference Question

6 What does the writer imply about the Declaration of Independence?

   a. Negotiating with England is very foolish.

   b. It estimates how many people will be free to vote.

   c. It is a principle that is more practical than ideal.

   d. It signifies the major ideas held by most Americans, even today.

The American Revolution (2)

By the summer of 1776, the colonists felt they could no longer expect England to negotiate a compromise. Thomas Jefferson was appointed to write a Declaration of Independence, and the document he produced was eloquent and persuasive. It combined powerful political ideas with clever propaganda and set a new standard for a free society. It supported the right to revolt, based on the principle that government depends on the consent of the governed. But that principle was more of an ideal than an accurate description of the colonists in 1776. Many of those who signed the Declaration did not really accept the statement that "all men are created equal." At the time about half a million people — one fifth of the population — were slaves. Yet of all America's historic documents, the Declaration of Independence remains the most treasured expression of the American dream.

1 The word **negotiate** in the passage is closest in meaning to

    a. arrange   b. repeal   c. transfer   d. botch

2 The word **compromise** in the passage is closest in meaning to

    a. composition   b. concession   c. admission   d. aversion

3 The word **eloquent** in the passage is closest in meaning to

    a. consummate   b. animated   c. expressive   d. corresponding

4 The word **persuasive** in the passage is closest in meaning to

    a. convincing   b. telltale   c. impervious   d. thoughtless

5 The word **propaganda** in the passage is closest in meaning to

   a. figures   b. epidemics   c. data   d. publicity

6 The word **revolt** in the passage is closest in meaning to

   a. rebel   b. resolve   c. rebuff   d. repulse

7 The word **principle** in the passage is closest in meaning to

   a. refund   b. belief   c. aberration   d. saturation

8 The word **consent** in the passage is closest in meaning to

   a. friction   b. proof   c. disapproval   d. agreement

Paraphrasing

Which best expresses the information in the underlined sentences?

1 It combined powerful political ideas with clever propaganda and set a new standard for a free society.

   a. The declaration had old ideas that revealed the basis for society.
   b. The U.S. is still struggling with its democracy.
   c. Too often political ideas get bogged down in debate.
   d. A combination of powerful ideas set the stage for a democracy.

2 Yet of all America's historic documents, the Declaration of Independence remains the most treasured expression of the American dream.

   a. The Declaration of Independence is a powerful document to treasure.
   b. Historic documents become irrelevant after several generations.
   c. The Declaration of Independence needs more refinement.
   d. The essential point to the declaration is that Jefferson wrote it.

Definitions and Examples

special

[spéʃəl]

- 영 of a distinct or particular kind or character
- 동 distinguished, exceptional

The gifted student was very **special**, particularly in physics.

재능이 타고난 그 학생은 매우 특별했으며, 특히 물리학에 뛰어났다.

a. 특별한

---

array

[əréi]

- 영 a large group, number, or quantity of people or things
- 동 wide range, collection

An **array** of tanks and armored vehicles were aligned on the border.

다수의 탱크와 장갑차가 국경에 정렬했다.

n. 다량, 다수

---

identify

[aidéntəfài]

- 영 to recognize as being a particular person or thing; verify the identity of
- 동 establish, find out

Identifying the cause of death is the C.S.I. investigator's job.

사인을 식별하는 것이 과학수사대 수사관의 임무이다.

v. 식별하다 발견하다

---

parallel

[pǽrəlèl]

- 영 extending in the same direction and never converging or diverging
- 동 aligned

Children are sitting in **parallel** rows, their eyes locked in a gaze at the teacher.

아이들은 나란히 앉아 선생님에게서 시선을 떼지 않았다.

a. 나란한

---

diffuse

[difjúːz]

- 영 to spread or scatter widely or thinly; disseminate
- 동 spread, emanate

I was taught how a scent **diffuses** through the air.

냄새가 어떻게 공기를 통해 퍼져나가는지 배웠다.

v. 발산하다

Astronomy & Physics Ⅲ

scatter [skǽtər]	영 to throw loosely about; distribute at irregular intervals 동 disperse The winds **scattered** the pollution from Chinese coal factories. 중국의 석탄 공장에서 발생한 공해가 바람을 타고 흩어졌다.	v. 흩어지다
transmit [trænsmít]	영 to convey or pass along, usually as information or news 동 send It is fairly easy to **transmit** radio waves. 라디오 전파를 전송하는 일은 상당히 쉽다.	v. 전송하다
translate [trænsléit]	영 to change the form, condition, nature, etc. of 동 change, convert She tries to **translate** efforts and actions into tangible results. 그녀는 자신의 노력과 행동이 가시적인 결과로 변할 수 있도록 노력한다.	v. 변하다
measure [méʒər]	영 to have measurement of 동 gauge, appraise The room **measures** 3.3m X 3.36m and can be used as a double bedroom. 그 방은 크기가 가로세로로 각각 3.3미터와 3.36미터이고, 2인용 침대를 갖춘 침실로 사용할 수 있다.	v. ~의 폭(길이)이다
frequency [frí:kwənsi]	영 the number of periods or regularly occurring events of any given kind in a unit of time 동 audio wave The **frequencies** from the NASA satellite carried out into space. 미국 항공 우주국 위성에서 송출된 주파수가 우주에 이르렀다.	n. 주파(수)

A. Choose the one word that best fits the sentence.

1 The two teams are standing in _____ lines, facing each other.

    a. curvy   b. wavy

    c. dispersed   d. parallel

2 If you _____ material, you disseminate it, sometimes in many directions.

    a. diffuse   b. deflect

    c. discover   d. deform

3 A(An) _____ event is usually one that is very unique.

    a. special   b. awkward

    c. clumsy   d. routine

4 If you send a(an) _____ of things, you send a large group of them.

    a. collector   b. array

    c. sundries   d. scum

5 _____ something is the first step in discovering what it is.

    a. Sousing   b. Identifying

    c. Poking   d. Polluting

B. Choose the one word that best fits the sentence.

1 If your waist _____ 28, your underwear size will be Size 6.

   a. calculates   b. adjusts

   c. regulates   d. measures

2 The ashes of her grandfather were _____ in the wind over the ocean.

   a. scattered   b. driven

   c. needed   d. converged

3 Much of the attraction of lasers is that they have very high and powerful _____.

   a. frequencies   b. executions

   c. regularities   d. weapons

4 They tried their best to _____ their words into action.

   a. distort   b. translate

   c. keep   d. cheat

5 When she aimed her flashlight into the night, it did not _____ a beam of light very far.

   a. reek   b. interfere

   c. transmit   d. hand on

1 How does a laser beam work?

    a. By diffusing light so that it is in tiny particles.

    b. By sending rays quickly through space.

    c. Through using parallel beams so they can travel long distances.

    d. Through using pulse beams that oscillate in wavy patterns.

Speaker's Purpose

2 Why does the writer explain laser beams?

    a. To demonstrate the amazing possibilities that could be realized if the technology works.

    b. To show how useful lasers can be used, particularly when transmitting data.

    c. To predict how lasers can cure cancerous lesions on patients.

    d. To demonstrate their rather limited possibilities.

Understanding Organization

3 How does the writer introduce laser beams?

    a. By showing how far university scientists have come with their research.

    b. Through comparing lasers and the basic technology of simple flashlights.

    c. By showing that mankind routinely comes up with new amazing technology.

    d. By talking about lasers as the one of the newest types of energy sources.

4 Listen again to part of the lecture. Then answer the question.
   What's the function of this passage?

   a. To explain how laser light can travel over great distances, unlike radio waves.
   b. To explain how laser light can travel up to 900 meters uninterrupted.
   c. To describe the limitations of radio and laser waves in low Earth orbit.
   d. To contrast the difficulties of laser research in the military.

Specific Information

5 According to the writer, what two ways can lasers be used in modern society? Choose 2 answers.

   a. By powering electric vehicles and mass transit.
   b. By transmitting pulses of power evenly.
   c. By using lasers in computer mice.
   d. Through using lasers as communications transmitters.

Inference Question

6 What does the writer imply about laser beams?

   a. Communication is probably the next big field for laser beams.
   b. Lasers are an array of new energy sources that should be used more widely.
   c. Flashlights are much lower tech, but as highly efficient as lasers.
   d. Electric power can be translated into laser light if only enough hydroelectricity were available.

Energy (2)

The laser beam, a special form of light, is the latest in an array of new energy sources, and scientists are identifying an amazing number of possibilities for it. The light waves of laser beams are exactly in phase with one another and so nearly parallel that they can travel for long distances in a straight line. In comparison, the beam of a flashlight diffuses after only a few meters because the light waves are of so many frequencies that they interfere with each other and become scattered. Lasers may come to be used to transmit pulses of power that would not decrease even over a great distance. To do this, electric power would be translated into laser light and then the process would be reversed at the receiving end. Lasers could also be used as communications transmitters. A laser's wavelength measures in the tenths of millionths of a centimeter, compared to radio waves, which span hundreds of meters. Thus, with lasers, a large volume of messages could be carried on a very narrow band of frequencies.

1 The word **special** in the passage is closest in meaning to
    a. queer   b. exceptional   c. horrendous   d. wonderful

2 The word **array** in the passage is closest in meaning to
    a. decimal   b. variation   c. wide range   d. gush

3 The word **identify** in the passage is closest in meaning to
    a. approach   b. compare   c. recognize   d. categorize

4 The word **parallel** in the passage is closest in meaning to
    a. aligned   b. whippy   c. uneven   d. vertical

5 The word **diffuse** in the passage is closest in meaning to

    a. combine   b. emanate   c. defuse   d. tally

6 The word **scatter** in the passage is closest in meaning to

    a. disperse   b. concede   c. reconcile   d. blow up

7 The word **transmit** in the passage is closest in meaning to

    a. go   b. repent   c. send   d. identify

8 The word **translate** in the passage is closest in meaning to

    a. change   b. apply   c. interpret   d. stagnate

Paraphrasing

Which best expresses the information in the underlined sentences?

1 To do this, electric power would be translated into laser light and then the process would be reversed at the receiving end.

    a. Building lasers means transforming electric power into a gaseous phase.
    b. Air cannot mix with the fine laser beam.
    c. The process of translating electric power into lasers must be reversed at the other end.
    d. It is not technically feasible to transfer electric power into lasers.

2 A laser's wavelength measures in the tenths of millionths of a centimeter, compared to radio waves, which span hundreds of meters.

    a. The width of a laser is at least a million times narrower than a centimeter.
    b. Radio waves are infinitely smaller than laser waves.
    c. Measuring the wavelength of various laser and radio waves is not too difficult.
    d. Radio waves are tenths of millionths of laser wavelengths.

Definitions and Examples

versatile	영 having or capable of many uses	a. 다용도의
[vɜ́:rsətl]	동 adaptable, all-around	
	This **versatile** appliance can be used to make tea, boil eggs and more.	
	이 다용도 기구로 차도 끓이고, 달걀도 삶고, 그 외 여러가지로 사용할 수 있다.	

chemical	영 relating to or used in chemistry	a. 화학의
[kémikəl]		
	The company uses **chemical** substances for research, developing new products.	
	그 회사는 제품 연구에 화학 물질을 사용하여 신제품을 개발한다.	

contain	영 to hold or include within its volume or area	v. 포함하다
[kəntéin]	동 include	
	The substance **contains** lots of protein.	
	그 물질에는 많은 양의 단백질이 포함되어 있다.	

release	영 to free from something that binds, fastens, or holds back	v. 방출하다 풀어놓다
[rilí:s]	동 let go, set free	
	Unknown fighters **released** toxic gases into the atmosphere.	
	정체를 알 수 없는 여러 대의 전투기가 대기에 유독성 기체를 방출했다.	

control	영 to exercise restraint or direction over; dominate; command	v. 제어하다
[kəntróul]	동 regulate	
	The pilot tried to **control** the airplane after losing power.	
	비행기 동력이 손실된 뒤 조종사는 비행기를 제어하려고 애썼다.	

toast	⑧ to brown, as bread or cheese, by exposure to heat	v. 굽다
[tóust]	⑧ bake	
	I ate way too many **toasted** pie crusts.	
	노릇노릇하게 구운 파이 크러스트를 지나치게 많이 먹었다.	

shade	⑧ the degree of darkness of a color, determined by the quantity of black or by the lack of illumination	n. 색조, 빛깔
[ʃéid]	⑧ color, hue	
	Her t-shirt is a light **shade** of blue.	
	그녀가 입은 티셔츠는 옅은 파란색 빛깔을 띤다.	

uncontrollable	⑧ incapable of being controlled or restrained	a. 통제할 수 없는
[ʌ̀nkəntróuləbəl]	⑧ wild, ungovernable	
	He had an **uncontrollable** urge to eat large pizzas with extra cheese.	
	치즈를 추가한 라지 사이즈 피자를 먹고 싶은, 통제할 수 없는 강한 충동을 느꼈다.	

combine	⑧ to bring into a state of unity	v. 결합하다
[kəmbáin]	⑧ merge, mix	
	Physics **combines** elements of both science and mathematics.	
	물리학에서는 과학과 수학, 두 학문의 요소를 결합한다.	

surrounding	⑧ environing things, circumstances, conditions, etc.	n. 주변
[səráundiŋ]	⑧ environment	
	After looking around for an hour, she couldn't identify her **surroundings**.	
	한 시간 동안 주위를 둘러보았지만, 그녀는 자신의 주변을 알아볼 수 없었다.	

A. Choose the one word that best fits the sentence.

1 It is the most _____ knife for paring, peeling and trimming ever made.

    a. nimble   b. versatile

    c. agile   d. capricious

2 Tattoo inks _____ unhealthy levels of toxic metals.

    a. contain   b. forge

    c. establish   d. intoxicate

3 If a material has many toxic elements to it, it probably is comprised of a

_____ .

    a. chemical   b. fiber

    c. mission   d. factor

4 If you get _____ from prison, you will no longer have to stay in your cell.

    a. reviewed   b. loosened

    c. released   d. assumed

5 If you are _____ by your boss, then you will likely have little freedom.

    a. manufactured   b. patronized

    c. controlled   d. contracted

Sentence Completion

B. Choose the one word that best fits the sentence.

1 If you change your _____ then you might be happier with your work environment.

   a. surroundings

   b. looks

   c. passage

   d. wardrobe

2 The sweater comes in two _____ of green.

   a. glares

   b. shades

   c. covers

   d. shadow lines

3 He usually has a sausage and egg _____ sandwich for breakfast along with cappuccino.

   a. diluted

   b. toasted

   c. sterilized

   d. preserved

4 When hydrogen _____ with chloride, it becomes highly volatile.

   a. separates

   b. identifies

   c. empathizes

   d. combines

5 His car was _____, a situation that led to him crashing into a tree.

   a. uncontrollable

   b. repaired

   c. malleable

   d. well-tuned

1 Why does paper turn yellow?

    a. Because paper molecules mix with oxygen through a gradual burning process.

    b. Because there are old coffee grains imbedded in the paper.

    c. Because the atmosphere around the paper is quite humid.

    d. Because paper combines with oxygen and becomes yellow through a slow burning process.

2 Why does the writer explain chemical reactions?

    a. To offer examples of coal and wood, meringue dessert cooking and paper oxidizing.

    b. To state that chemical reactions are versatile when mixed with other compounds.

    c. To show how chemistry teachers can excite students through interesting experiments.

    d. To explain the properties of coal and fire wood.

3 How does the writer introduce chemical reactions?

    a. By outlining how to make several forms of dynamite.

    b. Through suggesting that chemicals are the most vital and versatile form of energy.

    c. By mixing carbon, sulfur and other hydrocarbons.

    d. Through showing that geology and chemistry are linked.

4 Listen again to part of the lecture. Then answer the question.
   What's the function of this passage?

   a. To introduce how, under controlled circumstances, chemical energy
      can be highly useful.
   b. To state that chemical energy cannot be easily controlled.
   c. To describe the limitations cooking desserts like meringue.
   d. To contrast the techniques used in the kitchen to make meringue via
      chemical reaction.

5 According to the writer, what two factors contribute to the yellowing of
   paper? Choose 2 answers.

   a. Changes in temperature surrounding the paper.
   b. Paper combining with oxygen.
   c. Outside interference.
   d. The paper being a darker shade of brown.

6 What does the writer imply about chemical reactions?

   a. Chemical reactions are extremely volatile.
   b. Energy produced by chemical reactions is highly versatile and useful.
   c. Cooking food a light shade of brown is a form of experimentation.
   d. Chemical reactions are extremely applicable to home life.

Energy (3)

The most vital and versatile form of energy is offered by chemical reactions. The chemical energy contained in coal and wood can be released by a single match. At the other end of the spectrum is the diamond, whose energy can be released only when it is heated to its burning point, 650 degrees Celsius. Chemical energy can be easily controlled, and that is why cooks can toast meringue to the exact shade of brown they seek. On the other hand, it can also be uncontrollable, such as when it comes in the form of dynamite. At this very second, this page is releasing chemical energy. As it combines with the oxygen of the air, the page is becoming hotter than its surroundings, and as the years pass it will become yellow as a result of this slow burning.

1 The word **versatile** in the passage is closest in meaning to

    a. inflexible   b. volatile   c. all-around   d. accomplished

2 The word **contain** in the passage is closest in meaning to

    a. include   b. consume   c. exclude   d. eliminate

3 The word **release** in the passage is closest in meaning to

    a. seek   b. let go   c. apprehend   d. take back

4 The word **control** in the passage is closest in meaning to

    a. regulate   b. tame   c. unbridle   d. imprison

5 The word **toast** in the passage is closest in meaning to

    a. scorch   b. thaw   c. grill   d. bake

6 The word **shade** in the passage is closest in meaning to

    a. type   b. conundrum   c. color   d. mood

7 The word **uncontrollable** in the passage is closest in meaning to

    a. confirming   b. ungoverned   c. manageable   d. unyielding

8 The word **combine** in the passage is closest in meaning to

    a. unite   b. detach   c. mix   d. pile

Paraphrasing

Which best expresses the information in the underlined sentences?

1 Chemical energy can be easily controlled, and that is why cooks can toast meringue to the exact shade of brown they seek.

    a. Chemical energy is essential to cooking most desserts, especially toast.
    b. The brown shade of dessert food is highly dependent on chemicals.
    c. Chemical energy, properly controlled, is essential to making an excellent meringue.
    d. Controlling chemical reactions is part of the cooking process.

2 As it combines with the oxygen of the air, the page is becoming hotter than its surroundings, and as the years pass it will become yellow as a result of this slow burning.

    a. When this page becomes hotter, it will turn a bright yellow.
    b. The release of chemical energy, coupled with oxygen, results in the yellowing of matter.
    c. Too much heat can make this page turn yellowish brown.
    d. Paper changes when exposed to different surroundings, often yellowing over the years.

Definitions and Examples

medium [míːdiəm]	영 an intervening agency, means, or instrument by which something is conveyed or accomplished 동 means Words are a **medium** of expression. 단어는 표현을 나타내는 매개체이다.	n. 매개체, 수단
permeate [pə́ːrmièit]	영 to pass into or through every part of 동 penetrate The anthrax was **permeating** through the skin membrane. 탄저균은 피부막을 통해 몸 안으로 퍼지고(투과하고) 있었다.	v. 투과하다
communicate [kəmjúːnəkèit]	영 to transfer to another 동 transmit Children are more likely to **communicate** disease to others. 아이들은 다른 사람들에게 질병을 전파할 가능성이 높다.	v. 전하다, 옮기다
matter [mǽtər]	영 the substance of which any physical object consists or is composed 동 substance The desk was made up of solid **matter**. 그 책상은 고체 물질로 만들어졌다.	n. 물질
disprove [disprúːv]	영 to prove to be false or wrong 동 refute, invalidate It has been **disproved** that dinosaurs and man existed at the same time. 사람과 공룡이 동시대에 존재했다는 사실이 반증되었다.	v. 반증하다

incomprehensible

[ìnkamprihénsəbəl]

영 impossible to understand or comprehend
동 unintelligible

His long rambling speech was very **incomprehensible**.

그의 연설은 산만하여 아주 이해하기 어려웠다.

a. 이해할 수 없는

postulate

[pástʃəlèit]

영 to assume or assert the truth, reality, or necessity of, especially a basis of an argument
동 suppose, believe

Galileo **postulated** that the Earth was indeed round, not flat.

갈릴레오는 지구가 평평한 것이 아니라 사실은 둥글다고 가정했다.

v. 가정하다
주장하다

vanish

[vǽniʃ]

영 to cause to disappear
동 disappear, fade

He stirred quickly, and the light powder **vanished** almost instantly into the whirlpool he created. 빠르게 휘젓자, 그 가벼운 분말은 그가 만든 소용돌이 속으로 거의 일순간 사라져 버렸다.

v. 사라지다

publication

[pʌ̀bləkéiʃən]

영 the act of publishing or announcing publicly
동 announcement, reporting

The **publication** of the theory would have such an effect, if the theory were true.

그 이론이 사실이라면, 그 이론 발표가 엄청난 영향을 미칠 수도 있을 것이다.

n. 발표, 출판

common sense

[kámən séns]

영 sound judgment not based on specialized knowledge
동 practical wisdom

Instead of following every rule, it is acceptable to use **common sense** as you go about editing.

편집할 때에는 모든 규칙을 따르는 대신 상식을 따르는 것도 허용이 된다.

n. 상식

A. Choose the one word that best fits the sentence.

1   When one is _____ , they are sending information from one source
   to the next.

    a. withdrawing   b. communicating

    c. withstanding   d. commuting

2   If you have a theory that is _____ , then it is factually incorrect.

    a. disproved   b. shut out

    c. explained   d. cordoned

3   If gas is _____ , then it gets into everything, going through many
   solids and liquids.

    a. permeating   b. vibrating

    c. exiting   d. going out of

4   Painting is a _____ in which the mind can actualize itself.

    a. token   b. medium

    c. setting   d. foreboding

5   The world is comprised of _____ , (solids, liquids and gases).

    a. detritus   b. carcass

    c. possessions   d. matter

B. Choose the one word that best fits the sentence.

1 There's no point making another _____ ; no one will read it.

    a. publication   b. knock-off

    c. doubt   d. subversion

2 Being _____ , he was never fully understood by his coworkers.

    a. fluent   b. incomprehensible

    c. vanished   d. articulate

3 It has been _____ that an aether medium allows light to travel through space.

    a. decoyed   b. measured

    c. thrashed   d. postulated

4 They need time to grow at least to have _____ .

    a. immatureness   b. childishness

    c. common sense   d. impractical sense

5 The reputation he is seeking is actually like a bubble, easily broken and _____ soon.

    a. included   b. vanished

    c. established   d. appeared

1 What is the basis of electromagnetic theory?

    a. Matter can be set in motion and transmitted and heat also plays a role in this process.

    b. Time expands and heat is a core function of that process.

    c. The vacuum of space shrinks and contracts as time itself changes.

    d. Powerful magnets are key to changing how aether light is transmitted through space.

2 Why does the writer explain Maxwell's electromagnetic theory?

    a. To demonstrate that gravitation pull can move planets.

    b. To suggest that an "aether" enabled light can be transmitted through space.

    c. To try to comprehend the speed of light.

    d. To show faults in Einstein's 1905 published paper.

3 How does the writer introduce electromagnetic theory?

    a. By explaining Einstein's electromagnetic theory.

    b. Through the use of a quotation by James Clerk Maxwell on an aethereal medium.

    c. By predicting how the world explodes, then vanishes.

    d. By showing popular concepts in the early 20th century.

Listening Comprehension

4 Listen again to part of the lecture. Then answer the question.
What's the function of this passage?

    a. To show how light can be transmitted through space.

    b. We should rely on Einstein's theories to prove the mysteries of the world.

    c. Some theories, although sounding amazing, need further research.

    d. To contrast Einstein and Maxwell's mathematic theories.

5 According to the writer, what two factors contributed to Maxwell's electromagnetic theory? Choose 2 answers.

    a. Gross matter, like an aethereal medium, can be affected by heat.

    b. He thought an aether enabled light could be transmitted quickly.

    c. He predicted that permeating bodies of space were the key to time travel.

    d. He thought he detected patterns of motion in aethereal mediums.

6 What does the writer imply about electromagnetic theory?

    a. The world is comprehensible if you are a smart physicist.

    b. Mathematic theories are abundant, but like Maxwell's, many are untrue.

    c. Through hard work and proper peer review, theories can be proven.

    d. Many significant scientific theories are mathematically based.

Energy (4)

In 1865 James Clerk Maxwell wrote that "there is an aethereal medium filling space and permeating bodies, capable of being set in motion and of transmitting that motion from one part to another, and of communicating that motion to gross matter so as to heat it and affect it in various ways." In explaining his electromagnetic theory, Maxwell suggested that the existence of an "aether" enabled light to be transmitted through space. It was a popular concept — until Albert Einstein came along and disproved it. Einstein once said, "The most incomprehensible thing about the world is that it is comprehensible," but actually no other individual has made the world more difficult to understand. He postulated that time expands, the substance of the world explodes and vanishes, lengths contract, and common sense no longer matters. From the time of Einstein's first important publication in 1905 to the present, science has become the world of the mathematician.

1 The word **medium** in the passage is closest in meaning to

    a. means   b. center   c. middle   d. mass media

2 The word **permeate** in the passage is closest in meaning to

    a. ooze   b. penetrate   c. float   d. hamper

3 The word **communicate** in the passage is closest in meaning to

    a. receive   b. transmit   c. fortify   d. necessitate

4 The word **matter** in the passage is closest in meaning to

    a. silicon   b. substance   c. wonder   d. core

5 The word **disprove** in the passage is closest in meaning to

    a. refute   b. obstruct   c. counteract   d. saunter

6 The word **incomprehensible** in the passage is closest in meaning to

    a. unintelligible   b. passionate   c. impossible   d. unlikely

7 The word **postulate** in the passage is closest in meaning to

    a. drown   b. believe   c. ramble   d. tinker

8 The word **vanish** in the passage is closest in meaning to

    a. dissolve   b. disappear   c. emerge   d. materialize

Paraphrasing

Which best expresses the information in the underlined sentences?

1 He postulated that time expands, the substance of the world explodes and vanishes, lengths contract, and common sense no longer matters.

    a. With the expansion of time, worlds come to an end and the improbable becomes possible.

    b. Einstein didn't believe that the world would vanish one day.

    c. Everything will end once time expands and the world explodes.

    d. Common sense no longer matters if the world ends so quickly.

2 From the time of Einstein's first important publication in 1905 to the present, science has become the world of the mathematician.

    a. Einstein's publication of 1905 fundamentally changed the nature of science.

    b. It is important for scientists to publish in academic journals.

    c. Too much publishing helps diminish the strength of scientific theories.

    d. With Einstein's 1905 publication, science became reliant more and more on mathematics.

Native American Art

Definitions and Examples

art work
[áːrt wə̀ːrk]

- 영 works of art collectively, as paintings, sculptures, or drawings
- 동 artistic creation

The **art works** at the Guggenheim Museum are out of this world.

구겐하임 미술관에 전시된 예술 작품은 매우 훌륭하다.

n. 예술 작품

indigenous
[indídʒənəs]

- 영 originating in and characteristic of a particular region or country
- 동 native, aboriginal

The **indigenous** tribes of Canada and Australia have a long history.

캐나다와 호주에 거주하는 토착 부족은 긴 역사를 가지고 있다.

a. 토착의

native
[néitiv]

- 영 originating naturally in a particular country or region, as animals or plants
- 동 indigenous

There are also many species of plants here that are not **native** to the region.

여기에는 지역 고유의 품종이 아닌 초목도 많다.

a. 고유의

extremely
[ikstríːmli]

- 영 to a high degree or extent
- 동 very, highly

The system has an **extremely** big problem.

시스템에는 매우 심각한 문제점이 있다.

ad. 매우

bowl
[bóul]

- 영 a round container with a wide uncovered top
- 동 basin, dish

She particularly likes dark mahogany **bowls** for her salads.

그 여자는 짙은 색의 샐러드용 마호가니 사발을 특히 좋아한다.

n. 사발, 그릇

totem pole

[tóutəm pòul]

- 영 a long wooden pole with symbols and pictures carved and painted on it

The Haida natives built **totem poles** each year for their festival.

하이다 족은 매년 축제 기간에 토템폴을 세웠다.

n. 토템폴

* 토템: 미개인, 특히 북아메리카 원주민들이 세습적으로 숭배하는 자연물

contemporary

[kəntémpərèri]

- 영 of the present time
- 동 current, modern

Ian is a literary author who writes primarily **contemporary** novels.

이안은 주로 현대 소설을 쓰는 문학 작가이다.

a. 현대의

ritual

[rítʃuəl]

- 영 an established or prescribed procedure for a religious or other rite
- 동 ceremony

There are many interesting **rituals** in Native American cultures.

아메리카 원주민의 문화에는 흥미로운 의식이 많다.

n. 의식

second rate

[sékənd réit]

- 영 of lesser or minor quality, importance, or the like
- 동 inferior

That Chinese car is definitely **second rate** compared to a Volvo or Saab.

저 중국제 자동차는 볼보나 사브에 비하면 분명 2류이다.

a. 2류의

deserve

[dizə́:rv]

- 영 to be worthy of
- 동 merit, be entitled

I think the team **deserves** to make it to the playoffs this year.

내 생각에 그 팀은 올해 결승에 진출할 만하다.

v. ~할 만하다
마땅하다

A. Choose the one word that best fits the sentence.

1 Wheat was not _____ to China, so it took much longer to reach China.

      a. foreign
               b. peculiar

      c. native
                 d. disposed

2 We often use colorful salad _____ when setting a Mexican dinner party.

      a. ladles
                b. bowls

      c. blenders
              d. tea saucer

3 If you view some _____ in a museum, then you are seeing a reflection of culture.

      a. videos
                b. martial arts

      c. art works
              d. rubbishes

4 When you meet a(an) _____ person, their ancestors have been around for a long time.

      a. home-grown
           b. indigenous

      c. erudite
               d. expatriate

5 Stable insulin levels can have a(an) _____ powerful effect on cardiovascular health.

      a. dreadfully
           b. ornamentally

      c. abhorrently
            d. extremely

Sentence Completion

B. Choose the one word that best fits the sentence.

1 Buying a _____ car is a very good idea for a college student on a budget.

    a. high-end   b. finest

    c. second rate   d. brand-new

2 Since they were first noticed by European explorers in the 1700s, _____ may have been misunderstood as frightening statues worshipped as gods.

    a. native pipes   b. smoking guns

    c. totem poles   d. telegraph poles

3 _____ Literature is a course designed to familiarize the student with what some of our best writers are doing today.

    a. Classic   b. Contemporary

    c. Traditional   d. Conventional

4 They _____ to be given equal rights and opportunities and be treated fairly.

    a. deserve   b. rest

    c. abhor   d. threaten

5 Some _____ in South American cultures involve praying to dead spirits.

    a. rituals   b. partitions

    c. galas   d. hazing sessions

1 What was considered second rate in native culture?

    a. Native plants.

    b. Art forms using natural materials.

    c. The artwork on cave walls.

    d. Local embroidery patterns.

2 Why does the writer explain Native American art?

    a. To indicate the displeasure of art historians.

    b. To describe the daily life of normal Americans.

    c. To show the cultural richness of Native Americans.

    d. To illustrate patterns in native photography.

3 How does the writer introduce Native American art?

    a. To illustrate how American artists were extremely creative.

    b. By explaining about the term indigenous.

    c. By denigrating Native American artworks.

    d. Through describing various minerals used in art.

4 Listen again to part of the lecture. Then answer the question. What's the function of this passage?

    a. To show how clothing and jewelry was very valuable.

    b. To illustrate how Native art served many purposes.

    c. To describe the limitations of Native artisans.

    d. To contrast North and South American art forms.

Listening Comprehension

5 According to the writer, what two events did art have a prominent place in? Choose 2 answers.

   a. In Native American festivals.

   b. In Native American photographs.

   c. In Native American sites.

   d. In Native American rituals.

6 What does the writer imply about Native American art?

   a. Only modern Native American art uses natural materials.

   b. That traditional Native American art was culturally important.

   c. It needs to be promoted into contemporary art forms.

   d. He stresses the importance of ceremonies.

Native American Art

Native American art is any art works that are produced by the indigenous peoples of the Americas; the term usually refers to the people of North America but can be used to include the indigenous people of South America. Traditionally, these art works were composed of natural materials, such as native plants, paints made from local minerals, and animal parts; these Native American artists were extremely creative in their ability to produce many art forms from these materials, including clothing, jewelry, blankets, masks, baskets, bowls, and totem poles. Today, many Native American artists also produce contemporary art using painting on canvas and photographs. Although today Native American art is seen as part of the culture, just as any other contemporary art form, traditional Native American art served many purposes. Some were intended for use in daily life, others had importance in ceremonies and rituals. For centuries, Native American art was seen as second rate, not deserving to be considered with the great art traditions from other parts of the world, but today art historians recognize the beauty and significance of Native American art.

1   The word **art work** in the passage is closest in meaning to

    a. artistic creation   b. liberal arts
    c. graffiti   d. fake goods

2   The word **indigenous** in the passage is closest in meaning to

    a. adjoining   b. foreign   c. aboriginal   d. exotic

3   The word **native** in the passage is closest in meaning to

    a. acquired   b. indigenous   c. constitutional   d. nearby

4 The word **extremely** in the passage is closest in meaning to

    a. exclusively   b. reasonably   c. somehow   d. highly

5 The word **bowl** in the passage is closest in meaning to

    a. scoop   b. basin   c. watering hole   d. carton

6 The word **contemporary** in the passage is closest in meaning to

    a. modern   b. time-honored
    c. forward   d. temporary

7 The word **ritual** in the passage is closest in meaning to

    a. rite of passage   b. ceremony
    c. burial   d. inauguration

8 The word **second rate** in the passage is closest in meaning to

    a. inferior   b. luxurious   c. crude   d. exclusive

Paraphrasing

Which best expresses the information in the underlined sentences?

1 Today, many Native American artists also produce contemporary art using painting on canvas and photographs.

    a. The Native Americans were very instrumental in art circles.
    b. Artists are trying to establishing new artistic techniques.
    c. Too much paint on canvas causes the material to stretch.
    d. The art generated by Native Americans often used paint on canvas.

2 Although today Native American art is seen as part of the culture, just as any other contemporary art form, traditional Native American art served many purposes.

    a. The traditional art forms didn't serve any useful purposes.
    b. Art is often reevaluated after historians take another look at it.
    c. Today, Native American art is viewed as quite contemporary.
    d. Many cultures have long lost art that served many purposes.

Definitions and Examples

dramatic

[drəmǽtik]

영 very noticeable and surprising

동 striking, impressive

Increases in the human population have had **dramatic** effects on the environment.

인구 증가는 환경에 두드러진 영향을 미쳐왔다.

a. 현저한, 두드러진

---

immigrant

[ímigrənt]

영 a person who leaves one country to settle permanently in another.

동 emigrant

Many **immigrants** leave their country in order to make a better life.

많은 이민자들이 좀더 나은 생활을 꿈꾸며 조국을 떠난다.

n. 이민자

---

newcomer

[njú:kʌmər]

영 a person or thing that has recently arrived

The **newcomers** to the party were dressed appropriately.

파티에 새로 온 사람들은 파티에 어울리는 옷을 입었다.

n. 새로 온 사람
신출내기

---

diverse

[divə́:rs]

영 many and different

동 varied, various

New York City is comprised of many **diverse** communities.

뉴욕 시는 다수의 다양한 공동체로 이루어져 있다.

a. 다양한

---

undeveloped

[ʌndivéləpt]

영 lacking in development

동 unexploited, backward

Much of **undeveloped** Asia 50 years ago has now been transformed into burgeoning cities.

50년 전 대다수 미개발된 아시아 대륙이 이제는 급성장하는 도시로 변모했다.

a. 미개발의

substantial

[səbstǽnʃəl]

영 large in amount or degree
동 big, considerable

There is a **substantial** chance I will fail the calculus exam tomorrow.

내일 미적분 시험에서 떨어질 가능성이 상당히 높다.

a. 상당한

---

rule

[rúːl]

영 control, government, or dominion
동 reign, control

The country is suffering under the **rule** of a repressive dictator.

그 나라는 강압적인 독재자의 통치로 고통 받고 있다.

n. 통치

---

acquire

[əkwáiər]

영 to come into possession or ownership of
동 obtain

Petroleum giant Exxon **acquired** Mobil several years ago to form a new mega corporation.

몇 년 전 거대 석유 회사인 엑슨 사는 모빌 사를 흡수(획득)하여 거대 기업의 모습을 갖추었다.

v. 획득하다

---

annex

[ənéks]

영 to take (territory) as if by conquest
동 incorporate

Hitler **annexed** Austria, a nation traditionally and culturally bound to Germany.

히틀러는 독일과 전통적, 문화적으로 관계가 깊은 국가인 오스트리아를 합병했다.

v. 합병하다

---

set

[set]

영 completely prepared
동 ready

The car maker is **set** to launch a high-end SUV.

그 자동차 회사는 최고급 SUV 출시를 준비하고 있다.

a. 준비된

A. Choose the one word that best fits the sentence.

1 If you greet _____ , then you are welcoming people new to your area, home or work.

    a. employees   b. retirees

    c. residents   d. newcomers

2 If you live in a(an) _____ area, the land around you is probably vacant or farmland.

    a. advanced   b. cutting-edge

    c. packed   d. undeveloped

3 Overall population numbers have declined by approximately 30% because of a(an) _____ decrease in birth rates.

    a. charming   b. dramatic

    c. ecstatic   d. lukewarm

4 If you were _____ , then you came from another country.

    a. convicts   b. inmates

    c. immigrants   d. nationals

5 Throughout my travels to six continents, I have learned to embrace _____ cultures, ideas, and ethnic groups.

    a. diverse   b. ethnocentric

    c. intolerable   d. racist

B. Choose the one word that best fits the sentence.

1 Germany forcibly _____ countries, which was a factor in the start of World War II.

    a. liberated   b. annexed

    c. enriched   d. empowered

2 The territory is still comparatively underexplored; therefore, it has _____ potential for future discoveries of significant mineral deposits.

    a. substantial   b. negligible

    c. traceable   d. diminutive

3 Two hundred demonstrators were killed during protests against dictatorial _____.

    a. deregulation   b. submission

    c. rule   d. leniency

4 The minister left his post just two months before a new administration was _____ to take over.

    a. overdue   b. set

    c. behind schedule   d. relinquished

5 When she _____ her new sports car, she was ecstatic and bragged to everyone.

    a. ravaged   b. incinerated

    c. pawned   d. acquired

Listening Comprehension

1 What was the secret of American industry?

a. It had a ready and available workforce.

b. It had cheap and forced labor.

c. It had an unavailable workforce.

d. It had indentured workers.

2 Why does the writer explain turn of the century America?

a. To explain how immigration, coupled with cheap labor, can lead to greatness.

b. To illustrate how annexing Hawaii was useless.

c. To predict the dramatic rise in the number of immigrants.

d. To tell how diverse communities have added to the U.S.

3 How does the writer introduce turn of the century America?

a. By talking about a cheap, willing, and available workforce.

b. Through advocating the liberation of Cuba.

c. By outlining the amount of rapid change in the U.S.

d. Through explaining population and industrial growth.

the Function of Statement

4 Listen again to part of the lecture. Then answer the question.
   What's the function of this passage?

   a. To show how Spain could have retained its power.

   b. To illustrate the rise of a great international power.

   c. To describe the limitations of international power.

   d. To contrast population and industrial growth.

Specific Information

5 According to the writer, what two factors contributed to the rise of the U.S.
   as a world power? Choose 2 answers.

   a. Undeveloped areas in Puerto Rico.

   b. The liberation of Cuba from Spain.

   c. The advent of Cuban immigrants in Florida.

   d. The rise of a low cost industrial workforce.

Inference Question

6 What does the writer imply about turn of the century America?

   a. That American industrial power gave it leverage on the international
      scene.

   b. It is someone else's turn to be a leading power.

   c. That diverse communities have ruined the U.S.

   d. That America should play a greater role in foreign aid.

Late 19th Century America

The late 19th century was a period of rapid change for the United States both domestically and abroad. Domestically the nation saw a dramatic rise in the number of immigrants. These newcomers to America created diverse communities and helped to develop previously undeveloped areas, such as California. The rapid increase in the number of available workers also provided American industry with a cheap, willing, and available workforce. This period saw a substantial growth in American industry. By the end of the 19th century, the United States was one of the leading industrial powers in the world. During this period of population and industrial growth, the United States began to rise to a position of international power. Near the close of the 19th century, America helped to liberate Cuba from Spanish rule, and at the end of the Spanish-American War the United States acquired the Philippines. The United States also annexed Hawaii and Puerto Rico. The United States was now an international power both economically and militarily. The stage was set for America to play a major role on the international stage over the next century.

1 The word **dramatic** in the passage is closest in meaning to
   a. stirring   b. exhilarating   c. theoretical   d. striking

2 The word **immigrant** in the passage is closest in meaning to
   a. emigrant   b. colony   c. nationalist   d. dweller

3 The word **diverse** in the passage is closest in meaning to
   a. versed   b. uniform   c. varied   d. malformed

4 The word **undeveloped** in the passage is closest in meaning to

    a. emerging   b. enlightened   c. backward   d. primitive

5 The word **substantial** in the passage is closest in meaning to

    a. considerable   b. burly   c. chief   d. trifling

6 The word **rule** in the passage is closest in meaning to

    a. standard   b. constitution   c. suffrage   d. control

7 The word **acquire** in the passage is closest in meaning to

    a. acknowledge   b. succumb

    c. obtain   d. renounce

8 The word **annex** in the passage is closest in meaning to

    a. segregate   b. incorporate   c. further   d. accompany

Paraphrasing

Which best expresses the information in the underlined sentences?

1 By the end of the 19th century, the United States was one of the leading industrial powers in the world.

    a. The United States was a leading soft power by the 1900's.

    b. Near the middle of the 19th century, the U.S. had lost some of its influence.

    c. The United States was a leading power by the late 1800's.

    d. Being a leading industrial power is difficult.

2 During this period of population and industrial growth, the United States began to rise to a position of international power.

    a. The United States rose to international power when it conquered poverty.

    b. A period of population and industrial growth follows every powerful nation.

    c. The rise of many powerful nations is often linked to wealth and ambition.

    d. The United States became powerful due to its size and industry.

Chinese Art

Definitions and Examples

estimate
[éstəmèit]

영 an approximate judgment or calculation, as of the value, time or size

동 calculation, assessment

The NASA flight administrators had to make important **estimates** on the flight plan.

NASA 비행 관리자들의 비행 계획에 대한 추정은 중요한 일이었다.

n. 추정, 평가

civilization
[sìvəlizéiʃən]

영 a society in an advanced state of social development

동 culture

The Indus Valley in modern day Pakistan is the location of one of many early **civilizations**.

오늘날 파키스탄 지역인 인더스 계곡은 초기의 여러 문명 중 하나의 발생지이다.

n. 문명

influence
[ínfluəns]

영 a power affecting a person, thing, or course of events

동 power

Her **influence** on her husband was enormous in changing his life.

그녀가 남편에게 미친 영향은 남편의 삶을 바꾸어 놓을 정도로 대단했다.

n. 영향

Confucianism
[kənfjú:ʃənìzəm]

영 a system of ethics, founded on the teachings of Confucius, that influenced the traditional culture of China

Confucianism is one of the traditional Chinese religions.

유교는 중국의 전통 종교 가운데 하나이다.

n. 유교

depict
[dipíkt]

영 to represent in a picture or sculpture; to give a description of

동 portray, picture, describe

No other painter succeeded in **depicting** the lake so beautifully and with such passion.

그 어떤 화가도 그 호수를 이토록 아름답게, 열정을 담아 묘사하지는 못했다.

v. 묘사하다

achievement

[ətʃíːvmənt]

영 something which someone has succeeded in doing, especially after a lot of effort

동 accomplishment

Your **achievement** was very surprising given your past efforts in school.

과거 학창시절 쏟았던 노력을 고려하면 네가 성취한 것은 매우 놀라운 일이었다.

n. 성취

capture

[kǽptʃər]

영 to succeed in representing or expressing something intangible

동 catch

Many of the photos **captured** the atmosphere of the day.

그 사진 가운데 그 날 분위기를 잘 포착한 사진들이 많았다.

v. 포착하다
담아내다

calligraphy

[kəlígrəfi]

영 art of producing beautiful handwriting using a brush or a special pen

동 handwriting, penmanship

Being able to write in **calligraphy** would be an amazing talent to have.

서예를 할 수 있다면 놀라운 재능을 하나 갖게 된 것이다.

n. 서예, 서법

distinguishing

[distíŋgwiʃiŋ]

영 characteristic, as a definitive feature of an individual or group

동 distinctive

Her **distinguishing** feature was her very unusual hysterical laugh. 다른 사람과 구별되는 그녀의 특징은 웃음이 터지면
참지 못하고 깔깔대고 큰소리로 웃는 것이었다.

a. 구별되는

simplicity

[simplísəti]

영 the state, quality, or an instance of being simple

동 plainness

The **simplicity** of Hinduism and Buddhism makes it very attractive to some.

힌두교와 불교의 간소함에 매력을 느끼는 사람들도 있다.

n. 간소함

341

B. Choose the one word that best fits the sentence.

1 Early attachment of the child to his or her mother is a major _____ on the child's psychological health.

    a. influence   b. inflation

    c. swing   d. leeway

2 Once the gifts finally started to get handed out, my dad would set up the video camera to _____ the joyful moment.

    a. obliterate   b. wipe

    c. capture   d. ruin

3 When you make _____ about something, you make an approximate judgment about it.

    a. arrangements   b. certainties

    c. estimates   d. notes

4 If you live in one of the older _____ , you are likely from India, China, Iran or Italy.

    a. communism   b. chapels

    c. cells   d. civilizations

5 If you believe in _____ , then you are likely to be from a Chinese influenced culture.

    a. religion   b. Confucianism

    c. philosophy   d. orthodoxy

B. Choose the one word that best fits the sentence.

1 The _____ characteristics of the Chinese are their good business
sense and patience.

    a. ludicrous   b. presumptuous

    c. distinguishing   d. insane

2 The artist made an effort to _____ her impressions of nature and
gradually found a style of her own.

    a. vandalize   b. buffet

    c. depict   d. despise

3 There's one _____ I would like to make in life and that is climbing
Mt. Kilimanjaro.

    a. achievement   b. realization

    c. metaphor   d. triumph

4 Beauty lies in _____ without being crude and inane.

    a. disgrace   b. simplicity

    c. snub   d. nastiness

5 Being an expert in _____ takes many years of practice and a very
steady hand.

    a. choreography   b. writing

    c. academia   d. calligraphy

1 What did Chinese artists try and depict?

    a. Reflections of family life.

    b. Artistic scenes of their great emperors.

    c. Aspects of the human spirit.

    d. Scenes that minimize elegant simplicity.

Speaker's Purpose

2 Why does the writer explain Chinese art?

    a. To talk about flowers and landscapes.

    b. To show how varied Chinese art took a variety of forms.

    c. To contrast various Asian artistic techniques.

    d. To illustrate sculpture, metal arts, and paper techniques.

Understanding Organization

3 How does the writer introduce Chinese art?

    a. By showing how modern art has evolved into a lucrative business.

    b. By explaining the 5,000 year old history of Chinese civilization.

    c. Through analyzing how common subjects lived in China.

    d. Through talking about the spirits of Nature.

4 Listen again to part of the lecture. Then answer the question.

   What's the function of this passage?

   a. To introduce and depict aspects of the human spirit.

   b. To give an example of simplicity in Chinese culture.

   c. To describe painting, silk, calligraphy, pottery, and sculpture.

   d. To illustrate the importance art holds in Chinese culture.

Specific Information

5 According to the writer, what two factors were central for an artist to

   obtain? Choose 2 answers.

   a. An elegant simplicity.

   b. Art done on oil canvases.

   c. Art that specializes in pottery.

   d. Art that represents Nature.

Inference Question

6 What does the writer imply about Chinese art?

   a. Chinese art needs to evolve more.

   b. That it is highly artistic and impressionistic.

   c. That Nature is a simple thing to copy.

   d. Chinese art needs to become more refined.

Chinese Art

By some estimates, Chinese culture is five thousand years old, making it one of the oldest civilizations in existence. As with all civilizations, art is an important part of Chinese culture. There have been three main influences on Chinese art: Confucianism, Taoism, and Buddhism; the one constant in all Chinese art traditions has been the central place nature has played. The most common subjects for Chinese artists have been ones from nature, such as birds, flowers, and landscapes. Through these subjects chosen from nature, the Chinese artist would try to depict aspects of the human spirit. They believed that the spirits of nature give life to everything, so the highest achievement for a painter is to capture the feeling of nature. Chinese art has taken a variety of forms including painting, silk, calligraphy, pottery, sculpture, metal arts, and paper cuttings. One of the distinguishing features of Chinese art is an elegant simplicity.

1 The word **estimate** in the passage is closest in meaning to

    a. adjustment   b. evidence   c. calculation   d. arithmetic

2 The word **civilization** in the passage is closest in meaning to

    a. culture   b. savagery   c. insight   d. cultural shock

3 The word **influence** in the passage is closest in meaning to

    a. anxiety   b. emphasis   c. power   d. strain

4 The word **depict** in the passage is closest in meaning to

    a. enumerate   b. confide   c. verify   d. portray

5 The word **achievement** in the passage is closest in meaning to

    a. affection   b. affliction   c. task   d. accomplishment

6 The word **capture** in the passage is closest in meaning to

    a. catch   b. snatch   c. exonerate   d. attract

7 The word **calligraphy** in the passage is closest in meaning to

    a. sketch   b. fine print   c. penmanship   d. simile

8 The word **distinguishing** in the passage is closest in meaning to

    a. weird   b. idiosyncratic   c. neurotic   d. distinctive

Paraphrasing

Which best expresses the information in the underlined sentences?

1   The most common subjects for Chinese artists have been ones from Nature, such as birds, flowers, and landscapes.

    a. Depicting Nature is difficult for some abstract painters.

    b. Nature holds an important place in Chinese value systems.

    c. It is all too common for artists to depict Nature scenes.

    d. Nature holds an important place in the artistry of China.

2   Through these subjects chosen from Nature, the Chinese artist would try to depict aspects of the human spirit.

    a. Nature is just a medium to depict other themes like the human spirit.

    b. Spirits hold an important place in Chinese communities.

    c. Depicting the human spirit is hard for creative painters.

    d. Nature subjects are chosen because of state concerns.

Definitions and Examples

undergo

[ʌ̀ndərgóu]

圀 to be subjected to; experience; pass through

동 endure

She had to **undergo** plastic surgery again to correct the doctor's mistake.

성형 수술시 의사의 실수가 있었던 부분을 바로잡기 위해 그녀는 재수술을 받아야 했다.

v. 경험하다, 겪다

---

temperate

[témpərit]

圀 moderate in respect to temperature; not subject to prolonged extremes of hot or cold water

동 mild

The rainforest had a **temperate** climate, not too hot or cold. 그 열대림은 너무 춥지도 덥지도 않은, 온난한 기후였다.

a. 온난한

---

zone

[zóun]

圀 any continuous tract or area that differs in some respect, or is distinguished for some purpose

동 area

The **zone** around the residential area was put aside for commercial use.

거주 지역의 주변 구역은 상업용으로 따로 떼어놓은 곳이었다.

n. 구역

---

deciduous

[disídʒuːəs]

圀 trees and shrubs that shed the leaves annually

동 leaf-shedding

The trees in British Columbia are of the **deciduous** type.

브리티시 컬럼비아 주에 있는 나무는 잎이 떨어지는 낙엽성 나무이다.

a. 낙엽성의

---

shed

[ʃéd]

圀 to cast off or let fall (leaves, hair, feathers, etc.)

동 cast off

When an old feather is **shed**, a new one grows and replaces it.

오래된 깃털이 떨어지면 새 깃털이 자라 이를 대신한다.

v. (눈물, 낙엽, 털, 깃털, 허물 등을) 떨구다

Life Science Ⅲ

tropical [trǽpikəl]	영 pertaining to, characteristic of, occurring in, or inhabiting the tropics, esp. 동 equatorial, torrid Much of Brazil is **tropical** in nature with a wet and humid climate. 브라질은 영토의 대부분이 축축하고 습기 찬 기후를 띤 열대 지역이다.	a. 열대 지역의
abundant [əbʌ́ndənt]	영 present in great quantity; more than adequate; over sufficient 동 bountiful The wedding reception had an **abundant** amount of desserts and cakes. 그 결혼 피로연에는 후식과 케이크가 풍족하게 있었다.	a. 풍족한, 많은
story [stɔ́:ri]	영 a layer 동 level The library will rise to five **stories**, including a basement. 그 도서관은 지하층을 포함해 5층짜리 건물로 만들어진다.	n. 층
moss [mɔ́(:)s]	영 a very small soft green plant which grows on damp soil, or on wood or stone 동 lichen The young boy slipped on the **moss** when he ran over the boulder. 그 어린 소년은 바위를 뛰어 넘어가다가 이끼 위로 미끄러졌다.	n. 이끼
level [lévəl]	영 the position or height of such a line or plane 동 layer, story The food court is located in the first **level** of the mall. 식당가는 쇼핑몰 1층에 위치하고 있다.	n. 층, (수평면의)높이

A. Choose the one word that best fits the sentence.

1 The no-fly _____ is an area where planes are not allowed to fly.

    a. dimension   b. rectangle

    c. signpost   d. zone

2 I notice that during the winter months, my hair _____ a lot.

    a. gives out   b. cuts

    c. prospers   d. sheds

3 If you _____ surgery, then you have an operation.

    a. undergo   b. view

    c. survive   d. take on

4 If you live in a _____ region, then you will have pleasant weather.

    a. frigid   b. clammy

    c. temperate   d. scorching

5 If you have a(an) _____ tree, then it will shed its leaves.

    a. healthy   b. deciduous

    c. amphibious   d. sulfuric

B. Choose the one word that best fits the sentence.

1 Watch out for the wet _____ , or your bicycle tire might slip.

    a. rubber cement   b. moss

    c. mudflaps   d. hamper

2 One of the nicest climates to suntan in must surely be a(an) _____ one.

    a. bleak   b. tropical

    c. torrential   d. overcast

3 The water _____ continued to rise around New Orleans during the hurricane.

    a. pool   b. ranking

    c. level   d. boiler

4 I will meet you up on the 37th _____ of the office building.

    a. altitude   b. exposition

    c. latitude   d. story

5 There are _____ quantities of syringes in the hospital storage room.

    a. abundant   b. several

    c. dozen   d. squalid

1　What's unique about the layers of tropical forests?

  a.　There is not much activity in tropical forests.

  b.　They have up to eight layers, formed by the crowns of trees and shrubs.

  c.　Such forests are divided into separate hierarchies.

  d.　Tropical forests have many similar layers.

2　Why does the writer explain ecological differences?

  a.　Many plant species take refuge in the lower levels of the forest.

  b.　Abundant rainfall is key to having a dry tropical climate.

  c.　Seasonal change provides great variety in ecology.

  d.　There are diminishing differences in tropical ecologies.

3　How does the writer introduce the ecology of forests?

  a.　By describing the variety of tree insects.

  b.　By estimating the distance between tree levels.

  c.　By contrasting the amount of rainfall and the resulting life in the forests.

  d.　Through differentiating the crowns of trees.

4 Listen again to part of the lecture. Then answer the question.
   What's the function of this passage?

    a. To introduce alternative tree species in tropical forests.

    b. To give an example of the variety of animal and plant life in different climates.

    c. To describe the limitations of rainfall in dry climates.

    d. To contrast temperate and tropical animal life.

Specific Information

5 According to the writer, what two factors contribute to tropical forest growth? Choose 2 answers.

    a. Abundant rainfall.

    b. Dry and humid climates.

    c. Windy and coastal plains.

    d. Warm areas.

Inference Question

6 What does the writer imply about the ecology of forests?

    a. South America has a stunning display of habitats.

    b. Trees and shrubs often grow close together.

    c. Different seasonal changes result in differing types of trees and foliage.

    d. Temperate zones are only common in East Asia.

Ecology (1)

Areas that undergo seasonal change — winter, spring, summer, and fall — are called temperate zones. When there is enough rainfall, the natural ground cover of temperate zones is composed of deciduous trees, or trees that shed their leaves in the fall. This includes oaks, maples, and beeches. Tropical forests grow in warm areas where there is abundant rainfall, and can be found in South America, Asia, and Africa. Such forests are divided into separate "stories," with some having as many as eight levels. Each story is formed by the crowns of trees and shrubs growing closely together. Each story may serve as home to various plants — from ferns on the ground to mosses at higher levels — and various animals whose habits may differ from those living at levels above or below.

1 The word **undergo** in the passage is closest in meaning to

    a. conjecture   b. endure   c. continue   d. reject

2 The word **temperate** in the passage is closest in meaning to

    a. extreme   b. hot   c. coastal   d. mild

3 The word **zone** in the passage is closest in meaning to

    a. level   b. line   c. area   d. laxity

4 The word **deciduous** in the passage is closest in meaning to

    a. leaf-shedding   b. flaking   c. detaching   d. biological

5 The word **shed** in the passage is closest in meaning to

    a. pour   b. float up   c. cast off   d. pick up

6 The word **tropical** in the passage is closest in meaning to

    a. bitter   b. harsh   c. torrid   d. tundra

7 The word **abundant** in the passage is closest in meaning to

    a. sparse   b. seldom   c. minor   d. bountiful

8 The word **story** in the passage is closest in meaning to

    a. fable   b. level   c. height   d. point

Paraphrasing

Which best expresses the information in the underlined sentences?

1 Tropical forests grow in warm areas where there is abundant rainfall, and can be found in South America, Asia, and Africa.

    a. Tropical forests are highly dependent on lots of rainfall.

    b. These forests are usually found in the northern hemisphere.

    c. Tropical forests need clean air pathways.

    d. Tropical forests are well known for varied tree life.

2 Each story may serve as home to various plants — from ferns on the ground to mosses at higher levels — and various animals whose habits may differ from those living at levels above or below.

    a. The layers often rise to 13 stories or more.

    b. Oaks and maple trees are abundant in tropical forests.

    c. Ferns often dominate the habitat of other minor shrubs and plants.

    d. The many layers in tropical forests are home to various plants and animals.

Ecology (2)

Definitions and Examples

herd		
herd [hə́:rd]	영 **a number of animals kept, feeding, or traveling together; drove; flock** 동 **group** The **herd** of sheep were rounded up each morning by the Israeli shepherd. 그 이스라엘 양치기는 매일 아침 양 떼를 모았다.	**n.** 떼, 무리
post [póust]	영 **to place on watch or duty, watching over something** 동 **position, place** Government authorities **posted** patrols on the streets. 정부 당국이 거리에 순찰 병력을 배치했다.	**v.** 배치하다
stampede [stæmpí:d]	영 **to flee in a headlong rush** Suddenly all the horses **stampeded** from the place where they were kept for the night. 말들이 모두 밤새 갇혀있던 곳에서 갑자기 우르르 달아났다.	**v.** 우르르 달아나다 달아나게 하다
threaten [θrétn]	영 **to indicate impending evil or mischief** 동 **likely happen** Heavy rain **threatened** in unseasonably hot weather. 때아닌 폭염의 날씨속에 폭우가 내릴 것 같았다.	**v.** (위험이) 임박하다 (…) 할 듯하다
spear [spiər]	영 **a long pointed rod used as a tool or weapon** 동 **lance** She never quite learned how to properly throw a **spear** like the aborigines. 그녀는 원주민처럼 정확하게 창 던지는 법을 한번도 배워본 적이 없었다.	**n.** 창

stalk
[stɔ́:k]

ⓔ to pursue stealthily
ⓢ follow

He was charged with multiple counts of **stalking** women.

그는 여성들을 여러 차례 스토킹한 혐의로 기소되었다.

v. 몰래 접근하다
가만히 뒤를 밟다

conquistador
[kɑnkwístədɔ́:r]

ⓔ the 16th century Spanish conquerors of Central and South America
ⓢ conqueror

The natives of Peru were most afraid of the European **conquistador** and their magic guns.

페루 원주민들은 유럽의 정복자와 그들의 마법 같은 무기에 큰 두려움을 느꼈다.

n. 정복자

barter
[bá:rtər]

ⓔ to exchange goods without involving money
ⓢ trade, exchange

I **bartered** with them for something essential.

나는 꼭 필요한 물건을 그들과 교환했다.

v. (물물) 교환하다

launch
[lɔ́:ntʃ]

ⓔ to set going; initiate
ⓢ start, embark on

The organization has **launched** a new project to save threatened animals.

그 기관은 멸종 위기에 처한 동물을 구하기 위해 새로운 프로젝트를 시작했다.

v. 시작하다

slaughter
[slɔ́:tər]

ⓔ the killing of animals especially for food
ⓢ killing, slaying

There have been massive **slaughters** of birds in the country.

그 나라에서 새를 대량으로 도살했다.

n. 도살

A. Choose the one word that best fits the sentence.

1 The airline _____ the investigation to tackle the growing problem of thieves entering aircraft holds.

    a. launched   b. sent off

    c. distributed   d. bombarded

2 The financial firm had to _____ many guards during the sensitive business negotiations.

    a. incarcerate   b. post

    c. lodge   d. sign

3 The man _____ the animals into a log corral.

    a. attacked   b. stomped

    c. stampeded   d. stockpiled

4 He stole some jewels and tried to _____ them for food, but he had trouble finding a buyer.

    a. consume   b. barter

    c. search   d. seek

5 A large _____ of animals is similar to a large group of animals.

    a. handful   b. storage

    c. congregation   d. herd

B. Choose the one word that best fits the sentence.

1 _____ a woman after a bad breakup means you have problems with being rejected.

    a. Sanctioning   b. Exalting

    c. Stalking   d. Speeding

2 Four hurricanes and a major tropical storm _____ in August and September.

    a. threatened   b. summoned

    c. offered   d. promoted

3 Bird flu discovery has sparked mass chicken _____ in the area.

    a. consumption   b. farm

    c. hatch   d. slaughter

4 A _____ was a Spanish soldier, explorer, and adventurer who took part in the gradual invasion and conquest of much of the Americas and Asia Pacific.

    a. conquistador   b. lord

    c. battalion   d. brigade

5 The Kenyan tribal chief was very adept at throwing a _____.

    a. mortar   b. spear

    c. shotgun   d. bazooka

Listening Comprehension

1 Why did the fur companies want the bison?

    a. To sell back to the Native Americans.

    b. To make fur pelts and coats and make a profit.

    c. To predict how to manage the horse herds.

    d. To study conservation efforts aimed at the bison.

Speaker's Purpose

2 Why does the writer explain the role of the bison?

    a. To analyze how to stampede whole herds over cliffs.

    b. To better understand how bison and humans interacted.

    c. To predict the day when bison would become extinct.

    d. To compare hunting patterns between the White man and the Native American.

Understanding Organization

3 How does the writer introduce the bison?

    a. Through the use of stories written by Native Americans.

    b. By explaining its good sense of smell and hearing.

    c. By talking about the frequency of bison hunts.

    d. By showing patterns in eating habits.

Listening Comprehension

the Function of Statement

4 Listen again to part of the lecture. Then answer the question.

What's the function of this passage?

   a. To introduce an alternative application of how conquistadors killed the Native Americans.

   b. To give an example of how Native Americans hunted in the 17th century.

   c. To describe the limitations of bison hunting.

   d. To contrast buffalo and horse territorial habits.

Specific Information

5 According to the writer, for what two purposes the bison was used by the Native Americans? Choose 2 answers.

   a. Clothing and pistols.

   b. Lodging and batteries.

   c. Bedding and fuel.

   d. Lodging and food.

Inference Question

6 What does the writer imply about the fate of the bison?

   a. Horses were more highly sought after than the bison.

   b. They were valued by Native Americans and hunted sparingly until the fur companies came along.

   c. Descendants of those first horses chased the bison across the desert.

   d. The fur companies tried to save the slaughter of the bison.

Ecology (2)

The bison is a cautious animal, with an excellent sense of smell and hearing. A herd will post guards and stampede when danger threatens. For thousands of years, Native Americans hunted the bison on foot, using spears and arrows. Although they sometimes stampeded whole herds over cliffs, the Native Americans usually killed only one or two, after stalking them with great care. The Spanish conquistadors brought horses to the New World, and by the late 17th century, the Native Americans were using the descendants of those first horses to chase the bison across the plains. The animal became the source of the Native Americans' food, lodging, clothing, bedding, fuel, and equipment. Still, in spite of the frequency with which they were hunted by the Native Americans, the huge herds remained largely unaffected. When the great fur companies arrived with offers to barter for hides, however, it was the beginning of the end for large bison herds. From that point on, white hunters and Native Americans were to launch one of the greatest animal slaughters in history. However, with the help of some dedicated people, bison are growing in numbers today.

1 The word **herd** in the passage is closest in meaning to

    a. group   b. congregation   c. company   d. hunter

2 The word **post** in the passage is closest in meaning to

    a. pull   b. maim   c. place   d. construct

3 The word **threaten** in the passage is closest in meaning to

    a. likely happen   b. yell   c. surely dread   d. alleviate

4 The word **spear** in the passage is closest in meaning to

    a. lance   b. slingshot   c. rifle   d. grenade

5 The word **stalk** in the passage is closest in meaning to

    a. tease   b. irritate   c. follow   d. avert

6 The word **barter** in the passage is closest in meaning to

    a. stock   b. trade   c. discard   d. supply

7 The word **launch** in the passage is closest in meaning to

    a. disrupt   b. provide   c. halt   d. start

8 The word **slaughter** in the passage is closest in meaning to

    a. vengeance   b. conflict   c. killing   d. warfare

Paraphrasing

Which best expresses the information in the underlined sentences?

1 The animal became the source of the Native Americans' food, lodging, clothing, bedding, fuel, and equipment.

    a. The bison became a primary source for Native American livelihood.
    b. The bison fur was too warm in the summer months.
    c. Too much bison meat often made Native Americans sick with small pox.
    d. Some of the clothing Native Americans wore came from beaver, mink and bison.

2 When the great fur companies arrived with offers to barter for hides, however, it was the beginning of the end for the bison.

    a. Fur trading companies took advantage of many of the Native American tribes to sell them bedding and fuel.
    b. Bartering is an effective way to trade guns for animal hides.
    c. Some bison were rounded up and raised in farms by the fur trading companies.
    d. Fur trading companies traded with the Native Americans, thereby increasing the killing of bison.

Light and Vision(1)

Definitions and Examples

---

complex

[kəmpléks]

(영) composed of many different parts

(동) intricate, complicated

The biologist was setting up a **complex** series of experiments.

생물학자들은 복잡한 일련의 실험을 준비하고 있었다.

a. 복잡한

---

visual

[víʒuəl]

(영) of or pertaining to seeing or sight

(동) seen, optical

Visual learning is essential to a young child's education.

시각 학습은 어린 아이의 교육에 필수이다.

a. 시각의

---

link

[líŋk]

(영) to join by or as if by a link or links; unite

(동) connect

The new bridge will **link** the isolated village with the rest of the area.

새 다리는 고립된 마을과 그 지역의 나머지 일대를 연결해 줄 것이다.

v. 연결하다

---

intricate

[íntrìkət]

(영) having many interrelated parts or facets

(동) complicated, complex

The embroidery on the Bollywood movie star's dress was very **intricate**.

그 인도 영화 배우가 입은 옷에 놓여진 자수는 매우 복잡했다.

a. 복잡한

---

confused

[kənfjúːzd]

(영) being unable to think with clarity or act with understanding and intelligence

(동) perplexed, bewildered

The students were routinely **confused** by their teacher's instructions.

학생들은 선생님의 가르침에 혼란을 느끼기 일쑤였다.

a. 혼란스러운

Life Science Ⅲ

astronaut

[ǽstrənɔ̀ːt]

- ⑱ a person engaged in or trained for spaceflight
- ⑧ cosmonaut

The first **astronaut** to orbit space was from the Soviet Union.

우주로 나간 최초의 우주 비행사는 구 소련 출신이었다.

n. 우주 비행사

---

comprehend

[kàmprihénd]

- ⑱ to understand the nature or meaning of; grasp with the mind; perceive
- ⑧ understand

She found it difficult to **comprehend** the CEO's analysis of the project.

그녀는 그 프로젝트에 대한 최고 경영자의 분석을 이해하기 어려웠다.

v. 이해하다

---

contribute

[kəntríbjuːt]

- ⑱ to help bring about a result; act as a factor
- ⑧ help, benefit

Regular exercise **contributes** to better health.

규칙적인 운동은 건강 증진에 기여한다.

v. 기여하다

---

measure

[méʒər]

- ⑱ the degree to which you do something
- ⑧ degree, amount

The success of the operation depends in great **measure** on the skill of the doctor.

그 수술의 성공 여부는 거의 의사의 솜씨에 달렸다.

n. 양, 정도

---

pose

[póuz]

- ⑱ to assert, state, or put forward
- ⑧ present, propound

Potholes **pose** travelling problems for people and financial problems for city.

움푹 패인 도로는 사람들에게는 여행의 어려움을, 시에는 재정적 어려움을 제기한다.

v. 제시(제기)하다

A. Choose the one word that best fits the sentence.

1 When someone _____ the ropes to the anchors, then they make a connection.

    a. links   b. detaches

    c. fuses   d. sorts

2 When people get _____, they usually are not clear about things.

    a. blissful   b. hormonal

    c. ecstatic   d. confused

3 A(An) _____ series of mathematic formulas means that they are very difficult to solve.

    a. obvious   b. complex

    c. hazardous   d. straightforward

4 If you are a _____ person, they you remember things best when you see them.

    a. tactile   b. touchy

    c. visual   d. relative

5 If you are wearing _____ jewelry, then it has a complex and probably expensive design.

    a. rustic   b. intricate

    c. glittering   d. plain

B. Choose the one word that best fits the sentence.

1 The good policy has _____ to higher birth rates in the country.

    a. threatened   b. contributed

    c. wrecked   d. interrupted

2 There was much discussion about the safety of the _____ on the trip to Mars.

    a. horoscope   b. astronaut

    c. NASA   d. ecosystem

3 There's no point trying to _____ the complicated video image; it's too confusing.

    a. contort   b. cheat

    c. comprehend   d. misunderstand

4 Mounting tensions between the two countries may _____ a threat to the ongoing peace deal.

    a. reduce   b. chip away

    c. eliminate   d. pose

5 The _____ of our success on this project will be determined by our hard work.

    a. measure   b. longitude

    c. range   d. oblivion

Listening Comprehension

1 How does the human visual system help our mind?

    a. By giving us new sensations.

    b. Through estimating the neural connections in our head.

    c. By providing us with information to ask questions.

    d. By defining our role in the universe.

Speaker's Purpose

2 Why does the writer explain visual systems?

    a. To show how intricate and essential our vision and knowledge are.

    b. So we can see astronauts floating in outer space.

    c. To predict our future role in history.

    d. To learn about patterns of organization in our minds.

Understanding Organization

3 How does the writer introduce visual systems?

    a. By linking the visual system with how our brain works.

    b. By comparing the vision of cats at night with our own vision.

    c. By predicting how we comprehend images.

    d. By making donations to people who cannot see.

the Function of Statement

4 Listen again to part of the lecture. Then answer the question.
What's the function of this passage?

    a. To introduce weaknesses in cat vision.

    b. To give an example of various telescopes used in astronomy.

    c. To describe the complexity of human visual systems.

    d. To pose questions and find answers on television.

Specific Information

5 According to the writer, what two things does a cat see when watching television? Choose 2 answers.

    a. The cat starts to see horizontal lines.

    b. The cat gets confused.

    c. The cat starts to see mice on the screen.

    d. The cat gets disinterested.

Inference Question

6 What does the writer imply about visual systems?

    a. Visual systems are not that intricate.

    b. Some scientists estimate that cats have better vision than humans.

    c. Most of mankind's information is visually based and key to our understanding of our environment.

    d. To examine more closely how to contribute to research on the optical nerve.

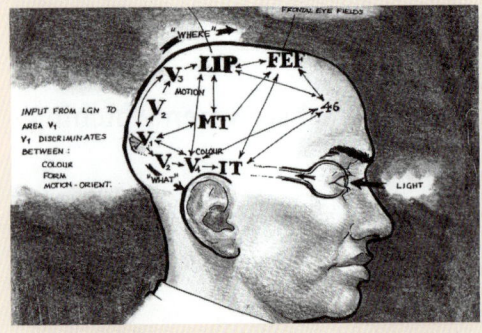

Light and Vision(1)

Of all the world's species, human beings have the most complex visual system. This system, linking the eye and various parts of the brain, allows people to organize and comprehend the many intricate elements of their environment. A cat seeing another cat on a television screen is either confused or disinterested, but when a human being sees an astronaut floating in space on the same television, he or she can comprehend the meaning of that image. The visual system also contributes in great measure to the human ability to pose questions and then work out ways to answer them. Curiosity about the role of mankind in the universe, for example, led to the development of telescopes. Questions about the nature of life resulted in microscopes to examine living cells.

1   The word **complex** in the passage is closest in meaning to
     a. subjective   b. doubtful   c. complicated   d. obscure

2   The word **visual** in the passage is closest in meaning to
     a. physical   b. insightful   c. contemplative d. optical

3   The word **link** in the passage is closest in meaning to
     a. dissect   b. connect   c. intermingle   d. rejoice

4   The word **intricate** in the passage is closest in meaning to
     a. complex   b. easy   c. savage   d. baffled

5   The word **confused** in the passage is closest in meaning to
     a. convinced   b. proving   c. perplexed   d. obvious

6 The word **astronaut** in the passage is closest in meaning to

    a. cosmonaut   b. maid   c. obstetrician   d. astrologist

7 The word **comprehend** in the passage is closest in meaning to

    a. adapt   b. gasp   c. mention   d. understand

8 The word **measure** in the passage is closest in meaning to

    a. calculation   b. portion   c. extension   d. degree

Paraphrasing

Which best expresses the information in the underlined sentences?

1   This system, linking the eye and various parts of the brain, allows people to organize and comprehend the many intricate elements of their environment.

    a. The saturation of information is often too much for the brain to absorb.
    b. Various parts of the brain are connected by nerves to relay information about our environment.
    c. Too many elements exist in our environment to take in all at once.
    d. Linking our eyes and brain segments is integral to understanding complex problems.

2   The visual system also contributes in great measure to the human ability to pose questions and then work out ways to answer them.

    a. Without information received through our eyes, we couldn't ask questions at all.
    b. Being informative is related to having good eyesight.
    c. Our visual system is acutely related to our ability to ask complex questions.
    d. Without information received through our various senses, we would be much less informed.

TOEFL 滿^만

Vocabulary

1

Answer Key

WorldCom

토플 단어 만점 받자!

TOEFL 滿
Vocabulary

1

Unit 01 — The Birth of the Universe   p.18

우주의 탄생

우리가 현재 알고 있는 우주는 약 150억 년 전에 주로 극히 소량의 헬륨과 수소만으로 구성된 빛나는 백열의 팽창하는 가스 구름에서 탄생했다고 과학자들은 가정한다. 그 때는 성운도 항성도 행성도 존재하지 않았다. 가스구름이 계속 팽창함에 따라 온도가 내려가기 시작했다. 약 1억 년 후에 최초의 천체가 그 가스 구름에서 응축되기 시작했다. 우리 태양계의 태양과 행성이 생겨나기 훨씬 전이다. 약 46억 년 전에 태양이 탄생됐고, 그 주변의 잔해들로부터 행성이 응결되기 시작했다. 항성과 행성의 형성과정은 지금도 계속되고 있다. 큰 망원경으로 아득히 먼 저편의 수소 가스 구름 속에서 발생하고 있는 항성의 창조과정을 지구에서 관찰할 수 있다.

Sentence Completion   p.14~15

A. 다음 문장에 가장 알맞은 단어를 고르시오.

1. 만일 무엇인가의 ____ 을/를 입증한다면, 그것의 실존은 의심의 여지가 없다.
   a. 동기   b. 존재   c. 백열광   d. 생존

2. 만일 당신의 시야를 ____ 다면, 좀 더 개방적인 사람이 될 것이다.
   a. 열다   b. 넓히다   c. 잠그다   d. 합치다

3. 만일 ____ 한다면, 무엇인가에 대해 가능성은 있으나 아직 증명되지는 않은 것에 대해 설명하는 것이다.
   a. 가정하다   b. 해설하다
   c. ~에 대해 생각하다   d. 주장하다

4. 우리는 그 야생동물이 남겨놓은 발자국 ____ 을/를 발견했다.
   a. 꾸러미들   b. 더미들   c. 흔적들   d. 계획들

5. 만일 당신이 무엇인가의 ____ 을/를 나타낸다면, 그것이 어떻게 창조되었는지를 보여주는 것이다.
   a. 존재   b. 형성   c. 타당성   d. 형태

B. 다음 문장에 가장 알맞은 단어를 고르시오.

1. 그 감독관은 자신의 ____ 성미 때문에 결국 해고당했다.
   a. 몹시 뜨거운   b. 위대한   c. 상냥한   d. 불같은

2. 만일 ____ 을/를 관찰한다면, 천문학의 경이로운 점을 발견할 것이다.
   a. 지질   b. 천체   c. 생물   d. 대양

3. 재능이 있는 일부 음악가들은 무료로 다운로드 할 수 있도록 자신의 ____ 을/를 기꺼이 온라인에 제공한다.
   a. 창조(물)   b. 장인정신   c. 출현   d. 조각

4. 만일 중국이 새로운 초강대국으로 ____ 한다면, 역내에 수백 년간 영향을 미칠 것이다.
   a. 발달하다   b. 몰락하다
   c. 비틀거리다   d. 나타나다(떠오르다)

5. ____ 빛은 어두운 방에서 공부하기에 충분치 않았다.
   a. 얇은   b. 무딘
   c. 백열광의   d. 회상하게 하는

Listening Comprehension   p.16~17

1. 우주가 생성될 때 초기의 기체 구름에 무슨 일이 벌어졌는가?
   a. 수소로 바뀌었다.
   b. 중력으로 인해 사라졌다.
   c. 팽창하고 냉각하면서 천체를 형성하였다.
   d. 태양 주위의 에너지로 인해 기체가 응고되었다.

2. 우주의 탄생을 아는 것이 중요한 이유는 무엇인가?
   a. 우리 자신에 대해 더 알기 위한 것
   b. 행성들이 최초에 어떻게 형성되었는지를 추정하기 위한 것
   c. 지구가 어떻게 변할지를 예상하기 위한 것
   d. 미래의 태양계에 대해 알기 위한 것

3. 작가는 우주의 탄생을 어떻게 소개하는가?
   a. 150억년 전 최초의 기체구름 팽창을 설명하면서
   b. 태양과 태양 주위에 있는 행성 파편의 출현을 언급하면서
   c. 망원경을 사용하여 행성을 관찰하는 것에 대해 말하면서
   d. 기체구름 응축에 대해 말하면서

4. 강의의 일부를 다시 듣고 문제에 답하시오. 이 구절의 기능은 무엇인가?
   a. 망원경 사용법을 정확하게 소개하기 위한 것
   b. 화학반응 및 기체의 확장에 대한 예를 들기 위한 것
   c. 태양계와 행성들의 최초 형성에 대해 알려주기 위한 것
   d. 태양의 형성과 지구의 형성을 비교하기 위한 것

5. 작가에 따르면 별에 대해 배우기 위해 어떠한 과학적 방법이 사용될까? 정답 두 개를 고르시오.
   a. 가상모델
   b. 천문학자를 위한 관측소
   c. 별 관측용 망원경
   d. 방향 측정용 나침반

6. 우주의 탄생에 대해 작가가 암시하는 바는 무엇인가?
   a. 행성 형성은 성급한 결론이었다.
   b. 행성이 만들어지는 데 수소는 필수적인 요소이다.
   c. 행성 형성은 점진적인 과정으로 오늘날까지도 계속되고 있다.
   d. 행성과 항성은 계속해서 확장, 냉각, 응고한다.

1. 본문의 '가정하다'와 가장 근접한 의미의 단어는?
   a. 추측하다   b. 증명하다   c. 확정하다   d. 확인하다

2. 본문의 '존재'와 가장 근접한 의미의 단어는?
   a. 검사   b. 실재   c. 생존   d. 현실

3. 본문의 '불타는'과 가장 근접한 의미의 단어는?
   a. 침침한   b. 성급한   c. 밝은   d. 타오르는

4. 본문의 '백열광을 발하는'과 가장 근접한 의미의 단어는?
   a. 시큼한   b. 진동하는   c. 밝은   d. (속이)텅 빈

5. 본문의 '확장하다'와 가장 근접한 의미의 단어는?
   a. 뻗어 내밀다   b. 열다   c. 나타나다   d. 계약하다

6. 본문의 '기미'와 가장 근접한 의미의 단어는?
   a. 더미   b. 덩어리   c. 발견물   d. 조금

7. 본문의 '천체의'와 가장 근접한 의미의 단어는?
   a. 지질의   b. 넓은   c. 별의   d. 천상의

8. 본문의 '나타나다'와 가장 근접한 의미의 단어는?
   a. 출현하다   b. 선언하다   c. 숨기다   d. 드러내다

Paraphrasing   p.19

1. 약 46억 년 전에 태양이 탄생됐고, 그 주변의 잔해들로부터 행성이 응결되기 시작했다.

   a. 46억 년 동안 기체구름이 행성을 만들었다.
   b. 태양 주위의 물질이 뭉쳐져 결국 행성을 형성했다.
   c. 은하계의 과다한 수분은 행성의 형성을 지연시켰다.
   d. 태양열 때문에 행성들이 파편들로 부터 응고했다.

2. 큰 망원경으로 아득히 먼 저편의 수소 가스 구름 속에서 발생하고 있는 항성의 창조과정을 지구에서 관찰할 수 있다.

   a. 망원경을 손쉽게 이용해서 많은 위성들을 볼 수 있다.
   b. 항성의 탄생은 수소 및 다른 기체들로 시작되었다.
   c. 항성의 탄생을 관찰하는 데에는 망원경이 유용하다.
   d. 큰 망원경만 있으면 수소를 관찰할 수 있다.

Unit 02   The Big Bang   p.26

빅뱅

대폭발설이란 우주의 기원을 설명하기 위해 접근하는 하나의 우주론이다. 이것에 의해 몇 가지 현상은 설명할 수 있지만, 많은 문제들이 아직 설명되지 않은 채로 남아 있다. 1929년 미국의 천문학자 에드윈 허블은 항성과 성운이 발하는 빛을 주의깊게 관찰했다. 이 관찰들을 이용해서, 그는 우주의 모든 물체가 엄청난 속도로 서로 멀어져 가고 있다고 판단했다. 그리고 그는 우주가 하나의 중심점으로부터 마치 폭발이라도 하듯이 확장하고 있다고 결론을 내렸다. 그 빅뱅-「대폭발」-은 모든 물질들이 무한히 작은 한 점에 응축되어 있었던 약 150억 년 전에 발생한 것으로 되어 있다. 도대체 무엇이 원인이 되어 그 점이 폭발한 것일까? 우주는 계속 확장될 것인가? 그렇지 않으면 앞으로 언젠가 수축하기 시작할 것인가? 확장과 수축을 무한히 반복할 것인가? 과학은 아직껏 이러한 의문들에 대한 답을 찾지 못하고 있다.

Sentence Completion   p.22~23

A. 다음 문장에 가장 알맞은 단어를 고르시오.

1. 만일 당신의 전화가 ____ 상태라면, 아마도 상대방은 당신과 이야기하고 싶지 않은 것이다.
   a. 응답이 없는   b. 보이지 않는
   c. 무지한   d. 실현되지 않는

2. 때때로 당신의 재정 상태를 정확하게 ____한다면, 만족스러운 예산을 짤 수 있을 것이다.
   a. (체로) 거르다   b. 해설하다
   c. 추정하다   d. 파괴하다

3. 당신이 ____ 을/를 연구한다면, 무엇인가 평범하지 않은 것을 연구하는 것이다.
   a. 발발   b. 사건   c. 현상   d. 경우

4. 만일 당신이 ____ 면, 성공하거나 실패할 때까지 도전하는 것이다.
   a. 포기하다   b. 시도하다   c. 유혹하다   d. 만들다

5. 그의 이론은 철저한 ____ 에 근거하지 않았기 때문에 무시되었다.
   a. 외관   b. 관찰   c. 겉모습   d. 고정관념

B. 다음 문장에 가장 알맞은 단어를 고르시오.

1. 만일 당신이 정기적으로 운동을 하지 않는다면, 근육이 ____ 것이다.
   a. 떨어지다   b. 수축하다
   c. 시작하다   d. 단념시키다

Answer Key

2. 그 다이너마이트 ____ 은/는 건물 전체를 파괴했다.
   a. 방출   b. 감전   c. 추적   **d. 폭발**

3. 만일 당신이 ____ 을/를 느끼기 시작한다면, 병원에 가서 출산할 때이다.
   a. 슬픔   b. 근육   **c. 수축(진통)**   d. 박동

4. 빅뱅 이론을 배우기 위해서는 더욱 열심히 공부를 해야 한다는 생각이 그는 문득 ____.
   a. 떠올랐다   b. 비판했다   c. 생각했다   d. 날이 샜다

5. 우리가 ____ 부유하다면, 우리의 삶이 어떨지에 대한 이야기를 나누고 있었다.
   a. 지속적으로   **b. 무한히(대단히)**
   c. 불안하게   d. 둔하게

Listening Comprehension   p.24~25

1. 빅뱅 이론이란 무엇인가?
   a. 여러 행성과 항성의 움직임을 관장하는 법칙
   b. 우주가 한 중심점에서부터 팽창하고 있다는 이론
   c. 신이 우주를 창조했다는 예측
   d. 150억년 전에 발생한 우주의 수축

2. 작가가 빅뱅 이론을 설명하는 이유는 무엇인가?
   a. 우주에서 여러 행성과 항성이, 왜 그리고 어떻게 움직이는지를 보다 잘 이해하기 위한 것
   b. 행성의 속도를 추정하기 위한 것
   c. 소행성의 수를 예측하기 위한 것
   d. 도처의 현상들을 관측하기 위한 것

3. 작가는 빅뱅 이론을 어떻게 소개하는가?
   a. 우주에 대해 과학자들이 사용하는 이론을 검토하면서
   b. 우주 폭발의 근원을 추정하면서
   c. 항성과 성운에서 발생하는 이상현상을 관측하면서
   d. 엄청난 속도의 패턴을 감지하면서

4. 강의의 일부를 다시 듣고 문제에 답하시오. 이 구절의 기능은 무엇인가?
   a. 새로운 우주론을 소개하기 위한 것
   b. 과학자들이 우주를 관측할 수 있는 방법 중 한 예를 제시하기 위한 것
   c. 우주의 소멸을 설명하기 위한 것
   d. 한 이론을 적용하여 우주의 기원에 대한 기존 정보를 설명하기 위한 것

5. 작가에 따르면 에드워드 허블의 이론에 기여한 주된 요소는 무엇인가? 정답 두 개를 고르시오.
   a. 그는 항성과 성운을 관측하였다.
   b. 그는 우주에 있는 물체들이 서로 멀어지고 있음을 추정하였다.
   c. 그는 우주가 두 지점에서부터 수축하고 있다고 예측하였다.
   d. 우주는 한 중심점에서부터 팽창하고 있었다.

6. 빅뱅 이론에 대해 작가가 암시하는 바는 무엇인가?
   a. 수축은 매우 흥미로우며, 추가 연구가 필요하다.
   b. 배워야 할 정보가 많다.
   c. 철저한 관측을 기반으로, 우주에 대한 최상의 이론을 제공한다.
   d. 우리는 화성과 토성에 대해 보다 많은 것을 배울 수 있다.

Vocabulary Test   p.26~27

1. 본문의 '시도하다'와 가장 근접한 의미의 단어는?
   a. 인내하다   b. 증명하다
   c. 하려고 애쓰다   d. 계속하다

2. 본문의 '현상'과 가장 근접한 의미의 단어는?
   a. 이상현상   b. 사물   c. 사건 발생   d. 축제

3. 본문의 '대답이 없는'과 가장 근접한 의미의 단어는?
   a. 안내된   b. 매력이 없는
   c. 신비한   **d. 알려진 바 없는**

4. 본문의 '관측'과 가장 근접한 의미의 단어는?
   a. 대답   **b. 검사**   c. 결과   d. 발견

5. 본문의 '추정하다'와 가장 근접한 의미의 단어는?
   a. 추가하다   b. 확신하다   **c. 생각하다**   d. 해산하다

6. 본문의 '폭발하다'와 가장 근접한 의미의 단어는?
   a. 터지다   b. 팽창하다   c. 내파하다   d. 죽다

7. 본문의 '발생하다'와 가장 근접한 의미의 단어는?
   a. 관측하다   **b. (사건이) 일어나다**
   c. 되다   d. 지나가다

8. 본문의 '무한히'와 가장 근접한 의미의 단어는?
   a. 오직   b. 세밀히   **c. 상당히**   d. 명확히

Paraphrasing   p.27

1. 그 빅뱅-「대폭발」-은 모든 물질들이 무한히 작은 한 점에 응축되어 있었던 약 150억 년 전에 발생한 것으로 되어 있다.
   a. 빅뱅은 한 번의 폭발에 이어 시작된 우주를 요약한 단어이다.
   b. 우주는 한 중심점에서 안쪽으로 폭발했다.
   c. 태양계는 수십 억년 전에 시작되었다.
   d. 여러 행성과 은하계는 무한히 작은 양의 물질에서 형성되었다.

2. 우주는 계속 확장될 것인가? 그렇지 않으면 앞으로 언젠가 수축되기 시작할 것인가? 확장과 수축을 무한히 반복할 것인가?
   a. 과학자들은 우주의 팽창과 수축을 연구하고 있다.
   b. 우주가 수축하면, 우주는 빅뱅 이전의 원초적 상태로 돌아갈 것이다.
   c. 우주가 주기적으로 계속 반복되는 기간을 거치는지 여부는 알려져 있지 않다.
   d. 우주는 계속 변화하고 있다.

Unit 03　The Origin of the Earth　p.34

지구의 기원

태양 같은 항성은 가스 구름으로부터 형성된다. 이 과정에서 잉여 가스가 그 별의 주위에 남는다. 이 남은 가스가 식어서 고체가 되어 지구와 같은 행성이 만들어진다. 약 40억 년 전에 지구가 형성되었을 때 그것은 비교적 차고 단단한 철과 그 밖의 물질을 포함한 큰 덩어리였다. 지구 본래의 덩어리에는 소량이지만 방사성 원소들도 있었다. 이 방사성 원소들은 몇백 만 년 동안에 걸쳐 부패했고 막대한 에너지를 방출했다. 그 에너지가 철을 용해시켰고, 표면에서 거의 4,000마일이나 아래에 있는 지구 중심에 침전되었다. 동시에 표면은 심한 지진으로 갈라졌다. 화산이 수소와 산소를 포함한 가스를 분출했고, 그 수소와 산소가 결합해서 물을 만들었다. 그리고 그 물이 축적되어 최초의 대양(大洋)이 생겨났다.

Sentence Completion　p.30~31

A. 다음 문장에 가장 알맞은 단어를 고르시오.

1. 어떤 물질은 액체나 기체로 만들어지고, 또 어떤 물질은 ____ 성분으로 만들어진다.
   a. 고체의
   b. 광범위한
   c. 영양분이 많은
   d. 부드러운

2. 당신의 머리카락에서 한 ____를 잘라 낸다면, 이는 머리카락을 상당 부분 자른 것이다.
   a. 견본
   b. 열기
   c. 덩어리(뭉치)
   d. 파편

3. 넓은 지대를 통과한다고 하면, 당신은 ____ 을/를 지나가는 것이다.
   a. 상여금
   b. 에이커
   c. 동네
   d. 지역

4. 만일 당신이 ____ 일을 한다면, 필요한 양보다 많이 하고 있는 것이다.
   a. 너무 제멋대로 하는
   b. 과다한
   c. 퇴행의
   d. 최소한의

5. 만일 당신이 ____ 다른 사람보다 빨리 뛴다면, 그 사람과 비교하였을 때 당신이 더 빠르다는 뜻이다.
   a. 급하게
   b. 비교적
   c. 느리게
   d. 빠르게

B. 다음 문장에 가장 알맞은 단어를 고르시오.

1. 저 차는 대기 중으로 배기가스를 ____.
   a. 가리켰다
   b. 빗나갔다
   c. 내뿜었다
   d. 진동시켰다

2. 원자력 발전소는 ____ 라고 내가 몇 번이나 말했니?
   a. 방사성이 있는
   b. 녹이 슨
   c. 비활성인
   d. 값비싼

3. 스파게티는 국수와 토마토 소스의 ____으로 만들어진다.
   a. 융합
   b. 조합
   c. 집단
   d. 용해

4. 방사성 물질은 우주에서 ____ , 행성 형성에 기여하였다.
   a. 구름으로 덮여
   b. 자연붕괴해서
   c. 원숙해져
   d. 즙을 내어

5. 학생들은, 수십 억년 전 지표면의 철 가운데 상당량이 ____ 는 사실을 배웠다.
   a. 조합했다
   b. 부드러워졌다
   c. 합쳐졌다
   d. 녹았다

Listening Comprehension　p.32~33

1. 지구는 어떻게 탄생되었는가?
   a. 지표면 밑에서 철이 융해되었다.
   b. 많은 양의 기체가 태양 주위를 소용돌이쳤다.
   c. 과다한 양의 기체가 냉각되어 철과 다른 물질이 합쳐진 덩어리를 형성하였다.
   d. 기체에서 여러 고체물질이 형성되었다.

2. 작가가 지구의 기원을 설명하는 이유는 무엇인가?
   a. 철과 기체를 연관시키기 위한 것
   b. 어떻게 우주의 물질이 서로 합쳐져 우리가 사는 행성을 형성했는지 추정하기 위한 것
   c. 지질학에 대해 좀더 많은 것을 예측하기 위한 것
   d. 태양계의 패턴을 발견하기 위한 것

3. 작가는 지구의 기원을 어떻게 소개하는가?
   a. 물리학 법칙이 수반되었다.
   b. 에너지 방출이 지구 형성을 도왔다.
   c. 항성에서 나오는 과다한 양의 기체가 때때로 지구와 같은 행성을 창조할 수 있다.
   d. 행성 창조에는 방사성 물질이 필수적이다.

4. 강의의 일부를 다시 듣고 문제에 답하시오. 이 구절의 기능은 무엇인가?
   a. 종교적 관점에서 지구의 기원을 소개하기 위한 것
   b. 태양 및 다른 항성의 형성에 대한 예를 제시하기 위한 것
   c. 화산활동을 묘사하기 위한 것
   d. 어떻게 기체가 철과 같은 다른 물질과 합쳐져서 지구의 물질을 형성하는지 설명하기 위한 것

5. 작가에 따르면 지구를 창조하는 데 기여한 요인은 무엇인가? 정답 두 개를 고르시오.
   a. 방사능 물질의 자연붕괴
   b. 지구 내부 맨틀의 융해
   c. 기체 냉각
   d. 기체 냉각과 화성암

6. 지구의 기원에 대해 작가가 암시하는 바는 무엇인가?
   a. 화학을 이해하는 것은 중요하다.
   b. 비활성 기체로 인해 최초의 지구는 하나의 큰 덩어리였다.

c. 기체와 금속의 변화에서 에너지가 생성되어 지구가 창조되었다.

d. 생물학을 이해하는 것은 중요하다.

1. 본문의 '과다한'와 가장 근접한 의미의 단어는?
   a. 여분의   b. 추출한
   c. 불필요한   d. 더욱 적은

2. 본문의 '지역'과 가장 근접한 의미의 단어는?
   a. 땅   b. 지대   c. 에이커   d. 구

3. 본문의 '고체의'와 가장 근접한 의미의 단어는?
   a. 단단한   b. 튼튼한
   c. 향상의 여지가 있는   d. 기체의

4. 본문의 '비교적'과 가장 근접한 의미의 단어는?
   a. 알맞게   b. 유사하게   c. 명백하게   d. 비교적

5. 본문의 '덩어리'와 가장 근접한 의미의 단어는?
   a. 입자   b. 고체   c. 큰 덩어리   d. 사물

6. 본문의 '부식하다'와 가장 근접한 의미의 단어는?
   a. 번성하다   b. 부서지다
   c. 썩다   d. 잃어버리다

7. 본문의 '융해되다'와 가장 근접한 의미의 단어는?
   a. 응고하다   b. 액화하다   c. 물을 주다   d. 굳다

8. 본문의 '(기체를)내뿜다'와 가장 근접한 의미의 단어는?
   a. 분출하다   b. 던지다   c. 흡수하다   d. 반영하다

1. 그 에너지가 철을 용해시켰고, 표면에서 거의 4,000마일이나 아래에 있는 지구 중심에 침전되었다.

   a. 그 에너지는 지구의 중앙으로 가라앉았다.
   b. 지표면 밑에서 엄청난 에너지로 인해 대부분의 철이 융해되었다.
   c. 지구의 중심부 중 일부분(지표면 밑 4,000마일)은 매우 뜨겁다.
   d. 지구의 상당 부분은 금속이 존재하기에 적합하지 않다.

2. 화산이 수소와 산소를 포함한 가스를 분출했고, 그 수소와 산소가 결합해서 물을 만들었다.

   a. 구름 내부의 기체 중 상당수가 응축과 화산 수증기로부터 생성된다.
   b. 공기에는 수소나 산소가 많지 않아서 화산이 형성된다.
   c. 물이 너무 많으면 기체 구름의 분출이 일어난다.
   d. 화산에서 여러 종류의 기체가 분출되어 물이 생성된다.

정복자들

   16세기에 유럽 군인들은 대서양을 횡단해서 신세계로 보물과 모험을 찾아 험난한 여행을 떠났다. Conquistador – 정복자를 뜻하는 스페인어인데 – 는 용감하고 무자비하며 탐욕스런 사람들이었다. 원주민 인디언들을 기독교로 개종시키려고 많은 기독교 사제들이 동행했다. 그들의 원정은 현재 멕시코가 된 곳에서부터 멀리 남부 캘리포니아, 콜로라도, 캔자스에까지 달했다. 당시 유럽에 유포되어 있던 신세계에 대한 얘기로는 그들이 실제로 만난 인조의, 그리고 자연의 경이를 사전에 알기가 거의 불가능했다. 아즈텍의 꿈같은 도시에서부터 그랜드캐넌의 멋진 장관까지, 정복자들은 일찌기 꿈꾸었던 그 어떤 땅보다도 훨씬 비옥한 땅을 발견했다.

A. 다음 문장에 가장 알맞은 단어를 고르시오.

1. 만일 당신이 ____ 사람이면, 많은 이들이 당신을 두려워하고, 또 어떤 이들은 당신을 동경하기도 할 것이다.
   a. 동정심 있는   b. 온정 있는   c. 병약한   d. 무자비한

2. 누군가 자신의 종교를 ____ 하기로 결심한다면, 그들은 새로운 종교로 바꾸기로 하는 것이다.
   a. 번역하다   b. 쇄신하다
   c. 개종하다   d. 새 방향으로 돌리다

3. 누군가 ____ 사람이면, 그들은 엄청난 고난이나 고통 따위를 두려워하지 않는 것이다.
   a. 행운의   b. 용감한   c. 소심한   d. 오만한

4. 당신이 ____ 처럼 싸운다면, 당신은 아마도 총 다루는 솜씨가 매우 뛰어난 것이다.
   a. 감독자   b. 기술자   c. 용병   d. 골키퍼

5. 만일 당신이 ____ 사람이면, 당신은 돈을 좋아하고 금전적 측면에서 이기적인 사람이다.
   a. 만족시킬 수 있는   b. 탐욕스러운
   c. 게걸스럽게 먹는   d. 기묘한

B. 다음 문장에 가장 알맞은 단어를 고르시오.

1. ____ 인, 포르투갈의 왕께서 궁에서 지금 당신의 방문을 받을 준비가 되었다.
   a. 다수   b. 폐하(웅장함)
   c. 유명인사   d. 예의 없음

2. 그는 강인한 팔을 가졌지만, ____ 부분이 허약하다.
   a. 더 작은   b. 아래(하체)의
   c. 하급의   d. 감소된

3. 다행히 유럽 탐험가들은 신세계에서 ____ 땅을 찾았다.
   a. 오래 써서 낡은   b. 더욱 가난한
   c. 더욱 풍요로운(비옥한)   d. 중산층의

4. 그는 산길 중간에서 알래스카 회색곰을 ____, 그래서 서둘러 도망쳤다.
   a. 우연히 만났고   b. 격려했고
   c. 빗나가게 했고   d. 안으로 밀어 넣었고

5. 가장 우수한 ____ 건물들 가운데 하나는 중국의 만리장성이다.
   a. 축적된   b. 합성된   c. 제조된   d. 인공의

Listening Comprehension   p.40~41

1. 정복자들은 누구를 데려 갔는가?
   a. 기독교 선교사들과 원주민들
   b. 신세계 항해에 도움을 주는 일부 탐험가들
   c. 기독교 선교사들과 기독교인들
   d. 정복자와 그들의 가족들

2. 작가가 정복자들을 설명하는 이유는 무엇인가?
   a. 인디언 원주민들이 초기에는 유럽인들을 환영했기 때문에
   b. 그들이 신세계 전 지역을 급습해 들어간 용감하고 담대한 사람들이었기 때문에
   c. 기독교인들과 미국 콜로라도 주 사람들 간의 중요한 무역 활동이 있었기 때문에
   d. 캘리포니아, 콜로라도, 캔자스 지역에서 종교가 말살 당했기 때문에

3. 작가는 정복자들을 어떻게 소개하는가?
   a. 유럽 용병들이 어떻게 배를 타고 들어오게 되었는지를 설명하면서
   b. 캔자스와 중서부 지역의 농가 수확량을 추정하면서
   c. 유럽 용병들이 금은보화를 얼마나 많이 찾아냈는지를 예측하면서
   d. 기독교 성직자들에 관한 이야기를 설명하면서

4. 강의의 일부를 다시 듣고 문제에 답하시오. 이 구절의 기능은 무엇인가?
   a. 유럽인들이 신세계에 끼친 영향을 소개하기 위한 것
   b. 사람이 만든 진기한 것들과 자연이 만든 신기한 것들에 관한 예를 제시하기 위한 것
   c. 인도인이 발견한 아즈텍 자연의 경이로움을 설명하기 위한 것
   d. 기독교 성직자들과 불교 승려들을 대비시키기 위한 것

5. 작가에 따르면, 여행 중 정복자들이 발견한 두 가지는 무엇인가? 정답 두 개를 고르시오.
   a. 아즈텍 문명
   b. 천연 자원이 거의 없는 땅
   c. 그랜드 캐년의 자연의 경이로움
   d. 풍부한 옥수수 농작물

6. 작가가 정복자에 대해 암시하는 바는 무엇인가?
   a. 정복자들이 새로운 땅을 발견한 것은 행운이었다.
   b. 탐험가들은 구식 기술에 의존해서 인디언들을 물리쳤다.
   c. 기독교는 사악한 종교였고, 인디언 이도교인들을 해하였다.
   d. 그들은 횡포하고 공격적인 침략자로 북 아메리카로 진격해 들어갔다.

Vocabulary Test   p.42~43

1. 본문의 '용병'와 가장 근접한 의미의 단어는?
   a. 노예   b. 상인
   c. 노동자   d. 용병

2. 본문의 '용감한'와 가장 근접한 의미의 단어는?
   a. 우승한   b. 소심한
   c. 두려움 없는   d. 압력에 쉽게 굴복하는

3. 본문의 '무자비한'와 가장 근접한 의미의 단어는?
   a. 잔인한   b. 교활한
   c. 자비로운   d. 특별한

4. 본문의 '탐욕스러운'와 가장 근접한 의미의 단어는?
   a. 열망하는   b. 괴로운
   c. 호색적인   d. 탐욕스러운

5. 본문의 '개종하다'와 가장 근접한 의미의 단어는?
   a. 개정하다   b. 수정하다
   c. 바꾸다   d. 고정시키다

6. 본문의 '남부의(밑의)'와 가장 근접한 의미의 단어는?
   a. 아래의   b. 너머
   c. 증가된   d. 네 번의

7. 본문의 '인공의'와 가장 근접한 의미의 단어는?
   a. 복제된   b. 재생산된
   c. 인공적인   d. 화학의

8. 본문의 '우연히 만나다'와 가장 근접한 의미의 단어는?
   a. 비틀거리며 걷다   b. 우연히 만나다
   c. 차다   d. 되튀다

Paraphrasing   p.43

1. 그들의 원정은 현재 멕시코가 된 곳에서부터 멀리 남부 캘리포니아, 콜로라도, 캔자스에까지 달했다.

   a. 멕시코 탐험은 보기에 멋진 모험이었다.
   b. 탐험가들은 스페인 영토에서 캘리포니아 북부 일대에 이르는 지역을 어행헸다.
   c. 캘리포니아 북부 지역 대다수 물이 16세기에 오염되었다.
   d. 멕시코인들은 그들의 땅을 지키기 위해서 좀 더 열심히 싸웠어야 했다.

2. 아즈텍의 꿈같은 도시에서부터 그랜드캐년의 멋진 장관까지, 정복자들은 일찌기 꿈꾸었던 그 어떤 땅보다도 훨씬 비옥한 땅을 발견했다.

　　a. 정복자들의 과학적 활동 덕분에 아즈텍의 삶은 보존되었다.
　　b. 새로운 땅의 발견은 심지어 그때 조차도 뻔한 결과였다.
　　c. 신세계는 어떤 지역에서 보다 자원이 풍부하고 아름다웠다.
　　d. 때로는 꿈이 현실이 될 수 있으므로 꿈을 꾸는 것은 좋은 일이다.

Unit 05	North America (1)	p.50

북아메리카 (1)

컬럼버스가 미국을 발견했을 때 인디언은 북미의 도처에 살고 있었다. 인류학자들은 당시의 인디언 인구에 대해서 오랫동안 논쟁을 벌여왔는데 지금은 많은 학자들이 1000만 명에서 2000만 명에 달하지 않을까 생각하고 있다. 이것은 초기의 추측보다 훨씬 많은 숫자이다. 인디언은 간단한 텐트에서부터 정교한 목조 가옥, 북부의 에스키모의 풀과 눈으로 만든 이글루에 이르기까지 환경에 적합한 다양한 주거지에 살고 있었다. 인디언은 오대호 주변과 훗날 미합중국이 되는 남서부에 집중하는 경향이 있었다. 내륙부에 사는 부족들은 강 유역에 무리지어 있었다. 강은 식량의 공급원이고 중요한 교통수단이기도 했다.

Sentence Completion　p.46~47

A. 다음 문장에 가장 알맞은 단어를 고르시오.

1. 만일 당신이 ＿＿＿ 면, 당신은 목소리를 높이고 매우 감정이 격양되기 쉽다.
　　a. 달래다　　　　　　　　b. 논쟁하다
　　c. 의견이 다르다　　　　　d. 창 시합을 하다

2. 당신이 ＿＿＿ 을/를 갖게 되면, 그것은 그 당시에 이용할 수 있는 가장 좋은 정보를 의미한다.
　　a. 어림짐작　　b. 추정치　　c. 풍문　　　d. 존중

3. 만일 당신이 ＿＿＿ 라면, 당신은 사람, 사회, 문화에 관련한 과학적 연구에 관심이 있는 것이다.
　　a. 생물학자　　b. 심리학자　　c. 인류학자　　d. 지리학자

4. 이 집에 귀신이 출몰한다는 단서는 그 집 ＿＿＿ 발견되었다.
　　a. 바로 안으로　　　　　b. 도처에서
　　c. 별문제로 하고　　　　d. 때때로

5. ＿＿＿ 이/가 도시에서 점점 더 커지면, 사람 수가 증가하는 것이다.
　　a. 주민　　　　　　　　b. 거주지
　　c. 인구　　　　　　　　d. 인구통계학

B. 다음 문장에 가장 알맞은 단어를 고르시오.

1. 세 가지 주요 지부가 미국 정부를 ＿＿＿.
　　a. 구획하다　　　　　　　b. 구성하다
　　c. 다시 나누다　　　　　d. 구성된다(consist in)

2. 그들의 ＿＿＿ 이/가 정부에 의해 파괴되어, 그 가족은 갈 곳이 없었다.
　　a. 구조물　　b. 승강기 통로　　c. 주거지(집)　　d. 헛간

3. 지하철은 서울에서 대중적인 ＿＿＿ 이다.
　　a. 전달　　　　　　　　b. 화물
　　c. 서신왕래　　　　　　d. 운송(교통)수단

4. 두바이에 있는 Burj Al Arab 호텔 보다 더 ＿＿＿ 호텔은 없다.
　　a. 이해하기 복잡한　　　　b. 정교한
　　c. 뒤얽힌　　　　　　　　d. 손재주가 있는

5. 그의 싸인을 받기 위해 사람들이 그 연예인 주변으로 ＿＿＿.
　　a. 흩어졌다　　b. 흩뜨렸다　　c. 폭로했다　　d. 밀집했다

Listening Comprehension　p.48~49

1. 인류학자는 무엇에 대해 주장했는가?
　　a. 유럽은 식량을 얻기 위해 인디언들과 싸웠어야 했다.
　　b. 환경에 적합한 거주지 수의 추정
　　c. 인디언 거주지들의 다양성과 규모
　　d. 강 주변 인구의 패턴

2. 작가가 북 아메리카 원주민들을 설명하는 이유는 무엇인가?
　　a. 인디언들이 얼마나 환경에 적합한 다양한 거주지에서 살았는지를 보여주기 위한 것
　　b. 그 지역사회의 운송수단을 추정하기 위한 것
　　c. 하나의 문명이 다른 문명을 어떻게 정복할 수 있는지를 예측하기 위한 것
　　d. 내륙 지역이 해안 지역보다 훨씬 좋았다는 것을 보여주기 위한 것

3. 작가는 북 아메리카 원주민들의 삶을 어떻게 소개하는가?
　　a. 콜럼버스 당시, 누가 그곳에 살았는지를 보여주면서
　　b. Great Lakes 근처에서 그들이 사용했던 사냥 방법을 분석하면서
　　c. 콜럼버스가 스페인 사람이었다는 것을 조명하면서
　　d. 정교한 원목 건축물에 대해 논의하면서

4. 강의의 일부를 다시 듣고 문제에 답하시오. 이 구절의 기능은 무엇인가?
　　a. '에스키모' 라는 단어를 대신하기 위해서 '이뉴잇' 이라는 용어를 소개하기 위한 것
　　b. 강 주변에 밀집해 있는 가옥들에 대한 예를 제시하기 위한 것
　　c. 원주민 부족들의 생활 여건을 설명하기 위한 것
　　d. 거주지들의 다양성을 대비시키기 위한 것

5. 작가에 따르면, 인디언 원주민들이 살았던 가옥 형태 두 가지는 무엇인가? 정답 두 개를 고르시오.

a. 진흙과 점토로 만들어진 큰 오두막
b. 캔버스 텐트
c. 정교한 원목 가옥
d. 아이스박스

6. 작가가 북 아메리카 원주민들에 대해 암시하는 바는 무엇인가?
   a. 인류학자들은 오랫동안 거주지의 규모를 둘러싸고 논쟁을 벌여왔다.
   b. 인디언 원주민들은 훌륭한 식량 공급망을 갖추고 유기적으로 잘 조직되어 있었다.
   c. 인류학자들은 인구가 그렇게 많지 않았다고 추측한다.
   d. 에스키모인들은 내륙 지역에 사는 인디언들보다 훨씬 더 건강식을 했다.

Vocabulary Test   p.50~51

1. 본문의 '도처에'와 가장 근접한 의미의 단어는?
   a. 도처에   b. 안에   c. 동안   d. 밖에

2. 본문의 '인류학자'와 가장 근접한 의미의 단어는?
   a. 조력자   b. 민족학자   c. 연구자   d. 언어학자

3. 본문의 '논쟁하다'와 가장 근접한 의미의 단어는?
   a. 논쟁하다   b. 소란피우다   c. 타협하다   d. 밀집하다

4. 본문의 '인구'와 가장 근접한 의미의 단어는?
   a. 추정   b. 설치동물   c. 거주자들   d. 숫자

5. 본문의 '추정치'와 가장 근접한 의미의 단어는?
   a. 단언   b. 견적   c. 육감   d. 사실

6. 본문의 '거주지'와 가장 근접한 의미의 단어는?
   a. 고민   b. 아파트   c. 내부   d. 집

7. 본문의 '정교한'과 가장 근접한 의미의 단어는?
   a. 복잡한   b. 낡은   c. 유행의   d. 구조화된

8. 본문의 '밀집하다'와 가장 근접한 의미의 단어는?
   a. 기다   b. 증명하다   c. 모이다   d. 흩어지다

Paraphrasing   p.51

1. 인류학자들은 당시의 인디언 인구에 대해서 오랫동안 논쟁을 벌여왔는데 지금은 많은 학자들이 1000만 명에서 2000만 명에 달하지 않을까 생각하고 있다. 이것은 초기의 추측보다 훨씬 많은 숫자이다.
   a. 많은 논의 후, 학술 조사는 새로운 증거가 있음을 암시한다.
   b. 인류학자들은 정확한 인디언 인구수를 놓고 오랫동안 논쟁을 벌여 왔다.
   c. 크리족의 식습관에 대해서는 알려진 바가 거의 없다.
   d. 많은 인구를 감안해 볼 때, 상당량의 식량이 있었다.

2. 내륙부에 사는 부족들은 강 유역에 무리지어 있었다. 강은 식량의 공급원이고 중요한 교통수단이기도 했다.
   a. 내륙 주민들은 종종 풍성한 강 주변에 위치해 살았다.
   b. 내륙에 살았던 부족들은 종종 강 주변 부족들과 싸움을 했다.
   c. 그들은 식량이 부족해서, 강 주변에 모여 살았다.
   d. 운송 수단 중심지 근처에 있는 연어가 그들이 먹는 음식의 대부분을 차지했다.

Unit 06   North America (2)   p.58

북아메리카 (2)

미국 서부의 개척은 1803년에 시작되었다. 대통령 토마스 제퍼슨이 프랑스에서 260만㎢ 이상의 토지를 매입하고 나서의 일이다. 루이지애나 구입으로 불리우는 토지 획득에 의해 합중국은 뉴올리언스에서 로키 산맥 북부까지의 토지를 손에 넣어 국토는 배 이상이 되었다. 제퍼슨은 이 황야의 유일한 횡단 루트를 찾으려고 자신의 비서인 메리웨더 루이스대위와 윌리엄 클라크 중위가 이끄는 탐험대를 조직했다. 이 두 명은 함께 초기의 인디언과의 전투를 경험했었다. 제퍼슨은 두 사람에게 우선 미주리 강을 수원(水原)까지 거슬러 올라가 다음에 하루 만에 서쪽의 산들을 넘어서 컬럼비아 강의 수원까지 보트를 타고 마지막으로 컬럼비아 강을 내려가서 태평양으로 나오는 것이었다.

Sentence Completion   p.54~55

A. 다음 문장에 가장 알맞은 단어를 고르시오.

1. 회사가 _____ 하면, 그 회사가 다른 회사를 매입하는 것이다.
   a. 소유격   b. 인수   c. 매진   d. 합병

2. 당신이 당신 집의 가치를 _____ 면, 그것은 가치를 두 배만큼 올렸다는 것이다.
   a. 포기했다   b. 두 배로 늘렸다
   c. 올렸다   d. 세 배로 늘렸다

3. 전쟁터에서 비즈니스로 전향하는 것은 대부분의 _____ 이/가 어느 시점에는 반드시 거쳐야 하는 것이다.
   a. 기술자   b. 소매업자
   c. 퇴역 군인   d. 양심적 병역거부자

4. 이것을 입는 사람들은 대부분 한 번에 2~4 상자 씩 _____ 했다.
   a. 자산   b. 접촉
   c. 수익   d. 매입(구매)

5. 사과의 시장 가격이 1달러에서 15달러에 ____ 때, 그것은 가격 범위가 굉장히 넓은 것이다.
   a. (범위가)이를   b. 아연실색케 하는
   c. 지배할   d. 확장할

B. 다음 문장에 가장 알맞은 단어를 고르시오.

1. 팀 리더가 신선한 광고 캠페인 계획의 ____ 때, 직원들은 열광했다.
   a. 강요했다   b. 윤곽을 그렸다
   c. 오용했다   d. 해결했다

2. 그들은 물거품이 이는 시냇가 근처 시골의 작은 오두막집을 ____.
   a. 사냥했다   b. 부채꼴로 펼쳤다
   c. 찾았다(구했다)   d. 분배했다

3. 수십 년 전에는, 일리노이스에서 캘리포니아까지 66번 ____ 을/를 따라 며칠씩 운전할 수도 있었다.
   a. 길   b . 산길
   c. 좁은 길   d. 자전거도로

4. 루이스와 클라크는 위험한 ____, 적대적인 인디언들, 그리고 로키 산맥을 헤치고 나아갔다.
   a. 나무들   b. 뒤뜰   c. 진흙   d. 황야

5. 대규모 순례 ____ 은/는 메이플라워호를 타고 여행에 나섰다.
   a. 여행   b. 한 손 가득   c. 탐험대   d. 전시

Listening Comprehension   p.56~57

1. 루이스는 제퍼슨 대통령과 무슨 관계 였는가?
   a. 그는 클라크의 조카였다.
   b. 그는 제퍼슨 비서의 선장이었다.
   c. 그는 백악관에서 부관으로 활동했다.
   d. 그는 제퍼슨의 개인 비서였다.

2. 작가가 미국 서부를 설명하는 이유는 무엇인가?
   a. 탐험대를 어떻게 조직해야 하는지를 보여주기 위한 것
   b. 그곳이 얼마나 무한한 가능성이 있는 아직 야생의 광대한 황야였는지를 보여주기 위한 것
   c. 영국 영토의 확장을 옹호하기 위한 것
   d. 누구나 새로운 사회를 만들 수 있다는 것을 보여주기 위한 것

3. 작가는 미국 서부의 시작을 어떻게 소개하는가?
   a. 프랑스의 관대함을 근거로 프랑스를 칭찬하면서
   b. 멕시코에 서부 지역을 반환하는 것을 옹호하면서
   c. 프랑스 대사와 제퍼슨의 관계를 설명하면서
   d. 루지애나 매입과 그것의 엄청난 효과를 설명하면서

4. 강의의 일부를 다시 듣고 문제에 답하시오. 이 구절의 기능은 무엇인가?
   a. 토마스 제퍼슨 대통령이 어떻게 2백 6천 킬로미터에 달하는 땅을 반환했는지를 소개하기 위한 것

b. 콜롬비아 강 수원에 도달하기 위한 클라크의 여정에 대한 예를 제시하기 위한 것
   c. 어떻게 국가들이 진실한 관계를 갖게 되었는지를 설명하기 위한 것
   d. 초창기 미국 서부의 멋진 탐험 역사를 보여주기 위한 것

5. 작가에 따르면, 루이스와 클라크가 탐험한 두 지역은 어디인가? 정답 두 개를 고르시오.
   a. 콜롬비아 강
   b. 몬타나와 캐나다 국경
   c. 북부 아이다호
   d. 미주리 강

6. 작가가 루이스와 클라크에 대해 암시하는 바는 무엇인가?
   a. 초기 인디언 전쟁에 참전한 군인들은 능력 있는 탐험가였다.
   b. 북부 로키 산맥은 여행하기에 어쩌면 보다 나은 행로였던 것 같다.
   c. 초기 아메리카 시대를 여는데 기여한 개척자들이 있었다.
   d. 조국을 배반한 영국인 변절자들이 있었다.

Vocabulary Test   p.58~59

1. 본문의 '매입'와 가장 근접한 의미의 단어는?
   a. 경매   b. 구매
   c. 샅샅이 뒤지기   d. 특매

2. 본문의 '인수(획득)'와 가장 근접한 의미의 단어는?
   a. 의무   b. 획득
   c. 유혹   d. 합병

3. 본문의 '이르다'와 가장 근접한 의미의 단어는?
   a. 달하다   b. 주류에 들어가다
   c. Z자 형태로 흐르다   d. 수축하다

4. 본문의 '두 배로 늘어나다'와 가장 근접한 의미의 단어는?
   a. 구부리다   b. 둘이서 있다
   c. 제휴하다   d. 두 배가 되다

5. 본문의 '찾다'와 가장 근접한 의미의 단어는?
   a. 눈에 보이게 하다   b. 찾다
   c. 기억하다   d. 관찰하다

6. 본문의 '황야'와 가장 근접한 의미의 단어는?
   a. 습지대   b. 정글
   c. 장난감 가게   d. 황무지

7. 본문의 '탐험대'와 가장 근접한 의미의 단어는?
   a. 선교사들   b. 기동 부대
   c. 조력자들   d. 탐사 무리들

8. 본문의 '퇴역 장군'와 가장 근접한 의미의 단어는?
   a. 저격수   b. 전문가
   c. 하사관   d. 퇴역 장군

p.59

1. 루이지애나 구입으로 불리우는 토지 획득에 의해 합중국은 뉴올리언즈에서 로키 산맥 북부까지의 토지를 손에 넣어 국토는 배 이상이 되었다.

   a. 그런 엄청난 규모의 땅을 양도한다는 생각은 오늘날에는 상상도 할 수 없는 일이다.
   b. 그런 큰 땅을 미국에 양도하다니, 멕시코는 착한 국가였다.
   c. 미국은 이 엄청난 땅 인수에 대해 매우 고마워하고 있음에 틀림없다.
   d. 그런 큰 규모의 땅 인수로 인해 미국의 규모가 두 배 늘어났다.

2. 제퍼슨은 두 사람에게 우선 미주리 강을 수원(水原)까지 거슬러 올라가 다음에 하루 만에 서쪽의 산들을 넘어서 컬럼비아 강의 수원까지 보트를 타고 마지막으로 컬럼비아 강을 내려가는 것이었다.

   a. 루이스와 클라크는 누구의 도움도 없이 등에 많은 물품을 실었다.
   b. 서부 산악지대를 넘어 콜롬비아로 가는 것이 그들의 계획이었다.
   c. 그런 여행은 특히 나이 많은 클라크에게 매우 힘든 일이었다.
   d. 카누가 부서진 후, 그들의 계획이 엇나갔다.

동물의 행동 (1)

동물의 행동에 관한 학문이 아직 초기단계에 있을 무렵, 연구자들은 두 학파로 나뉘어져 있었다. 유럽의 학자들은 본능적인 행동을 강조했고, 동물을 자연 상태에서 관찰·시험하는 방법을 선호했다. 한편 미국의 과학자들은 통제된 실험실에서 동물을 연구했다. 그러나 두 학파가 모두 존경하는 학자가 있었다. 오스트리아의 콘레드 Z. 로렌츠이다. 그는 동물의 행동은 생존을 위해 싸움으로써 결정되고 신체의 특징과 마찬가지로 적응진화의 산물이라는 생각에 기초한, 새로운 접근방법을 개척했다. 그는 개구리, 개, 오리, 원숭이, 그밖에 다양한 종류의 동물을 연구했다. 그가 이용한 방법 중 하나는 동물의 「언어」를 학습하는 것으로 그 방법에 의해 동물에게 더 잘 접근할 수 있었다. 그가 발견한 것 중 하나는 거위의 새끼가 엄마를 잃으면 그들은 그것을 대신할 것을 받아들인다는 사실인데, 실제로 그러한 새끼들이 로렌츠를 엄마로 간주하고 즐겁게 그를 따라 다녔다.

p.62~63

A. 다음 문장에 가장 알맞은 단어를 고르시오.

1. 어떤 사람이 ____ 면, 그는 박식하고 자신의 분야에서 전문가이다.
   a. 화학자   b. 학자   c. 어린이   d. 택시기사

2. 누군가 ____ 에서 일한다면, 그 곳에서 그는 연구하고 분석하는 일을 한다.
   a. 실험실   b. 사무실   c. 경마장   d. 역

3. 당신이 ____ 에 있다면, 당신은 매우 많이 어린 것이다.
   a. 유아기   b. 퇴직자 전용아파트
   c. 중년기   d. 무덤

4. 당신이 뭔가에 대해 ____ 을/를 두고 있었다면, 그것은 당신이 그것을 숙고했던 것이다.
   a. 갈망   b. 활주로   c. 생각   d. 환멸

5. 당신이 ____ 사람이면, 당신은 어떤 것에 대한 선천적인 직감과 감각을 가진 것이다.
   a. 재미있는   b. 유머 있는
   c. 본능적인   d. 창의적인

B. 다음 문장에 가장 알맞은 단어를 고르시오.

1. 어린 ____ 이/가 새 먹이통 옆에서 어미를 찾고 있었다.
   a. 아기 돼지   b. 새끼 거위   c. 망아지   d. 새끼 짐승

2. 그는 경극(중국오페라) 공연 티켓을 살지, 아니면 러시아 심포니 공연 티켓을 살지 ____ 할 수 없었다.
   a. 설립하다   b. 결정하다   c. 발견하다   d. 가정하다

3. 이 ____ 은/는 원래 것 보다 못하다.
   a. 대체물   b. 책임   c. 분리   d. 필수품

4. 어떤 곤충은 황무지에서 살아남기 위해 ____ 이 매우 높다.
   a. 적응성이(있는)   b. 고급의
   c. 융통성 없는   d. 경계선 상의

5. 청취에 가장 좋은 ____ 은/는 다른 사람의 말에 100퍼센트 집중하는 것이다.
   a. 명상   b. 전문기술   c. 기법   d. 지식

p.64~65

1. 과학자들은 왜 동물의 행동을 연구하는가?
   a. 유럽의 학술적 기법을 일축하기 위한 것
   b. 동물과 조류가 주변 자연 환경 속에서 어떻게 행동하는지 알기 위한 것
   c. 어린 새끼 거위들이 어떻게 새 부모를 찾는지 예측하기 위한 것
   d. 동물 "언어"를 아주 상세하게 연구하기 위한 것

2. 작가가 동물 행동의 테크닉을 설명하는 이유는 무엇인가?
   a. 과학집단 전체의 관심을 얻기 위한 것
   b. 새로운 과학적 접근법이 항상 가능하다는 사실을 보여주기 위한 것
   c. 이 주제에 관한 출판 기사에 대해 다른 과학자들이 어떻게 반응할 지 예측하기 위한 것
   d. 어린 새끼 거위와 로렌즈 간의 패턴을 보여주기 위한 것

3. 작가는 동물의 행동을 어떻게 소개하는가?
   a. 동물 행동에 대해 흔히 전해지고 있는 두 가지 접근 방식을 개괄하면서
   b. 어미 거위 한 마리가 낳는 새끼 거위의 수를 추산하면서
   c. 동물 생태, 특히 조류 관찰법을 예측하면서
   d. 환경에 따라 달라지는 동물 "언어"에 대해 이야기 하면서

4. 강의의 일부를 다시 듣고 문제에 답하시오. 이 구절의 기능은 무엇인가?
   a. 동물 행동은 크게 발달해서 분석하기 어려움을 지적하기 위한 것
   b. 조류 생태 연구 방법에 대해 과학자들 사이에 이견이 분분하다는 것을 보여주기 위한 것
   c. 동물 생태 연구와 관련하여 세 가지 학파가 존재한다는 것을 지적하기 위한 것
   d. 로렌즈는 짝짓기 습성 연구에 있어 창의적이었음을 보여주기 위한 것

5. 작가에 따르면, 동물 행동 연구에 흔히 사용되는 두 가지 요소는 무엇이었나? 정답 두 개를 고르시오.
   a. 통제된 실험실 조건에서의 동물 연구
   b. 새끼 조류의 물리적 특징 고찰
   c. 자연 환경 속에서 서식하는 동물에 대한 연구
   d. 세미나에서 동물에 대한 그룹 토의

6. 동물 행동에 대해 작가가 암시하는 바는 무엇인가?
   a. 새로운 기법을 이용하면 전혀 새로운 것을 발견할 수 있다.
   b. 자연 환경은 조류 연구에 있어 최적의 장소이다.
   c. 새로운 연구 방법을 통해 별로 많을 것을 배울 수는 없다.
   d. 통제된 실험실 조건은 조류 연구에 있어 유일하게 검증된 방법이다.

Vocabulary Test   p.66~67

1. 본문의 '초기'와 가장 근접한 의미의 단어는?
   a. 발견   b. 어린이   c. 성숙   d. 초기 단계

2. 본문의 '생각'과 가장 근접한 의미의 단어는?
   a. 측정   b. 증거   c. 관념   d. 정보

3. 본문의 '학자'와 가장 근접한 의미의 단어는?
   a. 대학   b. 학문가   c. 조력자   d. 학생

4. 본문의 '본능적인'와 가장 근접한 의미의 단어는?
   a. 행동의   b. 요구되는   c. 직관적인   d. 공통의

5. 본문의 '실험실'과 가장 근접한 의미의 단어는?
   a. 세면실   b. 사무실 공간   c. 컨디셔너   d. 테스트 실

6. 본문의 '결정하다'와 가장 근접한 의미의 단어는?
   a. 결정하다   b. 경멸하다   c. 애원하다   d. 포기하다

7. 본문의 '적응성 있는'와 가장 근접한 의미의 단어는?
   a. 엄격한   b. 융통성 있는   c. 이론적인   d. 비격식의

8. 본문의 '기법'와 가장 근접한 의미의 단어는?
   a. 판단   b. 유창함   c. 방법   d. 시스템

Paraphrasing   p.67

1. 그는 개구리, 개, 오리, 원숭이, 그밖에 다양한 종류의 동물을 연구했다.
   a. 청개구리의 짝짓기 습성이 가장 흥미롭다.
   b. 그는 포유류를 포함해 여러 종의 양서류, 네발짐승, 조류에 대해 연구했다.
   c. 연구에 이용할 수 있는 동물 종이 대단히 많았다.
   d. 그는 포유류를 포함해 여러 종의 고래, 벌, 조류에 대해 연구했다.

2. 그가 발견한 것 중 하나는 거위의 새끼가 엄마를 잃으면 그들은 그것을 대신할 것을 받아들인다는 사실이다.
   a. 흥미로운 발견은 거의 없었으며, 추가 조사도 필요 없었다.
   b. 전부는 아니더라도 많은 새끼 거위들이 새 어미 거위를 찾을 수 있다.
   c. 새끼 거위들이 새 어미를 찾기란 매우 어렵다.
   d. 길 잃은 새끼 거위들이 새 어미를 받아들이는 것은 흔한 일이다.

Unit 08   Animal Behavior (2)   p.74

동물의 행동 (2)

고래와 돌고래가 소리를 듣거나 내거나 할 수 있다는 것은 누구나 알고 있지만, 해양 포유동물이 무엇인가를 전달하거나 헤엄치거나 하는 데 소리를 어느 정도 사용하고 있는지는 제2차 세계대전 때까지 알려지지 않았었다. 전쟁 중에 잠수함을 탐지하기 위해 수중청음기가 발달되었는데, 이 기계는 해양 포유동물이 내는 방대한 양의 소리도 감지했다. 고래는 서로의 의사소통에 소나(수중음파 탐지장치)어를 쓸 뿐만 아니라, 소리를 내고 그 반사음, 바꿔 말하면 메아리로 장애물을 탐지한다는 사실을 알게 됐다. 이 현상은 고래가 때때로 「자살」하는 것처럼 보이는 이유를 설명하는데 도움이 될지도 모른다. 얕은 바다에 들어가 몸을 움직일 수 없게 되고, 해수에서 체중을 지탱할 수 없어 호흡불능에 빠져, 질식사하고 마는 것이다. 이런 좌초는 거의 언제나 완만한 경사의 모래땅이나 바닥이 진흙으로 되어 있는 곳에서 일어난다는 사실을 알게 되었다. 그러한 곳에서는 험한 바위 해안에서 얻을 수 있는 예리한 메아리를 얻지 못하기 때문이다.

A. 다음 문장에 가장 알맞은 단어를 고르시오.

1. ____ 에 타는 것은 수면 아래로 내려가, 물속에 잠기는 것이다.
   a. 장난감 배   b. 소형 범선   c. 스쿠너선   d. 잠수함

2. ____ 을/를 이용해서 수중의 음파를 탐지할 수 있다.
   a. 안내 밧줄   b. 수중음파탐지기
   c. 피아노   d. 발전소

3. 당신이 열심히 노력하는 ____ 은/는 곧 전념을 다하는 정도를 말한다.
   a. 정도   b. 위치   c. 가능성   d. 연합

4. ____ 은/는 수중의 여러 소리를 녹음하기 위해 사용되는 측정기이다.
   a. 수상비행기   b. 수중 청음기
   c. 클라리넷   d. 확성기

5. 당신이 ____ 재물을 가지고 있다면, 당신은 돈과 투자금이 매우 많은 것이다.
   a. 방대한   b. 적당한   c. 미세한   d. 작은

B. 다음 문장에 가장 알맞은 단어를 고르시오.

1. 그 어린 아이가 ____ 한 것은 큰 비극이었다. 그로 인해 가족 전체가 충격을 받았다.
   a. 유머   b. 질식   c. 발전   d. 공로

2. 잘 들어보면, 그 고래가 소리를 ____ 할 지도 모른다.
   a. (빛·열을)발하다   b. 내다
   c. 전달하다   d. (빛을)발하다

3. 매년 여름, 캘리포니아 해안가에는 고래 ____ 이 매우 많이 발생한다.
   a. 해변   b 내장   c. 성공   d. 스트랜딩

4. 내게 있어 어려워서 극복할 수 없는 ____ 은/는 없다.
   a. 분수대   b. 소환
   c. 장애물   d. 뜻밖의 횡재

5. 직장에서 당신이 가지고 있는 모든 기술을 다 ____ 하면, 승진도 가능하다.
   a. 제조하다   b. 남용하다   c. 뛰어넘다   d. 사용하다

1. 수중 청음기가 개발된 이유는 무엇인가?
   a. 잠수함이 고래와 돌고래를 피하는 데 도움을 주기 위한 것
   b. 생물학자들이 해양 및 조류 생태를 연구하는데 도움을 주기 위한 것
   c. 잠수함들 간의 통신 방식을 예측하기 위한 것
   d. 2차 세계대전이 발발했던 시기에 잠수함을 예측하기 위한 것

2. 고래와 돌고래는 왜 소리를 이용하는가?
   a. 에코를 이용해서 바다에서 여타 장애물들의 위치를 알아내기 위한 것
   b. 그 무리들 간의 보다 정교한 소통방식을 발달시키기 위한 것
   c. 다른 해양 동물을 찾아내는 방법을 예측하기 위한 것
   d. 바다에서 수중 청음기를 찾아내기 위한 것

3. 작가가 해양 동물을 어떤 식으로 소개하는가?
   a. 소나어(수중 음파어)에 대해 이야기 하면서
   b. 돌고래 무리 사이에서의 소통에 대해 이야기 하면서
   c. 2차 세계대전기간 동안 커뮤니케이션 장비에 대해 설명하면서
   d. 수중 음파 탐지기를 통해 고래 "언어" 속 패턴을 분석하면서

4. 강의의 일부를 다시 듣고 문제에 답하시오. 이 구절의 기능은 무엇인가?
   a. 때로는 과학적 장비가 해양 생태를 이해하는데 도움을 줄 수 있다는 것을 보여주기 위한 것
   b. 소나어에 대한 예를 제시하기 위한 것
   c. 무리들 속의 소통의 한계를 묘사하기 위한 것
   d. 고래와 돌고래의 생태를 대비시키기 위한 것

5. 작가에 따르면, 고래 스트랜딩의 원인이 되는 두 가지 요소는 무엇인가? 정답 두 개를 고르시오.
   a. 고래들이 해저에서 예리한 에코를 포착할 수 없는 장소들
   b. 서로 상충하는 신호를 보내는 잠수함들
   c. 경사가 완만한 모래 또는 진흙 바닥
   d. 다른 대형 고래들

6. 커뮤니케이션(소통)에 대해 작가가 암시하는 바는 무엇인가?
   a. 소나어에 대한 방대한 정보가 필요하다.
   b. 무리들 간의 소통은 지나치게 과대평가된 것이다.
   c. 고래와 돌고래의 소통에 대한 이해가 늘면, 그들을 구할 수도 있을 것이다.
   d. 고래 스트랜딩은 흔한 현상이 아니다.

1. 본문의 '정도' 와 가장 근접한 의미의 단어는?
   a. 범위   b. 안전   c. 방법   d. 총계

2. 본문의 '잠수함' 와 가장 근접한 의미의 단어는?
   a. 보트   b. 잠수정   c. 항해사   d. 배

3. 본문의 '방대한' 과 가장 근접한 의미의 단어는?
   a. 좁은   b. 짧은   c. 가는   d. 광범한

4. 본문의 '수중음파탐지기' 와 가장 근접한 의미의 단어는?
   a. 메아리   b. 잠수함 탐지기
   c. 이미터   d. 송신기

5. 본문의 '보내다' 와 가장 근접한 의미의 단어는?
   a. 보내다   b. 받다
   c. 즉석에서 하다   d. 제출하다

6. 본문의 '장애물'과 가장 근접한 의미의 단어는?
   a. 촉매제   b. 문   c. 원조   d. 장애

7. 본문의 '사용하다'와 가장 근접한 의미의 단어는?
   a. 방해하다   b. 사용하다   c. 촉진하다   d. 개선하다

8. 본문의 '질식'와 가장 근접한 의미의 단어는?
   a. 살인   b. 압착   c. 숨막힘   d. 제목

Paraphrasing   p.75

1. 이 현상은 고래가 때때로 「자살」하는 것처럼 보이는 이유를 설명
   하는데 도움이 될 지도 모른다. 얕은 바다에 들어가 몸을 움직일
   수 없게 되어, 질식사하고 마는 것이다.

   a. 이 이론은 고래들 사이에서 종종 발생하는 스트랜딩 현상에
      대한 설명을 돕는다.
   b. 얕은 물에 옴짝달싹할 수 없는 지경에 놓이는 현상은 쉽게
      수정된다.
   c. 해양 포유류 사이에서 "자살"은 흔치 않은 일이다.
   d. 고래가 가진 한 가지 단점은 "자살" 습성이 있다는 것이다.

2. 이런 좌초는 거의 언제나 완만한 경사의 모래땅이나 바닥이 진흙
   으로 되어 있는 곳에서 일어난다는 사실을 알게 되었다. 그러한
   곳에서는 험한 바위 해안에서 얻을 수 있는 예리한 메아리를 얻
   지 못하기 때문이다.

   a. 고래 피부의 침윤(수분 흡수)은 돌이 많은 해안에서는 적절치
      못하다.
   b. 완만한 경사 지대는 수중 음파가 부딪혀 반사되기에 적절치
      못한 장소다.
   c. 지나치게 얕은 물은 고래 건강에 좋지 않다.
   d. 고래는 어떤 형태의 물에서든 수중 음파 신호를 쉽게 포착한다.

Unit 09   Animal Behavior (3)   p.82

동물의 행동 (3)

동물은 본능으로 행동하지만, 인간은 지성으로 행동한다고들 한
다. 이는 완전히 사실이라고는 할 수 없지만(동물 가운데에는 지적인
행동을 하는 것도 있다), 본능이 동물에게 어떤 종류의 이점을 주고
있음도 잊어서는 안 된다. 예를 들어 나비는 성충이 되어 금세 날
수가 있고, 새끼 오리는 태어난 지 단 2시간 만에 완벽하게 물에
뛰어들 수가 있다. 한편 인간의 아이가 걸음을 배우려면 족히 1년
이상 걸린다. 인간은 생존에 관계되는 행동의 대부분을 학습해야만
하고, 많은 경우에 이것은 본능만큼 효율적이지는 않다. 그러나 인
간처럼 태어나서 즉각적으로 만족스러운 행동을 할 수 없는 동물은
많으며, 많은 동물의 행동패턴은 일생을 통해 변화한다. 개구리를
예로 들어보자. 부화하기 전 개구리는 바둥거리는 듯한 움직임을
보이는데 부화하면 몸을 구불거리며 헤엄치는 움직임으로 바뀌고
완전히 성장하면 개구리는 뛰는 움직임을 보여준다.

Sentence Completion   p.78~79

A. 다음 문장에 가장 알맞은 단어를 고르시오.

1. 새가 알을 ____ 하려고 한다면, 새끼를 낳는 중이다.
   a. 보내다   b. 경험하다   c. 양육하다   d. 부화하다

2. ____ 은/는 이제 막 태어난 것으로 동물이 아닌 사람을 말한다.
   a. 아장아장 걷는 아기   b. 10대
   c. 갓난아기   d. 쌍둥이

3. 나는 오늘 아침 너의 머리가 젖어있던 것에 ____.
   a. 주목했다   b. 무시했다
   c. 표시했다   d. 가치가 있었다

4. 당신이 ____ 방식으로 생각한다면, 당신은 매우 박식하고 똑똑
   한 사람이다.
   a. 정력적인   b. 지적인
   c. 기능적인   d. 수상쩍은

5. 그 박물관에서 최근의 고고학적 발견물 전체를 ____.
   a. 누설하다   b. 전시하다
   c. 달래다   d. 격분시키다

B. 다음 문장에 가장 알맞은 단어를 고르시오.

1. ____ 그 뱀을 피하려고 해봤자 아무 소용없다. 그것이 혼자
   저절로 사라지게 그냥 두어라.
   a. 부드러운   b. 신경질의
   c. 꿈틀거리고 있는   d. 맛있는

2. 대부분 이 전략이 ____ 일 거라고 생각지 않는다.
   a. 효과적인   b. 확장적인   c. 정통한   d. 가열된

3. 그 차량이 지금 ____ 중이다.
   a. 움직임   b. 레이저   c. 분열   d. 사건

4. 그 젊은 여성 임원이 경영관련 테스트를 통과하기 위해서는 매우 ____ 해야 했다.
   a. 느린   b. 유능한   c. 조리가 없는   d. 단정한

5. 그 아이는 태어날 때 ____ 머릿결을 갖고 태어났다.
   a. 곡선미있는   b. 물결 모양의   c. 흔들리는   d. 과감한

Listening Comprehension   p.80~81

1. 신생아가 걸음마를 하는데 걸리는 시간은 얼마인가?
   a. 잘 적응할 수 있는 행동 기술을 좀 더 익힐 때 까지
   b. 새끼 오리보다는 적게
   c. 기어 다니다가 걷는 데까지 이르는 시간은 약 1년 정도
   d. 나비와 거의 비슷한 정도의 시간

2. 작가가 동물의 지능에 대해 설명하는 이유는 무엇인가?
   a. 어릴 때, 더 좋은 걷기 방법을 배울 수 있다.
   b. 작가는 지능이 본능보다 더 낫다고 확신한다.
   c. 하늘을 날고 헤엄치는 경우에 있어, 인간보다 동물의 본능이 더 유리하다.
   d. 동물과 인간의 행동에 관해서는 아직도 밝혀져야 할 것들이 많이 남아있다.

3. 작가는 동물과 인간의 행동을 어떻게 소개하는가?
   a. 지능과 본능적 행동의 예를 개괄적으로 보여주면서
   b. 나비의 수명을 추산하면서
   c. 올챙이 진화에 대한 설명을 통해서
   d. 비교 양식을 통해서

4. 강의의 일부를 다시 듣고 문제에 답하시오. 이 구절의 기능은 무엇인가?
   a. 적응행동은 인간에게 있어 하나의 학습과정이다. 단, 동물의 경우 일부에 해당한다는 것
   b. 개구리는 필요를 충족시킬만한 움직임을 보여준다는 것
   c. "언어" 이론의 상대적 한계를 설명하는 것
   d. 개구리의 뛰어오르는 행동을 대비시키는 것

5. 작가에 따르면, 인간은 할 수 없는 불가능한 일을 하는 두 가지 동물은 무엇인가? 정답 두 개를 고르시오.
   a. 청개구리
   b. 새끼 오리
   c. 대다수 올챙이
   d. 나비

6. 작가가 동물의 지능과 관련하여 암시하는 바는 무엇인가?
   a. 사람들 보다 나비가 훨씬 훌륭하다.
   b. 지능은 본능적 방식보다 더 효과적이다.
   c. 인간만이 지적이라는 생각은 가정에 기초한 것이다.
   d. 심지어 올챙이도 학습에 있어 인간만큼 느리다.

Vocabulary Test   p.82~83

1. 본문의 '지적인'와 가장 근접한 의미의 단어는?
   a. 재기가 뛰어난   b. 가망 있는
   c. 가능성 있는   d. 지능이 떨어지는

2. 본문의 '주목하다'와 가장 근접한 의미의 단어는?
   a. 무시하다   b. 주의하다   c. 경시하다   d. 간과하다

3. 본문의 '부화하다'와 가장 근접한 의미의 단어는?
   a. 열다   b. 고안하다   c. 낳다   d. 추진하다

4. 본문의 '갓난아기'와 가장 근접한 의미의 단어는?
   a. 아기   b. 소문자   c. 미성년자   d. 사촌

5. 본문의 '효과적인'과 가장 근접한 의미의 단어는?
   a. 걸출한   b. 효과적인   c. 효과 없는   d. 번식하는

6. 본문의 '보여주다'와 가장 근접한 의미의 단어는?
   a. 숨기다   b. 공모하다   c. 나타내다   d. 평가하다

7. 본문의 '능력 있는'과 가장 근접한 의미의 단어는?
   a. 유능한   b. 비격식의   c. 감정적인   d. 이상한

8. 본문의 '꿈틀거리는'과 가장 근접한 의미의 단어는?
   a. 딱딱한   b. 유연한
   c. 몸을 피하는   d. 꿈틀거리는

Paraphrasing   p.83

1. 한편 인간의 아이가 걸음을 배우려면 족히 1년 이상 걸린다.
   a. 반면, 갓난아기가 걸음마를 하는 데는 적어도 1년이 걸린다.
   b. 올챙이는 자라서 개구리가 될 때 까지 걷지 못한다.
   c. 걷는 방법을 익히는데 너무 많은 시간이 소요된다.
   d. 반면, 인간이 걷는 데는 기껏해야 1년 정도다.

2. 부화하기 전 개구리는 바둥거리는 듯한 움직임을 보이는데 부화하면 몸을 구불거리며 헤엄치는 움직임으로 바뀌고 완전히 성장하면 개구리는 뛰는 움직임을 보여준다.
   a. 요점은 끊임없이 꿈틀거리는 행동을 연습한다는 것이다.
   b. 올챙이는 꿈틀거리고, 헤엄치고, 나중에 도약하는 것까지 빠르게 습득한다.
   c. 새끼 올챙이는 물결모양으로 수영하는 하는 것이 가장 좋다.
   d. 올챙이 때는 뛰어오르는 행동을 하는데 대부분의 시간을 보낸다.

Unit 10   Victorian Architecture   p.90

빅토리아 건축

19세기 후반 산업혁명은 최고조에 달했고, 많은 미국 실업가들이 엄청난 부자가 되었다. 1889년 미국에는 100명이 넘는 백만장자들이 있었고, 그들의 소득에는 세금이 부과되지 않았다. 부자들 대다수는 세련된 미의식이 부족했고 이것은 그들이 지은 별난 저택에서 여실히 드러나고 있다. 미국에는 유럽의 고전적인 양식과 현대양식이 어수선하게 혼합된 희귀한 빅토리아 건축이 생겼다. 이탈리아의 르네상스식 돔을 그리스풍의 기둥이 받치고, 고대 이집트풍의 뼈대에 세부는 스위스의 샬레풍으로 장식이 되어 있었다. 유일한 법칙은「많으면 많을수록 좋다」였던 모양이다. 실내는 저속한 풍요로움의 견본으로, 로마 시대의 조각과 일본의 종이우산, 프랑스의 장식장, 중국의 칸막이, 그리고 미국의 피아노 등, 고대와 현대, 외국제품과 국산품이 기묘하게 섞여 있었다.

Sentence Completion   p.86~87

A. 다음 문장에 가장 알맞은 단어를 고르시오.

1. 당신이 문화적 지식이 ____ 라는 말을 듣는다면, 당신은 그것에 대한 정보가 거의 없는 것이다.
   a. 사랑하다   b. 부족하다   c. 배치하다   d. 제공하다

2. 나는 그의 음악적 ____ 이/가 마음에 들지 않는다.
   a. 악취   b. 고난   c. 감각   d. 해탈

3. 당신의 일행이 지금 ____ 의 상황에 있다면, 모두가 좋은 시간을 보내고 있는 중이다.
   a. 고난   b. 최고조   c. 교도소   d. 긴장

4. 당신이 ____ 부자라면, 당신은 돈이 많고 풍족한 것이다.
   a. 새롭게   b. 빈약하게   c. 굉장히   d. 거의 없는

5. 친구가 당신을 ____ 이/가 있는 사람이라고 생각한다면, 당신은 세련되고 교양있는 사람이다.
   a. 세련(미)   b. 학식   c. 영리함   d. 간사함

B. 다음 문장에 가장 알맞은 단어를 고르시오.

1. 스위스나 이탈리아 알프스에 있는 ____ 에서 지내보면 매우 멋진 경험이 될 수 있을 것이다.
   a. 연못   b. 성문   c. 샬레   d. 학교

2. 사람들에게 잘 알려진 명성 높은 신발 ____ 은/는 분명 나이키이다.
   a. 분류   b. 별종   c. 광고주   d. 상표(종류)

3. 그 방은 장난감으로 ____ 있었다.
   a. 장비가 갖춰져   b. 벽판이 끼워져
   c. 덧대어져   d. 어질러져

4. 19세기 말 ____ 은/는 여러 가지 양식을 이상하게 조합해 놓은 것이었다.
   a. 디자이너   b. 교파   c. 건축   d. 매너리즘

5. ____ 기간 동안, 모네나 마네 같은 많은 유명 화가들이 명성을 얻었다.
   a. 일(월)식   b. 르네상스   c. 신석기 시대   d. 내란

Listening Comprehension   p.88~89

1. 고대 이집트 건축물은 무엇으로 장식되었는가?
   a. 스위스 샬레에서 쓰이는 보석류
   b. 스위스 성에 쓰이는 예술품
   c. 스위스 샬레에서 쓰이는 장식품
   d. 스위스 판잣집에서 쓰이는 조각상

2. 작가가 빅토리아 건축에 대해 설명하는 이유는 무엇인가?
   a. 예술적 측면에서 빅토리아 건축이 보기 흉하다는 것을 설명하기 위한 것
   b. 빅토리아 건축이 유럽의 고전 양식과 당대의 양식을 마구잡이로 섞어놓은 것임을 설명하기 위한 것
   c. 여기 저기 어질러져 있는 소장품에 대해 설명하기 위한 것
   d. 비싸기만 하고 보기 흉한 것들의 패턴을 보여주기 위한 것

3. 작가는 빅토리아 건축을 어떻게 소개하는가?
   a. 18세기 초, 대다수 사람들이 부유하였음을 설명하면서
   b. 19세기 초, 미국 사업가들이 매우 가난하였음을 보여주면서
   c. 고전적 건축과 당대의 건축이 유행이 될 것임을 예측하면서
   d. 산업혁명으로 인해 많은 이들이 어떻게 백만장자가 되었는지를 설명하면서

4. 강의의 일부를 다시 듣고 문제에 답하시오. 이 구절의 기능은 무엇인가?
   a. 이탈리아와 그리스 두 가지 양식을 조합하는 방법을 소개하기 위한 것
   b. 고대, 현대, 해외, 국내 네 가지 양식의 조합에 대한 예를 제시하기 위한 것
   c. 당대 그리스 양식의 한계를 설명하기 위한 것
   d. 스위스와 중국의 고대 병풍을 대비시키기 위한 것

5. 교수에 따르면, 부유한 미국인에게 부족했던 두 가지 요소는 무엇이었나? 정답 두 개를 고르시오.
   a. 미적 감각과 세련미
   b. 그들만의 독특한 건축 양식
   c. 세련미와 가치관
   d. 아주 작은 가옥 건축

6. 작가가 빅토리아 건축에 대해 암시하는 바는 무엇인가?
   a. 일본의 종이우산은 빅토리아 양식과 어울리지 않았다.
   b. 미국의 건축 양식은 다른 나라의 건축 양식을 많이 빌렸다.
   c. 부자는 더욱 세련되었다.
   d. 이탈리아 르네상스 돔은 볼품 없었다.

Vocabulary Test   p.90~91

1. 본문의 '최고조'와 가장 근접한 의미의 단어는?
   a. 개선   b. 한창   c. 느린 상태   d. 움직임

2. 본문의 '굉장히'와 가장 근접한 의미의 단어는?
   a. 지저분하게   b. 놀랄 만큼   c. 임의적으로   d. 때때로

3. 본문의 '부족하다'와 가장 근접한 의미의 단어는?
   a. 생각하다   b. 증명하다   c. 증진하다   d. 없다

4. 본문의 '세련'과 가장 근접한 의미의 단어는?
   a. 최고   b. 우아함   c. 어려움   d. 오만함

5. 본문의 '미적 관념'과 가장 근접한 의미의 단어는?
   a. 맛   b. 품격   c. 향기   d. 풍미

6. 본문의 '종류'와 가장 근접한 의미의 단어는?
   a. 광고   b. 조회   c. 낙인   d. 형태

7. 본문의 '건축'과 가장 근접한 의미의 단어는?
   a. 계획   b. 건물 설계   c. 가옥   d. 저택

8. 본문의 '어지르다'와 가장 근접한 의미의 단어는?
   a. 정돈하다   b. 어질러 놓다   c. 구성하다   d. 세우다

Paraphrasing   p.91

1. 고대 이집트풍의 뼈대에 세부는 스위스의 샬레풍으로 장식이 되어 있었다.

   a. 고대 이집트인들은 스위스를 꾸미는 기술이 매우 훌륭했다.
   b. 디자인 측면에서 스위스 샬레는 펜션(작은 호텔)과 비슷하다.
   c. 실내 장식 디자인상의 매우 많은 변화 때문에 끔찍한 결과물이 나온다.
   d. 이집트 양식의 사용은 스위스 디자인과 관련이 있다.

2. 유일한 법칙은 「많으면 많을수록 좋다」였던 모양이다.

   a. 크면 클수록 좋고, 특히 비용 역시 적을수록 좋다.
   b. 부자들은 대부분 큰 별장을 선호했다.
   c. "지나치다"는 단어의 정의가 없었던 것 같다. (즉, 지나친 것의 한계가 없는 정도로 대단히 과했다는 뜻)
   d. 지나치게 많은 과시용 주택은 도시를 흉하게 만든다.

Unit 11   Jazz Age Chronicler   p.98

재즈시대 기록자

F. 스코트 피츠제럴드는 1920년대의 젊은이들의 문화에 관해서는 좋은 의미로도 나쁜 의미에서도 크게 책임이 있다. 1920년에 24세의 피츠제럴드는 처녀작인 「낙원의 이 쪽」을 출판했고, 별안간 유명해졌다. 작가들 사이의 말을 빌리자면, 피츠제럴드는 「소위 미국 젊은이들의 왕」이 되었다. 그가 왕이라면 왕비는 그의 아름답고 기지가 풍부한 그리고 변덕스러운 아내 젤다이다. 국왕부처는 소설로뿐만 아니라 난폭한 행동으로도 유명했다. 그들은 택시의 후드에 올라타고 뉴욕의 5번가를 달리며 슬픈 장면에서 박장대소하고 농담에는 소리내어 울어 엉망으로 만들거나 파티에서 취해 요란스럽게 떠들거나 했다. 피츠제럴드는 이 사치스런 생활을 유지하기 위해, 많은 단편소설과 장편소설을 썼다. 그것이 시대를 기록하고 또 시대를 만드는 기능도 했던 것이다.

Sentence Completion   p.94~95

A. 다음 문장에 가장 알맞은 단어를 고르시오.

1. 비행기나 배와 같은 운송수단으로 ____ 소포를 부친다면, 도착하는데 24시간이 걸린다.
   a. 2주일에   b. 하룻밤 사이에
   c. 다음 주에   d. 48시간에

2. 정신과 의사가 너를 ____ 라고 진단한다면, 당신은 정서적으로 문제가 있는 것이다.
   a. 오만한   b. 건강한   c. 불안정한   d. 무기력한

3. 당신이 무언가로 인해 ____ 을/를 산다면, 당신은 그 일로 인해 비난을 받는 것이다.
   a. 파괴행위   b. 격찬   c. 비난   d. 분노

4. 당신이 직장에서 어떤 일을 한 것으로 인해 ____ 을/를 받는다면, 당신은 인정을 받는 것이다.
   a. 유죄   b. 승인   c. 책망   d. 인정

5. 어떤 사람이 매우 ____ 면, 그는 유머 있고 보통은 함께 이야기하면 즐거운 사람이다.
   a. 미친   b. 재치 있는
   c. 정신적인   d. 정신 이상의

B. 다음 문장에 가장 알맞은 단어를 고르시오.

1. ____ 축구 선수들이 함께 모여 있으면, 나중에 파티가 험악해질 수 있다.
   a. 행복한   b. 만취한   c. 기쁨에 넘친   d. 점잖은

2. 그의 _____ 이/가 나아지면, 우리는 그가 방에서 나와 저녁을 먹도록 해 줄 수 있다.
   a. 매너리즘　　b. 스타일　　c. 행동(태도)　　d. 상냥함

3. F. 스콧 피츠제럴드는 종종 밤늦게 까지 _____ 꾸민 파티를 열었다.
   a. 난폭하게　　　　　　　b. 약하게
   c. 민감하게　　　　　　　d. 사치스럽게

4. 그녀는 디자인 산업의 발전에(을) _____.
   a. 나누어 주었다　　　　b. 주었다
   c. 공헌했다　　　　　　　d. 먹었다

5. 파티 참석을 즐기는 옆집 사람들이 나이트클럽에서 돌아와 동네를 _____.
   a. 평온하게 했다　　　　b. 조직했다
   c. 혼란스럽게 만들었다　d. 진압했다

Listening Comprehension　　p.96~97

1. 피츠제럴드는 그의 생활에 필요한 돈을 어떻게 대었는가?
   a. 정신이 불안정한 아내의 이력을 홍보 수단으로 이용하면서
   b. 뉴욕에 있는 비싼 집을 세놓으면서
   c. 술파티를 주최하고 티켓을 판매하면서
   d. 소설과 에세이를 쓰면서

2. 작가가 재즈 시대를 설명하는 이유는 무엇인가?
   a. 귀족 부부가 좀 더 나은 대우를 받는 것을 설명하기 위한 것
   b. 1920년대는 재치 있고 유명한 사람에게 굉장히 좋은 시대였음을 보여주기 위한 것
   c. 부유함으로 인해 괴짜 같은 사람들이 많이 생겨났음을 설명하기 위한 것
   d. 성공한 소설가들이 얼마나 오만했는지 보여주기 위한 것

3. 작가는 재즈 시대를 어떻게 소개하는가?
   a. 뉴욕시 5번가를 묘사하면서
   b. 피츠제럴드의 처녀작 소설 "태양은 다시 떠오른다"를 소개하면서
   c. 피츠제럴드가 청년 문화에 끼친 영향을 설명하면서
   d. 피츠제럴드의 처녀작 소설 "낙원의 이쪽"을 소개하면서

4. 강의의 일부를 다시 듣고 문제에 답하시오. 이 구절의 기능은 무엇인가?
   a. 1920년대 생기발랄한 한 젊은 부부를 소개하기 위한 것
   b. 1920년대 도금시대에 대한 예를 제시하기 위한 것
   c. 지나친 부유함의 한계를 묘사하기 위한 것
   d. F. 스콧과 아내 젤다를 대비시키기 위한 것

5. 교수에 따르면, 피츠제럴드 부부의 행동을 방종하게 보이게 만드는 두 가지 요소는 무엇인가? 정답 두 개를 고르시오.
   a. 때를 가리지 않고 웃는 것
   b. "5번가" 영화에 대해 악평을 쓴 것
   c. 택시 후드에 올라타는 것
   d. 영화관에서 차분한 모습

6. 작가가 재즈 시대에 대해 암시하는 바는 무엇인가?
   a. 사치스럽게 즐기는 것은 모두가 소망해야 하는 것이다.
   b. 성공이 사치스런 생활방식으로 이어질 수도 있다.
   c. 그들의 삶은 훌륭했고 모두의 귀감이 되었다.
   d. 농담을 듣고 소리 내어 크게 웃는 것은 건강한 행동이다.

Vocabulary Test　　p.98~99

1. 본문의 '인정'과 가장 근접한 의미의 단어는?
   a. 인정　　b. 비난　　c. 책망　　d. 면죄

2. 본문의 '비난'과 가장 근접한 의미의 단어는?
   a. 가망　　b. 친화성　　c. 불화　　d. 비난

3. 본문의 '하룻밤 사이에'와 가장 근접한 의미의 단어는?
   a. 점차　　　　　　　b. 서두를 것 없이
   c. 주저하며　　　　　d. 거의 즉시

4. 본문의 '재치 있는'과 가장 근접한 의미의 단어는?
   a. 느린　　b. 영리한　　c. 저능의　　d. 우둔한

5. 본문의 '불안정한'과 가장 근접한 의미의 단어는?
   a. 안정된　　b. 어지러운　　c. 혼란한　　d. 지적인

6. 본문의 '행동'과 가장 근접한 의미의 단어는?
   a. 굼뜸　　b. 생각　　c. 행동　　d. 주장

7. 본문의 '혼란에 빠뜨리다'와 가장 근접한 의미의 단어는?
   a. 분리시키다　　b. 해체하다　　c. 어지럽히다　　d. 정돈하다

8. 본문의 '사치스럽게'와 가장 근접한 의미의 단어는?
   a. 사치스럽게　　b. 검약하게　　c. 수동적으로　　d. 유순하게

Paraphrasing　　p.99

1. 국왕부처는 소설로뿐만 아니라 난폭한 행동으로도 유명했다.
   a. 그 귀족 커플은 사람들을 환대하는 것으로 매우 유명했다.
   b. 귀족이 된다는 것은 심지어 영국에서 조차도 어려운 일이다.
   c. 피츠제럴드가 여는 파티의 대부분은 혼란하고 흥청망청 거렸다.
   d. 피츠제럴드 부부는 그들이 보인 행동 때문에 유명해졌다.

2. 그들은 택시의 후드에 올라타고 뉴욕의 5번가를 달리며 슬픈 장면에서 박장대소하고 농담에는 소리내어 울어 엉망으로 만들거나 파티에서 취해 요란스럽게 떠들거나 했다.
   a. 그들은 사치스럽고 교양 없게 행동했다.
   b. 택시 위에 올라타는 것은 한 가지 좋은 방법이다. 특히, 택시에 자리가 없을 때는 더욱 그렇다.
   c. 뉴욕시 5번가에서 택시 타기란 힘든 일이다.
   d. 술판이 벌어진 파티에서 사치스럽게 즐기는 것은 흔한 일이었다.

Real Jazzmen

진정한 재즈맨들

「심포닉 재즈」와 1920년대에 재즈로서 통용되었던 대부분 음악은 전혀 진짜 재즈라고 할 수 없었다. 진짜 재즈는 비교적 사람 눈에 띄지 않는 곳에서 만들어지고 있었다. 재즈는 이미 그 발상지인 뉴올리언즈에서 강을 올라갔는데, 여전히 할렘가와 시카고에 있는 흑인전용 댄스홀이나 노골적으로 「흑인 레코드」라고 이름붙여져 흑인가에서만 팔리는 레코드로 주로 들을 수 있었다. 폴 화이트맨 같은 콘서트 주최자가 이류의 재즈 콘서트를 열어서 연간 25만 달러나 벌어들이는 한편, 진짜 재즈맨들은 종종 돈 한 푼 없었다. 위대한 루이 암스트롱도 싸구려 쇼 밴드에서 연주할 수밖에 없었고, 빅스 바이더벡도 화려한 코넷의 음을 삼류 댄스 밴드를 위해 낭비하고 있었다. 진짜 재즈맨들은 짐을 지붕에 동여맨 고물 자동차로 몇 날 며칠을 여행했다. 하지만, 음악가들은 강했고, 그 음악도 강했으며 그것은 시대의 외면을 극복하고 살아남아 미국음악으로서 세계음악에 하나의 성공적인 공헌을 하게 되었다.

Sentence Completion   p.102~103

A. 다음 문장에 가장 알맞은 단어를 고르시오.

1. 만일 당신이 ____ 속에서 산다면, 당신은 비교적 조용하고 사람들의 눈에 띄지 않게 사는 것이다.
   a. 무명
   b. 우울한 시대
   c. 주목
   d. 지하실

2. 어떤 것이 ____ 다면, 분류해서 설명을 붙여놓은 것이다.
   a. 감춰진
   b. 라벨로 분류된
   c. 붙여진
   d. 쓰여 진

3. 당신이 ____ 음악을 작곡한다면, 당신은 매우 재능 있는 작곡가이다.
   a. 화학적
   b. 귀여운
   c. 불협화음의
   d. 교향악의

4. 세련된 매너 때문에 그는 신사로 ____.
   a. 깡충 뛴다
   b. 통한다
   c. 쭈그리고 앉다
   d. 응원한다

5. 만일 당신이 직장 동료에게 ____ 말한다면, 당신은 정직하고 솔직한 것이다.
   a. 종종
   b. 순진하게
   c. 솔직하게
   d. 속이며

B. 다음 문장에 가장 알맞은 단어를 고르시오.

1. 당신이 ____ 차를 탄다면, 여행 중간에 차가 분해돼 버린다고 해도 놀라지 마라.
   a. 금속제의
   b. 고급의
   c. 낡아빠진
   d. BMW

2. 예전엔 일본 자동차들이 ____ 했지만, 지금은 렉서스, 인피니티, 아쿠라 같은 일제차가 고급 차량에 속한다.
   a. 최고의
   b. 하급(저급)의
   c. 사치스런
   d. 최신 유행의

3. 일부 역사학자들은 미국의 ____ 시대가 끝나가고 있다는 사실에 한탄한다.
   a. 우울한
   b. 순식간의
   c. 영광스러운
   d. 가난에 허덕이는

4. 루이 암스트롱은 마침내 재즈를 통해 ____ 이력을 쌓아, 현재는 전 세계적으로 유명한 사람이 되었다.
   a. 하찮은
   b. 성공적인
   c. 지루한
   d. 복귀

5. 경적을 ____ 봤자 아무 소용없다.
   a. 울려(불어)
   b. 당겨
   c. 발산해
   d. 말해

Listening Comprehension   p.104~105

1. 화이트만과 같은 콘서트 주최자가 진정한 재즈인에 비해 유리한 점은 무엇인가?
   a. 그들은 뉴올리언즈 재즈를 홍보했다.
   b. 그들은 앨범을 판매하도록 루이 암스트롱을 격려했다.
   c. 그들은 막대한 돈을 벌기 위해 재즈 콘서트를 제작했다.
   d. 그들은 낡아빠진 고급자동차를 소유했다.

2. 작가가 재즈 아티스트에 대해 설명하는 이유는 무엇인가?
   a. 음악에 대한 미국의 공헌을 설명하기 위한 것
   b. 새로운 음악 시대의 탄생을 보여주기 위한 것
   c. 삼류 댄스 밴드의 조악함을 설명하기 위한 것
   d. 위대한 루이 암스트롱을 선전하기 위한 것

3. 작가는 재즈 아티스트를 어떻게 소개하는가?
   a. 암스트롱의 위대한 업적을 분석하면서
   b. 흑인들이 사는 동네에 대해 이야기하면서
   c. 재즈의 근원인 교향악 재즈에 대해 설명하면서
   d. 관심권 밖에 있는 음악에 대해 설명하면서

4. 강의의 일부를 다시 듣고 문제에 답하시오. 이 구절의 기능은 무엇인가?
   a. 음악과 관련하여, 인종들 간에 차이를 소개하기 위한 것
   b. 재즈인들이 낡아빠진 차량으로 어떻게 여행을 했는지에 대한 예를 제시하기 위한 것
   c. 프로모터가 되는 데 있어 한계를 설명하기 위한 것
   d. 다양한 음악적 장르를 대비시키기 위한 것

5. 교수에 따르면, 최초의 재즈 음악이 연주된, 두 곳은 어디였는가? 정답 두 개를 고르시오.
   a. 신시내티 소재 흑인 댄스 홀
   b. 음침하고 외진 곳에 위치한 공연장
   c. 오래된 시카고 악극 쇼
   d. 할렘에 위치한 흑인 댄스 홀

6. 작가가 재즈 아티스트에 대해 암시하는 바는 무엇인가?
   a. 진정한 음악가는 생계를 꾸려나가기 어렵다.
   b. 재즈가 처음 시작되던 시기는 음악가들에게 힘든 시기였다.
   c. 콘서트 프로모터가 되면 성공한다.
   d. 진짜 음악은 시카고에서 만들어 지고 있었다.

Vocabulary Test   p.106~107

1. 본문의 '교향악의(조화로운)'와 가장 근접한 의미의 단어는?
   a. 지저분한   b. 조화로운
   c. 불협화음의   d. 경이로운

2. 본문의 '통하다'와 가장 근접한 의미의 단어는?
   a. 제공되다   b. 갖추고 있다
   c. 대체되다   d. 간주되다

3. 본문의 '무명'과 가장 근접한 의미의 단어는?
   a. 우울함   b. 중간 상태
   c. 눈부심   d. 익명

4. 본문의 '솔직하게'와 가장 근접한 의미의 단어는?
   a. 자유로이   b. 경솔히 믿고
   c. 정직하게   d. 적절히

5. 본문의 '분류하다'와 가장 근접한 의미의 단어는?
   a. 조종하다   b. 꼬리표를 달다
   c. 인쇄하다   d. 같은 높이로 하다

6. 본문의 '하급의'와 가장 근접한 의미의 단어는?
   a. 내부의   b. 더 못한
   c. 잘 알려진   d. 수치스러운

7. 본문의 '멋진'과 가장 근접한 의미의 단어는?
   a. 악명 높은   b. 밝은   c. 훌륭한   d. 신성한

8. 본문의 '불다'와 가장 근접한 의미의 단어는?
   a. 내파하다   b. 들리다
   c. 울리다   d. 삑소리를 내다

Paraphrasing   p.107

1. 위대한 루이 암스트롱도 싸구려 쇼 밴드에서 연주할 수밖에 없었
   고, 빅스 바이더벡도 화려한 코넷의 음을 삼류 댄스 밴드를 위해
   낭비하고 있었다.
   a. 뭔가 수상쩍은 그 쇼 밴드는 사실 매우 과소평가 된 것이었다.
   b. 암스트롱은 그의 대단한 재능에도 불구하고, 2류 쇼 밴드에
      서 음악을 처음 시작했다.
   c. 빅스 바이더백은 자타가 공인하는 클라리넷 연주자였다.
   d. 코넷음악에 맞춘 노래는 오늘날 존중받는다.

2. 진짜 재즈맨들은 짐을 지붕에 동여맨 고물 자동차로 몇 날 며칠
   을 여행했다.

   a. 진정한 재즈인들은 공연장까지 오래되고 낡은 차로 여행을 했다.
   b. 낡아빠진 차는 특히 악기를 넣어두기 위해 고안된 것이었다.
   c. 진정한 재즈인들은 함께 여행을 하고 모텔에서 머물렀다.
   d. 많은 음악가들이 가장 힘들었던 부분은 힘든 도로 여행이었다.

Unit 13   Soil   p.114

토양

    미국 대평원의 목장과 농지의 표토 상태는 계속 악화되고 있다. 최근 몇 년 사이 가뭄과 강풍을 동반한 심한 폭풍에 의해 토양은 매우 심하게 황폐화 되었다. 가뭄일 때 농가는 작물의 모내기를 삼가는 경향이 있어 그 결과, 토양을 튼튼하게 고정시켜 줄 작물의 뿌리가 부족해 침식을 받기 쉬워진다. 겨울과 봄비에 의한 물의 침식작용은 토지의 손상을 더욱 심화시킨다. 그리고 비가 내리지 않을 경우 유해한 농약 잔류물이 토양에 그대로 남아 있게 된다. 그 레이트 플레인즈 고원지대의 농장과 목장에서는 1930년대의 심한 모래폭풍이 있은 이래로 이 정도로 많은 상층토를 잃은 적이 없었다. 우려해야 할 문제이다.

Sentence Completion   p.110~111

A. 다음 문장에 가장 알맞은 단어를 고르시오.

1. 농부의 농장에 ____ 이/가 있다면, 오랫동안 물이 없었다는 뜻이다.
   a. 벌레   b. 가뭄   c. 홍수   d. 상처 딱지

2. 당신에게 ____ 양의 돈이 있다면, 당신은 돈이 매우 많고 부자이다.
   a. 텅 빈   b. 단순한   c. 상당한   d. 궁핍한

3. 어떤 것의 상태가 ____ 하기 시작한다면, 그것이 부서지고 있다
   는 것이다.
   a. 조립하다   b. 결심하다   c. 악화되다   d. 외치다

4. 당신이 ____ 을/를 파내고 있다면, 당신은 토양의 윗부분을 파
   내고 있는 것이다.
   a. 묘목   b. 표토
   c. 꽃   d. (의료·목재 방부용)크레오소트

5. 당신이 ____ 두통이 있다면, 상태가 매우 심하고 고통스러운 것이다.
   a. 심각한   b. 경미한
   c. 중재 된   d. 고통이 없는

B. 다음 문장에 가장 알맞은 단어를 고르시오.

1. 도둑이 범죄 현장에 총기 ____ 을/를 남겼고, 그것이 경찰의 주요 단서가 되었다.
   a. 물질
   b. 잔여물
   c. 조직
   d. 머리카락 잔재물

2. ____ 의 주요 원인들 가운데 하나는 폭우와 바람, 그리고 진흙 사태이다.
   a. 충치
   b. 녹
   c. 침식
   d. 날씨

3. 그 묘목을 ____ 해봤자 아무 소용없다. 토양이 너무 건조하기 때문이다.
   a. 숙박시키다
   b. 바느질하다
   c. 파다
   d. 심다

4. 보통 그녀는 평생동안 ____ 의 순간을 피하려는 것 같았다.
   a. 명상
   b. 우려(두려움)
   c. 완화
   d. 평정

5. 인도 펀잡 지방의 덥고 건조한 평원에 내리는 비는 일반적으로 ____ 하다.
   a. 풍부
   b. 호우
   c. 부족
   d. 팽창

Listening Comprehension   p.112~113

1. 토양 침식을 악화시킬 수 있는 요인은 무엇인가?
   a. 많은 농작물을 심는 농부들
   b. 우수한 표토 속의 연약한 농작물 뿌리
   c. 화학물질이 가미된 표토
   d. 토양이 약한 상태에서 부는 높은 바람

2. 작가가 토양 침식을 설명하는 이유는 무엇인가?
   a. 농작물 재배할 때 농부들이 겪는 어려움들을 보여주기 위한 것
   b. 동절기 침식을 추정하기 위한 것
   c. 특정 옥수수 농작물의 수확량을 분석하기 위한 것
   d. 강우가 습지대에 어떤 식으로 추가 피해를 입히는지 보여주기 위한 것

3. 작가는 토양 침식을 어떻게 소개하는가?
   a. 농약 속 위험 잔여물을 설명하면서
   b. 텍사스와 알칸사스의 폭풍에 대해 설명하면서
   c. 대평원의 농경 패턴을 고찰하면서
   d. 1930년대 황진지대 당시를 열거하면서

4. 강의의 일부를 다시 듣고 문제에 답하시오. 이 구절의 기능은 무엇인가?
   a. 풍식에 대한 약점을 해결하는 한 가지 대안을 소개하기 위한 것
   b. 바람, 겨울, 봄비에 의한 침식과 관련된 예를 제공하기 위한 것
   c. 일상생활 속에서 사용되는 농약을 설명하기 위한 것
   d. 중서부 지방에서의 산업기술과 농업기술을 대비시키기 위한 것

5. 작가에 따르면, 풍식작용의 원인이 되는 두 가지 요소는 무엇인가? 정답 두 개를 고르시오.
   a. 가뭄에 취약한 농경지
   b. 농경지에 닥친 심한 폭풍
   c. 황진지대의 표토
   d. 품질 낮은 표토 속의 연약한 농작물 뿌리

6. 작가가 토양 침식에 대해 암시하는 바는 무엇인가?
   a. 우리 모두가 음식에 의존하는 이상, 침식 방지는 심각한 문제이다.
   b. 화학물질의 위험 잔여물이 곳곳에 많이 산재해 있다.
   c. 앞으로 수십 년간 강우량 부족현상이 있을 것이다.
   d. 황진지대 이후, 이 정도로 많은 표토 손실을 겪은 적이 없었다.

Vocabulary Test   p.114~115

1. 본문의 '표토'와 가장 근접한 의미의 단어는?
   a. 건조지대
   b. 혼합비료
   c. 표면 토양
   d. 자갈

2. 본문의 '나빠지다'와 가장 근접한 의미의 단어는?
   a. 악화되다
   b. 초래하다
   c. 썩다
   d. 개선되다

3. 본문의 '가뭄'과 가장 근접한 의미의 단어는?
   a. 건조제품
   b. 건조함
   c. 물기
   d. 이슬비

4. 본문의 '심각한'과 가장 근접한 의미의 단어는?
   a. 고집스러운
   b. 심한
   c. 인상적인
   d. 참을 만한

5. 본문의 '상당한'과 가장 근접한 의미의 단어는?
   a. 상당한 규모의
   b. 필수적인
   c. 주요한
   d. 비참한

6. 본문의 '침식'과 가장 근접한 의미의 단어는?
   a. 미쳐 날뜀
   b. 씻겨내려 감
   c. 추방함
   d. 건설함

7. 본문의 '심다'와 가장 근접한 의미의 단어는?
   a. 뽑다
   b. 털다
   c. 깊이 파고들다
   d. 재배하다

8. 본문의 '부족'과 가장 근접한 의미의 단어는?
   a. 풍부
   b. 부족
   c. 풍부
   d. 밀도

Paraphrasing   p.115

1. 가뭄일 때 농가는 작물의 모내기를 삼가는 경향이 있어 그 결과, 토양을 튼튼하게 고정시켜 줄 작물의 뿌리가 부족해 침식을 받기 쉬워진다.

   a. 식물 뿌리 부족으로 인해 풍식작용이 매우 높아진다.
   b. 종종 가뭄 이후에 상당한 강우기 내린디.

c. 비가 너무 많이 내리면 식물들 간의 "경쟁"이 유발된다.
d. 식물 뿌리가 너무 많으면 수원이 고갈된다.

2. 그레이트 플레인즈 고원지대의 농장과 목장에서는 1930년대의 심한 모래폭풍이 있은 이래로 이 정도로 많은 상층토를 잃은 적이 없었다. 우려해야 할 문제이다.

   a. 심지어 1930년 대 보다 더 표토 자원이 감소하고 있다.
   b. 대평원 농부들의 마음속에 우려가 존재한다.
   c. 농장과 목장에서 지나치게 많은 물을 사용한다.
   d. 대평원에서 조차, 표토 자원이 감소 추세다.

Unit 14   Groundwater   p.122

지하수

지하수는 인간이 이용할 수 있는 물의 주된 공급원이고, 죽음의 계곡 사막 아래에서 히말라야 산맥 정상까지 지하의 도처에서 발견되고 있다. 샘과 용수를 통과해 지표까지 올라와 대도시에 물을 공급할 뿐 아니라, 농장과 마을의 생활도 지탱하고 있다. 지하수는 지표의 물이 부족할 때의 중요한 관개 용수도 되므로, 사람들은 그 권리를 둘러싸고 싸우기도 했다. 배어 나와서 샘이 되거나 샘에서 나와 흐르는 이외에 지하수가 사람들의 눈에 띄는 일은 좀처럼 없지만 과학자들은 어디에 얼마나 축적되어 있는지, 얼마나 빨리 이동하고 있는지, 그 물은 어디에서 오는지, 몇 년 뒤에 어디에서 발견될지 등을 추정할 수 있다. 지하수는 매우 중요하므로, 관리·보존하기 위해 몇 백 명이나 되는 과학자들이 지도 작성 작업에 몰두하고 있다.

Sentence Completion   p.118~119

A. 다음 문장에 가장 알맞은 단어를 고르시오.

1. 욕실 수돗물이 ____ 면, 물이 매우 빠르게 흘러나오는 것이다.
   a. 방랑하다   b. 밀어닥치다
   c. 들어 올리다   d. 내던지다

2. 지구의 석유 자원이 ____ 면, 그것은 시추 때문에 고갈되는 것이다.
   a. 부족한   b. 개선되고 있는
   c. 풍부한   d. 반쯤 찬

3. 당신이 ____ 에 오른다면, 당신은 마침내 그것의 정상에 도달한 것이다.
   a. 바닥   b. 봉우리   c. 가장자리   d. 측면

4. 당신을 ____ 사람이 없다면, 당신을 도와줄 사람이 아무도 없다는 것이다.

a. 옮기는   b. 방해하는
c. 제공하는   d. 지탱(지원)해주는

5. 당신이 땅을 파서 ____ 에 도달한다면, 당신이 수원에 닿은 것이다.
   a. 먼지   b. 물방울   c. 지하수   d. 호스

B. 다음 문장에 가장 알맞은 단어를 고르시오.

1. 많은 지도제작자들은 지구 이곳저곳을 여행하면서 새로운 여러 지역의 ____ 일을 한다.
   a. 지도를 만드는   b. 흐리게 하는
   c. 어둡게 하는   d. 진압하는

2. 일상적으로 많은 농부들은 ____ 수로를 채우기 위해, 파이프를 통해 물을 나른다.
   a. 쓰레기   b. 화학물질   c. 관개   d. 오물

3. 갈라진 틈을 통해 ____ 을/를 막기 위해서, 벽에 콘크리트를 메워야 한다.
   a. 모욕하기   b. 감상하기
   c. 충당하기   d. 물의 스며들기

4. 아프리카에서 최근 코끼리와 치타를 보호하기 위한 ____ 노력이 있었다.
   a. 탐욕   b. 포화   c. 야만   d. 보호(관리)

5. 당신이 산악용 자전거 바퀴에 ____ 하면, 공기가 자전거 튜브를 부풀리게 할 것이다.
   a. 타격을 가하다면   b. 빈둥빈둥 보낸다면
   c. 못을 박는다면   d. 펌프질 한다면

Listening Comprehension   p.120~121

1. 왜 어떤 사람들은 지하수에 대한 권리를 둘러싸고 싸움을 하는가?
   a. 물을 대어야 할 농작물이 지나치게 많기 때문에.
   b. 일부 지역 사회에서는 물이 너무 비싸기 때문에.
   c. 사막지역에서의 농촌 생활을 지탱하는데 물은 대단히 중요하다.
   d. 물이 부족한 일부 지역에서는, 농작물을 키우기위해 지하수가 반드시 필요하다.

2. 작가가 지하수 사용을 설명하는 이유는 무엇인가?
   a. 인류의 이용 가능한 물 가운데 대부분은 지표면 아래에서 나오기 때문에
   b. 사람들이 수돗물에 대한 보존을 시작해야한다는 것을 제안하기 위한 것
   c. 지표면 아래, 사막지역 지하에서부터 해안선에 이르는 모든 지역에서 물 사용이 가능하다는 것을 보여주기 위한 것
   d. 관리 개선과 보존을 방해하기 위한 것

3. 작가는 지하수 사용을 어떻게 소개하는가?
   a. 히말라야에 사는 사람들이 어떻게 물을 사용하는지 보여주면서
   b. 관개기술의 진보에 대해 언급하면서
   c. 물이 부족한 상황에서, 미래에 닥칠 가뭄을 예측하면서
   d. 산에서 사막에 이르기까지 지하수를 발견할 수 있는 모든 장소를 설명하면서

4. 강의의 일부를 다시 듣고 문제에 답하시오. 이 구절의 기능은 무엇인가?
   a. 시간을 들여 장소 측량을 하는 과학자들이 수백 명임을 설명하기 위한 것
   b. 지하수 보호가 사회와 우리의 식량자원에 끼치는 중요성을 감안하여, 지하수 보호의 필요성을 제시하기 위한 것
   c. 보존 프로그램의 한계를 설명하기 위한 것
   d. 사막 수원 이용과 산악 수원 이용을 서로 대비시키기 위한 것

5. 작가에 따르면, 지하수 샘과 관련하여 과학자들이 측정하는 두 가지 면은 무엇인가? 정답 두 개를 고르시오.
   a. 지하수의 원래 위치
   b. 지하수가 보존되어 있는 이전 지역들
   c. 지하수의 유속
   d. 죽음의 계곡(데스밸리)에 있는 작은 지역사회들

6. 작가가 지하수 사용에 대해 암시하는 바는 무엇인가?
   a. 관리와 보존 문제는 정부 보조금의 확대가 반드시 있어야 할 사안이다.
   b. 우물이 고갈되는 속도를 예측해야 한다.
   c. 우물의 위치를 측량하는 데 많은 과학자들이 공을 들인다.
   d. 우물이나 샘에서 나오는 지하수를 적절히 사용하는 것이 인류에게 필수 불가결하다.

Vocabulary Test　　　p.122~123

1. 본문의 '봉우리'와 가장 근접한 의미의 단어는?
   a. 곡선　　　b. 측면　　　c. 꼭대기　　　d. 밑바닥

2. 본문의 '밀어닥치다(솟구치다)'와 가장 근접한 의미의 단어는?
   a. 부딪히다　　b. 쇄도하다　　c. 대면하다　　d. 밑줄 긋다

3. 본문의 '지탱하다'와 가장 근접한 의미의 단어는?
   a. 만족시키다　　　　　b. 악화시키다
   c. 개선시키다　　　　　d. 유지시키다

4. 본문의 '부족한'과 가장 근접한 의미의 단어는?
   a. 불충분한　　b. 엄청난　　c. 충분한　　d. 무해한

5. 본문의 '스며들다'와 가장 근접한 의미의 단어는?
   a. 거품이 일다　　　　　b. 스며들다
   c. 잔물결이 일다　　　　d. 울다

6. 본문의 '펌프질 하다'와 가장 근접한 의미의 단어는?
   a. 안으로 넣다　　　　　b. 밖으로 밀어내다
   c. 밀치다　　　　　　　d. 접종하다

7. 본문의 '지도를 만들다'와 가장 근접한 의미의 단어는?
   a. 도표로 만들다　　　　b. 대걸레로 닦다
   c. 조명하다　　　　　　d. 처리하다

8. 본문의 '보존(보호)'과 가장 근접한 의미의 단어는?
   a. 낭비함　　　b. 관찰　　　c. 저장　　　d. 보호

Paraphrasing　　　p.123

1. 배어 나와서 샘이 되거나 샘에서 나와 흐르는 이외에 지하수가 사람들의 눈에 띄는 일은 좀처럼 없지만 과학자들은 어디에 얼마나 축적되어 있는지를 추정할 수 있다.
   a. 과학자들이 물의 흐름을 예측할 수 있지만, 어디로 흘러가는지는 알지 못한다.
   b. 지하수의 양과 수원을 추정하는 것은 중요하다.
   c. 사막의 희박한 샘으로는 농부들이 필요한 물을 대지 못한다.
   d. 특정 지역에는 우물이 풍부하지만, 그 우물을 추출해내는 것은 그것과 별개의 문제이다.

2. 지하수는 매우 중요하므로, 관리·보존하기 위해 몇 백 명이나 되는 과학자들이 지도 작성 작업에 몰두하고 있다.
   a. 지도 제작 프로젝트에 자금조달 확대가 필요하다.
   b. 지하수 지역을 지도로 제작하는 것은 수원 관리에 핵심이다.
   c. 지하수 샘이 위치한 지역을 중앙 데이터베이스에 입력해야 한다.
   d. 과학자들이 작성한 지도는 겹쳐지는 부분이 지나치게 많다.

Unit 15 **Bodywater** p.130

체내 수분

가장 작은 아메바에서 가장 높은 나무까지 모든 종류의 동식물에게 있어 충분한 물의 공급은 필수 불가결이다. 모든 생물의 몸의 약 50%는 물이고, 인간은 체내 수분의 15%를 잃으면 죽고 만다. 물은 체내에서 이산화탄소와 산소, 염분 등 생명유지에 필요한 성분을 녹이고 분배한다. 물은 혈액순환과 노폐물의 제거, 근육을 움직이는 데 빼놓을 수 없다. 물 없이는 인간은 눈을 뜰 수조차 없다. 배설과 증발에 의해 생물이 잃는 수분은 계속 보충되어야만 한다. 이 끝없는 갈증은 생명의 기원이 바다에 있다는 데서 연유한 것으로 생각된다. 인체의 염분농도는 약 0.9%이고, 이 비율은 처음 생물이 바다에서 육지로 올라온 4억 년 전의 해수의 염분농도와 같다고 생화학자들은 믿고 있다. 때문에 어떤 의미에서 인간은 훨씬 옛날에 조상이 진화하는 바탕이 되었던 물을 지금도 체내에 갖고 있다는 얘기가 된다.

Sentence Completion   p.126~127

A. 다음 문장에 가장 알맞은 단어를 고르시오.

1. 과학시간에 _____ (으)로 실험을 하고 있다면, 기본적인 생물형태를 다루고 있는 것이다.
   a. 장난감   b. 유기체   c. 개체   d. 발사체

2. 배달원이 상품을 _____ 면, 그 상품을 목적지 까지 보내는 것이다.
   a. 나누다   b. 구매하다   c. 배달하다   d. 흩뿌리다

3. 프로 농구선수가 되기에 당신 키는 _____ 다.
   a. 박식한   b. 세련된   c. 충분한   d. 세포의

4. 당신의 _____ 장기가 손상이 되면, 중요한 내장이 다친 것이다.
   a. 중요한   b. 외부의   c. 하찮은   d. 부수적인

5. 어떤 것이 액체 속에서 _____ 면, 그 액체 속에 섞이고 있는 중인 것이다.
   a. 응고하다   b. 녹다   c. 해체하다   d. 만들다

B. 다음 문장에 가장 알맞은 단어를 고르시오.

1. 당신이 세계 여행을 _____ 면, 당신은 놀라운 문화를 많이 발견한 것이다.
   a. 삼가 했다   b. 후퇴했다   c. 과감히 했다   d. 주저했다

2. 당신 손의 _____ 을/를 막는다면, 혈액이 더 이상 그곳으로 흐르지 않을 것이다.
   a. 땀샘   b. 신경   c. 항로   d. 순환

3. 16킬로를 기진맥진한 상태로 달리고 나서, 물에 대한 그녀의 _____ 이/가 엄청나게 커졌다.
   a. 갈증   b. 땀   c. 고통   d. 혐오

4. 대부분 고대 _____ 가운데 지하수를 찾아내는데 굉장히 능했던 사람들도 있었다.
   a. 조력자들   b. 지인들   c. 조상들   d. 친구들

5. 얼룩말을 가지고 놀라운 화학적 연구를 실시한 _____ 이/가 한 명있다.
   a. 경리부장   b. 생화학자   c. 안무가   d. 언론인

Listening Comprehension   p.128~129

1. 신체는 어떤 중요 요소들을 전달하는가?
   a. 질소, 산소, 혈장
   b. 이산화탄소, 산소, 염분
   c. 일산화탄소, 산소, 염분
   d. 이산화탄소, 유황, 염분

2. 작가가 물의 기능에 대해 설명하는 이유는 무엇인가?
   a. 충분한 물 공급이 모든 동·식물에게 중요하다는 것을 설명하기 위한 것
   b. 유기체는 배변을 통해 물의 50%를 버린다는 것을 추정하기 위한 것
   c. 신체가 중요 요소들을 전달하고, 혈액을 순환시키고, 노폐물을 제거할 때, 수분이 절대적으로 필요하다는 것을 설명하기 위한 것
   d. 염분 수치가 혈액순환에 중요하다는 것을 설명하기 위한 것

3. 작가는 물의 기능을 어떻게 소개하는가?
   a. 물은 미세한 아메바에서부터 키 큰 나무에 이르기 까지, 모든 유기체에게 중요한 요소다.
   b. 물은 모든 생물체의 60%를 차지한다.
   c. 물은 거대 포유류와 동물군을 제외한 모든 유기체에게 중요하다.
   d. 인간은 그들의 조상이 갖고 있던 물을 여전히 체내에 갖고 있다.

4. 강의의 일부를 다시 듣고 문제에 답하시오. 이 구절의 기능은 무엇인가?
   a. 인간의 신체가 중요 영양분을 어떤 식으로 보충하는지 소개하기 위한 것
   b. 인간 체내의 염분 농도를 조사하기 위한 것
   c. 물이 생물에게 필수적임을 확실히 밝히기 위한 것
   d. 증발 이후, 증발된 부분이 어떤 식으로 계속해서 보충될 수 있는지를 대비시키기 위한 것

5. 작가에 따르면, 신체에서 빠져나가는 두 가지 요소는 무엇인가? 정답 두 개를 고르시오.

a. 근육 조직

b. 배설물

c. 질소

d. 증발

6. 작가가 물의 기능에 대해 암시하는 바는 무엇인가?
   a. 물은 혈액 세포 다음으로 가장 중요하다.
   b. 물이 없으면, 인간은 눈조차 뜰 수 없다.
   c. 모든 생물은 본질적으로 체내 수분과 영양분을 토대로 기능한다.
   d. 인류 조상들로부터 내려오는 물은 우리 생존에 기여한다.

Vocabulary Test   p.130~131

1. 본문의 '충분한'와 가장 근접한 의미의 단어는?
   a. 유용한   b. 부족한   c. 평균 이하의   d. 충분한

2. 본문의 '매우 중요한'와 가장 근접한 의미의 단어는?
   a. 이용할 수 없는   b. 전형적인
   c. 필수적인   d. 불필요한

3. 본문의 '유기체'와 가장 근접한 의미의 단어는?
   a. 종료   b. 건달   c. 포유류   d. 생물

4. 본문의 '녹다'와 가장 근접한 의미의 단어는?
   a. 녹다   b. 논박하다   c. 합병하다   d. 사라지다

5. 본문의 '배달하다'와 가장 근접한 의미의 단어는?
   a. 동반하다   b. 배달하다   c. 가져가다   d. 회수하다

6. 본문의 '순환'와 가장 근접한 의미의 단어는?
   a. 흐름   b. 행로   c. 분할   d. 할당

7. 본문의 '갈증'와 가장 근접한 의미의 단어는?
   a. 만족   b. 건조한 상태   c. 반감   d. 만족

8. 본문의 '조상'와 가장 근접한 의미의 단어는?
   a. 후손   b. 후임자   c. 선조   d. 후손

Paraphrasing   p.131

1. 배설과 증발에 의해 생물이 잃는 수분은 계속 보충되어야만 한다.

   a. 일단 유기체가 복제되면, 수분이 보충되어야 한다.
   b. 수분 상실은 대부분의 유기체에 흔한 일이다.
   c. 지나치게 많은 수분이 보충되는 것은 유기체 발달에 해롭다.
   d. 배설을 통해 잃은 수분은 보충되어야 한다.

2. 때문에 어떤 의미에서 인간은 훨씬 옛날에 조상이 진화하는 바탕이 되었던 물을 지금도 체내에 갖고 있다는 얘기가 된다.

a. 조상이 진화할 때, 그들이 그렇게 크게 변할 가능성은 거의 없다.

b. 본질적으로, 인간의 체내 수분은 그들 조상으로 거슬러 올라간다.

c. 우리 조상에게 있던 지나치게 많은 수분은 배출되어야 했다.

d. 조상들의 진화는 아주 오래 전 일이라, 지금 그들로부터 남겨진 것은 아무 것도 없다.

Unit 16   Machine (1)   p.138

기계 (1)

증기력시대는 제임스 와트와 함께 시작되었다고 일반적으로 생각되고 있지만, 증기력을 이용한 기술의 역사는 실제로는 훨씬 전으로 거슬러 올라간다. 고대 그리스에는 알렉산드리아의 헤론이 증기의 힘으로 움직이는 자동문 등의 장치에 관해 썼으며 수 세기가 지난 후에 갈릴레오, 토리첼리, 드 코가 증기 기술의 기본원리를 정했다. 그들이 17세기에 발견한 것으로, 물은 끓으면 증기로 바뀐다. 이 과정에서 증기는 팽창하고 1ℓ의 물이 약 1600ℓ의 증기를 생산할 수 있다. 그들은 또한 이 변화로 인해 엄청난 힘이 생성된다는 사실도 발견했다. 생성된 증기는 주전자의 뚜껑을 들어 올릴 뿐 아니라, 증기를 가두고 있는 보일러까지 날려 보낼 수 있다. 그리고 증기를 식히면 물로 돌아가는데 이 처리를 밀폐용기 안에서 하면 진공상태가 된다는 것도 발견했다.

Sentence Completion   p.134~135

A. 다음 문장에 가장 알맞은 단어를 고르시오.

1. 당신이 _____ 을/를 소유하고 있다면, 그것은 기계 장치 또는 기계이다.
   a. 회의   b. 개념   c. 기계   d. 확정

2. 당신이 어떤 과학적 _____ 을/를 읽는다면, 당신은 결론을 읽는 것이다.
   a. 문제들   b. 도입부   c. 연구결과   d. 신체

3. 당신이 많은 전자 _____ 을/를 소유하고 있다면, 당신은 얼리어답터(남들보다 신제품을 빨리 구입해서 써야 직성이 풀리는 소비자군)일 가능성이 높다.
   a. 데스크탑 컴퓨터   b. 고전작품
   c. 냉장고   d. 기계

4. 연필은 _____ 사용되는 용구이다.
   a. 멋지게   b. 회만저으로
   c. 괴롭히며   d. 일반적으로

5. 얼음은 녹아서 물로 ____.
   a. 변한다   b. 혁신한다
   c. 다시 배치한다   d. 옮긴다

B. 다음 문장에 가장 알맞은 단어를 고르시오.

1. 그 동물들은 새장 안에 ____ 있었다.
   a. 재생되어   b. 방해되어   c. 갇혀   d. 고무되어

2. 여성은 모든 직종의 99%에서 남성만큼이나 ____ 다.
   a. 양육하는   b. 미숙한   c. 무력한   d. 능력 있는

3. 그것은 지금까지 내가 읽어본 것들 가운데 17세기 중반 유럽에 관한 묘사가 가장 ____ 다.
   a. 멋진   b. 맛있는   c. 돈이 벌리는   d. 비싼

4. 만일 우리 사회가 혹시라도 디지털 방식이 아닌 전화기와 아날로그식 TV 사용으로 ____ 면, 끔찍할 것이다.
   a. 앞으로 도약하다   b. 진보하다
   c. 해방시키다   d. 되돌아가다

5. 30초 후에 폭탄이 ____.
   a. 나사를 돌렸다   b. 폭파했다
   c. 격투했다   d. 움켜쥐었다

Listening Comprehension   p.136~137

1. 그리스에서 어떤 발명품이 고안되었나?
   a. 팽창 기계
   b. 문을 여는 기계
   c. 강제로 문을 여는 병렬 장비
   d. 증기로 작동하는 문 폐쇄기

2. 작가가 증기 기계를 설명하는 이유는 무엇인가?
   a. 이탈리아 국민들이 토리첼리로 인해 얼마나 자긍심을 갖게 되었는지를 보여주기 위한 것
   b. 오늘날 증기력 사용을 평가하기 위한 것
   c. 증기력의 기본원리와 역사를 보여주기 위한 것
   d. 히로와 와트의 설명에 있어 그 패턴을 설명하기 위한 것

3. 작가는 증기 기계를 어떻게 소개하는가?
   a. 발명가인 히로에 대한 일반적 생각을 이야기하면서
   b. 발명가인 와트에 대한 일반적 생각을 논의하면서
   c. 물과 이온이 자연 상태로 되돌아가야 한다는 점을 제기하면서
   d. 증기와 하이브리드 배터리의 원리를 보여주면서

4. 강의의 일부를 다시 듣고 문제에 답하시오. 이 구절의 기능은 무엇인가?
   a. 증기가 300년 전보다 어떻게 보다 효율성이 높아졌는지에 대해 소개하기 위한 것
   b. 제임스 와트의 실패에 대한 예를 제시하기 위한 것

   c. 300년이 넘는 기간 동안, 증기가 인류와 어떤 식으로 함께 해 왔는지 소개하기 위한 것
   d. 보일러와 전기 토스터기의 위험을 대비시키기 위한 것

5. 교수에 따르면, 보일러 폭발에 원인이 되는 두 가지 요소는 무엇인가? 정답 두 개를 고르시오.
   a. 배출구가 없는 상태에서 증기 팽창
   b. 장기간 가둬 둔 증기
   c. 결함이 있는 보일러 뚜껑
   d. 짧은 시간 동안 가둬 둔 증기

6. 작가가 증기 기계에 대해 암시하는 바는 무엇인가?
   a. 1,600 리터의 증기를 생산하기 위해서는 깨끗한 물이 필요하다.
   b. 수 세기 전, 증기 기계는 단순하지만 기발한 생각이었다.
   c. 갈릴레오와 토리첼리는 그들의 설계를 완성하기 위해 최선을 다하지 않았다.
   d. 1/1,600리터의 비율로, 증기는 에너지 효율이 매우 높다.

Vocabulary Test   p.138~139

1. 본문의 '일반적으로'와 가장 근접한 의미의 단어는?
   a. 이해하듯이   b. 기묘하게   c. 대개   d. 드물게

2. 본문의 '기계'와 가장 근접한 의미의 단어는?
   a. 도구   b. PDA
   c. 문방구   d. 홀마크(증명서)

3. 본문의 '고안물'과 가장 근접한 의미의 단어는?
   a. 중재   b. 장비   c. 가둬두기   d. 귀공자

4. 본문의 '연구결과(발견물)'와 가장 근접한 의미의 단어는?
   a. 발견   b. 판결   c. 구하기   d. 평결

5. 본문의 '변환하다'와 가장 근접한 의미의 단어는?
   a. 반대로 하다   b. 변형시키다
   c. 결합시키다   d. 고정시키다

6. 본문의 '할 수 있는'과 가장 근접한 의미의 단어는?
   a. 무능한   b. 활성이 없는
   c. 재능이 있는   d. 할 수 있는

7. 본문의 '굉장히 멋진'과 가장 근접한 의미의 단어는?
   a. 필수적인   b. 놀라운
   c. 편재해 있는   d. 무시무시한

8. 본문의 '폭파하다'와 가장 근접한 의미의 단어는?
   a. 말다툼하다   b. 경적을 울리다
   c. 폭발하다   d. 팽창하다

1. 수 세기가 지난 후에 갈릴레오, 토리첼리, 드 코가 증기 기술의 기본원리를 정했다.

    a. 갈릴레오와 토리첼리는 증기 융합의 기본 개념을 개선시켰다.
    b. 증기 파이프 속으로 공기를 응축시킬 수 없다.
    c. 그 세 사람이 증기의 기본 개념들을 발견해 냈다.
    d. 갈릴레오와 드 코가 증기의 원리들을 개선시켰다.

2. 그들이 17세기에 발견한 것으로 물은 끓으면 증기로 바뀌고, 이 과정에서 증기는 팽창한다.

    a. 증기의 포화점은 37분 동안 끓은 이후다.
    b. 17세기에, 증기를 이용하기 위해 물 사용이 좀 더 용이했다.
    c. 보일러 속에 물이 지나치게 많으면, 증기로 변환될 수 없다.
    d. 물을 증기로 변환시키는 것은 17세기에 발견된 것이었다.

Unit 17   Machine (2)   p.146

기계 (2)

조립라인은 1913년에 헨리포드의 자동차 공장에서 탄생했다. 찰스 E(주철의 찰리) 소렌슨과 다른 현장 전문가의 도움으로, 포드는 조립라인을 오늘날까지도 사용하는 형태로 발전시켰다. 최초의 조립라인으로 만들어진 차는, 역사상 유명한 모델 T이다. 규격화된 교환 가능한 약 5000개의 부품으로 만들어진 이 차는 어떤 색으로도 변형이 가능했다. 「그것이 검은 색인 한은」이라고 포드는 말했다. 포드의 조립라인의 제1원칙은 공장 근로자가 일을 하기 위해 이동하는 것이 아니라 해야할 일이 근로자 쪽으로 이동하는 것이었다. 다른 기본 원칙은 불가피하지 않은 이상, 근로자는 한걸음 이상 움직일 필요가 없고 몸을 굽히고 일을 할 필요도 없다는 것이었다.

A. 다음 문장에 가장 알맞은 단어를 고르시오.

1. ____ 궁전이 있다면, 그것은 매우 오래되거나 역사적으로 중요하다는 의미이다.
    a. 개척적인   b. 두드러진   c. 역사적인   d. 학구적인

2. 만일 당신이 ____ 부품을 가지고 기계를 만든다면, 그 부품들은 다른 모델이나 브랜드에서도 작동(사용)될 것이다.
    a. 마시기에 알맞은   b. 양립할 수 없는
    c. 호환할 수 있는   d. 수송할 수 있는

3. 당신이 ____ 을/를 고용한다면, 당신은 특정한 일을 할 수 있는 훈련된 사람들을 고용하는 것이다.
    a. 아마추어   b. 신참자   c. 좌익   d. 전문가

4. 당신이 ____ 을/를 따라 일한다면, 당신은 한 줄로 서서 어떤 것들을 조립하는 것이다.
    a. 조립라인   b. 행렬   c. 본선   d. 송전선

5. ____ 방식들이 있다면, 그것들은 여타의 다른 곳에서도 그것을 똑같이 따라 하는 것이다.
    a. 다양한   b. 규격이 통일된
    c. 우연한   d. 비효율적인

B. 다음 문장에 가장 알맞은 단어를 고르시오.

1. 당신의 자녀가 어두운 골목이나, 낯선 사람들이 숨어있을 지도 모를 어떤 "위험한" 장소들을 ____ 하도록 하십시오.
    a. 피하다   b. 자주 가다
    c. 잡아채다   d. 큰 걸음으로 걷다

2. 그는 최근 능력 밖의 것을 요하는 ____ 을/를 떠맡고, 일에 대한 걱정으로 밤에 잠을 이루지 못한다.
    a. 기회   b. 일   c. 변화   d. 독창력

3. ____ 을/를 따르지 않으려 해봤자 아무 소용없다. 너의 상관이 너에게 큰 소리를 낼 것이기 때문이다.
    a. 규칙   b. 헌법   c. 조롱   d. 설명

4. 만일 너무 많이 ____ 하면, 당신은 결국 허리가 상하게 될 지도 모른다.
    a. 직립하다   b. 허리를 구부리다(웅크리다)
    c. 떨어뜨리다   d. 번갈아 하다

5. ____ 피할 수 있다면, "때를 벗기지 말라"는 것이지, "목욕을 하지 말라"는 것은 아니다.
    a. 터무니 없이   b. 지나치게   c. 무한히   d. 어떻게든

---

1. 소렌슨의 별명은 무엇을 본따 지어진 것인가?
    a. 철공의 기계   b. 일부 알루미늄
    c. 일부 뜨거운 주철   d. 연극에 출연하는 몇몇 배역

2. 작가가 조립라인을 설명하는 이유는 무엇인가?
    a. 모델 F가 어떻게 만들어졌는지를 보여주기 위한 것
    b. 산업이 어떻게 현대화되었는지를 보여주기 위한 것
    c. 일본이 그들의 자동차 산업을 현대화시키는 것을 도와주기 위한 것
    d. 산업 효율성의 패턴을 보여주기 위한 것

3. 작가는 조립라인을 어떻게 소개하는가?
   a. 어떻게 포드와 소렌슨이 조립라인을 만들었는지를 언급하면서
   b. 미시건에 있는 조립라인들을 평가하면서
   c. 직원들 휴식시간을 예측하면서
   d. 5000개의 독특한 부품들에 대해 언급하면서

4. 강의의 일부를 다시 듣고 문제에 답하시오. 이 구절의 기능은 무엇인가?
   a. 자동차 생산에 관련한 대안을 소개하기 위한 것
   b. 포드가 어떤 식으로 일을 직원에게 할당했는지를 보여주기 위한 것
   c. 조립라인의 한계를 설명하기 위한 것
   d. 생산 전문가의 방식들을 대비시키기 위한 것

5. 교수에 따르면, 헨리 포드가 조립라인에서 실시한 두 가지 규칙은 무엇인가? 정답 두 개를 고르시오.
   a. 한 걸음 이상 걸음을 떼지 마라.
   b. 화장실을 너무 많이 가지 마라.
   c. 허리를 구부려서 물건을 집지 마라.
   d. 두 개 중 하나는 검은 차로 만들어라.

6. 작가가 조립라인에 대해 암시하는 바는 무엇인가?
   a. 직원들의 요통 문제를 해결에 있어 큰 진보가 있었다.
   b. 직원들은 공장 작업장에서 마땅히 더 많이 움직일 수 있어야 한다.
   c. 이제 로봇이 사용되고 있어서, 조립라인은 구식이 되었다.
   d. 자동차 공장을 합리적으로 개선하는데 큰 진보가 있었다.

Vocabulary Test   p.146~147

1. 본문의 '조립라인'과 가장 근접한 의미의 단어는?
   a. 발명 라인   b. 집회 라인
   c. 생산 라인   d. 배관망 라인

2. 본문의 '전문가'와 가장 근접한 의미의 단어는?
   a. 전문가   b. 금광꾼
   c. 변호사   d. 컨설턴트(상담역)

3. 본문의 '역사적인'과 가장 근접한 의미의 단어는?
   a. 중요한   b. 거대한   c. 애처로운   d. 치명적인

4. 본문의 '호환할 수 있는'과 가장 근접한 의미의 단어는?
   a. 서투른   b. 양립할 수 없는
   c. 열릴 수 있는   d. 바꿀 수 있는

5. 본문의 '일(임무)'과 가장 근접한 의미의 단어는?
   a. 기계   b. 도구   c. 일   d. 가루반죽

6. 본문의 '규칙'과 가장 근접한 의미의 단어는?
   a. 책임   b. 처벌   c. 믿음   d. 원칙

7. 본문의 '어떻게든'과 가장 근접한 의미의 단어는?
   a. (실제는 어떻든)보기에   b. 있음직하지 않게
   c. 전에   d. 때때로

8. 본문의 '피하다'와 가장 근접한 의미의 단어는?
   a. 구별하다   b. 대면하다   c. 피하다   d. 반박하다

Paraphrasing   p.147

1. 규격화된 교환 가능한 약 5000개의 부품으로 만들어진 이 차는 어떤 색으로도 변형이 가능했다. 「그것이 검은 색인 한은」이라고 포드는 말했다.
   a. 자동차는 여러 가지 호환할 수 있는 많은 구조로 이루어져 있다.
   b. 포드는 호환할 수 있는 부품을 레인보우 색으로 만들었다.
   c. 포드 자동차는 검정 색으로만 주문 받을 수 있었고, 들어가는 부품도 많았다.
   d. 레인보우는 포드 자동차의 색상과 관련한 정책에서 기본이었다.

2. 포드의 조립라인의 제1원칙은 공장 근로자가 일을 하기 위해 이동하는 것이 아니라 해야할 일이 근로자 쪽으로 이동하는 것이었다.
   a. 포드 자동차의 구성은 크라이슬러의 구성을 이길 만큼 강하지 않다.
   b. 일을 직원에게 가져다주는 방식은 가장 효율적인 전략이었다.
   c. 효율성이 지나치면 직원은 나태해지고, 일도 서툴러지게 된다.
   d. 감독자들에게 각종 임무들을 가져다주는 것이 주요 책무였다.

Unit 18   Flying Machine   p.154

비행기

1903년에는 거의 아무도 인간이 하늘을 날으리라고는 믿지 않았다. 그런데 적어도 두 남자는 달랐다. 1903년 12월, 노스 캐롤라이나주 키티호크의 사막에서 라이트 형제 오빌과 윌버는 「비행기계」의 최종점검을 하고 있었다. 오하이오주 데이톤에 있는 자신들의 자전거가게에서 조립하여 테스트 비행을 위해 키티호크로 운반해 온 것이다. 오빌은 성공을 확신하고, 데이톤에 있는 아버지에게 절대 비밀로 하라고 전보를 쳤다. 그리고 12월 17일, 정말 갑자기 그것은 이루어졌다. 형제는 얄팍하고 볼품없는 기계를 조종하여 몇 번이나 아슬아슬한 비행을 계속했다. 가장 긴 비행은 59초동안 계속됐고 852피트(약244m)를 날았다. 이튿날 이것을 기사로 실은 신문은 미국 전역에서 불과 두 신문뿐이었다. 1908년에 형제가 그들 비행기의 개량형으로 정부관리에게 시범을 보이고야 비로소 세계인들은 인간이 정말로 하늘을 난다는 사실을 알게 되었다.

A. 다음 문장에 가장 알맞은 단어를 고르시오.

1. 당신이 어떤 일을 하도록 누군가 ____ 중이라면, 그들은 당신에게 그것을 하도록 요구하는 중인 것이다.
   a. 권하고 있는   b. 후원하고 있는
   c. 방해하고 있는   d. 진정시키고 있는

2. ____ 건물과 튼튼한 건물을 구분하는 것은 쉽다. 가령, 움푹 들어간 문, 위태로운 바닥, 그리고 휘어진 벽들이 그것을 보여준다.
   a. 내구성 있는   b. 견고한
   c. 약한   d. 튼튼한

3. 프로젝트에 당신이 마지막 ____ 을/를 한다면, 당신은 지금 그것을 끝 마치고 있는 중이다.
   a. 시작   b. 손질
   c. 순간   d. 양조주(음료)

4. 당신의 조부모께서 과거에 ____ 을/를 보냈다면, 그들은 2차 세계대전 이전에 살았던 것이다.
   a. 텔레파시   b. 케이블 카   c. 전보   d. 이메일

5. 만일 당신이 친구들 간에 ____ 을/를 지킬 수 있다면, 관계가 좋아질 것이다.
   a. 긴장   b. 적개심   c. 비밀   d. 침묵

B. 다음 문장에 가장 알맞은 단어를 고르시오.

1. 라이트 형제는 비행이 사실상 가능하다는 것을 인류 전체에게 ____ 하기 위해서 노력했다.
   a. 보여주다   b. 발굴하다   c. 발전시키다   d. 보류하다

2. 그 건물은 너무 ____ 해서 과거에 아무도 감히 거기에 머물려고 하지 않았을 것이다.
   a. 튼튼한   b. 실직적인
   c. 편리한   d. 날림으로 지은

3. 어떤 것이 ____ 면, 고르거나 수평이 아니라는 것이다.
   a. 고정된   b. 불안정한
   c. 환영하는   d. 고전하는

4. 만일 우리의 환경이 파괴되고 있다는 사실을 우리가 ____ 면, 우리가 환경을 구할 수 있을 지도 모른다.
   a. 비틀거리다   b. 자각하다
   c. 기뻐하다   d. 부인하다

5. 부족간 충돌과 내전으로 인해 많은 아프리카 국가들 간에 ____ 평화가 없다.
   a. 변덕스러운   b. 지속적인   c. 임시변통의   d. 소유의

1. 오빌은 아버지에게 무엇을 보냈는가?
   a. 전신부호
   b. 비밀을 설명하는 전보
   c. 정부 관계자 앞으로 보내는 서한
   d. 부실한 글라이더에 대해 알려주는 전보

2. 작가가 라이트 형제를 설명하는 이유는 무엇인가?
   a. 유인 비행은 어렵지만, 불가능하지는 않다는 것을 보여주기 위한 것
   b. 노스 캐롤라이나가 테스트 비행할 준비가 된 것을 보여주기 위한 것
   c. 오빌이 성공을 지나치게 확신했다는 것에 대해 설명하기 위한 것
   d. 어떤 공학 관련 업적도 모두 가능하다는 것을 보여주기 위한 것

3. 작가는 라이트 형제를 어떻게 소개하는가?
   a. 오빌의 엄마가 가졌던 의심을 설명하면서
   b. "하늘을 나는 기계"가 실패했다는 것을 보여주면서
   c. 다른 이들이 가졌던 여러 의심들을 보여주면서
   d. 조악하게 만들어진 비행기에 대해 설명하면서

4. 강의의 일부를 다시 듣고 문제에 답하시오. 이 구절의 기능은 무엇인가?
   a. 공적인 항공 정책에 대한 한 가지 대안을 소개하기 위한 것
   b. 오하이오에 있는 불안정한 항공기에 대한 예를 제시하기 위한 것
   c. 어떻게 두 남자가 다른 이들의 의심을 극복했는지를 설명하기 위한 것
   d. 비행 센터로서 오하이오와 노스 캐롤라이나를 대비시키기 위한 것

5. 교수에 따르면, Kitty Hawk 비행 소식이 일반에게 널리 공개될 수 있었던 두 가지 요소는 무엇인가?
   a. 정부의 시험 비행 주문
   b. 미국 정부에게 증명해 보여줌
   c. 라이트 형제들의 구매 권유
   d. 1908년 이후 늘어난 뉴스

6. 작가가 라이트 형제에 대해 암시하는 바는 무엇인가?
   a. 중력의 법칙이 비행 조종사들에게는 불리하게 작용한다.
   b. 인간의 비행 능력을 의심하는 것은 어리석다는 것
   c. 나무 비행기를 업그레이드한 비행기들이 지금은 인기다.
   d. 하늘을 날려는 시도조차 위험했다는 것

1. 본문의 '손질' 과 가장 근접한 의미의 단어는?
   a. 계획   b. (손·연장의)한 번 놀리기
   c. 감각   d. 비행

2. 본문의 '전보'와 가장 근접한 의미의 단어는?
   a. 전보   b. 이메일
   c. 메신저   d. 타이포그래피

3. 본문의 '권하다'와 가장 근접한 의미의 단어는?
   a. 낙담시키다   b. 협박하다   c. 경멸하다   d. 권고하다

4. 본문의 '비밀'과 가장 근접한 의미의 단어는?
   a. 기밀   b. 명상   c. 속보   d. 장엄

5. 본문의 '약한'과 가장 근접한 의미의 단어는?
   a. 가능한   b. 현란한
   c. 부서지기 쉬운   d. 무시무시한

6. 본문의 '날림으로 지은'과 가장 근접한 의미의 단어는?
   a. 튼튼한   b. 거짓의
   c. 견고하지 않은   d. 압제적인

7. 본문의 '불안정한'과 가장 근접한 의미의 단어는?
   a. 견고한   b. 위태위태한   c. 민감한   d. 안정된

8. 본문의 '계속하다'와 가장 근접한 의미의 단어는?
   a. 줄이다   b. 부족하다   c. 평가하다   d. 계속하다

Paraphrasing   p.155

1. 형제는 알팍하고 볼품없는 기계를 조종하여 몇번이나 아슬아슬한 비행을 계속했다. 가장 긴 비행은 59초동안 계속됐고 852피트(약 244m)를 날았다.

   a. 그 두 형제는 그들이 손수 제작한 것을 타고 용케 852 피트를 날았다.
   b. 따뜻한 공기는 비행기가 더 오랫동안 뜰 수 있도록 해준다.
   c. 새로 제작된 비행기는 종종 지나치게 많은 오버스티어(조종 핸들이 많이 꺾이는 것)를 야기한다.
   d. 그 형제는 종종 그들의 비행기를 꺼내 와서 불안정한 비행을 했다.

2. 이튿날 이것을 기사로 실은 신문은 미국 전역에서 불과 두 신문 뿐이었다.

   a. 그 짧은 비행에 관심을 보이는 TV보도가 너무나 많았다.
   b. 미국 언론은 하늘을 나는 기계에 대해 너무나 흥분했다.
   c. 그 놀라운 비행에 관심을 갖는 뉴스 기사는 거의 없었다.
   d. 그 비행이 휴일에 이루어져서, 두 개의 신문만이 그 소식을 전했다.

Unit 19   Mars   p.162

화성

큰 솥 같은 금성은 지구와 가장 가까운 행성이고, 화성은 지구와 가장 흡사한 행성이다. 화성에는 얼음의 결정, 즉 생명에 필요한 얼음물을 포함하는 얇고 차가운 대기가 있다. NASA의 우주선인 바이킹 1호와 바이킹 2호가 촬영한 섬뜩한 사진들이 한 때 화성에도 물이 있었을지 모른다는 설을 뒷받침하고 있다. 몇억 년 전에 화성은 강과 바다가 있는 온난한 세계였으며, 선진 문명이 있었을지도 모른다고 추측하는 사람들까지 있었다. 그러나 현재의 화성에는 복잡한 생명체의 존재를 나타내는 흔적이 없다. 화성에 무슨 일이 일어났는가? 실제로 화성인은 존재했는가? 과학자들은 화성이 어떤 자연의 대이변에 의해 희생된 것이 아닌가 추측하고 있다. 그렇지 않으면 화성인들이 동족끼리의 전쟁으로 서로를 파괴했을까? 이러한 의문점들에 대한 해답은 21세기 초로 예정되어 있는 유인 화성탐사계획을 기다려야 얻을 수 있을 것이다.

Sentence Completion   p.158~159

A. 다음 문장에 가장 알맞은 단어를 고르시오.

1. 당신이 소금 ____ 을/를 만들려 한다면, 물을 약 140도 까지 끓여야 한다.
   a. 콘플레이크   b. 이온   c. 결정체   d. 단백질

2. ____ 을/를 가지고 있다는 것과 특정 믿음에 대해 뒷받침할 만한 증거가 있는 것은 전혀 별개이다.
   a. 이론   b. 선언   c. 비준   d. 조리법

3. 만일 당신 차의 ____ 이/가 다른 차와 지나치게 가깝다면, 사고가 있을지 모른다.
   a. 볼륨   b. 근접성   c. 다수   d. 냄새

4. 당신이 어떤 것을 ____ 에 넣고 요리한다면, 당신은 일종의 큰 냄비를 사용하고 있는 것이다.
   a. 솥   b. 머그컵   c. 국자   d. 뚜껑

5. 이 나라에서는 대학 학위를 위해 영어가 일반적으로 하나의 ____ 이다.
   a. 화장품   b. 필수 조건   c. 관습   d. 변명

B. 다음 문장에 가장 알맞은 단어를 고르시오.

1. 만일 ____ 이/가 있다면, 우리나라의 미래가 위험에 처할 지도 모른다.
   a. 평온함   b. 격변   c. 흔적   d. 풍족

2. 그는 그 ____ 문제들을 풀 수 없다고 고백했다.
   a. 골절된   b. 수많은
   c. 느긋한   d. 구부러지지 않는

3. 가장 놀라운 ____ 가운데 하나는 분명 페르시아 제국일 것이다.
   a. 종교   b. 군   c. 문명   d. 철학

4. 전에 ____ 쇼는 연기자의 개인적인 문제로 인해 연기되었다.
   a. 추산된   b. 규제가 풀린 c. 망쳐진   d. 예정된

5. 그는 화성에 생명체가 있다고 ____.
   a. 추측했다   b. 음모를 꾸몄다
   c. 분열시켰다   d. 계획했다

Listening Comprehension   p.160~161

1. 화성에 생명체가 살 수 있는가?
   a. 바이킹 우주선에서 찍어 온 사진들은 아무 것도 증명하지 못한다.
   b. 지구와 근접해 있기 때문에, 화성에 생명체가 있을 수도 있다.
   c. 현재, 화성에 어떤 복잡한 생명체가 있다는 증거가 있다.
   d. 지금은 아니지만, 원시적인 형태의 생명체가 예전에는 일부 존재했을 수도 있다.

2. 작가는 왜 화성에 생명체가 있었을 지도 모른다고 생각하는가?
   a. 바이킹의 탐사처럼 더 많은 우주비행선을 보내는 것은 좋은 생각이다.
   b. (생명에 필요한) 물이 화성에 있다는 것은 단지 이론에 불과하다.
   c. 얼음 결정체로 가득한 화성의 대기는 물을 야기할 수도 있고, 또한 기본적인 삶을 가능하게 할 수도 있다.
   d. 미래에 과학자들은 화성으로 돌아가야 한다.

3. 작가는 화성의 생명체를 어떻게 소개하는가?
   a. 중력의 법칙을 설명하면서
   b. 화성이 지구와 비슷하기 때문에, 생명을 지탱해주는 비슷한 환경이 화성에 조성될 수도 있다.
   c. 우주선을 화성에 보내는 데 얼마의 비용이 드는 지를 예측하면서
   d. 화성에 존재하는 복잡한 생명체에 대해 언급하면서

4. 강의의 일부를 다시 듣고 문제에 답하시오. 이 구절의 기능은 무엇인가?
   a. 화성에 존재하는 생명체에 대한 설명을 시작하기 위한 것
   b. 어느 행성이 가장 지구와 비슷한지 알기 위한 것
   c. 나사(미 항공 우주국)의 탐사 프로그램을 설명하기 위한 것
   d. 우주의 얼음 결정체를 분석하기 위한 것

5. 작가에 따르면, 우주선에 의해 발견된 두 가지 요소는 무엇이었는가? 정답 두 개를 고르시오.
   a. 금성의 모양은 지구와 흡사하다.
   b. 한때 화성에 물이 존재했을 가능성이 크다.

c. 차가운 대기와 얼음 결정체들이 있었다.
   d. 유인 우주 비행을 통해 대 격변의 흔적이 발견되었다.

6. 작가가 화성에 대해 암시하는 바는 무엇인가?
   a. 지구와 금성에서 생명체의 존재가 유일하게 가능하다.
   b. 화성과 금성 간의 거리 예측
   c. 환경을 고려해 보건대, 화성에서 생명체의 존재가 가능했을지도 모른다.
   d. 화성에서의 강 형성 패턴

Vocabulary Test   p.162~163

1. 본문의 '솥'과 가장 근접한 의미의 단어는?
   a. 용기(그릇)   b. 행성   c. 바구니   d. 잡동사니

2. 본문의 '근접'과 가장 근접한 의미의 단어는?
   a. 즉시   b. 접합   c. 가까움   d. 틈

3. 본문의 '필수 조건'과 가장 근접한 의미의 단어는?
   a. 방향   b. 필요조건   c. 선택   d. 보조물

4. 본문의 '이론'과 가장 근접한 의미의 단어는?
   a. 대학   b. 증거   c. 이론   d. 주장

5. 본문의 '수많은'과 가장 근접한 의미의 단어는?
   a. 확인된   b. 제한된   c. 논박된   d. 무수한

6. 본문의 '문명'과 가장 근접한 의미의 단어는?
   a. 퇴보   b. 엘리트주의
   c. 문화   d. 야만

7. 본문의 '추측하다'와 가장 근접한 의미의 단어는?
   a. 기부하다   b. 추측하다
   c. 집중하다   d. 단언하다

8. 본문의 '격변'과 가장 근접한 의미의 단어는?
   a. 촉매제   b. 재난
   c. 선택   d. 위성

Paraphrasing   p.163

1. 과학자들은 화성이 어떤 자연의 대이변에 의해 희생된 것이 아닌가 추측하고 있다.

   a. 지구는 너무나 많은 격변으로 고통을 받았다.
   b. 일부 과학자들은 자연 재해가 그 행성의 존재에 기여했다고 믿는다.
   c. 지구 중심부에 있는 대부분 용암은 자연적 격변으로 인해 만들어신 것이었다.
   d. 과학계가 견지하고 있는 주요 이론은 격변을 일으키는 사건이 발생했다는 것이다.

2. 이러한 의문점들에 대한 해답은 21세기 초로 예정되어 있는 유인 화성탐사계획을 기다려야 얻을 수 있을 것이다.

   a. 인류의 기원에 관한 대다수 질문에 대한 해답은 심도 깊은 추가 우주 조사에서 비롯되어야 한다.
   b. 과학자들은 향후 50년 사이에 우주 탐사를 하기를 희망한다.
   c. 더 많은 증거를 밝혀내기 위해서, 우리는 좀 더 지구의 가장 깊숙한 곳까지 탐사해야 한다.
   d. 유인 우주 비행은 우주 탐사에 매우 효과적이다.

Unit 20 — Stars p.170

항성

항성은 조밀하고 소용돌이치는 가스 구름 속의 수소원자가 인력에 의해 가스구름의 중심부로 끌어당겨질 때 형성된다. 중심핵이 커짐에 따라, 더욱 많은 원자들이 끌려가고, 그것이 중심부로 떨어질 때 그것들은 속도를 내며 방대한 양의 에너지를 방출한다. 이 에너지가 기체를 따뜻하게 해 점점 온도가 높아지고 이윽고 수백 만 년 후에는 약 섭씨 1000만도에 달하게 된다. 맹렬한 열과 거대한 압력으로 말미암아 무수한 수소폭탄의 위력과 맞먹는 핵융합반응이 일어난다. 핵융합이 진행됨에 따라 수소와 헬륨이 핵반응을 통해 더욱 비중이 무거운 원자를 만들어내기 시작한다. 이 시점에서 진정한 하나의 항성이 탄생된다고 할 수 있다. 하지만 수소원자가 인력의 중심부를 향해 끌어당겨지는 과정은 수소가 완전히 없어질 때까지 계속된다. 성숙한 항성은 팽창하고 빨갛게 된다. 작고 오래된 항성은 조용히 소멸해 간다. 더 큰 항성들은 격렬히 폭발해서 우주의 저편으로 흩어져 간다.

Sentence Completion p.166~167

A. 다음 문장에 가장 알맞은 단어를 고르시오.

1. 만일 어떤 것이 ____ 다면, 그것이 뱅글뱅글 돌고 있는 것이다.
   a. 삼각형을 만들고 있는   b. 움직이고 있는
   c. 소용돌이치고 있는   d. 궁금해하고 있는

2. 만일 바깥 기온이 ____ 면, 매우 더운 것이다.
   a. 습기 찬   b. 돌풍이 부는
   c. 추운   d. 몹시 뜨거운

3. 만일 어떤 물질이 밀도가 거의 없고 가벼운 것의 정반대라면, 그것은 아마도 ____ 다.
   a. 짙은(밀도 높은)   b. 부드러운
   c. 관통할 수 있는   d. 숙련된

4. 물질의 구성 요소 가운데 일부는 ____ 같은 기본 요소를 포함한다.
   a. 증거   b. 원자   c. 전기   d. 방해 전파

5. 만일 당신이 ____ 사무실을 갖고 있다면, 아마도 그것은 당신의 본사일 것이다.
   a. 지점   b. 중심의   c. 치명적인   d. 부차적인

B. 다음 문장에 가장 알맞은 단어를 고르시오.

1. 중동 문제를 ____ 해결하기를 희망해 봤자 아무 소용없다.
   a. 조용히   b. 호전적으로
   c. 눈에 띄게   d. 적대적으로

2. 1마일은 약 1.6킬로미터에 ____ 다.
   a. 상당한(같은)   b. 다양한
   c. 있음직한   d. 양립할 수 없는

3. 시스템 상의 ____ 결점들로 인해 대량 리콜사태가 발생했다.
   a. 제한된   b. 셀 수 있는   c. 수없이 많은   d. 사려 깊은

4. 화산이 용암을 ____ 있다면, 살고 싶으면 빨리 도망치는 편이 낫다.
   a. 삼키고   b. 확장시키고
   c. 옆으로 비켜가고   d. 내뿜고

5. 별이 ____ 것이 관측되면, 블랙홀이 형성될 것이다.
   a. 솟아오르고 있는   b. 붕괴되고 있는
   c. 반짝이고 있는   d. 방향을 바꾸고 있는

Listening Comprehension p.168~169

1. 별은 어떻게 형성 되는가?
   a. 수소 원자의 붕괴가 농축된 덩어리를 야기한다.
   b. 수소 폭탄에 상당하는 핵반응 때문에 기온이 높아진다.
   c. 밀도가 높은 구름 속의 수소 원자들이 뭉쳐져서, 연쇄반응을 일으킨다.
   d. 중력이 별을 끌어당겨서, 그들을 한데 결합시킨다.

2. 작가가 별의 생성을 설명하는 이유는 무엇인가?
   a. 행성들 가운데 가장 작은 행성에 대해 배우기 위한 것
   b. 헬륨이 어떻게 결합해서 고밀도의 물질을 형성하는지를 설명하기 위한 것
   c. 별의 탄생과 소멸에 대해 설명하기 위한 것
   d. 행성 궤도 속의 패턴을 분석하기 위한 것

3. 작가는 별의 형성을 어떻게 소개하는가?
   a. 소용돌이치는 헬륨 가스 구름을 설명하면서
   b. 뜨거운 열과 원자핵 분열 이론을 통해서
   c. 태양의 구성에 대해 언급하면서
   d. 수소 원자 충돌과 부피 증가에 대해 언급하면서

4. 강의의 일부를 다시 듣고 문제에 답하시오. 이 구절의 기능은 무엇인가?

   a. 새로 탄생한 별이 어떻게 덩어리를 끌어당겨, 엄청난 양의 에너지를 만들어내는지를 설명하기 위한 것
   b. 덩어리가 커지면, 어떻게 에너지가 생성되는지를 설명하기 위한 것
   c. 중력 이론의 한계를 분석하기 위한 것
   d. 압력이 높으면 어떻게 핵융합 반응이 일어나는지에 대해 말하기 위한 것

5. 작가에 따르면, 어떤 두 가지 요소가 별 붕괴의 조짐을 보여주는가? 정답 두 개를 고르시오.
   a. 별의 중력이 더 강해진다.
   b. 모든 수소는 별 속에서 소모된다.
   c. 일부는 노란 색 속에서 폭발한다.
   d. 오래된 별은 점점 더 커지면서 붉은 색으로 변한다.

6. 작가가 별에 대해 암시하는 바는 무엇인가?
   a. 중력의 중심 에너지를 연구해야 한다.
   b. 별은 생성해서 소멸할 때까지 끊임없는 변화를 겪는다.
   c. 수소는 별 형성의 핵심이다.
   d. 에너지와 수소 원자 사이에 패턴이 존재한다.

Vocabulary Test   p.170~171

1. 본문의 '원자'와 가장 근접한 의미의 단어는?
   a. 질량   b. 분자   c. 묘사   d. 큰 덩어리

2. 본문의 '짙은'과 가장 근접한 의미의 단어는?
   a. 육중한   b. 빽빽한
   c. 약간의   d. 불 침투성의

3. 본문의 '소용돌이치는'과 가장 근접한 의미의 단어는?
   a. 삼각형의   b. 당황케 하는
   c. 소용돌이치는   d. 가라앉고 있는

4. 본문의 '중심의'와 가장 근접한 의미의 단어는?
   a. 외부의   b. 중간의   c. 작은   d. 부차적인

5. 본문의 '몹시 뜨거운'과 가장 근접한 의미의 단어는?
   a. 살을 에는 듯한   b. 타오르는 듯한
   c. 매우 추운   d. 부식성의

6. 본문의 '같은(상당하는)'과 가장 근접한 의미의 단어는?
   a. 같은   b. 다른   c. 약간의   d. 낙담한

7. 본문의 '수없이 많은'과 가장 근접한 의미의 단어는?
   a. 유한한   h. 제한된
   c. 셀 수 없이 많은   d. 약간의

8. 본문의 '붕괴되다'와 가장 근접한 의미의 단어는?
   a. 무너지다   b. 복종하다
   c. 유린하다   d. 밀어닥치다

Paraphrasing   p.171

1. 맹렬한 열과 거대한 압력으로 말미암아 무수한 수소폭탄의 위력과 맞먹는 핵융합반응이 일어난다.

   a. 수소 폭탄의 포화점은 핵융합 반응과 비슷하다.
   b. 핵융합 반응의 압력은 수많은 수소 폭탄에 상당한다.
   c. 수소 폭탄은 뜨거운 열과 마찰 현상의 주요 원인이 된다.
   d. 융합과 압력을 연결하기 위해서는 더 많은 연구가 필요하다.

2. 하지만 수소원자가 인력의 중심부를 향해 끌어당겨지는 과정은 수소가 완전히 없어질 때까지 계속된다.

   a. 별의 중력 중심부에는 수소 원자의 용해가 일어난다.
   b. 수소 원자는 수없이 많은 이온을 소모한다.
   c. 별이 중력 중심을 향해 붕괴된 이후, 모든 수소 원자는 소모된다.
   d. 붕괴는 전형적으로 수소 원자와 원거리에 있는 별을 필요로 한다.

Unit 21 — Energy (1) p.178

에너지 (1)

세계의 재생 불가능한 에너지원은 결국은 고갈될 것이라는 두려움이 고조되고 있는데 인간은 자연이 매일 만들어내는 방대한 에너지의 극히 일부 밖에 이용하지 않고 있다. 예를 들면, 하천이 만드는 에너지 가운데 인간이 이용하고 있는 것은 단지 1%나 2%인데, 이 수력에 의한 전력만 해도 우리들의 수요의 80%를 충족시키는 것이다. 풍력발전으로 현재 수력으로 만들어지고 있는 전력의 두 배의 양을 생산할 수 있고, 조류력을 이용할 수 있다면 세계의 에너지 수요의 절반을 충족시킬 수 있다. 그러나 뭐니 뭐니 해도 최대의 에너지원은 태양이다. 만약 세계 연료의 전 공급량을 한곳에 모으고 태양에너지에 맞먹는 비율로 태운다면, 3일 이내에 다 타고 말 것이다. 그러므로 세계의 재생 불가능한 에너지의 공급량이 줄어도 무한한 에너지를 개발할 수 있는 가능성이 남아 있다.

Sentence Completion p.174~175

A. 다음 문장에 가장 알맞은 단어를 고르시오.

1. 내가 사는 곳에는 바람이 거의 불지 않아서, 내가 가지고 있는 풍력 발전기는 이제껏 많은 에너지를 ____ 본 적이 없다.
   a. 소비해   b. 생각해
   c. 따로 떼어 놓아   d. 만들어내

2. ____ 이/가 들어오면, 바다 수면이 위 아래로 출렁인다.
   a. 조수   b. 늪   c. 건조함   d. 해초

3. 땅이 ____ 면, 그것은 구역이 매우 광대하고, 멀리까지 이어지는 것이다.
   a. 방대한   b. 혼잡한   c. 평화로운   d. 좁은

4. 당신이 어떤 것을 ____ 면, 당신이 그것을 모두 써 버린 것이다.
   a. 만들었다   b. 고갈했다
   c. 저장했다   d. 증대시켰다

5. 대부분의 주가 재생 가능한 에너지를 ____ 하는 것은 바람직한 일이다.
   a. 남용하다   b. 이용하다
   c. 망치다   d. 오염시키다

B. 다음 문장에 가장 알맞은 단어를 고르시오.

1. 전 세계 천연 석유 자원의 대부분은 ____ 다.
   a. 마시기에 알맞은   b. 재생 불가능한
   c. 골절된   d. 같은

2. 그녀는 그 영화에서 팬들의 기대를 ____ 하지 못했다.
   a. 수반하다   b. 충족시키다   c. 당황케 하다   d. 속이다

3. 그 문제의 중요성을 고려해 볼 때, 그의 과학적 관심이 그 문제에 ____ 것은 올바른 것이었다.
   a. 빗나간   b. 흩어진   c. 집중된   d. 퍼진

4. 풍력 에너지의 공급량이 ____ 다.
   a. 수수께끼의   b. 비바람에 씻긴
   c. 지루한   d. 무한한

5. 그 우주선은 빛의 속도에 ____ 할 수 없다.
   a. 필적하다   b. 기인하다   c. 상쇄하다   d. 평가하다

Listening Comprehension p.176~177

1. 전 세계 에너지 공급량에 대한 우려가 존재하는 이유는 무엇인가?
   a. 천연 에너지원으로는 돈을 거의 벌 수 없기 때문에
   b. 석유 회사들이 이익 증대를 원하기 때문에
   c. 최근의 우려를 고려할 때, 재생 불가능한 에너지의 대부분은 결국 사라지게 될 것이기 때문에
   d. 물과 바람을 자원으로 개발하고 싶어 하는 신생 사업이 많기 때문에

2. 작가가 천연 자원 사용을 강조하는 이유는 무엇인가?
   a. 풍력 에너지 회사들의 주식 수익이 매우 높을 수도 있기 때문에
   b. 수력 발전이 우리가 필요로 하는 에너지의 최고 80퍼센트까지 생산해 줄 수 있기 때문에
   c. 태양 에너지도 똑같이 강력하기 때문에
   d. 현재 우리가 17퍼센트가 넘는 수력에너지를 사용하고 있기 때문에

3. 작가는 에너지력을 어떻게 소개하는가?
   a. 얼마 지나지 않아 재생 불가능한 에너지가 부족해질 것임을 암시하면서
   b. 하루에 연소되는 연료가 어느 정도인지를 추산하면서
   c. 중동에 남아 있는 연료 공급량이 어느 정도인지 예측하면서
   d. 태양력과 풍력을 대비시키면서

4. 강의의 일부를 다시 듣고 문제에 답하시오. 이 구절의 기능은 무엇인가?
   a. 에너지원에 대한 대안 몇 가지를 소개하기 위한 것
   b. 수력 에너지 사용을 강조하기 위한 것
   c. 석유 기술의 한계를 설명하기 위한 것
   d. 과거 우리가 풍력을 어떻게 사용했는지를 대비시키기 위한 것

5. 작가에 따르면, 지구를 구하는 데 도움을 줄 수 있는 에너지 형태 두 가지는 무엇인가? 정답 두 개를 고르시오.
   a. 조력
   b. 풍차를 이용한 풍력
   c. 수력
   d. 오토바이에 태양전지판 사용

6. 작가가 에너지원에 대해 암시하는 바는 무엇인가?
   a. 여러 가지 장애물이 조력의 효과적 이용을 방해한다.
   b. 에너지 문제의 대부분은 고칠 수 없다.
   c. 우리가 독창력을 발휘한다면, 지구의 에너지 문제에 대한 해결책들도 있다.
   d. 대부분의 에너지 해결책은 비용이 많이 든다.

   a. 에너지와 관련하여 지구가 기댈 수 있는 희망은 새로운 에너지의 가능성을 개발하는 데 있다.
   b. 지구 에너지의 대부분은 아직도 사용되지 않고 남아있다.
   c. 지나치게 많은 대체 에너지원은 공급량 감소에 기여할 것이다.
   d. 전 세계 에너지 공급량이 빠르게 감소하고 있다.

Vocabulary Test   p.178~179

1. 본문의 '고갈하다'와 가장 근접한 의미의 단어는?
   a. 다 써버리다   b. 축적하다
   c. 피곤하게 하다   d. 비축하다

2. 본문의 '방대한'과 가장 근접한 의미의 단어는?
   a. 무거운   b. 큰   c. 빈약한   d. 묶인

3. 본문의 '만들어내다'와 가장 근접한 의미의 단어는?
   a. 생기게 하다   b. 결합시키다   c. 측정하다   d. 펑펑 쓰다

4. 본문의 '조수'와 가장 근접한 의미의 단어는?
   a. 조류   b. 해양   c. 물   d. 해초

5. 본문의 '이용하다'와 가장 근접한 의미의 단어는?
   a. 물을 주다   b. 오용하다   c. 이용하다   d. 괴롭히다

6. 본문의 '충족시키다'와 가장 근접한 의미의 단어는?
   a. 표준이상 달성하다   b. 범람시키다
   c. 만족시키다   d. 요구하다

7. 본문의 '집중시키다'와 가장 근접한 의미의 단어는?
   a. 섞다   b. 집중시키다
   c. 흩뜨리다   d. 가볍게 두드리다

8. 본문의 '필적하다'와 가장 근접한 의미의 단어는?
   a. 거스르다   b. 증명하다   c. 개선하다   d. 똑같다

Paraphrasing   p.179

1. 만약 세계 연료의 전 공급량을 한곳에 모으고 태양에너지에 맞먹는 비율로 태운다면, 3일 이내에 다 타고 말 것이다.

   a. 전 세계 연료 공급량이 며칠 만에 다 소모될 수 있다.
   b. 태양은 막대한 에너지를 저장하고 있다.
   c. 전 세계에 연소되는 모든 연료는 태양과 맞먹는 속도로 빠르게 모두 다 소진될 것이다.
   d. 지구는 태양 에너지와 필적하기 위해서 더 많은 에너지를 소비해야 한다.

2. 그러므로 세계의 재생 불가능한 에너지의 공급량이 줄어도 무한한 에너지를 개발할 수 있는 가능성이 남아 있다.

Unit 22   North America (3)   p.186

북아메리카 (3)

1800년대 중반, 서부는 아직 비교적 미정착 상태에 있었고 소수이긴 하지만 장래의 세대를 위해 이 땅의 자연의 경이를 지키려는 사람들이 있었다. 1864년 의회는 빙하에 새겨진 화강암 절벽으로 유명한 요새미티 계곡을 「국민이 이용하는 휴양지와 레크레이션」을 위한 공원으로 지정하고, 8년 후에는 간헐천과 온천으로 알려진 옐로우스톤 강의 수원을 지키기 위해 80만 9000 헥타르 이상의 토지를 할애했다. 개척민이 북미대륙을 횡단하여 진출함에 따라 황야는 찾아보기 힘들게 되고, 세코이아, 들소(버팔로), 큰 사슴은 도끼와 총이 금지된 지역에서만 살아 남았다. 이렇게 해서 미국의 공원 제도는 두 개의 중요한 기능을 하게 되었다. 미국 자연의 경이를 보여주는 것과 인간으로부터 자연을 지키는 것이다. 그러나 공원의 명확한 목적은 국민이 이용하도록 쓰이는 데 있다. 이 모순을 해소하려면 타협밖에 없고, 이는 국민들의 협력이 있어야만 국립공원 관리국이 달성할 수 있다.

Sentence Completion   p.182~183

A. 다음 문장에 가장 알맞은 단어를 고르시오.

1. 어떤 것이 _____ 때, 그것은 매우 드물고 멋진 것이다.
   a. 아는 체하는   b. 무뚝뚝한   c. 닮아빠진   d. 놀랄 만할

2. 일부 동성결혼 반대자들은 사회 전체가 전통적인 결혼의 정의를 _____ 해야한다고 믿는다.
   a. 망치다   b. 다시 정의하다
   c. 보호(보존)하다   d. 붕괴시키다

3. 그 주가 생긴 년도는 1981년도에 불과한데, 사람들에게 알려져 있지 않고 거의 _____ 지역이 지난 30여 년에 걸쳐 완전히 진화했다.
   a. 유명한   b. 사람이 살지 않는
   c. 인구가 많은   d. 돋보이는

4. 다음 _____ 에게 시구의 아름납고 녹특한 자연을 슬길 수 있는 기회를 주는 것이 우리의 의무이다.
   a. 조상   b. 자원   c. 세대   d. 시간의 틀

Answer Key

5. 물의 흐름이 대지와 얼음을 ____ 멋진 곡선을 만들어 냈다.
   a. 짓밟아서
   b. 상상해서
   c. 깎아 내서
   d. 소중히 간직해서

B. 다음 문장에 가장 알맞은 단어를 고르시오.

1. 그의 저서에서 불법 이민 문제에 대해 그가 ____ 입장과 비교해, 나는 유세 동안에 그 문제에 대해 그가 취한 입장과 중요한 차이가 있음을 발견했다.
   a. 충격받은
   b. 발산한
   c. 말했던(밝혔던)
   d. 가려운

2. 와이오밍 소재 옐로우스톤 국립공원에서 멋지게 물을 뿜어내는 ____ 을/를 볼 수 있다.
   a. 빙산   b. 소각   c. 간헐천   d. 밀밭

3. 비판자들은 예전 것과 비교해서 현재 대통령의 새로운 보건정책에는 약간의 ____ 이/가 있다고 주장했다.
   a. 흔적   b. 슬픔   c. 발전   d. 모순

4. 그 가족은 폭력 범죄가 ____ 한 곳이라면 어디든지 이사하기를 필사적으로 원하고 있다.
   a. 박차   b. 유행   c. 희귀(드묾)   d. 골칫거리

5. 물이 가득 찬 수로가 이 벽 주위를 감싸고 있어서, 그것이 군인과 말, 전쟁기계의 ____ 을/를 막아주는 방어 장벽의 역할을 했다.
   a. 방패   b. 진군   c. 절차   d. 불일치

Listening Comprehension   p.184~185

1. 세쿼이아, 바이슨(들소), 엘크는 왜 살아남았는가?
   a. 테오도르 루즈벨트가 그들을 위한 특별 공원을 설립했기 때문에
   b. 사냥과 벌목이 그것들의 서식지에서는 허용되지 않았기 때문에
   c. 엘크 고기는 인간들이 먹기에 너무 맛이 없었기 때문에
   d. 과학자들이 정확하게 엘크의 짝짓기 습성을 예측했기 때문에

2. 작가가 공원 시스템을 설명하는 이유는 무엇인가?
   a. 빙하에 의해 깎여진 화강암 절벽을 선전하기 위한 것
   b. 인간으로부터 자연을 보호하는 것이 매우 어렵다는 것
   c. 모든 사람에게 공원으로부터 이익을 얻을 수 있다는 것을 지적하기 위한 것
   d. 사람들이 그 지역에 있는 자연의 신비를 보호하지 못하게 하기 위한 것

3. 작가는 공원 시스템을 어떻게 소개하는가?
   a. 앨버타-몬태나 공원 시스템에 대해 언급하면서
   b. 자연 보호 구역을 지키는 데 의욕을 보이는 사람들에 대해 언급하면서
   c. 옐로우스톤 강에 대한 보존 방법을 예측하면서
   d. 국립공원 관리국을 비판하면서

4. 강의의 일부를 다시 듣고 문제에 답하시오. 이 구절의 기능은 무엇인가?
   a. 미국 자연의 신비로움을 보여주는 한 가지 시스템을 소개하기 위한 것
   b. 미국 자연의 신비로움을 외국인들에게 보여주기 위한 것
   c. 공원 내부의 광산업 한계를 설명하기 위한 것
   d. 얼마나 일부 국가들은 인간으로부터 자연을 보호하지 못하는지를 대비시키기 위한 것

5. 작가에 따르면, 요세미티 계곡을 성공 사례로 만든 두 가지 요소는 무엇인가? 정답 두 개를 고르시오.
   a. 자연 역사박물관
   b. 빙하가 만들어낸 화강암 절벽
   c. 전통을 자랑하는 핫도그, 햄버거 가판대
   d. 공공 휴양지들

6. 작가가 공원 시스템에 대해 암시하는 바는 무엇인가?
   a. 사람이 살지 않는 땅을 보존할 필요성이 있다는 것을 보여주기 위한 것
   b. 간헐천 속에 화학 물질이 요동친다는 것을 경고하기 위한 것
   c. 다른 유럽 국가들이 따라할 수 있는 모델을 보여주기 위한 것
   d. 자연과 인간이 함께 나란히 살아갈 수 있다는 것을 보여주기 위한 것

Vocabulary Test   p.186~187

1. 본문의 '사람이 살지 않는'과 가장 근접한 의미의 단어는?
   a. 무명의
   b. 판명되지 않은
   c. 주민이 없는
   d. 기능을 못하는

2. 본문의 '세대'와 가장 근접한 의미의 단어는?
   a. 동시대인   b. 생산   c. 사기꾼   d. 조상

3. 본문의 '놀랄 만한'과 가장 근접한 의미의 단어는?
   a. 의심스러운
   b. 놀랄 만한
   c. 환멸을 느낀
   d. 사랑스러운

4. 본문의 '깎아내다'와 가장 근접한 의미의 단어는?
   a. 잘라내다   b. 잘게 썰다   c. 부수다   d. 강조하다

5. 본문의 '보호하다'와 가장 근접한 의미의 단어는?
   a. 버리다   b. 고갈되다   c. 조달하다   d. 보존하다

6. 본문의 '전진'과 가장 근접한 의미의 단어는?
   a. 침략   b. 후퇴   c. 전진   d. 막다른 길

7. 본문의 '희귀한 것'과 가장 근접한 의미의 단어는?
   a. 풍족   b. 희귀   c. 고통   d. 초과

8. 본문의 '말하다'와 가장 근접한 의미의 단어는?
   a. 무효로 하다   b. 비난하다
   c. 단언하다   d. 분개하다

Paraphrasing   p.187

1. 개척민이 북미대륙을 횡단하여 진출함에 따라 황야는 찾아보기 힘들게 되고, 세코이아, 들소(버팔로), 큰 사슴은 도끼와 총이 금지된 지역에서만 살아 남았다.

   a. 많은 벌목꾼들이 나무와 풍요로운 숲을 대량으로 파괴시켰다.
   b. 세쿼이아, 바이슨(들소), 엘크는 캐나다의 지방 공원에서만 살아남았다.
   c. 모피를 얻기 위해 덫을 놓는 사람들이 수많은 엘크, 바이크(들소), 그리고 세쿼이아 나무를 절멸시켰다.
   d. 전 대륙을 가로질러 전진하는 정착민들이 많은 야생동물들을 사냥했다.

2. 이 모순을 해소하려면 타협밖에 없고, 이는 국민들의 협력이 있어야만 국립공원 관리국이 달성할 수 있다.

   a. 국립공원관리국은 타협할 수 있는 능력이 없다.
   b. 국립공원조성은 언제나 자연이냐, 현대화냐를 두고 한 가지를 선택해야 하는 일종의 거래이다.
   c. 공원관리국에서 아주 많은 대책을 내놓으면 야생 동물 수가 증가하게 될 것이다.
   d. 보다 큰 규모의 국립공원 가운데 일부에서는 더 많은 채굴이 필요하다.

Unit 23   The Puritans (1)   p.194

청교도 (1)

영국교회의 정화에 실패했기 때문에 청교도들은 그들 자신의 종교공동체 안으로 철수했다. 그리고 조국에서의 박해로부터 벗어나기 위해 북아메리카를 향해 출항했다. 많은 청교도들은 언젠가는 영국이 변할 것이며, 그들이 대항한 종교의 타락으로부터 해방되어 그들의 귀국을 환영할 것이라고 믿었다. 그들이 북아메리카의 황야에 생길 새 국가의 건설을 거들고 있다고 생각한 사람은 아무도 없었다. 1620년 12월 21일에 메사추세츠주의 플리머스 록에 상륙하기 전, 그들은 이미 미래의 공동체에 영향을 줄 전통의 기초를 구축했었다. 아직 그들의 배인 메이플라워호에 승선해 있었을 때 그들은 메이플라워 협정에 서명했고, 그 협정에서 공공의 이익을 위해 공동체에 의해 내려진 모든 결정사항에 따르겠다고 서약했다. 그 문서에 의해 민주적인 자치정부의 전통이 확립되었고 후세에 이어지게 되었다.

Sentence Completion   p.190~191

A. 다음 문장에 가장 알맞은 단어를 고르시오.

1. 만일 당신이 ____ 을/를 받는 상황에 놓여있다면, 당신은 고통과 괴로움을 겪고 있는 것이다.
   a. 수술   b. 집중 조명   c. 박해   d. 정의

2. 당신의 가족이 ____ 집단에 속한다면, 당신은 역사적인 미국 가정에 뿌리를 두고 있는 것이다.
   a. 케냐인   b. 청교도
   c. 루터교도   d. 호주 원주민

3. 만일 당신이 어떤 것을 ____ 면, 당신이 그것을 매우 깨끗하게 만드는 것이다.
   a. 더럽히다   b. 부드럽게 하다
   c. 깨끗이 하다   d. 바보처럼 보이게하다

4. 체스의 대가가 경기에서 ____ 하기로 결심한다면, 그 사람은 경기를 포기하는 것이다.
   a. 증가시키다   b. 감독하다   c. 나타나다   d. 물러나다

5. 당신이 당신의 ____ 으로 돌아간다면, 당신은 당신이 태어나서 자란 곳으로 돌아가는 것이다.
   a. 은신처   b. 조국   c. 국세청   d. 사무실

B. 다음 문장에 가장 알맞은 단어를 고르시오.

1. 많은 하키 선수들이 대단한 이력을 가지고 있지만, 웨인 그레츠키의 ____ 은/는 비견될 수 없을 정도였다.
   a. 절망   b. 원칙
   c. 유산(남긴 것)   d. 타고난 권리

2. 사람들이 기존 사회 제도를 존중하지 않기 때문에 많은 ____ 이/가 발생한다.
   a. 신뢰   b. 정직   c. 부패   d. 경쾌함

3. 한때 에티오피아에 속해 있었던 에리트레아는 현재 ____ 로 통치가 이루어진다.
   a. 정복자들   b. 자치
   c. 정의   d. 거대 기업들

4. 그녀가 새로 산 독일 셰퍼드 개의 ____ 은/는 모범이 될 만 했다.
   a. 동의   b. 복종   c. 허용   d. 열등

5. 수많은 청교도 ____ 은/는 범죄율이 낮고 학생들의 수업 참석률이 높은 것으로 유명했다.
   a. 오두막집들   b. 빈민가들
   c. 풍작   d. 지역사회들

1. 청교도들은 언제 영국으로 돌아갈 수 있을 거라고 생각했는가?
   a. 영국 왕이 그들에게 사면을 인가했을 때
   b. 더 이상 종교적 부패가 존재하지 않을 때
   c. 영국 국교회가 붕괴했을 때
   d. 뉴잉글랜드처럼 영국이 더 많은 자연의 신비로움을 가졌을 때

2. 작가가 청교도들을 설명하는 이유는 무엇인가?
   a. 그들이 부패와 박해에서 어떻게 도망쳤는지를 더 잘 이해할 수 있도록 하기 위한 것
   b. 미국 개인주의의 뿌리를 보여주기 위한 것
   c. 메이플라워호에 대해 더 많은 것을 배우기 위한 것
   d. 새로운 식민지를 찾는 방법을 예측하기 위한 것

3. 작가는 청교도들을 어떻게 소개하는가?
   a. 신세계로 향하는 메이플라워호의 항로를 고찰하면서
   b. 영국과 플리머스의 바위 사이의 거리를 추정하면서
   c. 청교도들이 어떻게 그들만의 지역사회로 들어가 버렸는지를 설명하면서
   d. 황야에서의 새 국가 건설을 분석하면서

4. 강의의 일부를 다시 듣고 문제에 답하시오. 이 구절의 기능은 무엇인가?
   a. 초기 영국 정착민들이 어떻게 공동으로 결정을 내렸는지를 소개하기 위한 것
   b. 미국의 토대로서의 플리머스의 바위에 대한 예를 제시하기 위한 것
   c. 새 종교를 만드는 것의 한계를 설명하기 위한 것
   d. 영국과 뉴잉글랜드 종교를 서로 대비시키기 위한 것

5. 작가에 따르면, 메이플라워 조약을 상징하는 두 가지 면은 무엇인가? 정답 두 개를 고르시오.
   a. 편협한 민주주의
   b. 복종이 가장 중요했다는 것
   c. 궁극적 목표로서의 자치
   d. 지역사회의 결정이 개인의 결정보다 우선했다는 것

6. 작가가 청교도들에 대해 암시하는 바는 무엇인가?
   a. 영국 교회는 항상 변함없는 기관이었다.
   b. 박해자들을 피하기 위해서 새 지역사회가 새로운 토대를 마련할 수도 있다.
   c. 그들은 현대적인 청교도 교회의 창립자였다.
   d. 자치는 독재적으로 사고하는 사회에 필수적이다.

1. 본문의 '깨끗이 하다'와 가장 근접한 의미의 단어는?
   a. 위생적으로 하다   b. 정화하다
   c. 개봉하다   d. 추방하다

2. 본문의 '물러나다'와 가장 근접한 의미의 단어는?
   a. 절멸시키다   b. 나아가다   c. 물러가다   d. 압수하다

3. 본문의 '박해'와 가장 근접한 의미의 단어는?
   a. 압박   b. 포기   c. 보상   d. 죄책감

4. 본문의 '조국'과 가장 근접한 의미의 단어는?
   a. 이웃   b. 상인단체   c. 지방   d. 고향

5. 본문의 '부패'와 가장 근접한 의미의 단어는?
   a. 솔직   b. 부정함   c. 뇌물   d. 친지

6. 본문의 '지역사회'와 가장 근접한 의미의 단어는?
   a. 열쇠공   b. 땅   c. 공산주의   d. 사회

7. 본문의 '복종'과 가장 근접한 의미의 단어는?
   a. 동의   b. 임무   c. 순종   d. 불법

8. 본문의 '유산'과 가장 근접한 의미의 단어는?
   a. 유산   b. 합법성   c. 기부   d. 적법

1. 1620년 12월 21일에 메사추세츠주의 플리머스 록에 상륙하기 전, 그들은 이미 미래의 공동체에 영향을 줄 전통의 기초를 구축했었다.
   a. 청교도들은 수년 간 지속될 전통의 시작점이었다.
   b. 플리머스의 바위는 중요한 코네티컷 해운 항만이었다.
   c. 자유를 너무 많이 인정하면 청교도의 기초가 원상태로 돌아가게 된다.
   d. 메이플라워 조약은 미국 헌법 제정에 기여했다.

2. 그 문서에 의해 민주적인 자치정부의 전통이 확립되었고 후세에 이어지게 되었다.
   a. 메이플라워 조약은 전국적 은행 시스템을 확립했다.
   b. 유산을 확립하는 것이 정착민들의 의도는 아니었다.
   c. 이 문서는 영국으로부터의 자치를 위한 토대를 세워주었다.
   d. 청교도들의 유산은 영원히 미국 역사 속에 고이 간직될 것이다.

The Puritans (2)

p.202

청교도 (2)

청교도주의가 미합중국에서 중요한 정치세력으로서의 힘을 잃은 뒤에도 그 문화는 여전히 미국인의 생활에 커다란 영향력을 미치고 있었다. 부정적인 면으로서, 대단한 열의와 성실함에도 불구하고, 청교도주의는 불행하게도 그 신자들이 영국을 떠나 탈피하려 했던 많은 편협한 태도를 조장했다. 하지만 청교도가 다른 종교단체에 대해서 관용적이지 않았기에 교회와 국가의 분리가 촉진되었고 정교분리는 현재의 미국 헌법에도 보장되어 있다. 좀더 긍정적인 특질로서는 청교도들은 전통적인 권위에 도전했고 개인의 자발성을 옹호했다. 그들의 향학열덕분에 의무교육을 정한 법률이 제정되었고 하버드를 비롯한 대학이 설립되었다. 청교도의 기질은 현대 미국인들의 몇 가지 특성−강한 윤리관과 완고함, 실용성을 중시하는 자세, 그리고 인도주의에 대한 호전적이라 할 만큼의 강한 열성 등에서 아직도 찾아볼 수 있다.

Sentence Completion   p.198~199

A. 다음 문장에 가장 알맞은 단어를 고르시오.

1. 만일 당신이 누군가에게 당신의 ____ 을/를 준다면, 당신은 그들에게 매우 고마움을 느끼는 것이다.
   a. 경멸   b. 열망   c. 슬픔   d. 진심

2. 당신이 강한 ____ 을/를 가지고 있다면, 당신은 자기주장이 강한 것이다.
   a. 범위   b. 태도   c. 애정   d. 적당

3. 8세기에 무역 상인들이 인도에 처음으로 소개한 이슬람교는 모굴제국 시기에 그 나라에서 막강한 종교적 ____ 이/가 되었다.
   a. 찬성   b. 분노   c. 영향력   d. 효능

4. 누군가 ____ 때, 그들은 많은 권력을 보유하고 매우 존경받는 사람들이다.
   a. 무명의   b. 영향력 있는   c. 빈정대는   d. 무력한

5. 누군가 ____ 사람이면, 그들은 마음이 좁은 것이다.
   a. 특이한   b. 반대의
   c. 편협한   d. 참을성 있는

B. 다음 문장에 가장 알맞은 단어를 고르시오.

1. ____ 은/는 청교도들이 매우 중요하다고 여겼던 것이다.
   a. 과음   b. 부패   c. 방종   d. 도덕성

2. 분기별 보고서가 마무리될 거라고 그녀가 ____, 그 보고서의 마무리가 한 달째 밀려있다.
   a. 의심했지만   b. 확대했시만
   c. 보장지만   d. 매혹시켰지만

3. 종교의 민주주의를 주장하는 운동가들은 인간의 자유를 ____, 즉, 대다수 사람들의 바램이 존중받아야 한다는 것이다.
   a. 대략 설명했다   b. 반대했다
   c. 추적했다   d. 옹호했다

4. 당신들의 ____ 은/는 어떤 좋은 결과도 만들어내지 못할 것이다. 오히려 관계를 악화시킬 뿐일 것이다.
   a. 사려깊음   b. 완고함   c. 배려   d. 용서

5. 인생의 성공자들은 보통 ____ 하는 사람들이다.
   a. 통과   b. 불이익
   c. 솔선수범   d. 뒷자리(나서지 않음)

Listening Comprehension   p.200~201

1. 헌법에서 국교는 왜 분리되었는가?
   a. 편협한 종교가 정부를 통제하는 일을 막기 위한 것
   b. 개신교 분파들 속에 존재하는 편협함을 막기 위한 것
   c. 뉴잉글랜드에서의 배움에 대한 열의를 막기 위한 것
   d. 영국이 식민지를 무력 지배하는 것을 막기 위한 것

2. 작가가 청교도들이 어떤 대접을 받았는지 설명하는 이유는 무엇인가?
   a. 종교적 관용을 가르치기 위한 것
   b. 미국의 가치관이 어디에서 유래했는지에 대해 더 많이 알기 위한 것
   c. 미국인들이 종교적으로 편협해질 것을 예측하기 위한 것
   d. 청교도들이 전통적 권위에 어떻게 도전했는지를 보여주기 위한 것

3. 작가는 청교도주의 윤리를 어떻게 소개하는가?
   a. 청교도주의 힘의 쇠락에 대해 언급하면서
   b. 하버드 대학과 같은 고등 교육 기관들의 미래를 추정하면서
   c. 강력한 도덕성을 옹호하면서
   d. 교회가 현재 어떻게 더 이상 종교적으로 강한 세력이 될 수 없는지에 대한 대략의 설명을 하면서

4. 강의의 일부를 다시 듣고 문제에 답하시오. 이 구절의 기능은 무엇인가?
   a. 다른 종교 집단에 대한 청교도의 관용을 소개하기 위한 것
   b. 교회가 어떻게 대학을 설립할 수 있는지에 대해 예를 제시하기 위한 것
   c. 국교 분리의 시작을 설명하기 위한 것
   d. 미국인들 인생의 중요한 한 부분을 대비시키기 위한 것

5. 작가에 따르면, 청교도 힘이 쇠락의 길을 걷게 되는데 원인이 된 두 가지 요소는 무엇인가? 정답 두 개를 고르시오.
   a. 독립직 사법제도
   b. 다른 종교 집단에 대한 불관용
   c. 청교도주의의 부상
   d. 미국 헌법이 그들의 영향력을 제한했던 것

6. 작가가 청교도주의에 대해 암시하는 바는 무엇인가?
   a. 배움에 대한 열의는 모두가 추구해야 한다.
   b. 미국의 강한 도덕성은 청교도주의에 그 뿌리를 두었다.
   c. 만일 나이 많은 청교도들이 오늘날 미국인들이 가지고 있는 일부 특징들을 보게 되면, 깜짝 놀랄 것이다.
   d. 아이러니컬하게도 편협함의 원인은 청교도 운동 때문이었다.

Vocabulary Test p.202~203

1. 본문의 '영향력'과 가장 근접한 의미의 단어는?
   a. 영향력   b. 제안   c. 개성   d. 지위

2. 본문의 '영향력 있는'과 가장 근접한 의미의 단어는?
   a. 취약한   b. 강력한   c. 강압적인   d. 의심스러운

3. 본문의 '성실'과 가장 근접한 의미의 단어는?
   a. 부정   b. 도전   c. 죄   d. 정직

4. 본문의 '편협한'과 가장 근접한 의미의 단어는?
   a. 성가신   b. 편견 없는   c. 견딜 수 있는   d. 속 좁은

5. 본문의 '태도'와 가장 근접한 의미의 단어는?
   a. 움직임   b. 민감성   c. 자세   d. 장애물

6. 본문의 '보장하다'와 가장 근접한 의미의 단어는?
   a. 고치다   b. 약속하다   c. 부드러워지다   d. 존경하다

7. 본문의 '옹호하다'와 가장 근접한 의미의 단어는?
   a. 개선하다   b. 주재하다   c. 멸망하다   d. 지지하다

8. 본문의 '솔선'과 가장 근접한 의미의 단어는?
   a. 선도   b. 사건   c. 성급함   d. 계획

Paraphrasing p.203

1. 좀 더 긍정적인 특질로서는 청교도들은 전통적인 권위에 도전했고 개인의 자발성을 옹호했다.

   a. 권력의 긍정적 관점은 종교가 우위를 차지할 수 없다는 것이다.
   b. 개인의 솔선수범은 청교도들의 핵심적인 일면이었다.
   c. 청교도들이 권위에 도전했지만, 정부를 이길 수는 없었다.
   d. 청교도가 지나치게 자주 권력 위에 군림했다.

2. 청교도의 기질은 현대 미국인들의 몇 가지 특성-강한 윤리관 (그리고 완고함), 실용성을 중시하는 자세, 그리고 인도주의에 대한 호전적이라 할 만큼의 강한 열성 등에서 아직도 찾아볼 수 있다.

   a. 청교도의 특징은 많은 미국 문화 속에서 구현된다.
   b. 사람들이 특징을 매우 과대평가하고 있다.
   c. 지나치게 많은 청교도의 특징들이 오늘날 까지도 분명하게 남아있다.
   d. 호전적 열의는 대다수 미국인들에게 도움이 되지 않는다.

| Unit 25 | Mammals | p.210 |

포유동물

포유동물은 다른 모든 생물과 마찬가지로 환경에 적응하지 않으면 멸종된다. 적응은 생존에 적합한 특징을 가진 동물이 자손을 만드는 경우에 생긴다. 반대로 생존에 부적합하거나 유해한 특징을 가진 생물은 대개, 거의 혹은 전혀 자손이 없다. 이것이 다윈의 진화론의 기초이다. 이 이론을 개설한 저서 「종의 기원」에서 다윈은 다음과 같이 썼다. 「유리한 개체의 차이 및 변이의 보존과 유해한 것의 파멸을 나는 「자연도태」 혹은 「적자생존」이라고 부르고 있다.」 다윈이 말하는 「적자」란 어떤 그룹 내에서 가장 크고, 가장 영리하고, 가장 강한 자라는 의미가 아니다. 그것보다는 어떤 종 가운데서 살아남는 자손을 가장 많이 만드는 것을 가리키는데 이 말을 사용했다. 만약 어떤 종이 어떤 환경에 적응할 수 있는 자손을 남길 수 없다면 그 종은 머지않아 멸종할 것이다.

Sentence Completion p.206~207

A. 다음 문장에 가장 알맞은 단어를 고르시오.

1. 당신이 당신의 파트너에게 매우 ____ 면, 당신은 상대방과 마음이 잘 맞는 것이다.
   a. 표를 요구받는
   b. 적합한
   c. 교묘히 처리된
   d. 자금을 받는

2. 당신은 ____ 상황을 잘 이용해서 너무 민감해질 수 있는 상황을 피해야 한다.
   a. 유리한
   b. 불길한
   c. 편협한
   d. 어처구니없는

3. 만일 당신이 ____ 면, 당신은 더 이상 존재하지 않을 것이다.
   a. 죽는다   b. 부활한다   c. 산다   d. 회복한다

4. 어떤 종이 특별한 ____ 을/를 보여준다면, 그것은 어떤 특징을 가지고 있는 것이다.
   a. 계산   b. 차원   c. 특징   d. 불합격

5. 당신이 많은 ____ 을/를 가지고 있다면, 당신에게는 자녀가 많은 것이다.
   a. 친척들
   b. 조상들
   c. 자식들
   d. 직장동료들

B. 다음 문장에 가장 알맞은 단어를 고르시오.

1. 다윈은 갈라파고스 섬에 있는 동물 ____ 가운데 어떤 것을 가장 많이 연구했는가?
   a. 선구자   b. 종속자   c. 속국   d. 종

2. 모든 돌의 색조가 _____ 하다.
   a. 편의시설　　　b. 다양　　　c. 양　　　d. 게으름

3. 경기장에서 상대팀 선수에게 태클을 가할 때, 그들에게 너무 _____ 않도록 노력해라.
   a. 텅 빈　　　　　　　b. 영향력 있는
   c. 해가 되는(상처 주는)　　d. 까다로운

4. 그가 잠시 _____ 하겠다고 말하긴 했지만, 나는 그가 그렇게 오래 자취를 감출지는 몰랐다.
   a. 사라져 있다　b. 싹트다　　c. 번성하다　　d. 감소하다

5. 우리는 아직도 가장 강하고 _____ 것만이 살아남는 일종의 정글 같은 현대 사회 속에서 살아가고 있다.
   a. 가장 취약한　　　　　　b. 가장 적응력 있는
   c. 가장 진부한　　　　　　d. 가장 유연한

Listening Comprehension　　p.208~209

1. 적자생존의 의미는 무엇인가?
   a. 때때로 약한 동물이 강한 동물을 정복한다.
   b. 동물의 왕국에서 다른 동물 보다 더 운이 좋은 동물도 있다.
   c. 다윈은 그의 이론을 완전히 확신하지는 못했다.
   d. 강한 동물일수록 환경에 완벽하게 적응하고, 약한 동물은 적응하지 못한다.

2. 작가가 진화론을 설명하는 이유는 무엇인가?
   a. 과학은 자연에 관한 다양한 것을 측정하고, 규명하고, 관찰하기 위해서 끊임없이 탐색한다.
   b. 자연도태 이론을 이해하는 것이 자연을 이해하는 열쇠이다.
   c. 다윈은 과학 저널에 그의 이론을 발표하기 위해 노력했다.
   d. 동물이 어떻게 진화하고 살아남는지에 관련하여 상충하는 이론들이 너무 많다.

3. 작가는 진화론을 어떻게 소개하는가?
   a. 적응은 열대지방에 사는 몸집 큰 동물들에게만 필요한 것이다.
   b. 자손의 중요성에 대해 토의하면서
   c. 만일 환경에 적합한 동물이 아니라면, 그 동물들은 환경에 적응하거나 아니면 소멸하게 된다.
   d. 자손이 그렇게 중요하지는 않다고 결론내리면서

4. 강의의 일부를 다시 듣고 문제에 답하시오. 이 구절의 기능은 무엇인가?
   a. 다윈의 이론에 따르면, 자손이 많으면 살아남아 적응할 확률이 더 크다는 것
   b. 다윈의 진화론은 주로 자손에 좌우된다는 것
   c. 다윈 이론의 한계를 설명하기 위한 것
   d. 다윈과 뉴턴이 과학적 증거를 어떻게 검토했는지를 대비시키기 위한 것

5. 작가에 따르면, 진화론의 특징을 나타내는 두 가지 요소는 무엇인가? 정답 두 개를 고르시오.
   a. 자연도태(약한 것이 소멸)
   b. 식물계에서의 분화
   c. 개별적으로 유리한 점들
   d. 행성들의 간격 패턴

6. 작가가 진화에 대해 암시하는 바는 무엇인가?
   a. 진화는 성경 내용과 상충하는 증명되지 않은 이론이다.
   b. 진화와 소멸 이론은 자연을 이해하는데 주요하다.
   c. 진화는 대체로 종교계에서 검증받지 못한 것이다.
   d. 동물계와 식물계에서 생존의 본질은 생활에 대한 적응이다.

Vocabulary Test　　p.210~211

1. 본문의 '죽다'와 가장 근접한 의미의 단어는?
   a. 죽다　　　　　　　　b. 약해지다
   c. 보충하다　　　　　　d. 재생시키다

2. 본문의 '특징'과 가장 근접한 의미의 단어는?
   a. 측면　　b. 인물비평　　c. 특징　　d. 기능

3. 본문의 '적합한'과 가장 근접한 의미의 단어는?
   a. 동등한　　b. 알맞은　　c. 비슷한　　d. 반대의

4. 본문의 '자식'과 가장 근접한 의미의 단어는?
   a. 종　　b. 친척들　　c. 집단들　　d. 자식들

5. 본문의 '유리한'과 가장 근접한 의미의 단어는?
   a. 유리한　　b. 기꺼이 하는　　c. 무뚝뚝한　　d. 반대의

6. 본문의 '변화(다양)'와 가장 근접한 의미의 단어는?
   a. 변형　　b. 이상함　　c. 부족　　d. 거부

7. 본문의 '해로운'과 가장 근접한 의미의 단어는?
   a. 유해한　　b. 부적절한　　c. 예기치 않은　　d. 학대하는

8. 본문의 '적응성 있는'과 가장 근접한 의미의 단어는?
   a. 엄격한　　　　　　b. 알맞은
   c. 꽉 죄인　　　　　　d. 유연성 없는

Paraphrasing　　p.211

1. 다윈이 말하는 「적자」란 어떤 그룹 내에서 가장 크고, 가장 영리하고, 가장 강한 자라는 의미가 아니다.
   a. 그의 말의 의미는 대가족이 역효과를 낸다는 것이었다.
   b. 그의 이론과 관련하여 할 일이 많다.
   c. 그는 다른 종들보다 자손 수가 많은 종에 대해 언급했다.
   d. 가장 영리한 동물이 항상 가장 오래 생존하는 것은 아니다.

2. 만약 어떤 종이 어떤 환경에 적응할 수 있는 자손을 남길 수 없다면 그 종은 머지않아 멸종할 것이다.

   a. 자연도태 이론이 주장하는 것은 동물들이 삶의 균형이 필요하다는 것이다.

   b. 대부분의 생태학적 서식지는 자연도태에 적합하지 않다.

   c. 동물들이 적응하지 못하면 죽게 될 것이라는 것이 자연도태 이론의 핵심이다.

   d. 자연의 정점은 강한 것이 어린 것을 잡아먹는다는 것이다.

| Unit 26 | The Grizzly Bear | p.218 |

회색곰

회색 곰은 북미의 서부와 유럽, 아시아의 일부에서 볼 수 있다. 겨울 동안, 그들은 신체 기능들이 계속 활동하고 있으며 체온이 정상으로 유지되고 있다는 사실을 제외하면 동면과 유사한 상태를 유지한다. 암회색 곰은 매년 6개월에서 9개월의 임신기간을 거쳐 한 배에 한 마리에서 네 마리 정도의 새끼를 낳는다. 회색 곰은 털로 덮인 큰 근육질의 체격을 갖고 있다. 다 자란 회색 곰은 보통 몸길이가 2.5m, 체중이 360kg이 되지만, 이 동물은 매우 민첩해서 삼림과 황량한 산 속에서도 재빨리 움직일 수 있다. 회색 곰은 궁지에 몰렸을 때 가장 위험스런 동물 중의 하나가 된다. 날카로운 발톱으로 공격하고 이빨로 잡아 뜯어 자신을 방어하려고 한다. 그러나 그러한 사나운 행동을 할 수 있는 반면에 길들이면 온순하게 말을 잘 듣는다.

Sentence Completion   p.214~215

A. 다음 문장에 가장 알맞은 단어를 고르시오.

1. 만일 당신이 ____ 액이 없다면, 당신은 아마도 죽은 것이다.
   a. 자금의   b. 세포의
   c. 물질의   d. 신체의(체액)

2. 그것은 맨 처음 착상해서, ____ 을/를 겪고, 태어나서, 양육과 발전으로 계속 이어진다.
   a. 잉태   b. 진행   c. 발달   d. 건설

3. 경제의 ____ 이/가 매우 좋고, 제조업도 잘 되고 있다.
   a. 상태   b. 부정   c. 강하   d. 불경기

4. 동물이 ____ 에 있을 때, 그것은 오랜 시간 잠을 자고 있는 것이다.
   a. 초만원   b. 동면   c. 고통   d. 농토

5. 동물이 ____ 을/를 낳으면, 그것은 새끼를 여러 마리 낳는 것이다.
   a. 웅덩이   b. (한 배에서 태어난)새끼
   c. 역병   d. 폭도

B. 다음 문장에 가장 알맞은 단어를 고르시오.

1. 카라코람 산맥의 ____ 을/를 오르려 해봤자 소용없다. 그곳은 매우 가파르다.
   a. 흔적   b. 개천   c. 경치   d. 지형

2. 한국 10대들의 ____ 신장은 지난 수십 년간에 걸쳐 몇 센티미터씩 커졌다.
   a. 대량의   b. 비정상적인
   c. 힘든   d. 평균(보통)의

3. 그 최고의 체조선수는 매우 빠르고 체조경기장에서 움직임이 ____ 했다.
   a. 낭비하는   b. 부주의한   c. 민첩한   d. 육중한

4. 그 ____ 회색 곰은 캐나다 평원에서 일상적으로 무스들을 많이 죽였다.
   a. 사나운   b. 근면한
   c. 온순한   d. 신뢰할 수 있는

5. 지면이 ____ 법의학 조사관들이 증거를 수집하는데 어려움을 겪었다.
   a. 부드러워서   b. 험해서
   c. 도로 포장이 잘돼서   d. 위생적이어서

Listening Comprehension   p.216~217

1. 동면은 무엇인가?
   a. 먹이를 구하기 위해서 일부 동물들이 취하는 일종의 습관이다.
   b. 동물의 서식지와 사냥 지역 사이의 거리를 말한다.
   c. 일부 포유류들이 휴식을 다소 오랜 동안 취하는 것이다.
   d. 다른 지역으로 이동하는 패턴이다.

2. 작가가 회색 곰을 설명하는 이유는 무엇인가?
   a. 그들만의 독특한 휴식취하는 방법과 왜 그들이 인상적인 킬러인지에 대해 언급하기 위한 것
   b. 곰의 경쟁자들에 대해 더 많이 알기 위한 것
   c. 그들의 잉태 기간은 매우 흔한 일이기 때문에
   d. 곰의 여러 패턴들을 추적하기 위해서, 과학자들은 수십 년간 곰을 연구해야 하기 때문에

3. 작가는 회색 곰을 어떻게 소개하는가?
   a. 국민들 대다수가 곰을 혐오하는데, 특히 몸집이 큰 곰을 혐오한다.
   b. 암컷 회색 곰에 대해 설명하면서
   c. 그것들은 전 세계에서 세 지역에서 발견된다.
   d. 회색 곰의 새끼들의 몸집이 점점 작아지는 패턴이 생기고 있다.

4. 강의의 일부를 다시 듣고 문제에 답하시오. 이 구절의 기능은 무엇인가?
   a. 회색 곰의 생태에 있어 기본적인 사항들을 소개하기 위한 것
   b. 어떻게 하면 우리가 회색 곰을 구할 수 있는지에 대한 예를 제시하기 위한 것
   c. 추운 겨울, 동면의 한계를 설명하기 위한 것
   d. 검은색 곰과 회색 곰을 대비시키기 위한 것

5. 작가에 따르면, 회색 곰들이 싸울 때 취하는 두 가지 방법은 무엇인가? 정답 두 개를 고르시오.
   a. 이빨을 사용
   b. 새끼를 완충지대로 사용하는 것
   c. 발톱을 사용
   d. 민첩한 행동과 숲 이곳저곳을 누비는 것

6. 작가가 회색 곰에 대해 암시하는 바는 무엇인가?
   a. 그들은 매우 위험하고 자기 영역에 대한 강한 습성을 갖고 있다.
   b. 아시아 지역에서 활동하는 회색 곰이 늘고 있다.
   c. 많은 곰들이 집에서 키우는 좋은 애완용이 되고 있다.
   d. 털이 많은 회색 곰도 있다.

Vocabulary Test   p.218~219

1. 본문의 '상태'와 가장 근접한 의미의 단어는?
   a. 장소   b. 상태   c. 지역   d. 위치

2. 본문의 '동면'과 가장 근접한 의미의 단어는?
   a. 겨울잠   b. 따뜻하게 함
   c. 악의   d. 낮잠

3. 본문의 '신체상의'와 가장 근접한 의미의 단어는?
   a. 해부의   b. 물 같은   c. 육체의   d. 추상적인

4. 본문의 '새끼'와 가장 근접한 의미의 단어는?
   a. 쓰레기   b. 선택   c. 아이들   d. 공급품

5. 본문의 '잉태'와 가장 근접한 의미의 단어는?
   a. 진화   b. 진보   c. 행동   d. 임신

6. 본문의 '보통의'와 가장 근접한 의미의 단어는?
   a. 드문   b. 일반적인
   c. 특이한   d. 불화를 일으키는

7. 본문의 '민첩한'과 가장 근접한 의미의 단어는?
   a. 지적인   b. 기어 다니는
   c. 빠른   d. 부드러운

8. 본문의 '험한'과 가장 근접한 의미의 단어는?
   a. 고르지 못한   b. 평평한
   c. 세련된   d. 거절할 수 있는

Paraphrasing   p.219

1. 겨울 동안, 그들은 신체 기능들이 계속 활동하고 있으며 체온이 정상으로 유지되고 있다는 사실을 제외하면 동면과 유사한 상태를 유지한다.
   a. 곰이 동면할 때, 완전 정지 상태로 들어간다.
   b. 공기 흐름 때문에 종종 곰이 동면에서 깨어날 수도 있다.
   c. 동면은 완전한 수면상태는 아니다. 여러 신체 기능이 그동안에도 계속 작동한다.
   d. 겨울에 체온이 종종 몇 도씩 증가한다.

2. 그러나 그러한 사나운 행동을 할 수 있는 반면에 길들이면 온순하게 말을 잘 듣는다.
   a. 곰의 사나운 행동도 전문가에 의해 길들여 질 수 있다.
   b. 곰의 격한 성미는 대부분 과학적 방식으로 치료 가능하다.
   c. 지나치게 광활한 지역은 수컷 회색 곰한테 좋지 않다.
   d. 그 엉뚱한 행동에도 불구하고, 곰은 사랑스런 친구이다.

Unit 27   Life in the Sea   p.226

바다 생물

바닷속 생물의 다양함과 아름다움은 끝없는 경이로움의 원천이다. 바다에 살고 있는 생물의 수는 하늘에 있는 별의 숫자보다 많다. 바다에는 여러 종류의 다양한 커다란 동물들은 말할 것도 없고, 현미경의 도움으로나 볼 수 있는 작은 무수한 생물들이 많다. 바다에 사는 가장 큰 동물은 남극의 흰 수염고래로서 평균 몸길이가 약 30미터, 체중 135톤으로, 지상 최대의 동물이라고 하는 공룡 체중의 3배를 훨씬 넘는다. 바다의 생물은 상상할 수 있는 온갖 크기, 모습, 형태를 하고 있다. 불가사리는 살아 있는 돌의 숲이라고 칭하는 핑크 산호의 가지들에 달라붙어 있고, 보기에도 무서운 아귀는 크고 납작한 머리를 갖고 있으며 그 거대한 입에는 날카롭고 뾰족한 이빨이 있고, 먹이를 찾으러 깊은 바닷속을 배회하고 있다.

Sentence Completion   p.222~223

A. 다음 문장에 가장 알맞은 단어를 고르시오.

1. 웅덩이에 열대산 물고기가 ____ 있으면, 그것은 그런 물고기로 가득 차 있는 것이다.
   a. 활기찬   b. 비우고 있는   c. 희박한   d. 들끓는

2. 당신의 소유지에서 ____ 을/를 내쫓는다면, 당신은 그 사람을 내보내는 것이다.
   a. 표면   b. 불운   c. 거주자   d. 접촉

3. 당신이 _____ 시간에 걸쳐 운전을 한다면, 당신은 매우 오랜 시간 운전하고 있는 것이다.
   a. 끝없는   b. 셀 수 있는   c. 포함하는   d. 목적 있는

4. 그들은 멋진 궁전과 위엄 있는 교회들을 _____ 을 가지고 응시했다.
   a. 위험   b. 경이로움   c. 현상   d. 창의력

5. 만일 당신 회사가 _____ 달러의 판매고를 올렸다면, 그것은 매우 성공한 회사이다.
   a. 보통의   b. 1조의   c. 부적절한   d. 빈약한

B. 다음 문장에 가장 알맞은 단어를 고르시오.

1. 두루마리 화장지 한 장이 그녀의 하이힐에 _____.
   a. 껴안았다   b. 잡았다
   c. 풀었다   d. 달라 붙어있었다

2. 그 조직은 그 나라에 보내는 인도적 _____ 을/를 절반 이상 늘렸다.
   a. 원조(도움)   b. 제재조치   c. 위협   d. 봉쇄

3. 코뿔소가 한때 고대 중국에서 _____ 사실을 알고 있었니?
   a. 비틀거린   b. 마구 때린   c. 큰 실수한   d. 돌아다닌

4. 그 제빵사는 케이크를 _____, 그것을 오븐에 넣었다.
   a. 평평하게 만들었고   b. 큰 걸음을 걸었고
   c. 희미하게 했고   d. (물을)튀겼고

5. 바다 전체에 사는 해양 생물을 모두 세는 것은 _____ 일이 아니다.
   a. 성급한   b. 상상할 수 있는
   c. 믿을 수 없는   d. 사악한

Listening Comprehension   p.224~225

1. 바다 속에 사는 것 가운데 가장 멋진 포유류는 무엇인가?
   a. 길이가 최고 30미터에 이르는 남극의 흰 수염고래
   b. 호주 연안선을 따라 늘어서 있는 산호초
   c. 평범한 주황색 불가사리
   d. 머리 부분이 납작한 이상한 모양의 아귀

2. 작가가 바다 생물에 대해 설명하는 이유는 무엇인가?
   a. 많은 다양한 생물 형태에 초점을 맞추기 위한 것
   b. 생김새가 무시무시한 아귀에 대해 언급하기 위한 것
   c. 흰 수염고래와 다른 생물들의 관계를 예측하기 위한 것
   d. 해저에 사는 새로운 생물 형태들의 패턴에 대해 언급하기 위한 것

3. 작가는 바다 생물을 어떻게 소개하는가?
   a. 지구상에 존재하는 엄청나게 많은 생물들을 언급하면서
   b. 해양에 사는 생물들의 수를 계산하면서
   c. 미래 바다의 건강 상태를 예측하면서
   d. 공룡과 흰 수염고래를 비교하면서

4. 강의의 일부를 다시 듣고 문제에 답하시오. 이 구절의 기능은 무엇인가?
   a. 과학자들이 바다 생물의 대부분을 이미 분류했다는 것
   b. 해양의 신비로움에 관련해 우리의 호기심을 자극하기 위한 것
   c. 우리 해양에 흥미롭고 아주 다양한 바다 생물이 있다는 것
   d. 공룡이 흰 수염고래보다 훨씬 더 흥미롭다는 것

5. 작가에 따르면, 바다 생물 중 매우 흥미로운 두 가지 형태는 무엇인가? 정답 두 개를 고르시오.
   a. 남극 흰 수염고래
   b. 푸른 돌고래
   c. 산호 가지에 붙어있는 불가사리
   d. 해마

6. 작가가 바다에 대해 암시하는 바는 무엇인가?
   a. 대부분의 바다 생물도 육지 생물만큼 흥미롭다.
   b. 산호 가지들은 인류가 초래한 오염 때문에 위험에 처해있다.
   c. 그는 흰 수염고래가 멸종할 것이라고 예측한다.
   d. 그는 불가사리의 생태 주기 패턴을 추적한다.

Vocabulary Test   p.226~227

1. 본문의 '끝없는'과 가장 근접한 의미의 단어는?
   a. 간헐성의   b. 일시적인   c. 무한한   d. 진행 중인

2. 본문의 '경이'와 가장 근접한 의미의 단어는?
   a. 감탄   b. 승인   c. 성공   d. 투쟁

3. 본문의 '들끓는'과 가장 근접한 의미의 단어는?
   a. 교육하는   b. 들끓는
   c. 참석하는   d. 한가히 거니는

4. 본문의 '도움'과 가장 근접한 의미의 단어는?
   a. 기아   b. 장애   c. 조수   d. 도움

5. 본문의 '거주자'와 가장 근접한 의미의 단어는?
   a. 궤양   b. 주민
   c. 자택소유자   d. 번역가

6. 본문의 '돌아다니다'와 가장 근접한 의미의 단어는?
   a. 찾다   b. 퍼지다
   c. 배회하다   d. 복종시키다

7. 본문의 '상상(생각)할 수 있는'과 가장 근접한 의미의 단어는?
   a. 불가능한   b. 믿기 힘든
   c. 충분한   d. 상상할 수 있는

8. 본문의 '달라붙다'와 가장 근접한 의미의 단어는?
   a. 분리시키다   b. 세게 치다
   c. 달라붙다   d. 통과하다

1. 바다에 사는 가장 큰 동물은 남극의 흰 수염고래로서 평균 몸길이가 약 30미터, 체중 135톤으로, 지상 최대의 동물이라고 하는 공룡 체중의 3배를 훨씬 넘는다.

   a. 고래는 대부분 몸집이 크지만, 흰 수염고래 보다는 작다.
   b. 가장 큰 해양 포유류는 몸집이 가장 컸던 공룡보다 몸무게가 3배 더 나간다.
   c. 가장 큰 해양 포유류는 몸집이 가장 컸던 공룡보다 길이가 3배 더 길다.
   d. 남극의 흰 수염고래는 포유류 가운데 식성이 가장 좋다.

2. 불가사리는 살아 있는 돌의 숲이라고 칭하는 핑크 산호의 가지들에 달라붙어 있고, 보기에도 무서운 아귀는 크고 납작한 머리를 갖고 있으며 그 거대한 입에는 날카롭고 뾰족한 이빨이 있고, 먹이를 찾으러 깊은 바다 속을 배회하고 있다.

   a. 해저에는 다양한 바다 생물이 넘쳐 난다.
   b. 아귀는 그 큰 이빨로 산호를 손쉽게 먹어치운다.
   c. 바다 생물이 너무 많으면 바다의 생물학적 균형을 해치게 된다.
   d. 핑크 산호는 대부분 흰 수염고래를 위해 플랑크톤을 끌어당긴다.

엔지니어 (1)

1876년, 토마스 에디슨은 뉴저지 주의 멘로 공원에 현재의 공업기술연구소의 원형이라 할 수 있는 「발명공장」을 설립했다. 그는 거기에 약간의 젊은 조수와 12명의 기계공을 모아 발명에 관한 일만을 했다. 에디슨의 목표는 「열흘마다 하나의 작은, 거의 반년마다 하나의 큰 발명」이었고, 그는 이것을 간단히 달성했다. 87년에 공장을 떠날 무렵에는 에디슨은 실용적인 백열전구와 전기 계통과 축음기를 포함한 약 400개의 특허를 취득했다. 하지만 에디슨의 가장 위대한 발명은 문제해결에 체계적으로 임했던 점이다. 하나의 문제와 가능한 해결책을 모든 면에서 조사하고, 자신의 발명과 관련이 있는 특수한 문제에서도 해결하려는 노력을 아끼지 않았다. 예를 들면 발전기, 휴즈, 전선관을 개발함으로써 전등을 그저 신기한 것이 아니라 실용적인 실체로 만들었던 것이다.

A. 다음 문장에 가장 알맞은 단어를 고르시오.

1. ____ 은/는 BMW 자동차를 해체하고, 밤새 엔진을 재정비한다.
   a. 개업의들   b. 변호사들   c. 현역 군인들   d. 기계공들

2. 당신이 어떤 상품에 대해 처음으로 ____ 을/를 가지고 있다면, 당신은 독점권을 갖는 것이다.
   a. 시민권   b. 특허   c. 법안   d. 장려금

3. 만일 당신이 ____ 을/를 만들고 있다면, 당신은 그것의 첫 번째 복제품을 만들고 있는 것이다.
   a. 기준   b. 변칙
   c. 견본   d. 대체적 범위

4. 그가 들어가자, ____ 멤버들이 자리에서 일어났다.
   a. 분산된   b. 모여 있던   c. 파괴된   d. 축적된

5. 만일 당신이 ____ 을/를 이루기 시작한다면, 당신은 어떤 것을 하기 위해서 노력하는 것이다.
   a. 목표   b. 축적   c. 정상   d. 횡재

B. 다음 문장에 가장 알맞은 단어를 고르시오.

1. 냉방 시설 시스템을 위해 당신이 ____ 을/를 설치할 때, 반드시 충분한 도구가 있어야 한다.
   a. 견본들   b. 도관들   c. 깔때기들   d. 하수 오물

2. 대학살은 특정 인종 집단, 주로 유태인들을 절멸시키기 위해 계산된, 매우 ____ 계획이었다.
   a. 방향의   b. 조직적인   c. 돌로 덮여진   d. 존경받는

3. 대평원에 위치한 그 발전소는 ____ 으로, 그 나라에서 처음 동물의 배설물을 연소시킨 곳이다.
   a. 획일   b. 관습   c. 신기한 것   d. 항로

4. ____ 이/가 꺼지면, 병원 운영에 필요한 전력을 전혀 얻지 못하게 될 것이다.
   a. 공급업자들   b. 서류분쇄기들
   c. 발전기들   d. 도랑들

5. 수백만 명이 그 파괴된 도시에서 벗어나려고 ____ 있었다. 그 도시는 생활에 기본적으로 필요한 것들 중 대부분이 붕괴되었다.
   a. 노력하고   b. 팔다리를 절단하고
   c. 빈둥거리고   d. 공상하고

1. 에디슨의 가장 중요한 발명품은 무엇인가?
   a. 마루 밑 난방 시스템   b. 전신주
   c. 백열전구   d. 비행기 레이더 시스템

2. 작가가 에디슨을 설명하는 이유는 무엇인가?
   a. 백열등의 비실용성을 보여주기 위한 것
   b. 공학적 측면에서, 에니슨의 성공이 얼마나 대단한 것인지 보여주기 위한 것

c. 그가 겪은 좌절감을 드러내기 위한 것

d. 뉴저지 소재 공학 연구실을 홍보하기 위한 것

3. 작가는 에디슨을 어떻게 소개하는가?

a. 그의 "발명 공장"에 대해 언급하면서

b. 조수와의 관계를 설명하면서

c. 전기에 관련하여, 그의 성공을 예측하면서

d. 400건의 특허 출원을 칭찬하면서

4. 강의의 일부를 다시 듣고 문제에 답하시오. 이 구절의 기능은 무엇인가?

a. 독특한 문제에 대한 해결법을 소개하기 위한 것

b. 에디슨의 문제 해결에 대한 짜임새 있는 접근법에 대한 예를 제시하기 위한 것

c. 백열전구의 한계를 설명하기 위한 것

d. 에디슨과 벨의 기술을 대비시키기 위한 것

5. 교수에 따르면, 백열전구 발견에 기여한 두 가지 요소는 무엇인가? 정답 두 개를 고르시오.

a. 헌신적인 연구 직원 한 명이 있었다는 것

b. 축음기에서 전송 기술을 이용한 것

c. 발명품에 대한 철저한 조사 과정

d. 어떤 시간의 간격을 두고 발명 목표를 정한 것

6. 작가가 에디슨에 대해 암시하는 바는 무엇인가?

a. 오늘날 독창적인 발명가들이 더 많이 필요하다는 것

b. 인내가 결국 멋진 발명품이라는 좋은 성과를 만들어낸다.

c. 열흘마다 작은 발명품을 만드는 것으로는 충분치 않다.

d. 발전기, 퓨즈, 도관들을 개발하는 것은 힘든 과정이다.

Vocabulary Test p.234~235

1. 본문의 '원형'과 가장 근접한 의미의 단어는?

a. 회의주의   b. 원본   c. 시력검사표   d. 삽화

2. 본문의 '모으다'와 가장 근접한 의미의 단어는?

a. 협조하다   b. 따로 떼어두다

c. 모으다   d. 성공하다

3. 본문의 '기계공'과 가장 근접한 의미의 단어는?

a. 엔지니어   b. 머리 수건   c. 전문적 방법   d. 권위자

4. 본문의 '목표'와 가장 근접한 의미의 단어는?

a. 이론적 근거   b. 우두머리   c. 성명   d. 목적

5. 본문의 '특허'와 가장 근접한 의미의 단어는?

a. 판권   b. 법   c. 특정 분야   d. 제안

6. 본문의 '조직적인'과 가장 근접한 의미의 단어는?

a. 주어진   b. 똑똑 떨어진

c. 정리된   d. 사전 모의한

7. 본문의 '노력하다'와 가장 근접한 의미의 단어는?

a. 어슬렁거리다   b. 간청하다

c. 노력하다   d. 받쳐 주다

8. 본문의 '발전기'와 가장 근접한 의미의 단어는?

a. 전력 생산기   b. 촉매제

c. 회로   d. 비행기 동체

Paraphrasing p.235

1. 하지만 에디슨의 가장 위대한 발명은 문제해결에 체계적으로 임했던 점이다.

a. 아직 에디슨은 대단한 발명품을 만들어 내지 못했다.

b. 그의 체계적인 접근은 지나치게 조직적이었다.

c. 에디슨은 위대한 발명가였지만, 또한 가난한 경영자였다.

d. 문제 해결은 에디슨이 매우 잘 했던 것이었다.

2. 하나의 문제와 가능한 해결책을 모든 면에서 조사하고, 자신의 발명과 관련이 있는 특수한 문제에서도 해결하려는 노력을 아끼지 않았다.

a. 에디슨의 발명과 관련된 문제들은 결코 해결되지 않았다.

b. 에디슨이 하려 했던 것은 모든 변형에 대한 해결책을 찾으려 노력하는 것이었다.

c. 너무나 많은 조사를 통해 확인되지 않은 해결책을 얻을 수 있다.

d. 발명품을 보면서 에디슨을 연상하는 사람들도 있었다.

Unit 29 Engineer (2) p.242

엔지니어 (2)

기술은 숙련자로부터 수습공에게 전해지고 있었기 때문에 18세기 후기까지, 공학은 지적 직업이 아니라 수공업직으로 간주되었다. 그러나 1794년, 최초의 기술자 양성학교가 설립되었다. 파리의 에콜 폴리테크닉이다. 미국에서는 30년 늦게 렌셀러 폴리테크닉 인스티튜트라는 최초의 기술학교가 개교했다. 오늘날에는 미국에서만도 280개를 넘는 학교에서 6만 5,000개의 공학계 학위가 수여되고 있다. 메사추세츠 공과대학(MIT)같은 학교는 새로운 타입의 기술자를 만들어 내기 위해 힘쓰고 있다. 그곳의 학생들은 과학의 개념과 실제의 응용에 대해서 집중적인 교육을 받으며 그와 동시에 인문과학에 대해서도 폭넓게 공부한다. 학생들의 미적 가치관과 레크레이션 감각이 발달하도록 도움으로써 이 미래의 기술자들이 사회가 직면하는 방대한 문제들에 좀더 능숙하게 대처할 수 있으리라고 MIT의 교수진은 생각하고 있다.

A. 다음 문장에 가장 알맞은 단어를 고르시오.

1. 누군가 ____ 에 신경 쓰고 있다면, 그들은 아이디어, 생각, 믿음을 생각하고 있는 것이다.
   a. 일관성   b. 양심   c. 개념   d. 징병제

2. 당신이 상당한 직업 ____ 을/를 가지고 있다면, 당신은 특정 업무에서 매우 훈련받은 사람이다.
   a. 간청   b. 서투름
   c. 칸막이 공간   d. 기술

3. 당신이 상당한 여행 ____ 이/가 있다면, 당신은 새로운 문화를 배우게 될 것이다.
   a. 친척관계   b. 고전 문학   c. 경험   d. 폭로

4. 당신이 직장에서 ____ 로 고려된다면, 당신은 인턴처럼 그 일이 처음인 것이다.
   a. 견습생   b. 소프트웨어 개발자
   c. 세계적 관여주의자   d. 편집장

5. 만일 당신이 열려있는 ____ 마음을 갖고 있다면, 당신은 많은 것을 배우게 될 것이다.
   a. 좁은   b. 넓은
   c. 불명예스러운   d. 분리된

B. 다음 문장에 가장 알맞은 단어를 고르시오.

1. MIT가 ____ 강의를 개설한 덕분에 그 해 입학률이 더 높아졌다.
   a. 공간적인   b. 방대한
   c. 얇은   d. 평범한

2. 만일 마드리드에 있는 박물관을 방문하게 되면, 피카소가 그린 게르니카의 ____ 아름다움에 넋을 잃을 것이다.
   a. 물에 잠긴   b. 지나치게 신경질적인
   c. 낡아빠진   d. 미적인

3. 독서에 어려움을 느끼는 사람들 중, ____ 독서 프로그램에 소속된 37명이 보통 수준의 지도 그룹에 소속된 12명을 앞질렀다.
   a. 집중적인   b. 널찍한
   c. 아무렇게나 하는   d. 사건 많은

4. 페루에 배치된 전파 망원경 위성 ____ 이/가 우주 깊은 곳을 향하고 있었다.
   a. 부족   b. 결핍
   c. 의복   d. 다량

5. 만일 당신이 에베레스트 산을 오르기 전에 ____ 않다면, 재난이 일어날 공산이 크다.
   a. 흥분하지   b. 마지못해 하지
   c. 준비되어 있지   d. 소환되지

1. MIT가 지금 가르치려는 것은 무엇인가?
   a. 구조 공학이 결부된 인문학
   b. 특정 과학적 개념에 대한 훈련
   c. 오래된 기술 습득을 위한 실용적 개념들
   d. 토목 공학이 결부된 인문학 수업

2. 작가가 공학을 설명하는 이유는 무엇인가?
   a. 더 많은 공업 전문대학에서의 성장을 장려하기 위한 것
   b. 응용부분에 많이 노출되도록 하기 위한 것
   c. 한 전문분야의 발전을 보여주기 위한 것
   d. 프랑스와 미국 학교의 패턴을 묘사하기 위한 것

3. 작가는 공학을 어떻게 소개하는가?
   a. 프랑스에 가도록 학생들을 격려하면서
   b. 단순직이 전문직으로 발전하는 것을 보여주면서
   c. 미국에 들어가는 방법을 가르쳐주면서
   d. 학생들을 MIT 시험에 대비할 수 있도록 하면서

4. 강의의 일부를 다시 듣고 문제에 답하시오. 이 구절의 기능은 무엇인가?
   a. 공학 학교의 다양한 교육 방법을 소개하기 위한 것
   b. 렌셀러 공대를 다시 개교하기 위한 것
   c. 공학 학교의 한계를 설명하기 위한 것
   d. 집중적인 과학 훈련 학문들을 대비시키기 위한 것

5. 교수에 따르면, 학생들이 받게 되는 두 가지 학문 형태는 무엇인가? 정답 두 개를 고르시오.
   a. 실용적인 일부 개념들
   b. 미적 감각과 디자인
   c. 정정당당함과 재미
   d. 다양한 사회 문제

6. 작가가 공학에 대해 암시하는 바는 무엇인가?
   a. 에꼴 폴리테크닉이 MIT 보다 우세하다하는 것
   b. 1794년 이후로 기술이 쇠퇴했다는 것
   c. 미적 가치관이 엔지니어에게 중요할 수 도 있다는 것
   d. 미래의 엔지니어들은 예술에 대해 정통하게 될 것이라는 것

1. 본문의 '기술'과 가장 근접한 의미의 단어는?
   a. 습관   b. 서투름   c. 기술   d. 슬픔

2. 본문의 '도제(견습생)'와 가장 근접한 의미의 단어는?
   a. 훈련생   b. 상담역   c. 중재자   d. 전문자

3. 본문의 '집중적인'과 가장 근접한 의미의 단어는?
   a. 기민한   b. 주의 깊은
   c. 변덕스러운   d. 집중적인

Answer Key

4. 본문의 '개념'과 가장 근접한 의미의 단어는?

   a. 암시   b. 생각   c. 인상   d. 추측

5. 본문의 '넓은'과 가장 근접한 의미의 단어는?

   a. 근원적인   b. 좁은   c. 혼란시키는   d. 광범한

6. 본문의 '체험(경험)'과 가장 근접한 의미의 단어는?

   a. 자백   b. 거절   c. 경험   d. 뉘우침

7. 본문의 '미적인'과 가장 근접한 의미의 단어는?

   a. 미적인   b. 솔직한   c. 악마의   d. 시각적인

8. 본문의 '준비된'과 가장 근접한 의미의 단어는?

   a. 원숙해진   b. 생각을 품은

   c. 준비된   d. 마지못해 하는

Paraphrasing   p.243

1. 메사추세츠 공과대학(MIT)같은 학교는 새로운 타입의 기술자를 만들어 내기 위해 힘쓰고 있다.

   a. MIT 소속 관리자들은 새로운 타입의 기술자들을 대량 배출해 내기 위해서 노력하는 중이다.

   b. MIT 소속 관리자들은 학교를 혁신시키고 있는 중이다.

   c. MIT의 엔지니어들은 학교의 교과과정을 개조하는 중이다.

   d. MIT와 같은 학교들이 새로운 타입의 기술자들을 대량 배출해 내기 위해서 노력하는 중이다.

2. 그곳의 학생들은 과학의 개념과 실제의 응용에 대해서 집중적인 교육을 받으며 그와 동시에 인문과학에 대해서도 폭넓게 공부한다.

   a. 과학 개념들만으로는 충분치 않다.

   b. 집중 훈련은 속성으로 배우는 국제 학생들을 위한 것이다.

   c. 인문학부는 예술 지향적인 학생들에게 이상적이다.

   d. 학생들이 개념을 이해하기 위해서는 더 많은 경험이 필요하다.

Unit 30   Roman Citizenship   p.250

로마 시민권

   고대 로마의 시민권은 오직 소수의 특권 계층만이 누릴 수 있었다. 로마 제국 내에 거주하는 사람들은 세 개의 계급, 즉 노예, 로마 제국 거주자, 시민으로 나눌 수 있었다. 노예는 재산으로 취급되었지만 약간의 제한된 권리를 갖고 있었다. 하지만 놀랍게도 주인이 해방한 노예는 자동으로 완벽한 로마 시민권자가 되었다. 로마 제국 영토에 거주하는 사람들은 2등 시민권 같은 제한된 형태의 로마 시민권을 받을 수 있었다. 완벽한 로마 시민권은 제국에서 특권 계층의 소유물이었다. 여자는 남자와 다른 계급에 속했고 절대로 완벽한 시민권을 받을 수 없었다. 이런 시민권으로는 투표를 할 수 없었고 공직에 나갈 수도 없었다. 로마 시민권을 얻을 수 있는 방법은 다양했다. 로마 시민권자의 남자 아이는 전부 자동으로 시민권을 받을 수 있었고, 해방 노예와 해방 노예의 남자 아이 또한 완벽한 로마 시민권을 받을 수 있었다. 그리고 제국을 위해 훌륭한 일을 한 사람에게도 시민권이 주어졌다. 로마는 점차 모든 식민지 거주자들에게도 시민권을 주기 시작했고, 3세기경 안토니우스 시민법을 통해 제국의 모든 남자에게 시민권을 주었다.

Sentence Completion   p.246~247

A. 다음 문장에 가장 알맞은 단어를 고르시오.

1. 그가 내 _____ 을/를 망가뜨리기 위해서 그것에 손을 대는 것을 보자, 나는 매우 화가 났다.

   a. 고물   b. 소유물   c. 신경   d. 약점

2. 그 인종차별주의 정치인은 이민자들을 _____ 시민으로 대한 것에 대해 비난받았다.

   a. 2등의   b. 배타적인   c. 자격 있는   d. 주요한

3. 당신이 사회에서 _____ 을/를 가진다면, 당신은 존중 받는 것이다.

   a. 분류   b. 지위(위신) c. 원한   d. 오명

4. 그와 그의 아내는 연간 부부소득이 6만 달러로, 중산 _____ 에 속한다.

   a. 여단   b. 무리   c. 계층   d. 대대

5. 당신이 사회에서 _____ 계층 출신이면, 지나치게 오만한 행동을 하지 않도록 노력하라.

   a. 사이가 멀어진   b. 가난한

   c. 교정하는   d. 특권의

B. 다음 문장에 가장 알맞은 단어를 고르시오.

1. K2 같은 산을 오르는 것은 당신이 _____ 노력해서 올라야 하는 것이다.

   a. 낙담하여   b. 대충

   c. 점진적으로(점점)   d. 호전적으로

2. 영어 공부에 대한 계획을 세워두지 않으면, 캐나다에 가서 ＿＿
을/를 신청해봤자 아무 소용없다.
   a. 성적   b. 시민권   c. 추방   d. 소유권

3. 로마 시민의 자식들은 남자일 경우, ＿＿ 시민권을 부여 받았다.
   a. 명예롭지 못하게   b. 무력으로
   c. 활기 없이   d. 자동적으로

4. 기상 상태가 매우 험악해서, 그린 랜드에는 ＿＿ 이/가 거의 없다.
   a. 거주민들   b. 자택 소유자
   c. 대여자   d. 채권자

5. 입학 위원회가 그의 학교 성적이 지나치게 ＿＿ 것에 대해 의문
을 제기 했다.
   a. 헛된   b. 뛰어난
   c. 시무룩한   d. 판권이 있는

Listening Comprehension   p.248~249

1. 누가 세 개의 계층으로 나뉘어 졌는가?
   a. 황제, 노예, 첩
   b. 노예, 거주자, 시민
   c. 여성, 아이들, 외국인 노예
   d. 노예, 거주자, 시민

2. 작가가 로마 시민권을 설명하는 이유는 무엇인가?
   a. 남성 거주자들이 제국을 지배했다는 것을 보여주기 위한 것
   b. 여성들에 대한 대우와 관련하여 로마 황제들을 비난하기 위한 것
   c. 완전한 시민권 부여의 중요성을 증명하기 위한 것
   d. 대다수 남성들이 어떻게 특권에서 제외되었는지를 언급하기
      위한 것

3. 작가는 로마 시민권을 어떻게 소개하는가?
   a. 그 지역에서의 삶에 대해 언급하면서
   b. 로마 시민권이 얼마나 일부에게만 제한되었는지를 보여주면서
   c. 완전한 로마 시민권을 받는 방법을 언급하면서
   d. 노예 소유의 장점을 보여주면서

4. 강의의 일부를 다시 듣고 문제에 답하시오. 이 구절의 기능은 무
엇인가?
   a. 칙령의 새 법을 소개하기 위한 것
   b. 노예와 시민의 삶에 있어서의 눈에 띄는 차이점들을 보여주
      기 위한 것
   c. 공직에 몸담는 것의 한계를 설명하기 위한 것
   d. 신속히 시민권을 부여받는 시민들에 대해 설명하기 위한 것

5. 작가에 따르면, 로마 여성에게 부여되지 않은 두 가지 권리는 무
엇인가? 정답 두 개를 고르시오.
   a. 그들은 투표할 수 없었다.
   b. 그들은 원로원의원의 자식들을 낳을 수 없었다.
   c. 시민이 될 수 없었다.
   d. 채소를 키울 수 없었다.

6. 작가가 로마 시민권에 대해 암시하는 바는 무엇인가?
   a. 여성이 남성과 다른 계층으로 분류되지 말았어야 했다는 것
   b. 시민권이 대체로 한 사람의 인생을 결정짓는 요소였다는 것
   c. 로마 영토가 노예를 위한 것이었다는 것
   d. 공직에 머무르는 것이 매우 심각한 일이었다는 것

Vocabulary Test   p.250~251

1. 본문의 "지위"와 가장 근접한 의미의 단어는?
   a. 조각상   b. 보유   c. 지위   d. 현상유지

2. 본문의 "계층"과 가장 근접한 의미의 단어는?
   a. 집회   b. 강의   c. 카스트   d. 평가

3. 본문의 "소유물"과 가장 근접한 의미의 단어는?
   a. 속성   b. 특징   c. 소유물   d. 심의

4. 본문의 "2등의"와 가장 근접한 의미의 단어는?
   a. 더 높은   b. 열등의   c. 기준의   d. 우수한

5. 본문의 "특권이 있는"과 가장 근접한 의미의 단어는?
   a. 소외된   b. 차상위의
   c. 혜택 받는   d. 과대평가된

6. 본문의 "시민권"과 가장 근접한 의미의 단어는?
   a. 관리   b. 의료 제공자
   c. 감금   d. 시민권

7. 본문의 "자동적으로"와 가장 근접한 의미의 단어는?
   a. 틀에 박혀   b. 자동으로
   c. 습관적으로   d. 명목상으로

8. 본문의 "뛰어난"과 가장 근접한 의미의 단어는?
   a. 누추한   b. 우수한   c. 평균의   d. 가려진

Paraphrasing   p.251

1. 여자는 남자와 다른 계급에 속했다.
   a. 여성이 대다수 남성보다 더 많은 권리를 부여받았다.
   b. 로마에서는 여성이 남성보다 우위에 있었다.
   c. 여성은 남성과 별개의 계층으로 대우받았다.
   d. 일부 여성은 남성보다 우월했던 것 같다.

2. 절대로 완벽한 시민권을 받을 수 없었다. 이런 시민권으로는 투
표를 할 수 없었고 공직에 나갈 수도 없었다.
   a. 그들은 법적 국민이 아니었기 때문에 투표할 수 없었다.
   b. 그들은 지방 선거에서 투표할 수 없었다.
   c. 완전한 법적 권리를 부여받는 것이 금지되어 있었다.
   d. 완전한 시민권을 부여받지 못한 것이 그들의 투표권에 불리
      하게 작용했나.

<table>
<tr><td>Unit 31</td><td>Water (1)</td><td>p.258</td></tr>
</table>

물 (1)

미국 최초의 대형 수력발전소는 1895년에 나이아가라 폭포에 건설되었다. 1968년까지 미국에서는 1500개 이상의 수력발전소가 가동되었고, 75년까지는 1조kwh의 전력이 생산되어 각 가정에 전기를 공급하고, 공장을 가동시켰다. 이 전력량 가운데 원자력 발전소를 포함한 증기력 발전소가 84.5%를 공급하고, 수력발전소가 약 15%를 생산, 합쳐서 하루에 110억kl의 물을 사용했다. 거대한 수력 발전댐은 현대공학의 경이 가운데 하나이다. 후버 댐은 특히 뛰어난 예로서 네바다 주와 아리조나 주 사이를 흐르는 콜로라도 강의 강바닥에서부터 221m의 높이로 솟은 후버 댐은 서반구에서 가장 높은 수력발전 댐이며, 유수의 관광지가 되어 연간 수 천 명이나 되는 관광객을 끌어들이고 있다.

Sentence Completion   p.254~255

A. 다음 문장에 가장 알맞은 단어를 고르시오.

1. 그 홀을 ____ 하는 불 때문에 연기 냄새가 공기 중에 가득하고, 그 연기로 인해 목이 간질거린다.
   a. 흐리게 하다　　　　　b. 먼지를 떨다
   c. 밝게 비추다　　　　　d. 그림자를 드리우다

2. 그 회사는 자금 부족으로 인해 그 공장을 ____ 할 원자재조차 조달하기 힘들게 되었다.
   a. 물을 주다　　b. 파괴하다　　c. 근절하다　　d. 가동하다

3. 당신 집에 ____ 동력이 있다면, 그것은 물의 힘으로 발생하는 전기를 공급받는 것이다.
   a. 물 같은　　　　　　　b. 수력 발전의
   c. 두들겨 펼 수 있는　　 d. 배터리의

4. 만일 당신이 에너지를 ____ 면, 당신은 그것을 발생시키는 것이다.
   a. 생산하다　　　　　　　b. 좌절시키다
   c. 끝내다　　　　　　　　d. 부활시키다

5. ____ 반응이 일정 강도에 다다르면, 그것은 "달아나 버리는"데, 다시 말해 위기의 상황이 벌어질 수 있는 것이다. 그것은 치명적일 수 있다.
   a. 핵의　　　b. 초기의　　　c. 초목의　　　d. 수소의

B. 다음 문장에 가장 알맞은 단어를 고르시오.

1. 작은 화산 분출이 그 호수 ____ 에서 발생했을 지도 모른다고 생각하는 사람들도 있다.
   a. 침대　　　b. 산호　　　c. 황무지　　　d. 바닥

2. 그 여자는 왼쪽 약지에 ____ 다이아몬드 반지를 끼고 행복해 했다.
   a. 융해하는　　b. 침착한　　c. 큼지막한　　d. 축 늘어진

3. 그 건물은 현대 건축의 ____ 로써, 열띠게 홍보되고 있다.
   a. 감각　　　b. 자갈　　　c. 경이　　　d. 강등

4. 최근에, 중국 수력발전 댐 근처에 새로운 관광 ____ 이/가 많이 있다.
   a. 명소들　　b. 속임수들　　c. 성질　　　d. 항소인들

5. 그 나이대 치고, 그녀의 아버지가 마라톤 기록을 세운 것은 매우 ____ 것이었다.
   a. 끔찍한　　　　　　　　b. 인상적인
   c. 대수롭지 않은　　　　　d. 감질 나는

Listening Comprehension   p.256~257

1. 후버 댐이 인상적인 이유는 무엇인가?
   a. 서반구에 있는 수력발전 댐 가운데 가장 높다.
   b. 하루에 물 110억 킬로리터를 제공한다.
   c. 그 댐의 높이를 보기 위해 많은 관광객들이 떼를 지어 몰려든다.
   d. 콜로라도에 많은 전력을 제공한다.

2. 작가가 수력발전소를 설명하는 이유는 무엇인가?
   a. 그것들은 건축공학이 만들어낸 경이이다.
   b. 나이아가라 폭포는 시간당 1조 킬로와트의 전력을 생산한다.
   c. 그것들은 미국의 중요 전력원이다.
   d. 그것들은 공학적으로 훌륭한 업적으로, 1895년으로 거슬러 올라간다.

3. 작가는 수력발전소를 어떻게 소개하는가?
   a. 후버댐으로 수천 명의 방문객을 유치하려 노력하면서
   b. 나이아가라 폭포를 시작으로, 수력발전소의 역사를 개괄하면서
   c. 미국과 캐나다의 수력발전 시스템을 대비시키면서
   d. 콜로라도 댐의 관광 패턴을 분석하면서

4. 강의의 일부를 다시 듣고 문제에 답하시오. 이 구절의 기능은 무엇인가?
   a. 애리조나와 네바다의 수력전기 프로젝트를 대비시키기 위한 것
   b. 현대 공학이 보여주는 여러 경이로움 가운데 하나에 대한 예를 제시하기 위한 것
   c. 수력발전 댐의 필요성과 중요성을 설명하기 위한 것
   d. 허버트 후버 미국 대통령을 소개하기 위한 것

5. 작가에 따르면, 미국 전력 수요에 도움이 되는 발전소 형태 두 가지는 무엇인가? 정답 두 개를 고르시오.
   a. 풍차 발전소
   b. 증기 발전소
   c. 옥수수 에탄올 발전소
   d. 핵발전소

6. 작가가 수력발전소에 대해 암시하는 바는 무엇인가?
   a. 증기 발전소는 충분히 이용되고 있진 않지만, 우리의 미래 에너지 수요에 중요한 열쇠이다.
   b. 가장 높은 수력발전 댐은 서반구에 있다.
   c. 수력발전소는 엄청난 양의 전력을 생산해 낼 수 있다.
   d. 공학적 진보가 제대로 이루어지면, 미국은 하루 210억 킬로리터의 물을 생산할 수 있다.

Vocabulary Test   p.258~259

1. 본문의 "만들어내다"와 가장 근접한 의미의 단어는?
   a. 소비하다   b. 발생시키다   c. 심다   d. 진압하다

2. 본문의 "밝게 비추다"와 가장 근접한 의미의 단어는?
   a. 선동하다   b. 비추다
   c. 어둡게 하다   d. 명확히 하다

3. 본문의 "가동하다"와 가장 근접한 의미의 단어는?
   a. 작동시키다   b. 중단하다   c. 고무하다   d. 강요하다

4. 본문의 "핵의"와 가장 근접한 의미의 단어는?
   a. 생물학적인 b. 작은   c. 강력한   d. 원자력의

5. 본문의 "거대한"과 가장 근접한 의미의 단어는?
   a. 소모적인   b. 거대한   c. 소형의   d. 연간의

6. 본문의 "경이"와 가장 근접한 의미의 단어는?
   a. 경이   b. 지점   c. 비명   d. 한계

7. 본문의 "인상적인"과 가장 근접한 의미의 단어는?
   a. 지배적인   b. 보잘 것 없는
   c. 두드러진   d. 최신 유행의

8. 본문의 "바닥"과 가장 근접한 의미의 단어는?
   a. 해안   b. 측선   c. 침대   d. 바닥

Paraphrasing   p.259

1. 거대한 수력발전 댐은 현대공학의 경이 가운데 하나이다.

   a. 식수 부족을 겪게 될 날이 올 것이다.
   b. 수력발전 댐은 놀라운 공학적 업적이다.
   c. 더 많은 대체 에너지를 조사하고 거기에 자금을 제공해야 했다.
   d. 댐이 너무 많으면 강의 생태학적 환경에 피해를 준다.

2. 후버 댐은 서반구에서 가장 높은 수력발전 댐이며, 유수의 관광지가 되어 연간 수 천 명이나 되는 관광객을 끌어들이고 있다.

   a. 관광객 수에 대한 적절한 통제가 이뤄지지 않으면, 그 댐은 관광객으로 뒤덮여질 것이다.
   b. 후버 댐의 서쪽 가장자리 부분에 균열이 발생하고 있다.
   c. 후버 댐은 실패한 공화당 출신 대통령의 이름을 본 딴 것이었다.
   d. 서반구에서 가장 높은 댐에 많은 사람들이 방문한다.

Unit 32   Water (2)   p.266

물 (2)

가뭄은 정상적인 기상패턴으로부터의 일탈이라고 통상 여겨져 왔지만, 실제로는 매년 세계의 어딘가에서 발생하고 있고, 장소에 따라서는 거의 정기적으로 반복된다. 예를 들면, 중앙아프리카 북부의 사헬지대는 1910년부터 1913년까지 심한 가뭄을 만났고, 1938년부터 1942년에도 또 다시 가뭄의 피해를 입었다. 미국에서는 1930년대와 1950년대에 혹독한 가뭄이 서부를 덮쳤다. 언제 어디에서 가뭄이 일어날지를 예측할 수는 없다. 기후학자의 대부분은 1890년부터 1945년에 걸쳐 지구의 대부분을 뒤덮은 온난한 기후는 장기저온경향으로부터의 일탈이었다고 생각하고 있다. 이 저온경향의 중단은 화석연료를 태웠기 때문에 대기 중의 이산화탄소의 농도가 상승함으로써 발생한 듯하다. 이산화탄소는 태양열을 차단하는 경향이 있다. 「온실효과」라고 불리 우는 현상이다. 세계가 따뜻해지느냐 추워지느냐에 관계없이, 기후가 조금이라도 변화하면 기상패턴이 혼란스러워지고 물의 공급 등 환경에 직접 영향을 줄 것은 확실하다.

Sentence Completion   p.262~263

A. 다음 문장에 가장 알맞은 단어를 고르시오.

1. 만일 당신이 피자 한판 중에 많은 ____ 을/를 먹는다면, 당신은 상당량의 피자를 먹은 것이다.
   a. (액체)1회분   b. 마찰   c. 분량   d. 긴축

2. 만일 당신이 음식 위에 ____ 핫 소스를 뿌린다면, 당신은 너무 맵지 않은 소수를 원한 것이다.
   a. 날카로운   b. 매운
   c. 감각을 마비시키는   d. 순한

3. 만일 당신이 가던 길에서 ____ 한다면, 당신은 원래 방향에서 벗어난 것이다.
   a. 이탈   b. 전진   c. 차이점   d. 선언

4. 많은 종들이 공통적으로 보여주는 ____ 이/가 있다.
   a. 지침서   b. 패턴   c. 진부한 표현   d. 4인조

5. ____ 이/가 날씨 보도를 한다면, 그들은 기상학자처럼 행동하는 것이다.
   a. 엔지니어   b. 고객   c. 기후학자   d. 조각가

B. 다음 문장에 가장 알맞은 단어를 고르시오.

1. 내복이라고 불리는 아래 위가 붙어있는 긴 속옷은 열을 ____, 몸을 따뜻하게 하는데 탁월한 기능을 가지고 있다.
   a 잡아두고   b 붕괴시키고
   c. 못 들어오게 하고   d. 난도질하고

2. 종종 가뭄을 잘 견뎌내기 위해 _____ 목표를 세우는 현명한 농부들이 많다.
   a. 술 취한   b. 이상한   c. 장기적인   d. 낡아빠진

3. 한국 사회의 최근 한 가지 _____ 은/는 점점 더 많은 여성들이 공공장소에서 공공연하게 담배를 피우는 것이다.
   a. 사설   b. 공감   c. 추세   d. 습관화

4. 그런 터무니없는 규정은 사회의 가치관과 질서의식을 위협하고 _____ 때문에, 제거되어야 한다.
   a. 혼란하게 하다   b. 요새화하다
   c. 소중히 간직하다   d. 강화하다

5. 언젠가 전 세계가 _____ 자원 대부분이 고갈되는 상황을 맞게 될 것임을 부인해 봤자 아무 소용없다.
   a. 풍력   b. 섭정   c. 자극   d. 화석연료

Listening Comprehension   p.264~265

1. 미국에서 가뭄이 발생한 이유는 무엇인가?
   a. 중북부 지역의 높은 기온
   b. 자동차에서 나오는 화석연료 배기가스와 습기가 혼합된 것
   c. 열대 지방의 높은 기온
   d. 이산화탄소 농도의 상승 가능성

2. 작가가 기후 변화를 설명하는 이유는 무엇인가?
   a. 지역에 따라, 전 세계 기온이 따뜻해지거나 혹은 추워진다는 것을 말하기 위한 것
   b. 인간의 화석연료 사용이 어떻게 기후를 변화시키고 있는지를 보여주기 위한 것
   c. 대기 속에 화석연료 농도를 언급하기 위한 것
   d. 과학자들이 대체 풍력 기계를 조사할 수 있는 기회를 제공하기 위한 것

3. 작가는 기후 변화를 어떻게 소개하는가?
   a. 기후 패턴에 있어 가뭄은 정상적인 현상이 아님을 설명하면서
   b. 가뭄이 물 공급에 끼치는 영향을 추정하면서
   c. 가뭄이 캘리포니아의 물웅덩이에 미치는 피해 정도를 예측하면서
   d. 아프리카 북중부 지역의 가뭄 패턴을 보여주면서

4. 강의의 일부를 다시 듣고 문제에 답하시오. 이 구절의 기능은 무엇인가?
   a. 언제, 어디서 가뭄이 발생하는지를 예측하는 것이 불가능하다는 점을 설명하기 위한 것
   b. 가뭄의 빈발에 관한 예를 제시하기 위한 것
   c. 가뭄 예방 기술의 한계를 설명하면서
   d. 기후 상의 작은 변화가 어느 정도 힘이 있는지를 보여주기 위한 것

5. 작가에 따르면, "온실효과"라는 현상의 원인이 되는 두 가지 요소는 무엇인가? 정답 두 개를 고르시오.
   a. 대기권 내에서의 농도
   b. 태양열을 잡아두는 이산화탄소
   c. 이산화탄소의 농도를 측정하는 것
   d. 화석연료 연소

6. 작가가 기후 변화에 대해 암시하는 바는 무엇인가?
   a. 전 세계가 (특히 사헬 지역에서) 더 추워지는 것이 아니라, 더욱 더워지고 있다.
   b. 물 공급량이 빠르게 줄고 있다.
   c. 과학자들은 언제 또는 어디서 가뭄이 발생할 지 예측할 수 없다.
   d. 인류에 의해 야기된 기후 상의 작은 변화가 기후 패턴을 혼란하게 만들 수 있다.

Vocabulary Test   p.266~267

1. 본문의 "이례"와 가장 근접한 의미의 단어는?
   a. 유래   b. 기계   c. 벗어남   d. 밀도

2. 본문의 "패턴(양식)"과 가장 근접한 의미의 단어는?
   a. 수집   b. 형태   c. 효과   d. 이해

3. 본문의 "분량"과 가장 근접한 의미의 단어는?
   a. 절반   b. 액체 1회분   c. 과제   d. 부분

4. 본문의 "기후학자"와 가장 근접한 의미의 단어는?
   a. 기상학자   b. 토플러
   c. 피부과의사   d. 산부인과의사

5. 본문의 "따뜻한"과 가장 근접한 의미의 단어는?
   a. 까다로운   b. 극도의
   c. 온난한   d. 부서지기 쉬운

6. 본문의 "추세"와 가장 근접한 의미의 단어는?
   a. 짜증   b. 경향
   c. 임차   d. 정신적 충격

7. 본문의 "잡아두다"와 가장 근접한 의미의 단어는?
   a. 숨을 헐떡거리다   b. 잡다
   c. 철회하다   d. 도망치다

8. 본문의 "혼란하게 하다"와 가장 근접한 의미의 단어는?
   a. 혼란시키다   b. 정돈하다
   c. 반박하다   d. 격분시키다

Paraphrasing   p.267

1. 기상학자의 대부분은 1890년부터 1945년에 걸쳐 지구의 대부분을 뒤덮은 온난한 기후는 장기저온경향으로부터의 일탈이었다고 생각하고 있다.

a. 지금의 온난한 기후가 확고히 자리 잡는다.

b. 온난한 기후는 최근의 현상으로 사라지게 될 것이다.

c. 지나치게 기후가 온난하면 가뭄이 많이 발생하게 될 것이다.

d. 기후학자들은 온난한 기후는 저온 추세에 역행하는 것이라고 믿는다.

2. 이산화탄소는 태양열을 차단하는 경향이 있다. 「온실효과」라고 불리 우는 현상이다.

a. 이산화탄소는 열을 잡아두어, 저온 효과를 야기한다.

b. 깨끗한 공기는 배출된 이산화탄소를 몰아낼 수 있다.

c. 온실 가스는 차가운 공기에 의존하는 작은 설치류에게는 위험한 것이다.

d. 이산화탄소는 열을 잡아두어, 고온 효과를 야기한다.

Unit 33 — Water (3) p.274

물 (3)

몇 십억 리터라는 오염물질이 폐수와 함께 전 세계의 수로에 버려지고 있다. 미처리된 하수에서부터 눈에 보이지 않는 유독화학물질까지 오염물질은 다양한 형태를 취하고 있다. 그중 대부분은 유기물이며 분해되어 무해하게 되는 것도 있지만 나머지는 활발히 성장해 급속하게 번식하며 수중의 산소를 다 쓰고 물고기를 죽인다. 나머지 오염물질은 무기물이며, 분해되지 않는다. 새로운 농약과 비료를 비롯해 물속에서 발견되는 신제품에 쓰이는 화학물질은 점점 늘고 있고, 질산염, 불화물(佛化物), 인산염도 지하수 오염에 의해 물에 혼합되어 있다. 이러한 오염물질은 먹이사슬을 통해 인체에 들어가고, 신경조직 안에 축적되는 경향이 있다. 이들 화학물질의 인체에 대한 영향에 관해서는 아직 충분히 해명되지 않고 있다.

Sentence Completion p.270~271

A. 다음 문장에 가장 알맞은 단어를 고르시오.

1. 만일 배가 ____ 위에서 움직인다면, 배가 강이나 시내 위를 따라 움직이는 것이다.
   a. 방공호   b. 사교장   c. 수로   d. 고속도로

2. 만일 당신이 ____ 다면, 아무도 당신을 볼 수 없을 것이다.
   a. 불명확한   b. 보이지 않는
   c. 발견할 수 있는   d. 추적할 수 있는

3. 만일 당신이 당신의 ____ 을/를 재활용한다면, 당신은 그것을 계속해서 다시 사용하는 것이다.
   a. 신성모독   b. DVD
   c. 의무   d. 쓰레기(폐품)

4. 당신이 마시는 물에 ____ 이/가 있으면, 그것은 어쩌면 해로운 것일지 모른다.
   a. 효모   b. 강장제   c. 오염물질   d. 파파야

5. 최근에, 국제 시장의 ____ 재료 가격이 보편적 수요 증가로 인해 껑충 뛰어 올랐다.
   a. 편재하는   b. 원료 그대로의(원자재)
   c. 유독한   d. 과도한

B. 다음 문장에 가장 알맞은 단어를 고르시오.

1. 사회에서 겪는 좌절감이 약자에게 분출되는 ____ 는 것은 문제다.
   a. 약하게 쉿 소리가 나다   b. 경향이 있다
   c. 진정되다   d. 열망하다

2. 물속에 이미 존재하고 있는 박테리아는 ____ 물질을 이용해서 증식하고, 동시에 물속의 산소를 제거한다.
   a. 유기체의   b. 해로운
   c. 변동이 있는   d. 무생물의

3. 그 새끼 고양이는 ____, 널 할퀴지 않을 테니, 잘 다뤄 줘.
   a. 제멋대로 해서   b. 해롭지 않아서
   c. 해로워서   d. 명료해서

4. 만일 의사가 당신 척추에 있는 ____ 을/를 다치게 한다면, 당신은 몸이 마비될 수도 있다.
   a. 섬유   b. 신경조직
   c. 모공   d. 대형 손수건

5. 기업 농업은 많은 ____ 을/를 사용하여 농장이나 농작물에 뿌린다.
   a. 도구   b. 기생충   c. 비료   d. 점액

Listening Comprehension p.272~273

1. 오염물질은 어떤 형태로 발생하는가?
   a. 오염물질은 하이브리드 차와 디젤 트럭에서 생길 수 있다.
   b. 오염물질은 정화되지 않은 하수와 보이지 않는 해로운 화학물질에서 생길 수 있다.
   c. 오염물질은 우주공간에서 생길 수 있다.
   d. 오염물질은 화장실과 실습 클리닉에서 생길 수 있다.

2. 작가가 오염물질을 설명하는 이유는 무엇인가?
   a. 먹이 사슬을 통해 인체에 들어가는 오염물질에 대해 말하기 위한 것
   b. 오염물질을 발생시키는 기업들에게 가할 처벌에 대해 토의하기 위한 것
   c. 인류가 어떻게 오염물질을 제거할 수 있을지를 예측하기 위한 것
   d. 분해되는 오염물질과 분해되지 않는 오염물질을 비교하기 위한 것

3. 작가는 오염물질을 어떻게 소개하는가?
   a. 일부 오염물질들은 얼마나 무기성이고, 분해되지 않는지에 대해 분석하면서
   b. 오염물질들이 얼마나 여러 가지 형태를 취하는지에 대해 토의하기 위한 것
   c. 오염물질들이 얼마나 무해한 지를 설명하면서
   d. 우리 물 시스템 내에서의 액체 폐기물 오염물질에 대해 언급하면서

4. 강의의 일부를 다시 듣고 문제에 답하시오. 이 구절의 기능은 무엇인가?
   a. 급수에 들어가는 질산염, 불화물, 인산염을 소개하기 위한 것
   b. 물속에서 증식하는 오염물질의 예를 제시하기 위한 것
   c. 물고기를 죽이는 것의 한계를 설명하기 위한 것
   d. 지하수 오염과 해양 오염을 대비시키기 위한 것

5. 작가에 따르면, 해로운 두 가지 오염물질은 무엇인가? 정답 두 개를 고르시오.
   a. 산소를 소모하고 물고기를 죽이는 오염물질
   b. 액체 효소로 구성된 오염물질
   c. 급속히 증식하는 오염물질
   d. 화학물질에도 쉽게 영향을 받지 않는 오염물질

6. 작가가 오염물질에 대해 암시하는 바는 무엇인가?
   a. 오염물질은 급속히 증식하고 물속의 산소를 전부 소모한다.
   b. 수인성 오염물질로 인해 공공 보건이 위험에 처해있다.
   c. 우리의 수로를 깨끗하게 정화시킨다면 그것은 기적일 것이다.
   d. 소량의 오염물질이 먹이 사슬을 통해 인체에 들어간다.

Vocabulary Test p.274~275

1. 본문의 "쓰레기(폐기물)"와 가장 근접한 의미의 단어는?
   a. 농산물   b. 묽은 수프   c. 쓰레기   d. 낭비

2. 본문의 "오염물질"과 가장 근접한 의미의 단어는?
   a. 요소   b. 오염균   c. 청결   d. 장기

3. 본문의 "수로"와 가장 근접한 의미의 단어는?
   a. 수로   b. 연쇄   c. 도랑   d. 좁은길

4. 본문의 "정화(가공)되지 않은"과 가장 근접한 의미의 단어는?
   a. 비양심적인   b. 증명되지 않은
   c. 요리되지 않은   d. (폐물이)가공 처리되지 않은

5. 본문의 "보이지 않는"과 가장 근접한 의미의 단어는?
   a. 공표된   b. 눈에 보이지 않는
   c. 분비된   d. 불투명한

6. 본문의 "무해한"과 가장 근접한 의미의 단어는?
   a. 의심스러운   b. 슬픔에 잠긴
   c. 해가 없는   d. 불쾌한

7. 본문의 "비료"와 가장 근접한 의미의 단어는?
   a. 거름   b. 비옥
   c. 대리인   d. 헤로인

8. 본문의 "경향이 있다"와 가장 근접한 의미의 단어는?
   a. 가망 없다   b. 참석하다
   c. 경향이 있다   d. 애타게 하다

Paraphrasing p.275

1. 그중 대부분은 유기물이며 분해되어 무해하게 되는 것도 있지만 나머지는 활발히 성장해 급속하게 번식하며 수중의 산소를 다 쓰고 물고기를 죽인다.
   a. 일부 오염물질은 유기체로, 무해한 구성요소로 쉽게 분해된다.
   b. 오염물질은 수백만 개로 쉽게 증식될 수 있다.
   c. 일부 오염물질은 무기체로, 쉽게 분해되고 물고기를 죽인다.
   d. 많은 오염 분자들은 보통 물속의 산소를 모두 가져가 버린다.

2. 이러한 오염물질은 먹이사슬을 통해 인체에 들어가고, 신경조직 안에 축적되는 경향이 있다.
   a. 먹이사슬은 생존을 위해 필수적인 구성요소이다.
   b. 오염물질이 물에서 인체로 들어가는 것은 자연적인 과정이다.
   c. 오염물질이 지나치게 많으면 신경조직에 해롭다.
   d. 인간은 먹는 음식에 무엇이 들어가는지에 대해 신경을 더 많이 써야한다.

Unit 34 Thomas Jefferson p.282

토마스 제퍼슨

토마스 제퍼슨은 독립선언의 기초자이고 제3대 미합중국의 대통령으로서 폭넓은 흥미와 재능을 가진 인물이었다. 그는 정치가였고, 책략가, 건축가, 철학자, 그리고 발명가였다. 그러나 또한 심한 자기모순을 갖고 있기도 했다. 예를 들면 독립선언 중에서 「…모든 사람들은 평등하게 태어났다」고 썼으면서, 자신은 노예를 소유하고 있었다. 또한 신은 인간에게 「생명, 자유 및 행복의 추구」와 같은 천부적 권리를 주었다고 썼으면서 그 자신은 신의 존재에 대해 의문을 품고 있는 회의론자였다. 제퍼슨은 정부 내에서 검약을 주창했으면서, 한편에서 루이지애나 구입에 1,500만 달러라는 당시로서는 엄청난 금액을 지출했다. 비평가들은 그가 아무런 가치도 없는 황무지에 돈을 낭비했다고 비난했다. 그러나 루이지애나 구입은 미합중국의 영토를 2배 이상으로 확대한 현명한 투자였다.

A. 다음 문장에 가장 알맞은 단어를 고르시오.

1. 당신이 집을 짓기 위해 ____ 이/가 필요하다면, 그것은 당신이 집을 설계할 사람이 필요한 것이다.
   a. 출장 요리사   b. 건축가   c. 배관공   d. 엔지니어

2. 어떤 것이 ____ 일 때, 그것은 매우 놀랍고 충격스러운 경험이다.
   a. 기운찬   b. 윙윙거리는
   c. 신경에 거슬리는   d. 활동적인

3. 당신이 ____ 총기 수집품을 갖고 있다면, 당신은 무기를 매우 많이 갖고 있는 것이다.
   a. 일상적인   b. 광범위한   c. 독특한   d. 고대의

4. 당신이 ____ 로 불린다면, 당신은 영향력과 수완이 있고, 강력한 사람이다.
   a. 방화범   b. 수배자   c. 변절자   d. 정치가

5. 누군가 ____ 로서 칭송받는다면, 그들의 깊은 사고능력이 높이 평가되는 것이다.
   a. 종속자   b. 중개자   c. 철학자   d. 학생

B. 다음 문장에 가장 알맞은 단어를 고르시오.

1. 만일 당신이 돈을 쓰고 나서 저축하는 습관이 있다면, 많은 ____ 의 돈을 저축할 수 없을 것이다.
   a. 액수   b. 공제   c. 계산   d. 원조

2. 인간은 공기, 물, 토지, 생물 다양성, 숲, 산, 그리고 빙하와 같은 훌륭한 천연자원들을 ____ 것이다.
   a. 한탄하는   b. 부여받은   c. 지배된   d. 정복된

3. 토마스 제퍼슨은 하느님의 존재를 믿지 않았다. 즉, 하느님의 존재에 관하여 그는 ____ 였다.
   a. 해학가   b. 명인   c. 회의론자   d. 성직자

4. 인간이 지구 자원을 계속 ____ 때, 기후는 인간에게 더 이상 우호적이지 않은 방식으로 변할 수도 있다.
   a. 품다   b. 탕진하다   c. 보존하다   d. 재생하다

5. 돈에 대한 그의 철학은 ____ 에 근거하여, 하루에 5달러 이상은 절대 쓰지 않는다.
   a. 취소   b. 자만   c. 부   d. 절약

1. 일각에서 루이지애나 구입을 돈 낭비에 지나지 않다고 생각하는 이유는 무엇인가?
   a. 프랑스는 그것을 미국에 매각한 뒤, 돌려받기를 원한다.
   b. 천 5백만 달러라는 금액은 1700년대 당시에는 엄청난 금액이었다.
   c. 미국 땅이 더 있을 필요가 없다고 생각하는 사람들이 많았다.
   d. 제퍼슨의 성공을 원치 않는 사람들도 있었다.

2. 작가가 제퍼슨을 설명하는 이유는 무엇인가?
   a. 제퍼슨의 돈 관리 부실을 대비시키기 위한 것
   b. 제퍼슨이 어떻게 백인들을 위한 기본 인권 수호 운동을 펼쳤는지를 보여주기 위한 것
   c. 행복추구 이론의 장점을 보여주기 위한 것
   d. 어떻게 제퍼슨이 국민 모두의 형편을 개선시키기 위해 노력했는지를 설명하기 위한 것

3. 작가는 제퍼슨을 어떻게 소개하는가?
   a. 하느님의 적이자, 종교 조직에 대한 비판자로서
   b. 굉장한 플랜테이션과 노예의 소유자로서
   c. 그가 얼마나 정부 재원을 탕진했는지를 설명하면서
   d. 독립선언문 작성자로서, 그리고 대통령으로서의 그의 역할을 개괄하면서

4. 강의의 일부를 다시 듣고 문제에 답하시오. 이 구절의 기능은 무엇인가?
   a. (지금 생각해 볼 때)제퍼슨의 그 현명했던 결정을 소개하기 위한 것
   b. 일반인들도 위대한 일을 할 수 있다는 예를 제시하기 위한 것
   c. 더 많은 땅 획득의 필요성을 설명하기 위한 것
   d. 제퍼슨의 결혼생활에서 나타나는 위선을 대비시키기 위한 것

5. 작가에 따르면, 대통령으로서 제퍼슨이 성취한 두 가지는 무엇인가? 정답 두 개를 고르시오.
   a. 그는 링컨과 함께 노예를 해방시켰다.
   b. 정부가 지출을 현명하게 할 것을 주장했다.
   c. 그는 독립선언문을 작성했다.
   d. 그는 루이지애나 땅을 구입했다.

6. 작가가 제퍼슨에 대해 암시하는 바는 무엇인가?
   a. 모든 인간은 태어날 때부터 공평하지 않다.
   b. 그는 일부 모순된 부분이 있음에도 불구하고 훌륭한 사람이었다.
   c. 과거에 더 훌륭한 대통령들이 있었을 수도 있다.
   d. 역사적으로 제퍼슨의 궁은 과대평가된 것이다.

1. 본문의 "광범위한"과 가장 근접한 의미의 단어는?
   a. 열린   b. 해외의   c. 거대한   d. 광대한

2. 본문의 "정치가"와 가장 근접한 의미의 단어는?
   a. 정치인   b. 헤로인   c. 지질학자   d. 변절자

3. 본문의 "건축가"와 가장 근접한 의미의 단어는?
   a. 기안자   b. 구조 엔지니어
   c. 건물 설계자   d. 전기 기사

4. 본문의 "철학자"와 가장 근접한 의미의 단어는?
   a. 거지   b. 개업의   c. 조련사   d. 사상가

5. 본문의 "부여하다"와 가장 근접한 의미의 단어는?
   a. 수여하다   b. 요구하다   c. 빼앗다   d. 바라보다

6. 본문의 "회의론자"와 가장 근접한 의미의 단어는?
   a. 낙관론자   b. 회의가   c. 추종자   d. 숭배자

7. 본문의 "절약"과 가장 근접한 의미의 단어는?
   a. 방종   b. 추구   c. 관대   d. 검약

8. 본문의 "탕진하다"와 가장 근접한 의미의 단어는?
   a. 낭비하다   b. 소환하다   c. 개선하다   d. 분개하다

Paraphrasing p.283

1. 또한 신은 인간에게 −생명, 자유 및 행복의 추구−와 같은 천부적 권리를 주었다고 썼으면서 그 자신은 신의 존재에 대해 의문을 품고 있는 회의론자였다.

   a. 생명, 자유, 행복 추구는 노예들을 위한 것이다.
   b. 하느님은 사람들에게 절대 박탈할 수 없는 기본권을 주었다.
   c. 자유가 너무 많으면 폭동이 일어날 것이다.
   d. 하느님의 존재에 대해 의문을 제기하는 것이 정상이다.

2. 비평가들은 그가 아무런 가치도 없는 황무지에 돈을 낭비했다고 비난했다.

   a. 그 비평가들은 마음속에 악의를 품은 매우 시기심 강한 사람들이었다.
   b. 제퍼슨을 비난하는 사람들은 그가 내린 결정의 지혜로움을 볼 수 없었다.
   c. 지나치게 많은 돈이 나무나 알려지지 않은 산림지에 쓰이고 있었다.
   d. 지출의 핵심은 돈을 전부 다 써버리는 것이다.

Unit 35 The American Revolution (1) p.290

미국 혁명 (1)

미국 독립혁명은 매우 복잡하고 아주 충격적인 사건이었다. 식민지의 권리를 지키기 위한 잇단 폭동이 발단이 되어 서서히 정치상의 독립을 요구하는 전면적인 전쟁이 되어 갔다. 뒤에 일어나는 대부분의 혁명과는 달리 미국 독립전쟁은 법률준수에 신경을 썼다는 점에서 특징적이었다. 식민지 개척자들은 영국인으로서 보장되고 있다고 믿는 권리를 위해 싸웠다. 당시 미국 식민지 개척자들의 대부분에게 조지 3세를 비난하는 일 등은 상상조차 못할 일이었고, 국가주의의 고양에도 불구하고 자신들의 고난을 왕의 탓으로 돌리는 저명한 식민지 개척자들은 극히 소수에 불과했다. 많은 유혈전투 후에도 제1회 대륙회의는 영국으로부터의 독립요구를 부결했고, 화해가 원만히 성립될 때까지 식민지에 대한 무력행위를 끝낼 것을 국왕에게 계속 요청했다.

Sentence Completion p.286~287

A. 다음 문장에 가장 알맞은 단어를 고르시오.

1. 어떤 것이 큰 ____ 을/를 가진다면, 그것은 영향력이 매우 큰 것이다.
   a. 가식   b. 비열함   c. 접촉   d. 영향

2. 군이 ____ 공격을 시작할 때, 그들은 무력을 총동원해서 적과 대면하는 것이다.
   a. 전면적인   b. 부분적인   c. 지방적인   d. 불완전한

3. 만일 상황이 ____ 으로 가득 하다면, 그것은 해결하기 매우 어려운 것이다.
   a. 밀도   b. 복잡함   c. 약속   d. 관용

4. 만일 당신이 ____ 힘을 가지고 있다면, 당신은 근력운동에 능할 것이다.
   a. 조건부의   b. 미약한   c. 어마어마한 d. 작은

5. 만일 ____ 이/가 있다면, 보통 정부 내에 수많은 유혈사태와 변화가 있는 것이다.
   a. 합법   b. 저항운동   c. 기념일   d. 연회

B. 다음 문장에 가장 알맞은 단어를 고르시오.

1. 식민지 시대에, 최초의 미국 ____ 가운데 대대수는 영국 국왕이 너무 오만하다고 생각했다.
   a. 최고 경영자들   b. 변절자들
   c. 식민지 이주자들   d. 팬

2. 퇴직할 때, 그 대단한 기념식 덕분에 저명한 그 법학대학 학장은 ____ 보였다.
   a. 빛이 바랜   b. 두드러져   c. 배반당한   d. 폐지된

3. ____ 의 좋은 점 가운데 하나는 온 나라가 어떤 대의에 대해 마음이 하나가 된다는 것이다.
   a. 이타주의　　　　　　　　b. 이기주의
   c. 민족주의(애국심)　　　　d. 지방적 기질

4. 그 부서의 장이 지원자의 98퍼센트를 ____ 싶어 한다는 것은 터무니없다.
   a. 평가하고　　　　　　　　b. 해당하고
   c. 받아들이지 않고(거절하다)　d. 동원하고

5. ____ 판사가 판결을 내리자, 사람들은 그 결정에 완전히 승복했다.
   a. 홀대받는　　　　b. 유명한　　　c. 터무니없는　　d. 무능한

Listening Comprehension　　p.288~289

1. 식민지 이주민들은 왕이 어떤 행동을 취하기를 원했는가?
   a. 어퍼 캐나다(온타리오주의 별칭)의 합병을 끝내는 것
   b. 식민지에 대한 군사 행동을 종료하는 것
   c. 재임하여 통치하는 것
   d. 프랑스와 같은 유럽 주변국들을 침략하지 않는 것

2. 작가가 미국 혁명을 설명하는 이유는 무엇인가?
   a. 미국 내 민족주의 발전을 상술하기 위한 것
   b. 영국에 대한 경의를 평가하기 위한 것
   c. 어떻게 미국인들이 그들의 법적 권리를 위해 투쟁했는지를 보여주기 위한 것
   d. 전 세계 저항운동의 패턴을 보여주기 위한 것

3. 작가는 미국 혁명을 어떻게 소개하는가?
   a. 혁명의 엄청난 효과를 설명하면서
   b. 정치 독립의 장점을 보여주면서
   c. 제 1차 대륙회의에 대해 언급하면서
   d. 국왕이 가한 고통을 보여주면서

4. 강의의 일부를 다시 듣고 문제에 답하시오. 이 구절의 기능은 무엇인가?
   a. 영국인들이 조지 왕을 얼마나 찬미했는지를 소개하기 위한 것
   b. 식민지 이주민들의 권리를 수호하는 것에 관한 예를 제시하기 위한 것
   c. 미국혁명과 법에 대한 관심부족을 설명하기 위한 것
   d. 개혁이 어떻게 국가 전체를 변화시킬 수 있는지를 보여주기 위한 것

5. 작가에 따르면, 식민지 이주민들이 지키려 했던 두 가지는 무엇인가? 정답 두 개를 고르시오.
   a. 영국인으로서의 법적 권리　　b. 식민지를 위한 분리 과세
   c. 민족주의 정서의 감소　　　　d. 점차적인 정치적 독립

6. 작가가 미국 혁명에 대해 암시하는 바는 무엇인가?
   a. 혁명 이후, 복잡한 변화가 발생했다.
   b. 독립을 위한 공동의 노력

   c. 법에 대한 깊은 존중이 필요하다.
   d. 영국인들에게는 권리가 보장되어서는 안된다.

Vocabulary Test　　p.290~291

1. 본문의 "복잡"과 가장 근접한 의미의 단어는?
   a. 무욕　　　　b. 복잡　　　　c. 불분명　　　d. 행동

2. 본문의 "어마어마한"과 가장 근접한 의미의 단어는?
   a. 막대한　　　　　　　　b. 허약한
   c. 보잘 것 없는　　　　　d. 감금된

3. 본문의 "영향"과 가장 근접한 의미의 단어는?
   a. 자동차 추돌사고　　　b. 자동차 펜더
   c. 맛　　　　　　　　　　d. 영향

4. 본문의 "저항운동"과 가장 근접한 의미의 단어는?
   a. 버릇없는 행동　　　　b. 반란
   c. 순종　　　　　　　　　d. 위협

5. 본문의 "전면적인"과 가장 근접한 의미의 단어는?
   a. 불행한　　b. 광범위한　　c. 총력을 다한　　d. 희박한

6. 본문의 "두드러진"과 가장 근접한 의미의 단어는?
   a. 추월당한　　　　　　　b. 눈에 띄는
   c. 비난받는　　　　　　　d. 증거로 제공된

7. 본문의 "민족주의"와 가장 근접한 의미의 단어는?
   a. 애국심　　　　　　　　b. 배반
   c. 지배광　　　　　　　　d. 호전적 애국주의

8. 본문의 "유명한"과 가장 근접한 의미의 단어는?
   a. 전통적인　　b. 기업적인　　c. 중요한　　d. 주변의

Paraphrasing　　p.291

1. 뒤에 일어나는 대부분의 혁명과는 달리 미국 독립전쟁은 법률준수에 신경을 썼다는 점에서 특징적이었다.

   a. (프랑스, 러시아)혁명이 광범위한 부패로 이어지는 경우가 매우 잦다.
   b. 민주주의 헌법은 특정 법률보다 더 중요하다.
   c. 법에 대한 지나친 관심은 절대 나쁜 것이 아니다.
   d. 미국 혁명은 법의 중요성을 강조한 것으로 유명했다.

2. 당시 미국 식민지 개척자들의 대부분에게 조지 3세를 비난하는 일 등은 상상조차 못할 일이었다.

   a. 조지 3세는 포용력이 없는 사람이었다.
   b. 유럽 전역에 왕들은 오만하고 너무나 강력했다.
   c. 조지 3세는 비난받을 리 없었다.
   d. 조지 3세는 가끔 백성들의 말에 귀 기울였다.

Unit 36   The American Revolution (2)   p.298

미국 혁명 (2)

1776년 여름에 미국의 식민지 개척자들은 영국이 타협을 위한 교섭에 응할 거라곤 더 이상 기대할 수 없다고 느끼고 있었다. 독립선언을 기초하기 위해 임명된 사람은 토마스 제퍼슨으로서 그가 쓴 문서는 능변이었고 설득력이 있었다. 그 선언은 강력한 정치사상과 교묘한 슬로건을 결합하여 자유로운 사회를 위한 새로운 기준을 세웠다. 또한 정부는 피통치자들의 동의에 의존한다는 원칙에 바탕을 두고 혁명권을 용인했다. 그러나 그 원칙은 1776년의 미국을 정확히 표현한 것이라기보다는 이상에 가까웠다. 그 선언에 서명한 사람들의 대부분이 「인간은 모두 평등하게 태어났다」라는 기술을 그대로 받아들인 것은 아니었다. 당시 약 50만명, 인구의 5분의 1이 노예였다. 하지만 미국의 역사적인 문서 가운데에서 독립선언은 현재도 아메리칸 드림을 표현한 것으로서 가장 중요시되고 있다.

Sentence Completion   p.294~295

A. 다음 문장에 가장 알맞은 단어를 고르시오.

1. 만일 당신이 ____ 시를 쓴다면, 정밀하면서도 아름다운 시어가 자연스럽게 표현되는 것이다.
   a. 광대한   b. 비꼬는
   c. 표현력이 뛰어난   d. 추잡한

2. 누군가 ____ 을/를 전달한다면, 그것은 사람을 선동하고 자극하는 것일 가능성이 크다.
   a. 정확한 정보   b. 진상   c. 선전(물)   d. 전문 용어

3. 어떤 경우라도 계약 ____ 이 가장 적합한 방침이라고는 말할 수 없다.
   a. 협상을 하는 것   b. 파괴하는 것
   c. 조롱하는 것   d. 외면하는 것

4. 누군가 ____ 발표를 한다면, 청중을 설득하겠다는 뜻이다.
   a. 탐구적인   b. 가능성 없는
   c. 오해를 일으키는   d. 설득력 있는

5. 많은 전문가들은 양측이 그 민감한 사안에 대해 ____ 을/를 찾을 공산이 크다는 장미빛 전망을 내놓았다.
   a. 논쟁   b. 타협(점)   c. 충돌   d. 멸시

B. 다음 문장에 가장 알맞은 단어를 고르시오.

1. 정부는 ____ 이/가 광우병같은 건강을 위협하는 질병에 노출되지 않도록 하는데 책임이 있다.
   a. 피고인   b. 피지배자(국민)
   c. 관리자   d. 고인

2. 정부가 억압할 때 국민은 ____ 할 권리가 있다.
   a. 복종하다   b. 순응하다
   c. 혁명을 일으키다   d. 급격히 증가하다

3. 미국 헌법에 존재하는 한 가지 ____ 에 따르면 국민은 궁극적으로 자신의 운명을 스스로 선택한다.
   a. 원칙   b. 사기   c. 해방   d. 근본주의

4. 본인이 소유하고 있는 수많은 물건과 견줘, 그녀는 유독 24캐럿짜리 다이아몬드 목걸이를 가장 ____.
   a. 지원하다   b. 탄핵하다
   c. 귀중하게 여기다   d. 격노하다

5. 그 십대 소녀들은 비욘세 콘서트에 가도 된다는 어머니의 ____ 을/를 받지 못했다.
   a. 적신호   b. 동의   c. 반대 의견   d. 동요

Listening Comprehension   p.296~297

1. 독립 선언문의 표현은 어떠했는가?
   a. 어색하고 장황했다.
   b. 독창적인 문구로 유익했다.
   c. 표현력이 뛰어나고 설득력이 있었다.
   d. 품위가 떨어지고 모욕적이었다.

2. 작가가 독립 선언문을 설명하는 이유는 무엇인가?
   a. 미합중국 헌법 제정자가 어떻게 강력한 정치사상을 생각해냈는지 보여주기 위한 것
   b. 50만 명이 참정권을 박탈당한 과정을 설명하기 위한 것
   c. 신생 국가가 얼마나 감명적인 문서를 작성했는지 보여주기 위한 것
   d. 훌륭하게 작성한 법안의 패턴을 보여주기 위한 것

3. 작가는 독립 선언문을 어떻게 소개하는가?
   a. 노예 제도 폐지를 옹호하면서
   b. 제퍼슨이 노예 수를 늘리고 싶어 했다는 사실을 나타내면서
   c. 식민지 주민과의 협상을 설명하면서
   d. 수정안을 제시하면서

4. 강의의 일부를 다시 듣고 문제에 답하시오. 이 구절의 기능은 무엇인가?
   a. 문서 작성 시 노예도 반드시 포함되어야 한다는 제안을 하기 위한 것
   b. 제도에서 소외당한 50만 명에 대한 예를 제시하기 위한 것
   c. 헌법 문서 작성의 한계를 설명하기 위한 것
   d. 미국인의 삶을 길잡이하는 영향력 있는 문서에 대해 알리기 위한 것

5. 작가에 따르면, 독립 선언문에 담긴 두 가지 사상은 무엇인가? 정답 두 개를 고르시오.
   a. 정치인은 표현력이 뛰어나야 한다.
   b. 모든 사람은 평등하게 태어났다.

c. 국민이 국가를 선택하지, 국가가 국민을 선택하는 것은 아니다.
d. 주요 문서를 승인하려면 동의가 필요하다.

6. 작가가 독립 선언문에 대해 암시하는 바는 무엇인가?
   a. 영국과의 협상은 어리석은 짓이었다.
   b. 얼마나 많은 사람이 자유롭게 투표하게 될 지를 추정한다.
   c. 그것은 이상보다는 실용적인 원칙이다.
   d. 그것은 오늘날까지 미국인 대부분이 갖고 있는 주된 사고들을 나타낸다.

Vocabulary Test   p.298~299

1. 본문의 "협상하다"와 가장 근접한 의미의 단어는?
   a. 조정하다   b. 폐지하다
   c. 옮기다   d. 망치다

2. 본문의 "타협"과 가장 근접한 의미의 단어는?
   a. 구성   b. 양보   c. 승인   d. 반감

3. 본문의 "표현력이 뛰어난"과 가장 근접한 의미의 단어는?
   a. 완전한   b. 살아 있는
   c. 표현이 풍부한   d. 일치하는

4. 본문의 "설득력이 있는"과 가장 근접한 의미의 단어는?
   a. 설득력있는   b. 고자질하는
   c. 영향을 받지 않는   d. 경솔한

5. 본문의 "선전(슬로건)"과 가장 근접한 의미의 단어는?
   a. 숫자   b. 유행병   c. 자료   d. 홍보

6. 본문의 "혁명을 일으키다"와 가장 근접한 의미의 단어는?
   a. 반란을 일으키다   b. 해결하다
   c. 거절하다   d. 격퇴하다

7. 본문의 "원칙"과 가장 근접한 의미의 단어는?
   a. 환불   b. 신념   c. 탈선   d. 침윤

8. 본문의 "동의"와 가장 근접한 의미의 단어는?
   a. 마찰   b. 증거   c. 거절   d. 동의

Paraphrasing   p.299

1. 그 선언은 강력한 정치사상과 교묘한 슬로건을 결합하여 자유로운 사회를 위한 새로운 기준을 세웠다.

   a. 독립 선언문에는 식민지 사회의 원칙을 보여주는 낡은 사상이 있었다.
   b. 미합중국은 민주주의를 확립하고자 오늘날까지 투쟁하고 있다.
   c. 다양한 정치사상이 논쟁으로 인해 발목 잡히는 일이 허다하다.
   d. 강력한 사상이 서로 결합하여 민주주의의 기반을 다진다.

2. 하지만 미국의 역사적인 문서 가운데에서 독립선언은 현재도 아메리칸 드림을 표현한 것으로서 가장 중요시되고 있다.

   a. 독립 선언문은 강력한 힘을 가진 문서로 귀중하게 여겨야 한다.
   b. 몇 세대가 지나면 역사적인 가치가 있는 문서는 무의미해진다.
   c. 독립 선언문은 더 다듬어야 한다.
   d. 독립 선언문의 요지는 제퍼슨이 작성한 문서라는 점이다.

Unit 37   Energy (2)   p.306

에너지 (2)

빛의 특수한 형태인 레이저광선은 일련의 새로운 에너지원 중에서도 최신의 것이고, 과학자들은 그에 대한 놀라울 정도의 많은 가능성들을 밝혀내고 있다. 레이저광선의 광파는 서로의 위상이 완전히 동일하며 그리고 거의 평행하기 때문에 긴 거리를 직진할 수 있다. 이에 비해 회중전등의 섬광은 광파의 주파수가 매우 많고 서로 간섭하여 분산되어 버리므로 불과 몇 미터 앞에서 확산되어 버린다. 레이저는 원거리에서도 전도손실이 없는 전송에 쓰이게 될 수도 있다. 이를 위해서는 전력을 레이저광으로 변환하고, 수신측에서 반대의 것을 행한다. 또한 레이저는 정보전달 수단(통신 송신기)으로서도 이용할 수 있다. 레이저의 파장은 전파가 몇 백 미터인데 비해 1cm의 1000만분의 1이다. 따라서 레이저를 사용하면 대량의 메시지를 매우 좁은 주파수대에서 보낼 수 있다.

Sentence Completion   p.302~303

A. 다음 문장에 가장 알맞은 단어를 고르시오.

1. 양 팀은 마주본 채 ____ 형태로 줄지어 서 있다.
   a. 굽은   b. 물결 모양의
   c. 흩어진   d. 나란한

2. 어떤 물질을 ____ 면, 이 물질을 퍼뜨린다는 뜻으로 때로는 사방으로 퍼져나간다.
   a. 발산하다   b. 빗나가다
   c. 발견하다   d. 흉하게 변하다

3. ____ 사건이란 보통 매우 독특한 사건을 뜻한다.
   a. 특별한   b. 곤란한   c. 꼴사나운   d. 일상적인

4. 어떤 물건을 ____ 으로 보내면, 많이 보내는 것이다.
   a. 수집기   b. 다량(다수)   c. 잡동사니   d. 거품

5. 어떤 대상을 ____ 이/가 그것의 정체를 밝히는 첫 번째 단계이다.
   a. 흠뻑 적시는 것   b. 식별하는 것
   c. 찌르는 것   d. 오염시키는 것

B. 다음 문장에 가장 알맞은 단어를 고르시오.

1. 허리 둘레가 28 ____ 면, size6 속옷을 입으면 될 것이다.
   a. 계산하다   b. 조정하다
   c. 규제하다   d. ~의 폭이다

2. 바다에서 그 여자의 할아버지 유골이 바람에 ____ 했다.
   a. 흩어진   b. 조종된   c. 요구된   d. 합쳐진

3. 레이저가 갖는 큰 장점은 매우 길고 강한 ____ 이/가 있다는 것이다.
   a. 주파수   b. 집행   c. 정규   d. 무기

4. 그들은 말을 행동으로 ____ 데 최선을 다했다.
   a. 왜곡하는   b. 옮기는   c. 보존하는   d. 속이는

5. 어둠을 향해 손전등을 비췄지만 빛은 그리 멀리까지 ____ 하지 못했다.
   a. 악취를 풍기다   b. 방해하다
   c. 전송하다(전달되다)   d. 넘겨주다

Listening Comprehension   p.304~305

1. 레이저 광선은 어떻게 작동하는가?
   a. 작은 입자 상태가 되도록 빛을 흩뜨리면서
   b. 공간을 통과하도록 광선을 빠르게 쏘면서
   c. 먼 거리를 갈 수 있도록 평행한 광선을 사용하면서
   d. 파도 모양처럼 진동하는 펄스 광선을 사용하면서

2. 작가가 레이저 광선을 설명하는 이유는 무엇인가?
   a. 기술이 발전하면 놀라운 일이 일어날 수 있다는 점을 설명하기 위한 것
   b. 데이터를 전송할 때 특히 레이저가 얼마나 유용하게 사용될 수 있는 지를 보여주기 위한 것
   c. 암환자의 손상된 부분을 레이저가 어떻게 치료하는지 예측하기 위한 것
   d. 레이저 광선의 다소 불확실 가능성을 설명하기 위한 것

3. 작가는 레이저 광선을 어떻게 소개하는가?
   a. 우주 과학자들의 연구가 어느 정도까지 이르렀는지를 보여주면서
   b. 레이저와 간단한 손전등에 적용된 기초적인 기술을 서로 비교하면서
   c. 인류가 일상적으로 새로운 기술을 개발해 온 사실을 보여주면서
   d. 레이저를 가장 최신 형태의 에너지원 가운데 한 가지로 언급하면서

4. 강의의 일부를 다시 듣고 문제에 답하시오. 이 구절의 기능은 무엇인가?

a. 라디오 전파와는 다르게 레이저 광선이 얼마나 먼 거리까지 이르는지 설명하기 위한 것
b. 레이저 광선이 어떻게 방해받지 않고 최대 900미터 까지 이를 수 있는지 설명하기 위한 것
c. 지구 궤도 저점에서 라디오와 레이저 전파의 한계를 설명하기 위한 것
d. 군사적 레이저 연구의 난점을 대비시키기 위한 것

5. 작가에 따르면, 현대 사회에서 사용하는 레이저의 두 가지 용도는 무엇인가? 정답 두 개를 고르시오.
   a. 전기 차량과 대중교통 수단에 전력을 공급하면서
   b. 전기 펄스를 고르게 전송하면서
   c. 컴퓨터 마우스에 레이저를 사용하면서
   d. 통신 송신기로서 레이저를 사용하면서

6. 작가가 레이저 광선에 대해 암시하는 바는 무엇인가?
   a. 레이저 광선 활용 분야로 아마도 통신이 뜨게 될 것이다.
   b. 레이저는 그 사용 영역을 넓혀야 할 새로운 에너지원이다.
   c. 손전등에 사용되는 기술은 떨어지지만 레이저만큼 효율이 높다.
   d. 수력 전기만 충분히 공급해 준다면 전력을 레이저 광선으로 변환할 수 있다.

Vocabulary Test   p.306~307

1. 본문의 "특별한"과 가장 근접한 의미의 단어는?
   a. 기묘한   b. 특별한   c. 끔찍한   d. 훌륭한

2. 본문의 "다량"과 가장 근접한 의미의 단어는?
   a. 십진법   b. 변화   c. 광범위   d. 분출

3. 본문의 "식별하다"와 가장 근접한 의미의 단어는?
   a. 접근하다   b. 비교하다   c. 인식하다   d. 분류하다

4. 본문의 "나란한"과 가장 근접한 의미의 단어는?
   a. 정렬한   b. 탄력 있는   c. 울퉁불퉁한   d. 수직의

5. 본문의 "발산하다"와 가장 근접한 의미의 단어는?
   a. 결합하다   b. 방사하다
   c. 위기를 해제하다   d. 기록하다

6. 본문의 "흩어지다"와 가장 근접한 의미의 단어는?
   a. 흩뜨리다   b. 시인하다   c. 중재하다   d. 폭파하다

7. 본문의 "전송하다"와 가장 근접한 의미의 단어는?
   a. 가다   b. 뉘우치다   c. 보내다   d. 식별하다

8. 본문의 "변하다"와 가장 근접한 의미의 단어는?
   a. 변화하다   b. 적용하다   c. 해석하다   d. 정체하다

1. 이를 위해서는 전력을 레이저광으로 변환하고, 수신측에서 반대의 것을 행한다.

   a. 레이저를 발사한다는 뜻은 전력을 기체 모양으로 변환한다는 것이다.
   b. 공기와 레이저는 섞일 수가 없다.
   c. 반대쪽 끝에서는 전력을 레이저로 변환하는 과정을 역으로 바꿔야 한다.
   d. 전력을 레이저로 변환하지 못하는 이유는 기술이 부족해서가 아니다.

2. 레이저의 파장은 전파가 몇 백 미터인데 비해 1cm의 1000만분의 1이다.

   a. 레이저 폭은 1cm를 기준으로 적어도 100만 배 정도 좁다.
   b. 라디오 전파는 레이저 전파에 비해 굉장히 작다.
   c. 다양한 레이저 파장과 라디오 파장을 측정하는 일은 비교적 쉽다.
   d. 라디오 전파는 레이저 파장의 1000만분의 1이다.

Unit 38   Energy (3)   p.314

에너지 (3)

가장 중요하고 용도가 많은 에너지 형태는 화학반응에 의해 얻을 수 있다. 석탄과 나무에 함유된 화학에너지는 성냥 한 개비로 방출할 수 있다. 그 반대의 극에 있는 것이 다이아몬드로서 섭씨 650℃라는 발화점까지 가열하지 않으면 에너지를 방출하지 않는다. 화학에너지는 제어가 간단하다. 그래서 요리사는 머랭을 원하는 대로 노릇노릇하게 구울 수 있는 것이다. 한편 다이나마이트의 형태를 취했을 때처럼 제어 불가능한 에너지도 있다. 지금 이 순간에 이 페이지도 화학에너지를 방출하고 있다. 페이지가 공기 중의 산소와 화합하여 주위보다 뜨거워지고 이 화력이 약한 연소의 결과로 시간이 지나면 노랗게 변색된다.

Sentence Completion   p.310~311

A. 다음 문장에 가장 알맞은 단어를 고르시오.

1. 껍질을 깎고 모양을 다듬는 ____ 칼 가운데 이 제품이 가장 좋다.
   a. 민첩한   b. 다용도의
   c. 재빠른   d. 변덕스러운

2. 문신용 잉크에는 건강에 문제가 생길 정도의 금속을 ____.
   a. 포함하다   b. 단조하다
   c. 설립하다   d. 취하게 하다

3. 금속에 유해한 물질이 많으면 ____ 물질로 구성될 가능성이 있다.
   a. 화학   b. 섬유   c. 임무   d. 요소

4. 감옥에서 ____ 면, 감방에서 더 이상 있을 이유가 없다.
   a. 검토된   b. 느슨해진
   c. 석방된(풀려나)   d. 가정된

5. 상사에게 ____ 것은 자유가 거의 없는 것이나 다름없다.
   a. 제조되는   b. 보호되는
   c. 제어되는   d. 계약되는

B. 다음 문장에 가장 알맞은 단어를 고르시오.

1. ____ 에 변화를 주면, 근무 환경에 더욱 만족하게 될 수도 있다.
   a. 주변   b. 용모
   c. 구절   d. 옷장

2. 스웨터가 두 가지의 녹색 ____ 을/를 띤다.
   a. 섬광   b. 색조(빛깔)
   c. 뚜껑   d. 그림자 윤곽선

3. 그는 보통 아침마다 소시지와 계란을 곁들여 ____ 샌드위치를 카푸치노 커피와 함께 먹는다.
   a. 희석된   b. 구운   c. 살균된   d. 보존된

4. 수소와 염화물이 ____ 하면, 휘발성이 매우 높아진다.
   a. 분리하다   b. 식별하다
   c. 감정 이입하다   d. 결합하다

5. 그는 자기 차를 ____ 해서, 나무에 충돌하는 사태가 발생했다.
   a. 통제할 수 없는   b. 수리한
   c. 두들겨 펼 수 있는   d. 맵시 있는

Listening Comprehension   p.312~313

1. 종이는 왜 노란색으로 변하는가?
   a. 점차적인 연소과정을 통해, 종이분자와 산소가 섞이기 때문에
   b. 오래된 커피 열매가 종이에 깊숙이 파묻혔기 때문에
   c. 종이 주변의 공기가 습하기 때문에
   d. 종이가 산소와 결합한 다음 약한 연소 과정을 거쳐 노란색으로 변한다.

2. 작가가 화학 반응을 설명하는 이유는 무엇인가?
   a. 석탄과 나무, 머랭 과자와 종이 산화에 대한 예를 제시하기 위한 것
   b. 다른 화합물과 섞이면 화학 반응이 다양하게 나타나는 점을 설명하기 위한 것
   c. 재미있는 실험을 통해 화학 선생님이 학생의 흥미를 끌 수 있는 방법을 보여주기 위한 것
   d. 석탄과 장작의 속성을 설명하기 위한 것

3. 작가는 화학 반응을 어떻게 소개하는가?
   a. 다이너마이트를 몇 가지 형태로 제조하는 방법을 개괄하면서
   b. 화학 물질은 가장 중요하고 다용도로 쓰이는 에너지임을 시사하면서
   c. 탄소와 황 그리고 다른 탄화수소를 섞으면서
   d. 지질학과 화학이 서로 연관되어 있음을 보여 주면서

4. 강의의 일부를 다시 듣고 문제에 답하시오. 이 구절의 기능은 무엇인가?
   a. 통제 상황 하에서 화학물질이 얼마나 유용할 수 있는 지를 소개하기 위한 것
   b. 화학 에너지는 사람이 쉽게 제어할 수 없다고 알리기 위한 것
   c. 머랭과 같은 디저트를 만드는 데 있어 한계를 설명하기 위한 것
   d. 화학반응을 통해, 머랭을 만들기 위해 부엌에서 사용되는 기술들을 대비시키기 위한 것

5. 작가에 따르면, 종이가 노란색으로 변하는 두 가지 원인은 무엇인가? 정답 두 개를 고르시오.
   a. 종이 주변의 온도 변화
   b. 종이와 산소의 결합
   c. 외부 간섭
   d. 갈색보다 짙은 색조를 띠는 종이

6. 작가가 화학 반응에 대해 암시하는 바는 무엇인가?
   a. 화학 반응은 매우 불안정하다.
   b. 화학 반응으로 생긴 에너지는 활용도가 높고 유용하다.
   c. 밝은 갈색 빛깔을 띠도록 음식을 요리하는 것은 일종의 실험 형태이다.
   d. 화학 반응은 가정 생활에 적용할 수 있는 부분이 상당히 많다.

Vocabulary Test   p.314~315

1. 본문의 "다용도의"와 가장 근접한 의미의 단어는?
   a. 완고한   b. 휘발성의   c. 만능의   d. 성취된

2. 본문의 "포함하다"와 가장 근접한 의미의 단어는?
   a. 함유하다   b. 소비하다   c. 제외하다   d. 제거하다

3. 본문의 "방출하다"와 가장 근접한 의미의 단어는?
   a. 찾다   b. 풀어주다   c. 체포하다   d. 돌려 받다

4. 본문의 "제어하다"와 가장 근접한 의미의 단어는?
   a. 규제하다   b. 길들이다
   c. 구속에서 풀다   d. 투옥하다

5. 본문의 "굽다"와 가장 근접한 의미의 단어는?
   a. 햇볕에 그슬리다   b. 녹다
   c. (고기를)석쇠로 굽다   d. (빵을)굽다

6. 본문의 "색조"와 가장 근접한 의미의 단어는?
   a. 유형   b. 수수께끼   c. 색   d. 분위기

7. 본문의 "통제할 수 없는"과 가장 근접한 의미의 단어는?
   a. 확인하는   b. 지배받지 않는
   c. 다루기 쉬운   d. 완고한

8. 본문의 "결합하다"와 가장 근접한 의미의 단어는?
   a. 합치다   b. 떼다
   c. 섞다   d. 말뚝을 박다

Paraphrasing   p.315

1. 화학에너지는 제어가 간단하다. 그래서 요리사는 머랭을 원하는 대로 노릇노릇하게 구울 수 있는 것이다.
   a. 화학 에너지는 대다수의 후식, 특히 토스트를 만드는 데 반드시 필요하다.
   b. 후식의 갈색 빛깔은 화학물질에 따라 달라진다.
   c. 잘 다루기만 한다면, 화학 에너지는 맛있는 머랭을 굽는 데 꼭 필요하다.
   d. 화학 반응을 다루는 일은 요리 과정의 일부이다.

2. 페이지가 공기 중의 산소와 화합하여 주위보다 뜨거워지고 이 화력이 약한 연소의 결과로 시간이 지나면 노랗게 변색된다.
   a. 이 책장이 온도가 더 높아지기 시작하면 색이 밝은 노란색으로 변한다.
   b. 산소와 결합하여 화학 에너지가 방출되면 노란색을 띠는 물질이 만들어진다.
   c. 온도가 높아지면 이 책장은 노란빛이 도는 갈색으로 변한다.
   d. 종이가 여러 환경에 노출될 때 색이 변하는데, 몇 년이 지나면 주로 노란색으로 변한다.

Unit 39   Energy (4)   p.322

에너지 (4)

    1865년 제임스 클락 멕스웰은 이렇게 썼다. 「공간을 채우고, 물체에 침투하는 에테르라는 매질(媒質)이 있다. 그것은 움직임을 시작하고 그 움직임을 어느 부분에서 다른 부분으로 전달해 그 움직임을 물질에 전달하고 그것을 가열해 다양한 방법으로 그것에 영향을 줄 수 있는 것이다」. 그의 전자기 이론을 설명하는 가운데 맥스웰은 「에테르」가 존재하기 때문에 빛은 공간을 이동할 수 있음을 시사했다. 이 생각은 인기를 모았지만 그것도 알버트 아인슈타인이 나타나 오류를 입증할 때까지의 일이었다. 아인슈타인은 일찌기 「우주에 관해서 가장 이해할 수 없는 것은 우주는 이해할 수 있다는 것이다.」라고 말했는데 실제로 그 사람 이상으로 우주를 이해하기 어렵게 만든 사람도 없다. 그는 시간은 팽창한다, 우주의 물질은 폭발하고 소멸한다, 길이는 축소한다, 상식은 이제 쓸모가 없다고 주장했다. 아인슈타인이 1905년에 최초의 중요한 발표를 했을 때부터 현재까지 과학은 수학자의 영역이 되어 있다.

Sentence Completion　p.318~319

A. 다음 문장에 가장 알맞은 단어를 고르시오.

1. 누가 ____ 있을 때, 그들이 다른 곳으로 정보를 보내고 있는 것이다.
   a. 후퇴하고　　　　　b. 전하고
   c. 저항하고　　　　　d. 통학하고

2. 만일 당신이 ____ 이론을 가지고 있다면, 그것은 사실이 아니라는 것이다.
   a. 반증된　　　　　　b. 쫓아내는
   c. 설명된　　　　　　d. 교통이 차단된

3. 기체가 ____ 있다면, 그것은 수많은 고체, 액체를 통과하고, 모든 것의 안으로 들어가는 것이다.
   a. 투과하고　　　　　b. 진동하고
   c. 나가고　　　　　　d. 밖으로 나가고

4. 그림은 하나의 ____ 로, 그 속에서 생각을 구체적인 형태로 실현할 수 있다.
   a. 징표　　　　　　　b. 매개체
   c. 장소　　　　　　　d. 육감

5. 세계는 (고체, 액체, 기체의) ____ 로 구성되어 있다.
   a. 찌꺼기　　　　　　b. 시체
   c. 소유물　　　　　　d. 물질

B. 다음 문장에 가장 알맞은 단어를 고르시오.

1. 다른 ____ 을/를 해봤자 아무 소용없다. 아무도 그것을 읽지 않을 것이다.
   a. 발표　　b. 모조품　　c. 의심　　d. 전복

2. 그는 ____ 사람으로, 직장 동료들은 그를 완전히 이해하지 못했다.
   a. 유창한　　　　　　b. 이해할 수 없는
   c. 사라진　　　　　　d. 명료한

3. 에테르 매개체 때문에 빛이 공간을 통과하여 움직일 수 있다고 ____ 왔다.
   a. 유인되어　　　　　b. 측정되어
   c. 채찍질당해　　　　d. 주장되어

4. ____ 을/를 가지게 되는 데에는 최소한의 시간이 필요하다.
   a. 미숙함　　　　　　b. 유치함
   c. 상식　　　　　　　d. 비실용적 감각

5. 그가 쫓는 명성은 실상 거품과 같아서, 그 거품은 쉽게 부서져 곧 ____.
   a. 포함했다　　　　　b. 사라졌다
   c. 확립되었다　　　　d. 나타났다

Listening Comprehension　p.320~321

1. 전자기 이론의 기본원리는 무엇인가?
   a. 물질이 움직여서 다른 곳으로 전달될 수 있고, 열 또한 이 과정에서 핵심 역할을 한다.
   b. 시간이 팽창하고, 열이 그 과정의 핵심 기능이다.
   c. 시간이 바뀌면서 진공이 수축된다.
   d. 빛이 공간을 통해 옮겨지는 방식을 변화시키는 핵심은 강력한 자석이다.

2. 작가가 맥스웰의 전자기 이론을 설명하는 이유는 무엇인가?
   a. 중력이 행성을 움직일 수 있다는 것을 보여주기 위한 것
   b. "에테르"에 의해 움직이는 빛이 공간을 통해 투과될 수 있다는 것을 주장하기 위한 것
   c. 빛의 속도를 이해하려고 하기 위한 것
   d. 아인슈타인의 1905년 발표 논문의 결점들을 보여주기 위한 것

3. 작가는 전자기 이론을 어떻게 소개하는가?
   a. 아인슈타인의 전자기 이론을 설명하면서
   b. 에테르 매질에 대한 제임스 클락 맥스웰의 인용문을 사용해서
   c. 어떻게 세계가 폭발해서 사라지게 되는지를 예측하면서
   d. 20세기 초, 대중적인 개념들을 보여주면서

4. 강의의 일부를 다시 듣고 문제에 답하시오. 이 구절의 기능은 무엇인가?
   a. 빛이 어떻게 공간을 통해 투과될 수 있는지를 보여주기 위한 것
   b. 우리는 전 세계의 불가사의한 것들을 증명해 보이기 위해 아인슈타인의 이론에 의존해야 한다.
   c. 멋진 이론으로 들리지만, 일부 이론들은 추가 조사가 필요하다.
   d. 아인슈타인과 맥스웰의 수학이론을 대비시키기 위한 것

5. 작가에 따르면, 맥스웰의 전자기 이론에 기여하는 두 가지 요인은 무엇인가? 정답 두 개를 고르시오.
   a. 에테르 매질처럼 전체 물질도 열에 의해 영향을 받을 수 있다.
   b. 그는 에테르에 의해 움직이는 빛은 빠르게 투과될 수 있다고 생각했다.
   c. 그는 시간 여행의 열쇠는 공간을 투과하는 물체라고 예측했다.
   d. 그는 자신이 에테르 매질의 동작패턴을 추적한다고 생각했다.

6. 작가가 전자기 이론에 대해 암시하는 바는 무엇인가?
   a. 당신이 머리 좋은 물리학자라면, 세계는 이해하기 쉽다.
   b. 수학 이론은 많지만, 맥스웰의 이론처럼 사실이 아닌 것이 많다.
   c. 성실히 연구하고 동료 연구원들의 검토를 거쳐, 이론이 증명될 수 있다.
   d. 두드러진 수많은 과학 이론들은 수학을 근거로 한 것이다.

Vocabulary Test　p.322 323

1. 본문의 "매개체(매질)"와 가장 근접한 의미의 단어는?
   a. 수난　　b. 중심　　c. 중간　　d. 대중매체

2. 본문의 "투과하다"와 가장 근접한 의미의 단어는?
   a. 스며 나오다   b. 통과하다
   c. 떠오르다   d. 방해하다

3. 본문의 "옮기다"와 가장 근접한 의미의 단어는?
   a. 받다   b. 전하다
   c. 강화하다   d. 필요로 하다

4. 본문의 "물질"과 가장 근접한 의미의 단어는?
   a. 실리콘   b. 물질
   c. 경의   d. 핵심

5. 본문의 "반증하다"와 가장 근접한 의미의 단어는?
   a. 반박하다   b. 방해하다
   c. 거스르다   d. 거닐다

6. 본문의 "이해할 수 없는"과 가장 근접한 의미의 단어는?
   a. 알기 어려운   b. 열렬한
   c. 불가능한   d. 가망 없는

7. 본문의 "주장(가정)하다"와 가장 근접한 의미의 단어는?
   a. 익사시키다   b. 생각하다
   c. 어슬렁거리다   d. 만지작거리다

8. 본문의 "사라지다"와 가장 근접한 의미의 단어는?
   a. 용해하다   b. 사라지다
   c. 나타나다   d. 구체화하다

Paraphrasing   p.323

1. 그는 시간은 팽창한다, 우주의 물질은 폭발하고 소멸한다, 길이
   는 축소한다, 상식은 이제 쓸모가 없다고 주장했다.

   a. 시간의 팽창과 함께, 세계가 종말을 고하고, 불가능하게 보이
      는 것들이 가능하게 된다.
   b. 아인슈타인은 세계가 하루사이에 사라질 거라 생각지 않았다.
   c. 일단 시간이 팽창하고 세계가 폭발하면 모든 것이 끝날 것이다.
   d. 만일 세계가 너무나 빠르게 종말을 고하면, 상식은 더 이상
      중요치 않다.

2. 아인슈타인이 1905년에 최초의 중요한 발표를 했을 때부터 현
   재까지 과학은 수학자의 영역이 되어 있다.

   a. 아인슈타인의 1905년 발표는 기본적으로 과학의 본질을 바
      꿔놓았다.
   b. 과학자들이 학술지에 발표하는 것은 중요하다.
   c. 지나치게 많은 이론 발표는 과학 이론의 힘을 감소시키는데
      기여한다.
   d. 아인슈타인의 1905년 발표와 함께, 과학은 수학에 점점 더
      의존하게 되었다.

Unit 40   Native American Art   p.330

아메리카 원주민 예술

아메리카 원주민의 예술은 아메리카 대륙에 거주하는 원주민들
이 창작한 모든 예술 작품을 뜻한다. 그리고 보통은 북아메리카에
거주하는 사람들을 의미하지만 남아메리카에 거주하는 원주민들도
포함하여 말할 수도 있다. 전통적으로 이러한 예술 작품은 그 지방
고유의 식물, 지방 특유의 광물로 만든 도료, 동물에게서 얻은 재
료와 같은 자연 재료로 만들어졌다. 아메리카 원주민 예술가들은
창의력이 뛰어나기 때문에 자연 재료를 옷과 장신구, 담요와 가면,
바구니와 접시, 토템폴과 같은 다양한 형태의 작품으로 창작한다.
오늘날에는 많은 수의 아메리카 원주민 예술가들이 유화와 사진을
이용한 현대적인 작품을 창작하기도 한다. 현재는 아메리카 원주민
예술을 문화의 일부로 간주하지만, 현 시대의 다른 예술 형태와 마
찬가지로 과거의 전통적인 아메리카 원주민 예술은 다양한 목적으
로 사용되었다. 일부는 실생활에서 사용되었고 다른 일부는 여러
의식에서 중요한 의미를 차지했다. 수세기 동안 아메리카 원주민
예술은 다른 지역에서 위대한 예술 양식으로 그 가치를 인정받지
못하고 2류 취급을 당했지만, 오늘날의 미술 사학자들은 아메리카
원주민의 예술이 갖고 있는 미와 중요성을 인식하고 있다.

Sentence Completion   p.326~327

A. 다음 문장에 가장 알맞은 단어를 고르시오.

1. 밀은 중국 _____ 것이 아니기 때문에, 그것이 중국에 닿는 데 더
   오랜 시간이 걸렸다.
   a. 외국의   b. 특이한
   c. 고유의   d. 경향이 있는

2. 우리는 종종 멕시코 식 저녁 파티를 준비할 때, 다채로운 샐러드
   _____ 을/를 사용한다.
   a. 국자   b. 그릇   c. 믹서기   d. 찻잔 접시

3. 만일 당신이 박물관에서 _____ 을/를 잠시 본다면, 당신은 문화
   의 일면을 보고 있는 것이다.
   a. 비디오   b. 무술   c. 예술품   d. 쓰레기

4. 당신이 _____ 사람을 만난다면, 그들의 조상은 오랜 세월 이 곳
   에 존재해 온 것이다.
   a. 집에서 만든   b. 토착의(토착민)
   c. 박식한   d. 국외로 추방된

5. 안정된 인슐린 수치는 심혈관 건강에 _____ 강력한 영향을 끼칠
   수 있다.
   a. 끔찍하게   b. 장식적으로
   c. 증오스러운   d. 매우

B. 다음 문장에 가장 알맞은 단어를 고르시오.

1. _____ 자동차를 구입하는 것은 예산이 빠듯한 대학생에게는 좋은 아이디어이다.
   a. 고급의
   b. 가장 좋은
   c. 2류의(평범한)
   d. 최신의

2. 1700년대 처음으로 그것들이 유럽 탐험가들의 눈에 띈 이후로, _____ 은/는 신으로 숭배되는 무시무시한 조각상으로 오해받았을지 모른다.
   a. 천연 파이프
   b. 결정적 증거
   c. 토템폴
   d. 전신주

3. _____ 문학은 오늘날 최고의 작가들 가운데 일부는 무엇을 하고 있는지 학생들에게 잘 알려주기 위해서 개설된 강좌이다.
   a. 고전의
   b. 현대의
   c. 전통적인
   d. 관습적인

4. 그들은 평등한 권리와 기회를 부여받고 공평하게 대우받아 _____.
   a. 마땅하다
   b. 쉬다
   c. 질색하다
   d. 위협을 주다

5. 남미 문화 가운데 일부 _____ 은/는 죽은 혼령에게 기도하는 특징이 있다.
   a. 의식
   b. 분할
   c. 축제
   d. 신고식

Listening Comprehension   p.328~329

1. 원주민 문화에서 2류로 생각되는 것은 무엇인가?
   a. 토종식물
   b. 천연 재료를 이용한 예술품
   c. 벽에 그려진 삽화
   d. 지방의 자수 패턴

2. 작가가 아메리카 원주민 예술을 설명하는 이유는 무엇인가?
   a. 미술사가들의 불만을 지적하기 위한 것
   b. 보통 미국인들의 일상을 묘사하기 위한 것
   c. 미국 원주민들의 풍요로운 문화를 보여주기 위한 것
   d. 원주민 사진술의 패턴을 보여주기 위한 것

3. 작가는 아메리카 원주민 예술을 어떻게 소개하는가?
   a. 얼마나 미국 예술가들이 매우 독창적이었는지를 보여주기 위한 것
   b. "토착의"라는 용어에 대해 설명하면서
   c. 미국 원주민들의 예술품들을 더럽히면서
   d. 미술에 사용된 여러 가지 광물질을 묘사하면서

4. 강이이 일부를 다시 듣고 문제에 답하시오. 이 구절의 기능은 무엇인가?

a. 옷과 보석류가 얼마나 당시 매우 귀중한 것이었는지 보여주기 위한 것
b. 원주민 예술이 얼마나 다양한 목적에 부합되게 사용되었는지를 보여주기 위한 것
c. 원주민 장인들의 한계를 보여주기 위한 것
d. 북미와 남미의 예술형태를 대비시키기 위한 것

5. 작가에 따르면, 예술이 어떤 두 가지 행사에서 중요한 위치를 차지했는가? 정답 두 개를 고르시오.
   a. 미국 원주민 축제에서
   b. 미국 원주민 사진에서
   c. 미국 원주민 지역에서
   d. 미국 원주민 의식에서

6. 작가가 아메리카 원주민 예술에 대해 암시하는 바는 무엇인가?
   a. 현대 아메리카 원주민 예술에서만 천연 재료를 이용한다.
   b. 전통적인 아메리카 원주민 예술은 문화적으로 중요한 것이었다는 것
   c. 현대 예술 형태로 증진되어야 한다.
   d. 그는 의식의 중요성을 강조한다.

Vocabulary Test   p.330~331

1. 본문의 "예술 작품"과 가장 근접한 의미의 단어는?
   a. 예술적인 창조물
   b. 교양
   c. 낙서
   d. 모조품

2. 본문의 "토착의"와 가장 근접한 의미의 단어는?
   a. 인접한
   b. 외국의
   c. 토착의
   d. 이국적인

3. 본문의 "고유의"와 가장 근접한 의미의 단어는?
   a. 후천적인
   b. 토착의
   c. 헌법의
   d. 근처의

4. 본문의 "매우"와 가장 근접한 의미의 단어는?
   a. 배타적으로
   b. 합리적으로
   c. 어쨌든
   d. 매우

5. 본문의 "그릇(사발)"과 가장 근접한 의미의 단어는?
   a. 국자
   b. 둥글넓적한 그릇
   c. 사교장
   d. 큰 상자

6. 본문의 "현대의"와 가장 근접한 의미의 단어는?
   a. 현대의
   b. 유서 깊은
   c. 앞쪽의
   d. 일시적인

7. 본문의 "의식"과 가장 근접한 의미의 단어는?
   a. 통과의례
   b. 의식
   c. 매장
   d. 취임

8. 본문의 "2류의"와 가장 근접한 의미의 단어는?
   a. 열등한
   b. 고급의
   c. 천연 그대로의
   d. 배타적인

Paraphrasing   p.331

1. 오늘날에는 많은 수의 아메리카 원주민 예술가들이 유화와 사진을 이용한 현대적인 작품을 창작하기도 한다.

   a. 미국 원주민들은 예술계에 매우 도움이 된다.
   b. 예술가들은 새로운 미술 기법을 확립시키기 위해 애쓰고 있다.
   c. 유화와 사진이 너무 많으면 재료가 늘어나게 된다.
   d. 미국 원주민들이 만들어낸 미술은 종종 캔버스 위에 물감을 사용하는 것이었다.

2. 현재는 아메리카 원주민 예술을 문화의 일부로 간주하지만, 현시대의 다른 예술 형태와 마찬가지로 과거의 전통적인 아메리카 원주민 예술은 다양한 목적으로 사용되었다.

   a. 전통적인 미술 형태는 유용하게 사용되지 못했다.
   b. 예술은 역사가들의 재검토 뒤에 다시 평가받는다.
   c. 오늘날, 미국 원주민 미술은 매우 현대적인 것으로 간주된다.
   d. 여러 모로 도움이 되는 예술을 잃어버리고 지내온 문화가 많다.

Unit 41   **Late 19th Century America**   p.338

19세기 말 미국

19세기 말은 미국이 국내 및 해외에서 빠른 변화를 겪은 시기였다. 국내에서는 이민자의 수가 급격히 증가하였다. 이 이주민들은 다양한 공동체를 만들었고 캘리포니아 주와 같은 미개발 지역을 개발하는 데 일조했다. 가용 노동력의 수가 빠르게 증가하면서, 미국은 의욕적인 노동력도 낮은 임금으로 확보할 수 있었다. 이 시기 동안 미국의 산업은 상당한 발전을 이루었다. 19세기 말경 미국은 세계에서 주요 산업 강대국 가운데 하나였다. 이 시기 동안 인구 성장과 산업 발전을 바탕으로 미국은 세계적인 강대국으로 부상하였다. 19세기가 끝날 무렵, 미국은 스페인의 통치를 받고 있는 쿠바의 독립을 원조했고, 미국–스페인 간 전쟁 후반에는 필리핀을 획득했다. 또한 미국은 하와이와 푸에르토리코를 합병했다. 당시 미국은 경제와 군사 양 부문에서 세계적인 강대국이었다. 이로써 다음 세기에 미국이 세계에서 중요한 역할을 수행할 무대가 마련되었다.

Sentence Completion   p.334~335

A. 다음 문장에 가장 알맞은 단어를 고르시오.

1. 만일 당신이 ____ 을/를 맞이한다면, 당신은 당신이 사는 지역이나 집, 또는 직장에 새로 온 사람들을 환영하는 것이다.
   a. 고용인   b. 퇴직자
   c. 주민   d. 새로 온 사람

2. 만일 당신이 ____ 지역에 산다면, 당신 주변 땅은 아마도 텅 비어있거나 농토일 것이다.
   a. 발전한   b. 첨단의   c. 혼잡한   d. 미개발된

3. 출산율의 ____ 감소로 인해 전체 인구수가 거의 30퍼센트 감소했다.
   a. 멋진   b. 현저한
   c. 황홀한   d. 미적지근한

4. 만일 당신이 ____ 라면, 당신은 다른 나라 출신이다.
   a. 죄수   b. 수감자   c. 이민자   d. 국민

5. 여섯 개 대륙을 여행하면서, 나는 ____ 문화, 아이디어, 인종 집단들을 포용하는 법을 배우게 되었다.
   a. 다양한   b. 자민족중심주의의
   c. 참을 수 없는   d. 인종차별주의의

B. 다음 문장에 가장 알맞은 단어를 고르시오.

1. 독일이 여러 국가들을 강제로 ____ 던 것이 제 2차 세계대전 발발의 한 요인이었다.
   a. 석방했다   b. 합병했다
   c. 부유하게 만들었다   d. 권력을 위임했다

2. 그 영토는 아직도 비교적 미개발된 국가여서, 앞으로 많은 광산지를 발견할 ____ 잠재력을 갖고 있다.
   a. 상당한   b. 하찮은
   c. 추적할 수 있는   d. 소형의

3. 독재적 ____ 에 반대하는 시위 동안에 200명의 시위자가 사망했다.
   a. 규제완화   b. 복종   c. 통치   d. 관용

4. 새 장관이 업무 인수인계를 받을 ____ 상황에서, 그 장관은 새 장관 취임 두 달을 앞두고 장관직에서 물러났다.
   a. 지불 기한이 넘은   b. 준비가 된
   c. 예정보다 늦게   d. 양도된

5. 그녀가 새로 산 스포츠카를 ____ 때, 그녀는 매우 황홀해하며 모두에게 자랑했다.
   a. 황폐화시켰다   b. 소각했다
   c. 저당 잡았다   d. 획득했다(가졌다)

Listening Comprehension   p.336~337

1. 미국 산업의 비밀은 무엇이었나?
   a. 준비된 가용 노동력이 있었다.
   b. 저임금으로 강제로 노동시킬 수 있었다.
   c. 불가용 노동력이 있었다.
   d. 계약 노동자들이 있었다.

2. 작가가 세기의 변화 과정(20세기 초)에 있던 미국을 설명하는 이유는 무엇인가?
   a. 저임금 노동과 더불어 얼마나 이민자 수가 엄청나게 늘어났는지를 설명하기 위한 것
   b. 하와이 합병이 얼마나 쓸모없는 것이었는지에 대해 설명하기 위한 것
   c. 이민자 수의 급격한 증가를 예측하기 위한 것
   d. 다양한 지역사회가 미국에 얼마나 기여했는지를 말하기 위한 것

3. 작가는 20세기 초 미국을 어떻게 소개하는가?
   a. 직업을 원하는 저임금 가용 노동력에 대해 언급하면서
   b. 쿠바의 해방운동을 옹호하면서
   c. 미국 내의 급격한 변화들을 개괄하면서
   d. 인구증가와 산업 발전을 설명하면서

4. 강의의 일부를 다시 듣고 문제에 답하시오. 이 구절의 기능은 무엇인가?
   a. 어떻게 하면 스페인이 권력을 유지할 수도 있었을지 보여주기 위한 것
   b. 강력한 세계열강으로의 부상을 보여주기 위한 것
   c. 세계열강의 한계를 설명하기 위한 것
   d. 인구증가와 산업 발전을 대비시키기 위한 것

5. 작가에 따르면, 미국이 세계열강으로 부상하는데 기여한 두 가지 요소는 무엇인가? 정답 두 개를 고르시오.
   a. 푸에르토리코의 미개발 지역들
   b. 쿠바의 스페인으로부터의 해방운동
   c. 플로리다 주에 쿠바 이주민들의 출현
   d. 값싼 산업 노동자들의 증가

6. 작가가 20세기 초 미국에 대해 암시하는 바는 무엇인가?
   a. 미국 산업의 힘으로 인해 국제무대에서의 자국 영향력이 커졌다는 것
   b. 어떤 강력한 지배세력에게 누군가 의존하는 것
   c. 다양한 공동체들이 미국을 파괴시킨 것
   d. 미국이 해외 원조에 더 큰 역할을 해야 한다는 것

Vocabulary Test p.338~339

1. 본문의 "현저한"과 가장 근접한 의미의 단어는?
   a. 감동시키는   b. 기분을 돋우는
   c. 이론적인   d. 두드러지는

2. 본문의 "이민자"와 가장 근접한 의미의 단어는?
   a. 이주자   b. 식민지   c. 민족주의자   d. 거주자

3. 본문의 "다양한"과 가장 근접한 의미의 단어는?
   a. 정통한   b. 똑같은   c. 다양한   d. 기형의

4. 본문의 "미개발의"와 가장 근접한 의미의 단어는?
   a. 신흥의   b. 개화된   c. 뒤떨어진   d. 원시적인

5. 본문의 "상당한"과 가장 근접한 의미의 단어는?
   a. 상당한   b. 건장한   c. 주요한   d. 하찮은

6. 본문의 "통치"와 가장 근접한 의미의 단어는?
   a. 기준   b. 헌법   c. 참정권   d. 지배

7. 본문의 "획득하다"와 가장 근접한 의미의 단어는?
   a. 인정하다   b. 굴복하다   c. 얻다   d. 포기하다

8. 본문의 "합병하다"와 가장 근접한 의미의 단어는?
   a. 분리하다   b. 통합시키다   c. 촉진하다   d. 동행하다

Paraphrasing p.339

1. 19세기 말 경 미국은 세계에서 주요 산업 강대국 가운데 하나였다.
   a. 미국은 1900년대 까지 유력한 조용한 대국이었다.
   b. 19세기 중반을 즈음하여, 미국은 일부 영향력을 잃었다.
   c. 미국은 1800년대 말까지 주요 강대국이었다.
   d. 주요 산업 강대국이 된다는 것은 힘든 일이다.

2. 이 시기 동안 인구 성장과 산업 발전을 바탕으로 미국은 세계적인 강대국으로 부상하였다.
   a. 미국은 빈곤을 이겨내고, 세계열강으로 부상했다.
   b. 강력한 국가 뒤에는 인구와 산업 성장의 기간이 있다.
   c. 여러 강국의 부상은 부와 야망과 종종 관련이 있다.
   d. 미국은 그 규모와 산업으로 인해 강해졌다.

Unit 42 Chinese Art p.346

중국 예술

부의 추측으로는 중국의 문화는 5,000년 전에 시작되었고 지금까지 존재하는, 가장 오래된 문명 가운에 하나라고 한다. 다른 모든 문명과 마찬가지로 예술은 중국 문화에서 중요한 부분을 차지한다. 세 가지 요인이 중국의 예술에 중요한 영향을 미쳤다. 그 요인은 바로 유교, 도교, 불교로 중국의 모든 예술 양식에 반드시 포함된 요소이자 중심에 위치하는 요소이다. 중국 예술가들이 가장 흔히 사용하는 주제는 새, 꽃, 풍경과 같은 자연이다. 이처럼 자연에서 선택한 주제를 통해 중국 예술가들은 인간의 정신적인 면을 묘사하려고 했다. 이들은 자연의 기에서 모든 사물이 생명을 얻는다고 믿었기 때문에, 화가들의 최종 목표는 자연의 느낌을 그대로 옮기는 것이었다. 중국의 예술에는 그림, 비단, 서예, 도자기, 조각, 금속 공예, 종이 공예 등 실로 다양한 형태가 존재한다. 중국 예술의 가장 뛰어난 점은 우아한 여백의 미이다.

Answer Key

Sentence Completion p.342~343

A. 다음 문장에 가장 알맞은 단어를 고르시오.

1. 아이가 어렸을 때 엄마에게 느끼는 애착은 아이의 정신 건강에 주요한 ____ 으로 작용한다.
   a. 영향   b. 인플레이션
   c. 변동   d. 여유

2. 마침내 선물이 전달되기 시작하자, 아빠는 즐거운 한때를 ____ 위해, 비디오카메라를 설치했다.
   a. 지우다   b. 닦다
   c. 포착하다   d. 망치다

3. 당신이 어떤 것에 대해 ____ 할 때, 당신은 그것에 대해 대략 판단을 내리는 것이다.
   a. 정리   b. 확신
   c. 추정   d. 주목

4. 만일 당신이 오래된 ____ 가운데 한 곳에서 산다면, 당신은 인도, 중국, 이란, 이탈리아 출생일 가능성이 크다.
   a. 공산주의   b. 예배당
   c. 감방   d. 문명

5. 만일 당신이 ____ 을/를 믿는다면, 당신은 중국 영향을 받은 문화에서 태어났을 가능성이 높다.
   a. 종교   b. 유교
   c. 철학   d. 정설

B. 다음 문장에 가장 알맞은 단어를 고르시오.

1. 중국의 ____ 특징들은 그들의 대단한 비즈니스 감각과 인내이다.
   a. 터무니없는   b. 건방진
   c. 구별되는   d. 제정신이 아닌

2. 그 예술가는 자연에서 받은 인상을 ____ 하기 위해 노력하며, 점차적으로 자신만의 스타일을 발견해 나갔다.
   a. 고의적으로 파괴하다   b. 치다
   c. 묘사하다   d. 경멸하다

3. 삶에서 내가 ____ 하고 싶은 한 가지가 있는데, 그것은 킬리만자로를 등반하는 것이다.
   a. 성취   b. 깨달음   c. 은유   d. 승리

4. 아름다움은 조잡하지도 공허하지도 않은, ____ 에 있다.
   a. 수치   b. 간소함
   c. 호되게 꾸짖음   d. 더러움

5. ____에서 전문가가 되는 데는 수년간의 인내와 흔들림 없는 손놀림이 필요하다.
   a. 안무   b. 작문
   c. 학구적 세계   d. 서예

Listening Comprehension p.344~345

1. 중국 예술가들은 무엇을 묘사해내려고 애썼는가?
   a. 가족의 생활 모습을 반영하는 것
   b. 위대한 황제들의 예술적 모습들
   c. 인간의 정신적인 측면들
   d. 우아한 간소함을 극소화하는 모습들

2. 작가가 중국 예술을 설명하는 이유는 무엇인가?
   a. 꽃과 풍경에 대해 언급하기 위한 것
   b. 얼마나 다양한 중국 예술이 다양한 형태를 취하는지를 보여주기 위한 것
   c. 다양한 아시아의 예술 기법들을 대비시키기 위한 것
   d. 조각, 금속예술, 종이기술을 보여주기 위한 것

3. 작가는 중국 예술을 어떻게 소개하는가?
   a. 얼마나 현대 예술이 수익이 남는 사업으로 발전했는지를 보여주면서
   b. 5000년 역사의 중국 문명을 설명하면서
   c. 얼마나 흔한 주제들이 중국에 있었는지를 분석하면서
   d. 자연의 기에 대해 설명하면서

4. 강의의 일부를 다시 듣고 문제에 답하시오. 이 구절의 기능은 무엇인가?
   a. 인간의 정신적 측면을 소개하고 묘사하기 위한 것
   b. 중국 문화에 깃든 간소함에 대해 예를 제시하기 위한 것
   c. 그림, 실크, 서예, 도기, 조각을 설명하기 위한 것
   d. 중국 문화에서 예술이 점하는 중요성을 보여주기 위한 것

5. 작가에 따르면, 예술가들이 획득하는 두 가지 중요 요소는 무엇인가? 정답 두 개를 고르시오.
   a. 우아한 간소함(여백의 미)
   b. 유화용 캔버스 위에 행해진 예술
   c. 도기 전문 예술
   d. 자연을 묘사하는 예술

6. 작가가 중국 예술에 대해 암시하는 바는 무엇인가?
   a. 중국 예술은 더욱 진화해야 한다.
   b. 중국 예술이 매우 예술적이고 인상에 근거한 것이라는 것
   c. 자연은 복제하기에 쉽다는 것이라는 것
   d. 중국 예술이 더 많이 세련되어져야 한다는 것

Vocabulary Test p.346~347

1. 본문의 "추정"과 가장 근접한 의미의 단어는?
   a. 적응   b. 증거
   c. 추측   d. 산수

2. 본문의 "문명"과 가장 근접한 의미의 단어는?
   a. 문화   b. 미개함
   c. 통찰   d. 문화충격

3. 본문의 "영향"과 가장 근접한 의미의 단어는?
   a. 걱정　　　　　　　　b. 강조
   c. 힘　　　　　　　　　d. 긴장

4. 본문의 "묘사하다"와 가장 근접한 의미의 단어는?
   a. 열거하다　　　　　　b. 신임하다
   c. 증명하다　　　　　　d. 묘사하다

5. 본문의 "성취"와 가장 근접한 의미의 단어는?
   a. 애정　　　　　　　　b. 고통
   c. 임무　　　　　　　　d. 성취

6. 본문의 "포착하다"와 가장 근접한 의미의 단어는?
   a. 잡다　　　　　　　　b. 낚아채다
   c. 해방시키다　　　　　d. 끌어당기다

7. 본문의 "서예(서법)"와 가장 근접한 의미의 단어는?
   a. 밑그림　　　　　　　b. 작은 활자
   c. 서법　　　　　　　　d. 직유

8. 본문의 "구별되는"과 가장 근접한 의미의 단어는?
   a. 불가사의한　　　　　b. 기이한
   c. 신경증의　　　　　　d. 구별이 있는

Paraphrasing　　　　　　p.347

1. 중국 예술가들이 가장 흔히 사용하는 주제는 새, 꽃, 풍경과 같
   은 자연이다.

   a. 일부 추상 화가들이 자연을 묘사하기란 힘들다.
   b. 자연은 중국 가치관 체계에 중요한 위치를 차지한다.
   c. 예술가들이 자연의 풍경을 묘사하는 것은 흔한 것이다.
   d. 자연은 중국의 예술성에 중요한 위치를 차지한다.

2. 이처럼 자연에서 선택한 주제를 통해 중국 예술가들은 인간의
   정신적인 면을 묘사하려고 했다.

   a. 자연은 인간의 정신과 같은 여타 주제를 묘사하는데 있어 단
      순히 매개체의 역할을 한다.
   b. 정신적 측면은 중국 공동체 내에서 중요한 위치를 차지한다.
   c. 독창적인 화가들이 인간의 정신을 묘사하기란 힘들다.
   d. 자연에서 주제를 선택한 이유는 주 정부의 우려 때문이다.

생태학 (1)

　봄·여름·가을·겨울의 4계절의 변화가 있는 지역을 온대라고
한다. 충분한 강우가 있을 때 온대의 지면을 뒤덮는 자연은 떡갈나
무, 단풍나무, 너도밤나무 등 가을에는 잎이 떨어지는 낙엽수로 이
루어지는 숲이다. 열대우림은 강우량이 풍부하고 따뜻한 지역에 자
라며 남아메리카, 아시아, 아프리카에서 볼 수 있다. 이런 숲은 여
러 개의 「층」으로 나뉘어져 있고 그 중에는 여덟 개나 되는 층을
가진 것도 있다. 각 층은 수관(樹冠)과 밀생(密生)하는 관목으로 구
성되고, 지상의 양치류에서부터 상층의 이끼에 이르는 다양한 식물
과 서식하는 높이에 따라 습성이 다른 다양한 동물들에게 있어 집
과 같은 역할을 하고 있다.

Sentence Completion　　　p.350~351

A. 다음 문장에 가장 알맞은 단어를 고르시오.

1. 비행 금지 ____ 은/는 비행기들의 비행이 허용되지 않는 지역
   이다.
   a. 차원　　　b. 직사각형　　　c. 푯말　　　d. 구역

2. 겨울철에 내 머리카락이 많이 ____ 은/는 것을 알게 되었다.
   a. 배부하다　　　　　　b. 자르다
   c. 번성하다　　　　　　d. 빠지다(떨구다)

3. 만일 당신이 수술을 ____ 면, 당신은 수술을 받는 것이다.
   a. 경험하다　　b. 지켜보다　　c. 살아남다　　d. 맡다

4. 만일 당신이 ____ 지역에 산다면, 그 지역의 날씨가 쾌적할 것이다.
   a. 추운　　　　　　　　b. 차고 끈적끈적한
   c. 온난한　　　　　　　d. 매우 더운

5. 만일 당신이 ____ 나무를 가지고 있다면, 그 나무는 잎이 떨어
   지는 나무일 것이다.
   a. 건강한　　　b. 낙엽성의　　c. 양서류의　　d. 유황의

B. 다음 문장에 가장 알맞은 단어를 고르시오.

1. 젖은 ____ 을/를 조심해. 그렇지 않으면 자전거 바퀴가 미끄러
   질지도 몰라.
   a. 고무 접착제　b. 이끼　　c. 흙받이　　d. 바구니

2. 선탠하기에 가장 좋은 기후 가운데 하나는 분명 ____ 기후이다.
   a. 차가운　　b. 열대지역의　c. 급류의　　d. 흐린

3. 허리케인 동안, 뉴 올리언즈 주변의 물 ____ 이/가 계속 상승했다.
   a. 웅덩이　　b. 순위　　c. 높이(수위)　　d. 보일러

Answer Key

4. 그 빌딩 37 _____에서 너를 만나도록 할게.
   a. 고도   b. 박람회
   c. 위도   d. 층

5. 병원 창고에 _____ 양의 주사기가 있다.
   a. 많은   b. 몇 개의
   c. 12개의   d. 누추한

Listening Comprehension   p.352~353

1. 열대우림 층의 독특한 점은 무엇인가?
   a. 열대우림에 별다른 활동이 없다.
   b. 최고 여덟 개의 층이 있으며, 그것은 수관과 관목으로 형성된 것이다.
   c. 그러한 산림은 별개의 분류 체계로 나누어진다.
   d. 열대우림에는 유사한 층이 많이 있다.

2. 작가가 생태학적 차이점들을 설명하는 이유는 무엇인가?
   a. 많은 종의 식물들이 산림 하층부에 자리하고 있다.
   b. 건조한 열대지역 기후의 핵심은 풍부한 강우량이다.
   c. 계절적 변화는 생태에 엄청난 다양성을 제공한다.
   d. 열대지역 생태 내부의 차이점들이 점점 줄어들고 있다.

3. 작가는 산림 생태를 어떻게 소개하는가?
   a. 다양한 나무 벌레를 묘사하면서
   b. 각 층의 나무들 간의 거리를 추정하면서
   c. 강우량과 그에 따른 산림 속 생물들을 대비시키면서
   d. 수관들을 식별하면서

4. 강의의 일부를 다시 듣고 문제에 답하시오. 이 구절의 기능은 무엇인가?
   a. 열대우림 내의 재배종들을 소개하기 위한 것
   b. 기후에 따라 서로 다른 다양한 동·식물에 대한 예를 제시하기 위한 것
   c. 건조한 기후에서의 강우량의 한계를 묘사하기 위한 것
   d. 온난한 지역과 열대지역의 동물생태를 대비하기 위한 것

5. 작가에 따르면, 열대우림이 자라는데 기여하는 두 가지 요소는 무엇인가? 정답 두 개를 고르시오.
   a. 풍부한 강우량
   b. 건조하고 습기 많은 기후
   c. 바람이 많이 부는 연안 평야
   d. 따뜻한 지역

6. 작가가 산림 생태에 대해 암시하는 바는 무엇인가?
   a. 남미는 서식지를 매우 잘 드러내 보여주는 지역이다.
   b. 나무와 관목은 종종 밀생한다.
   c. 서로 다른 기후 변화로 인해 나무와 잎의 형태가 달라진다.
   d. 온난한 지역은 동아시아에서 유일하게 흔하다.

Vocabulary Test   p.354~355

1. 본문의 "겪다"와 가장 근접한 의미의 단어는?
   a. 추측하다   b. 겪다   c. 계속하다   d. 거절하다

2. 본문의 "온난한"과 가장 근접한 의미의 단어는?
   a. 극도의   b. 더운   c. 연안의   d. 온후한

3. 본문의 "구역"과 가장 근접한 의미의 단어는?
   a. 레벨   b. 선   c. 지역   d. 소홀함

4. 본문의 "낙엽성의"과 가장 근접한 의미의 단어는?
   a. 잎을 떨어뜨리는   b. 조각으로 벗겨지는
   c. 떼어내는   d. 생물학적인

5. 본문의 "떨구다"와 가장 근접한 의미의 단어는?
   a. 쏟아 붓다   b. 떠오르다   c. 버리다   d. 줍다

6. 본문의 "열대지역의"와 가장 근접한 의미의 단어는?
   a. 지독한   b. 거친
   c. 타는 듯이 뜨거운   d. 동토대

7. 본문의 "많은"과 가장 근접한 의미의 단어는?
   a. 희박한   b. 거의 없는   c. 작은 편의   d. 풍부한

8. 본문의 "층"과 가장 근접한 의미의 단어는?
   a. 우화   b. 층   c. 높이   d. 지점

Paraphrasing   p.355

1. 열대우림은 강우량이 풍부하고 따뜻한 지역에 자라며 남아메리카, 아시아, 아프리카에서 볼 수 있다.
   a. 열대우림은 강우량에 매우 좌우된다.
   b. 이런 산림은 보통 북반구에서 발견된다.
   c. 열대우림은 청정한 공기의 경로가 필요하다.
   d. 열대우림은 다양한 나무들로 유명하다.

2. 각 층은 수관(樹冠)과 밀생(密生)하는 관목으로 구성되고, 지상의 양치류에서부터 상층의 이끼에 이르는 다양한 식물과 서식하는 높이에 따라 습성이 다른 다양한 동물들에게 있어 집과 같은 역할을 하고 있다.
   a. 그 층이 종종 13층 이상 까지 올라간다.
   b. 오크와 단풍나무는 열대우림에서 풍부하다.
   c. 양치류는 종종 여타 작은 관목과 식물의 서식지를 점령한다.
   d. 열대우림의 많은 층에는 다양한 동·식물이 서식한다.

Ecology (2)

p.362

생태학 (2)

들소는 뛰어난 후각과 청각을 가진 조심성 있는 동물이고, 무리 한테는 여러 감시망을 배치해, 위험이 닥치면 일제히 도망친다. 몇 천 년 동안이나, 인디언들은 창과 활을 사용하여 걸어서 들소 사냥 을 했다. 때로는 들소떼를 몽땅 절벽으로 몰아넣은 적도 있었지 만 보통은 세심한 주의를 기울이며 접근해, 한 마리나 두 마리 밖 에 죽이지 않았다. 스페인 정복자들이 신세계에 말을 갖고 들어갔 고, 17세기까지는 인디언도 최초의 말의 자손에 올라타 평원에서 들소를 쫓았다. 들소는 인디언의 식료, 주거, 의류, 침구, 연료, 도 구 등의 공급원이 되었다. 그러나 빈번히 인디언에게 잡혔는데도 불구하고, 큰 무리는 거의 영향을 받지 않았다. 그런데 유력한 모피 업자가 모피와의 물물교환품을 갖고 오자, 그것이 들소 멸종의 발 단이 되었다. 그 이후 백인 사냥꾼들과 인디언들은 사상 최대라고 할 수 있는 대학살에 나서게 되었다. 그러나 일부 헌신적인 사람들 의 도움으로 오늘날 들소의 수가 증가하고 있다.

Sentence Completion p.358~359

A. 다음 문장에 가장 알맞은 단어를 고르시오.

1. 그 항공사는 항공기 화물실로 몰래 들어오는 도둑들이 점점 늘 어나는 문제를 해결하기 위한 조사에 ____ .
   a. 착수(시작)했다   b. 발송했다
   c. 분배했다   d. 폭격했다

2. 그 금융회사는 민감한 사업 협상을 진행하는 동안, 많은 경호원 들을 ____ 해야 했다.
   a. 감금하다   b. 배치하다
   c. 숙박시키다   d. 서명하다

3. 그 남자는 동물들을 우리 안쪽으로 ____.
   a. 공격했다   b. 짓밟았다
   c. 달아나게 했다(몰아넣었다)   d. 비축했다

4. 그는 보석 몇 개를 훔쳐서 그것들을 음식으로 ____ 하려 했지 만, 구매자를 찾기가 쉽지 않았다.
   a. 소비하다   b. 교환하다
   c. 찾다   d. 구하다

5. 많은 ____ 의 동물들이란 많은 그룹의 동물들과 같다.
   a. 한줌   b. 저장
   c. 모임   d. 무리

B. 다음 문장에 가장 알맞은 단어를 고르시오.

1. 매우 추하게 이별을 한 이후에, 여자를 ____ 은/는 당신이 누군 가에게 거절당하는 것을 받아들이는데 문제가 있다는 것을 의미 한다.
   a. 인정하는 것   b. 칭찬하는 것
   c. 스토킹하는 것   d. 촉진하는 것

2. 8월과 9월에 네 번의 허리케인과 한 번의 강한 열대 폭풍이 ____ 것 같았다.
   a. 발생할   b. 소환한
   c. 제공할   d. 촉진할

3. 조류독감 발견은 그 지역에서의 닭 대량 ____ 을/를 촉발시켰다.
   a. 소비   b. 농장
   c. 부화   d. 도살

4. ____ 란 스페인의 군인이자, 탐험가이자, 또 모험가로서, 점진적 인 침략행위와 아메리카 · 아시아 태평양의 대다수 지역을 정복 하는 일에 참여했다.
   a. 정복자   b. 군주
   c. 대대   d. 여단

5. 케냐 부족의 장은 ____ 을/를 던지는데 명수였다.
   a. 박격포   b. 창
   c. 산탄총   d. 바주카포

Listening Comprehension p.360~361

1. 모피회사가 바이손(들소)을 원했던 이유는 무엇인가?
   a. 미국 원주민들에게 되팔기 위한 것
   b. 털가죽과 코트를 만들어 이익을 남기기 위한 것
   c. 말 무리를 다루는 방법을 예측하기 위한 것
   d. 들소를 목표로 한 보호 노력을 연구하기 위한 것

2. 작가가 들소의 역할을 설명하는 이유는 무엇인가?
   a. 절벽 너머로 소떼들을 몰아가는 방법을 분석하기 위한 것
   b. 들소와 인간이 서로에게 어떻게 영향을 끼쳤는지에 대한 이 해를 높이기 위한 것
   c. 들소가 멸종될 그 날을 예측하기 위한 것
   d. 백인과 미국 원주민들 간의 사냥 패턴을 비교하기 위한 것

3. 작가는 들소를 어떻게 소개하는가?
   a. 미국 원주민들이 쓴 이야기들을 이용하면서
   b. 뛰어난 후각과 청각을 설명하면서
   c. 들소사냥 빈도수를 언급하면서
   d. 식습관의 패턴을 보여주면서

4. 강의의 일부를 다시 듣고 문제에 답하시오. 이 구절의 기능은 무엇인가?
   a. 정복자들이 어떤 식으로 미국 원주민들을 죽였는지에 대한 한 가지 대안을 소개하기 위한 것
   b. 17세기 미국 원주민들의 사냥방법에 대한 예를 제시하기 위한 것
   c. 들소 사냥의 한계를 설명하기 위한 것
   d. 버팔로와 말의 영역지배 습성을 대비시키기 위한 것

5. 작가에 따르면, 원주민들은 들소를 어떤 두 가지 목적으로 사용했는가? 정답 두 개를 고르시오.
   a. 의류와 권총
   b. 주거와 배터리
   c. 침구와 연료
   d. 주거와 식료

6. 작가가 들소의 운명에 대해 암시하는 바는 무엇인가?
   a. 들소보다 말이 더 인기가 많았다.
   b. 미국 원주민들은 들소들을 소중히 여겼고, 모피회사들이 등장할 때 까지는 조금씩 사냥했다.
   c. 최초 말의 자손들은 사막을 가로질러 들소를 쫓았다.
   d. 모피회사들은 들소의 도살을 막기 위해 애썼다.

Vocabulary Test   p.362~363

1. 본문의 "무리"와 가장 근접한 의미의 단어는?
   a. 무리   b. 모임   c. 친구   d. 사냥꾼

2. 본문의 "배치하다"와 가장 근접한 의미의 단어는?
   a. 당기다   b. 불구로 만들다
   c. 배치하다   d. 건설하다

3. 본문의 "임박하다"와 가장 근접한 의미의 단어는?
   a. 일어날 것 같다   b. 소리치다
   c. 분명 두려워하다   d. 완화하다

4. 본문의 "창"과 가장 근접한 의미의 단어는?
   a. 창   b. 새총   c. 권총   d. 수류탄

5. 본문의 "몰래 접근하다"와 가장 근접한 의미의 단어는?
   a. 괴롭히다   b. 짜증나게 하다
   c. 뒤따르다   d. 외면하다

6. 본문의 "교환하다"와 가장 근접한 의미의 단어는?
   a. 비축하다   b. 교환하다   c. 버리다   d. 공급하다

7. 본문의 "시작하다"와 가장 근접한 의미의 단어는?
   a. 분열시키다 b. 제공하다   c. 중지하다   d. 시작하다

8. 본문의 "도살"과 가장 근접한 의미의 단어는?
   a. 복수   b. 충돌   c. 살해   d. 전쟁

Paraphrasing   p.363

1. 들소는 인디언의 식료, 주거, 의류, 침구, 연료, 도구 등의 공급원이 되었다.
   a. 들소는 미국 원주민들의 생계에 주요 공급원이 되었다.
   b. 들소 털은 여름철 너무 더웠다.
   c. 많은 들소 고기 때문에 종종 미국 원주민들이 천연두를 앓았다.
   d. 미국 원주민들이 입는 의류 가운데 일부는 비버, 밍크, 들소로 만들었다.

2. 그런데 유력한 모피업자가 모피와의 물물 교환품을 갖고 오자, 그것이 들소 멸종의 발단이 되었다.
   a. 모피 무역 회사들은 침구와 연료를 팔기 위해 많은 미국 원주민 부족들을 이용했다.
   b. 물물 교환은 총을 동물 가죽으로 바꾸는데 효율적인 방법이다.
   c. 모피 무역 회사들이 일부 들소를 몰아서, 농장에서 사육했다.
   d. 모피 무역 회사들은 미국 원주민들과 물물 교환을 했고, 그래서 들소 도살이 증가했다.

Unit 45   Light and Vision(1)   p.370

빛과 시각 (1)

　지구상의 모든 종(種) 가운데에서 인간은 가장 복잡한 시각시스템을 갖고 있다. 눈과 뇌의 각 부분을 연결하는 이 시스템에 의해 인간은 주위에 있는 다수의 복잡한 요소를 조직하고 이해할 수 있다. 고양이는 TV에 비친 다른 고양이를 보더라도 당황하거나 흥미를 보이지 않거나 둘 중의 하나겠지만, 인간은 TV에서 우주공간을 떠도는 우주비행사의 모습을 보면, 그 화상의 의미를 이해할 수 있다. 또한 인간의 시각시스템은 문제를 제기하여 거기에 답하는 방법을 생각해내는 인간의 능력에 지대한 공헌도 하고 있다. 예를 들면 우주에서의 인류의 역할에 대한 호기심으로부터 망원경이 개발되었고, 생명의 본질에 관한 의문에서 살아있는 세포를 조사하는 현미경이 생겨났다.

Sentence Completion   p.366~367

A. 다음 문장에 가장 알맞은 단어를 고르시오.

1. 누군가 닻에 줄을 _____ 때, 그들은 닻과 줄을 연결을 하는 것이다.
   a. 연결하다   b. 떼어내다
   c. 융합시키다   d. 분류하다

2. 사람들이 ____ 상황일 때, 그들은 어떤 것에 대해 명확하지 않은 것이다.
   a. 행복한   b. 호르몬에 의한
   c. 황홀한   d. 혼란스러운

3. 일련의 ____ 수학 공식들은 그것들을 풀어내기 매우 어렵다는 것을 뜻한다.
   a. 분명한   b. 복잡한
   c. 모험적인   d. 정직한

4. 당신이 ____ 사람이라면, 당신은 뭔가를 보았을 때 매우 잘 그것들을 기억하는 사람이다.
   a. 촉각적인   b. 성 잘 내는
   c. 시각적인   d. 상대적인

5. 만일 당신이 ____ 보석을 하고 있다면, 그 보석은 복잡하고 또 어쩌면 디자인이 고가일 지도 모른다.
   a. 거칠게 만든   b. 복잡한
   c. 반짝이는   d. 평범한

B. 다음 문장에 가장 알맞은 단어를 고르시오.

1. 그 훌륭한 정책은 국내 출생률 증가에 ____.
   a. 위협했다   b. 기여했다
   c. 좌절시켰다   d. 방해했다

2. 화성 여행 중, ____ 의 안전에 대한 많은 토론이 있었다.
   a. 별점   b. 우주 비행사
   c. 나사(미 항공우주국)   d. 생태계

3. 그 복잡한 비디오 이미지를 ____ 하려 해봤자 아무 소용없다. 너무 헷갈린다.
   a. 곡해하다   b. 속이다
   c. 이해하다   d. 오해하다

4. 그 두 국가 간의 긴장 고조가 현재 진행 중인 평화 협상에 위협을 ____ 지 모른다.
   a. 감소시키다   b. 조금씩 깎아내다
   c. 제거하다   d. 제기하다

5. 이 프로젝트에 대한 우리 성공의 ____ 은/는 우리가 얼마나 열심히 하느냐에 달려 있을 것이다.
   a. 정도   b. 경도   c. 범위   d. 망각

Listening Comprehension   p.368~369

1. 인간의 시각 시스템이 우리 정신에 어떻게 도움을 주는가?
   a. 우리에게 새로운 깊긱들을 제공하면서
   b. 우리 머릿속의 신경계 연결을 추정하면서
   c. 우리에게 질문할 정보를 제공하면서
   d. 우주에서 우리의 역할을 정의하면서

2. 작가가 시각 시스템을 설명하는 이유는 무엇인가?
   a. 우리의 시각과 지식이 얼마나 복잡하고 필수적인지를 보여주기 위한 것
   b. 그래서 우리는 우주비행사가 우주에서 떠있는 모습을 볼 수 있다.
   c. 역사에서의 미래 우리의 역할을 예측하기 위한 것
   d. 우리 정신 속의 조직 패턴에 대해 알기 위한 것

3. 작가는 시각 시스템을 어떻게 소개하는가?
   a. 시각시스템과 우리 뇌가 기능하는 방식을 연결하면서
   b. 늦은 저녁시간, 고양이의 시각과 우리 인간의 시각을 비교하면서
   c. 우리가 어떻게 이미지를 이해하는지를 예측하면서
   d. 눈이 보이지 않는 사람들에게 기부를 하면서

4. 강의의 일부를 다시 듣고 문제에 답하시오. 이 구절의 기능은 무엇인가?
   a. 고양이 시각의 약점들을 소개하기 위한 것
   b. 천문학에서 사용되는 다양한 망원경의 예를 제시하기 위한 것
   c. 인간의 시각 시스템의 복잡함을 설명하기 위한 것
   d. 질문하고 TV 상에서 해답을 발견하기 위한 것

5. 작가에 따르면, TV를 볼 때 고양이가 보는 두 가지는 무엇인가? 정답 두 개를 고르시오.
   a. 고양이는 수평선을 보기 시작한다.
   b. 고양이는 혼란스러워 한다.
   c. 고양이는 화면상에서 쥐를 보기 시작한다.
   d. 고양이는 무관심해 진다.

6. 작가가 시각 시스템에 대해 암시하는 바는 무엇인가?
   a. 시각 시스템은 그렇게 복잡하지 않다.
   b. 일부 과학자들은 고양이가 인간보다 시력이 더 좋다고 생각한다.
   c. 인간이 얻는 정보의 대부분은 시각을 통해 얻어지는 것이고, 우리의 환경을 이해하는 데 있어 핵심이 된다.
   d. 시신경 연구에 기여하는 방법을 보다 자세히 조사하는 것

Vocabulary Test   p.370~371

1. 본문의 "복잡한"과 가장 근접한 의미의 단어는?
   a. 주관적인   b. 의심을 품은
   c. 복잡한   d. 분명치 않은

2. 본문의 "시각의"와 가장 근접한 의미의 단어는?
   a. 물리적인   b. 통찰력 있는
   c. 명상적인   d. 시각의

3. 본문의 "연결하다"와 가상 근접한 의미의 단어는?
   a. 절개하다   b. 연결하다
   c. 혼합하다   d. 기쁘게 하다

4. 본문의 "복잡한"과 가장 근접한 의미의 단어는?
   a. 복잡한   b. 쉬운   c. 미개한   d. 당황한

5. 본문의 "혼란스러운"과 가장 근접한 의미의 단어는?
   a. 확신한   b. 증명하는
   c. 어찌할 바 모르는   d. 분명한

6. 본문의 "우주 비행사"와 가장 근접한 의미의 단어는?
   a. 우주 비행사   b. 하녀   c. 산과 의사   d. 점성술사

7. 본문의 "이해하다"와 가장 근접한 의미의 단어는?
   a. 적응시키다   b. 헐떡거리다   c. 언급하다   d. 이해하다

8. 본문의 "정도"과 가장 근접한 의미의 단어는?
   a. 추측   b. 분량   c. 확장   d. 정도

Paraphrasing   p.371

1. 눈과 뇌의 각 부분을 연결하는 이 시스템에 의해 인간은 주위에 있는 다수의 복잡한 요소를 조직하고 이해할 수 있다.

   a. 포화상태에 이른 정보를 뇌가 흡수할 수는 없다.
   b. 뇌의 다양한 부분들이 신경으로 연결되어, 우리 주변 환경에 대한 정보를 그대로 전달해 준다.
   c. 한 번에 모든 것을 흡수하기에는, 우리 환경에 존재하는 요소들이 너무 많다.
   d. 우리의 눈과 뇌의 각 부분들을 연결하는 것은 복잡한 문제를 해결하는 데 있어 필수적이다.

2. 또한 인간의 시각시스템은 문제를 제기하여 거기에 답하는 방법을 생각해내는 인간의 능력에 지대한 공헌도 하고 있다.

   a. 눈을 통해 습득된 정보가 없으면, 우리는 전혀 문제를 제기할 수 없다.
   b. 정보를 제공해 준다는 것은 시력이 좋다는 것과 관련되어 있다.
   c. 우리의 시각 시스템은 복잡한 질문을 할 수 있는 능력과 민감하게 연결되어 있다.
   d. 우리의 다양한 감각을 통해 습득된 정보가 없으면, 우리는 아는 것이 훨씬 줄어들 게 될 것이다.

TOEFL 滿^만
Vocabulary

WorldCom

#1005, Kolon Digital Tower Villant II, 222-8. Guro-gu, Seoul, Korea
Tel.02-3273-4300 Fax.02-3273-4303 www.wcbooks.co.kr